ORGANIZATION
THEORY

John H. Jackson
University of Wyoming

Cyril P. Morgan
University of Colorado

ORGANIZATION THEORY

A Macro Perspective
for Management

PRENTICE-HALL, INC., *Englewood Cliffs, New Jersey* 07632

Library of Congress Cataloging in Publication Data

JACKSON, JOHN HAROLD.
  Organization theory: a macro perspective for management.

  Includes bibliographies and index.
  1. Organization. I. Morgan, Cyril P. (date)
joint author. II. Title.
HD31.J23   658.4   77-27559
ISBN   0-13-641407-9

Printed in the United States of America

10   9   8   7   6   5   4   3   2

PRENTICE-HALL INTERNATIONAL, INC., *London*
PRENTICE-HALL OF AUSTRALIA PTY. LIMITED, *Sydney*
PRENTICE-HALL OF CANADA, LTD., *Toronto*
PRENTICE-HALL OF INDIA PRIVATE LIMITED, *New Delhi*
PRENTICE-HALL OF SOUTHEAST ASIA PTE. LTD., *Singapore*
WHITEHALL BOOKS LIMITED, *Wellington, New Zealand*

To

Linda, Jeff, Jodie, and Cody

and

Sharon, Patrick, Sean, and Matthew

CONTENTS

section two
THE MANAGEMENT
OF ORGANIZATIONAL DESIGN

chapter 3
Bureaucracy and Structure, 75

chapter 4
Basic Processes in Business Organization Design, 101

chapter 5
Patterns of Business Organization Design, 126

**section four
ORGANIZATIONAL CONTINUITY**

**chapter 10
Organizational Goals
and Effectiveness, 319**

**chapter 11
Organizational Survival
and Change, 346**

PREFACE

> The conclusion is apparent: that large economic organizations are here to stay, and that, short of an almost inconceivable revolution in public opinion, there is no way of getting rid of them. They have arisen in response to certain profound human needs—not so much economic needs as deeper, one might almost say "spiritual," needs. They have arisen also because of an increased ability to organize, and this ability is not going to be lost. It is of the utmost importance, therefore, that we examine what problems such organized groups create in economic and political life and in individual conduct.*
>
> Kenneth Boulding, *The Organizational Revolution*

This book was written to provide managers and administrators as well as scholars a perspective on organization that they probably have not had before. The field of organization theory in its present form is quite new, as witnessed by the recent increase in university courses, scholarly articles, and organization units devoted to its understanding.

The term *organization theory* itself is not new but is often associated in the minds of management academics with "principles of organization." The material contained in this book is not oriented toward principles of organization but rather toward what has been labeled in sociology "complex organizations." That title was rejected because it was the intent of the authors to summarize and adapt and integrate that information with management literature not for sociologists but for managers and administrators in organizations of all types.

The perspective is a *macro* perspective. Unlike organizational behavior

*From page 208 in *The Organizational Revolution* by Kenneth Boulding. Copyright © 1953 by the Federal Council of the Churches of Christ in America. By permission of Harper & Row, Publishers, Inc.

(a field of study that considers the individual and the small group as the unit of analysis) organization theory considers the *organization* itself as the unit of analysis. This provides, in our opinion, a very useful additional perspective for the management or administrative decision maker. We would never argue that organization theory should be the only perspective a decision maker should have, but its inclusion in management/administrative knowledge provides a useful balance to the more *micro* view of the organizational behavioralists.

The book evolved from efforts by the authors to develop and conduct a course in organization theory at the Universities of Wyoming and Colorado, respectively. Tempered by the judgment of our colleagues and students, it has continued to evolve. Our approach has been interdisciplinary in the selection of material, and we have carefully reviewed and included ideas from some of the classic works in the field because they form its conceptual base. Too often classic ideas, although still relevant, receive less attention as authors "update" the field. We feel knowledge is cumulative. We have also covered contemporary materials that illustrate the "cutting edge" of research and controversial areas; this has been done, in part, through the use of "dialogue" selections at the end of each section of material. These selections, written by leading names in each area, were chosen to either expand or take issue with the presentation we made in that section.

There are eleven chapters, which are, in turn, organized into four sections for pedagogical purposes and to provide order to the field. In the first section a preliminary look at *organizations in human affairs* is taken to familiarize the reader with the "why" and "what" of organizations. Furthermore, the reader is provided with an overview of the process of studying organizations and thereby given a basis for evaluating the research works he encounters in the book.

In the second section we deal with *managerial considerations in designing an organization*. The third chapter views organization as bureaucracies and considers the nature of organizational structure. Here, we try to acquaint the reader with the real meaning of bureaucracy and the scope of the literature on organizational structure. Chapter 4 deals with processes involved in designing business organizations (although most of the ideas apply to others as well). A contrast is drawn between academic and "real world" organizing concerns. Chapter 5 deals with the practitioner's problems of grouping activities by function or by divisions and how it is commonly done.

In the next section we present variables that have been viewed as *"imperatives" for managers in designing or understanding organizations*. Chapter 6 considers the importance of the technology an organization uses and chapter 7 the importance of the size of the organization. Chapter 8 deals with the effects the environment in which an organization operates (including other organizations) has upon its operations, etc. Chapter 9 focuses on three intraorganizational issues that have had imperative status at one point or another: power, control, and rules. These were selected from the many possible intraorganizational issues because of their importance and their interrelatedness.

In section four the general area of *organizational continuity* is discussed. Chapter 10 covers the issues surrounding organizational goals and effectiveness for profit *and* nonprofit organizations. Chapter 11 considers organizational survival and change.

We feel that these eleven topics cover most of the important issues in organization theory. Indeed, simply trying to define the field was no easy task since we felt it really had not been well done to date. The critical reader will learn that even though we had intended a complete resource, we have only skimmed the surface on some topics. Each of us argued for materials that are not included. A great many more dialogue selections received serious consideration and could have been chosen but the volume would have become too long.

In addition to the dialogue feature, we have tried to present the material, which can sometimes be quite difficult and detailed, in a readable fashion through the use of "summary blocks" (which are abstracts of long, or perhaps statistically complex articles) in order to provide a convenient acquaintanceship with the important points about complex organizations.

Our approach has been to focus on the macro aspects of organizations and tie together the classic and contemporary works of both conceptual and empirical natures. To us this was a worthwhile cause, but the final test of an idea is its utility to others. We trust that readers and colleagues will provide us with the feedback needed to evaluate our approach.

Finally, we would like to express thanks to some people whose work and inputs helped us get this task accomplished. Sue Adams, Glenn Runkewich, and Kevin Taylor contributed a number of important ideas. Dick Montanari, Robert Dailey, and W. Anthony Kulisch read a great deal of the material and made important suggestions. Our friend and colleague Craig Schneier made major recommendations. We received excellent reviews and suggestions from Bob Taylor at the United States Air Force Academy, Robert Guest at Dartmouth College, Craig Lundberg at Oregon State University, Arlyn Melcher at Kent State University, John Stockman at California State University, Sacramento, and Mary Beth Beres at Temple University, which surely improved the quality of the book. That we were unable to incorporate all their ideas is a reflection on our abilities and not theirs. Finally, we would like to acknowledge the support and guidance of the Prentice-Hall editorial staff, particularly Earl Kivett, Ted Jursek, and Joan Lee.

section one

To begin the book we have chosen to explore some issues that hopefully will convince you that understanding the phenomenon of organization is useful. Chapter 1 describes the differences between the *micro* perspective on organizations, which focuses on the individual and associated small group phenomena, and the *macro* perspective, which focuses on the organization itself as the unit of analysis. The history and pervasiveness of organization is developed, and conditions important to the process of organizing are covered. Finally, organizational growth is discussed.

Chapter 2 deals with problems associated with our knowledge of organizations. The process of gaining knowledge about organizations is described, and the methods by which this knowledge is typically collected are noted. We have chosen to include this material at this point in the book to provide you with a basis for evaluating much of the material that will be presented later. Our purpose was to try to make you a more knowledgeable consumer of the organization theory material that follows.

The objectives for section one are to answer the general questions:

1. Are organizations worth learning about?
2. How good is our knowledge of organizations?

THE SIGNIFICANCE
OF ORGANIZATION
IN HUMAN AFFAIRS

chapter one

A PRELIMINARY LOOK AT ORGANIZATIONS

The focus of this book is organizations. Not people in organizations, but the organizations themselves. There are in existence already a number of sources of information about the behavior of people in organizations. There are considerably fewer available sources that pull together the knowledge in which organizations themselves have been the unit of analysis. That is the task we undertake here.

What is to be gained by using the organization as the unit of analysis? Don't people make up organizations? And if that's true, then shouldn't the study of people be the proper unit for analyzing organizations? Certainly people do make up organizations, and, indeed, you can't have organizations without people. The study of people in organizations *is* a proper and vital study for managers and administrators. However, organizations are *more* than simply an aggregation of individuals who make up each organization; therefore, studying *only* people without looking at the organizations in which they do their work deals with only half the problem of managing people in work organizations.

Organizations have characteristics of their own over and above the characteristics of the people that make them up. For example, organizations have a distinct structure; they have rules and organizational norms that have developed over time; they have a life cycle of their own that goes beyond the lives of individuals; and they probably have goals, policies, procedures, and practices. They exist in an environment that affects many of these other characteristics. They are usually engaged in processing some kind of input and turning it into an output. They interact with other organizations, and they have to change internally to keep up with external pressures. Because organizations are a unit of analysis separate and apart from the psychology of organization members, the study of organizations is a useful study for managers and administrators. Understanding the essential issues in initially designing or reorganizing existing organizations is critical to managers in middle and upper organizational levels.

As we have suggested, the study of human beings in work organizations has taken two forms. A "micro" perspective on behavior in work organizations looks at *human beings themselves as a point of* study. It concerns itself with each individual's psychological makeup, and the other "individual-oriented" variables that determine how he is likely to react in a given situation. Variables such as an examination of how an individual learns, how he is motivated, and different kinds of leadership strategies designed to produce a kind of behavior in the individual that the leader wants, might be examined in the micro view. Yet, managers manage *more* than people; they manage the design of the work environment in which work takes place.

Kurt Lewin has argued that behavior is a function of an interaction between variables in the individual and variables in the environment:

$$B = f(I, E).$$

For a manager to really understand and analyze what takes place in work organizations, he or she must understand not only the individual but the characteristics of the environment in which the individual exists as well. For the purpose of management and administration in work organizations, that environment is the *work organization* itself.

The study of individuals in organizations is rather well developed and is recognized as a discipline called organizational behavior. Our purpose here is to draw together and integrate the literature that considers the *organization* itself as the unit of analysis. In so doing we will make every effort to avoid overlapping with the organizational behavior literature, not because the two streams of literature should not be joined at some point—*they should*—but because very little literature exists that takes a management/administrative perspective in viewing the "macro" unit of analysis—the organization itself. In this book we will confine our analysis to work organizations and not concern ourselves with the other forms of organization that people form for other purposes.

The body of knowledge we have labeled a macro perspective on organizations is quite scattered and in need of an attempt to order it in some fashion. Therefore, we will present an eclectic viewpoint drawing from many sources and will try to use empirical studies for our information where they are available. Unfortunately, because the study of organizations is in a very early stage of development, empirical studies of the caliber we would like are not always available. When this is the case, we will use theoretical or nonempirical bases for development of understanding.

Other Reasons to Learn About Organizations

Most of us will find that we will spend much of our lives working in organizations of some sort, yet many people go through life never really understanding much about these organizations. For example, why do organizations take the forms they do? How do the external pressures on organizations reflect upon members? What kinds of alternatives are available for designing, managing, and administering organizations?

An interesting argument for studying organizations is advanced by William H. Whyte, Jr., in one of the classic best sellers of the 1950s: *The Organization Man.* Whyte argues that we must understand organizations if we are to be able to deal with them on a personal basis. See Block 1-1 for an excerpt from Whyte's thoughts.

Not everyone agrees that organizations themselves are an appropriate unit of analysis for management and administration. Chris Argyris, for example, has argued that the two levels of analysis proposed here are inappropriate: "Individuals and social systems are independent of each other in trivial ways. Certainly it is true that any given individual may come and go, but the system exists. The system will exist as long as the individuals in it behave according to its requirements."[1] Argyris seems to be saying that *individuals* make up organizations and *must* therefore be the basis for understanding organizations. He further argues, "It may be inaccurate to state that one can study organizations-as-wholes, if one selects to ignore the admittedly critical parts of organization. Individual's behavior, small group behavior, intergroup behavior, represent important parts that help create the whole."[2] Argyris believes that the only viable, reasonable way to study behavior in organizations is to look at the micro level of analysis. There are others who agree with his views.

But William Wolf has argued that approaches like Argyris' provide a very limited perspective on behavior in organizations.

> The complexity of formal organizations poses problems in their study. First, it is not valid to fractionate an organization and then reify the parts. The whole is more than the sum of the parts. It is the interaction of the parts with each other and with the complex of which they are a part that constitutes organization. In short, an organization is a dynamic field. It should be studied as a whole Gestalt. It will not yield to simple cause and effect reasoning. To change one part is to change interaction among other parts and to change the whole. One cannot comprehend the whole by dealing with the parts in isolation.[3]

Wolf believes that it does make sense to study organizations, that studying only people will provide us with inappropriate answers.

block 1-1

THE ORGANIZATION MAN

People *do* have to work with others, yes; the well-functioning team *is* a whole greater than the sum of its parts, yes—all this is indeed true. But is it truth that now needs belaboring? Precisely because it is an age of organization, it is the other side of the coin that needs emphasis. We do need to know how to cooperate with The Organization but, more than ever, so do we need to know how to resist it. Out of context this would be an irresponsible statement. Time and place are critical, and history has taught us that a philosophical individualism can venerate conflict too much and cooperation too little. But what is the context today? The tide has swung far enough the other way, I submit, that we need not worry that a counteremphasis will stimulate people to an excess of individualism.

The energies Americans have devoted to the cooperative, to the social, are not to be demeaned; we would not, after all, have such a problem to discuss unless we had learned to adapt ourselves to an increasingly collective society as well as we have. An ideal of individualism which denies the obligations of man to others is manifestly impossible in a society such as ours, and it is a credit to our wisdom that while we preached it, we never fully practiced it.

But in searching for that elusive middle of the road, we have gone very far afield, and in our attention to making organization work we have come close to deifying it. We are describing its defects and virtues and denying that there is—or should be—a conflict between the individual and organization. This denial is bad for the organization. It is worse for the individual. What it does, in soothing him, is to rob him of the intellectual armor he so badly needs. For the more power organization has over him, the more he needs to recognize the area where he must assert himself against it. And this, almost because we have made organization life so equable, has become excruciatingly difficult.

To say that we must recognize the dilemmas of organization society is not to be inconsistent with the hopeful premise that organization society can be as compatible for the individual as any previous society. We are not hapless beings caught in the grip of forces we can do little about, and wholesale damnations of our society only lend a further mystique to organization. Organization has been made by man; it can be changed by man. It has not been the immutable course of history that has produced such constrictions on the individual as personality

The answer we have suggested to the question "Why study organizations?" is that the macro analysis provides a vital perspective for managers and administrators that is not generally considered elsewhere. With Lewin, we would assert that if the understanding and analysis of what goes on in work organizations is to ever reach its potential, it will require an understanding of not only the individuals in the organizations but an understanding of the important variables in the organization itself.

A Model for Presenting the Macro Perspective

In presenting the macro-level organizational material, we will follow the sequence presented in Figure 1-1. The roman numerals in Figure 1-1 correspond to sections in the text. We will consider four major issues in the chapters that follow:

1. The significance of organization in human affairs
2. The management of organization design
3. The imperatives: critical dimensions for understanding organizations
4. Organizational continuity

The major subdivisions for each of these topics are presented in Figure 1-1 to provide you with a "road map" of the direction our discussion will take.

In this first chapter we will follow a sequence of topics designed to start the reader thinking about organizations in macro terms. First, we will deal with a case example of a developing organization to make the point that organization is inevitable. Then to further substantiate the point, we will look back in history to examples of organizing know-how from the recorded past. Then we will consider conditions necessary for organizations to evolve, including the organizing process itself. Finally, we turn to a subject that has stirred theoretical as well as managerial interest—organizational growth.

figure 1-1

A MODEL FOR PRESENTING THE MACRO PERSPECTIVE ON ORGANIZATIONS

I. The Significance of Organization in Human Affairs

  1. A preliminary look at organizations
     (inevitability, history, growth)

  2. Limits on our knowledge of organizations
     (scientific inquiry, research methods, special problems with organizations)

General objectives: To determine (1) Are organizations worth learning about?
(2) How good is our knowledge of organizations?

II. The Management of Organizational Design

  3. Bureaucracy and structure
     (an "ideal" organization, what is structure?)

  4. Basic processes in business organization design
     (traditional approaches to design, job design, activity grouping)

  5. Patterns of business organization design
     (the functional organization, the divisional organization, overlays)

General objectives: To determine (1) What "should" organizations look like?
(2) How are organizations usually built?

III. The Imperatives: Critical Dimensions for Understanding Organizations

  6. Technology
     (support for the imperative, the doubtful imperative, toward a broader meaning for technology)

  7. Organization size
     (size and structure, administrative component)

  8. The environment and interorganization relations
     (what is environment? interorganizational relationships)

  9. Intraorganizational issues: power, control, rules
     (compenents of power, kinds of control, why rules?)

General objective: To determine (1) What things about organizations have been found to be keys to understanding them?

IV. Organizational Continuity

  10. Goals and effectiveness
      (different approaches to effectiveness, a close look at goals, nonprofit effectiveness)

  11. Organizational survival and change
      (survival as a goal, reasons organizations fail to survive, the process of change)

General objective: To determine (1) What is required for an organization to survive?

Perhaps a good place to start the discussion of organizations is to convince you that there is a certain inevitability about organizations. One of the supposed lifelong dreams of the organization man is to some day be able to break away from the organization for which he works and to "go it on his own." However, the individual would probably find that "going it on his own" includes another organization. Let's consider a hypothetical example.

Beginnings of the Organization

Frank Jones is a cog in one of the wheels of American Corporation International. Frank is an engineer and has been with the organization for 15 years. In his spare time he enjoys inventing things. He finally succeeds in inventing what he considers to be an electronic component for computers that is vastly superior to anything now available on the market.

He succeeds in getting a patent on the invention and begins to manufacture them in his garage on a very limited basis. Frank finds that working after he gets home from American Corporation in the evenings and working Saturdays and Sundays, he can produce roughly 50 of the components a week. Frank soon learns that he can sell many more than the 50 that he is able to produce in the amount of time that is available to him. Even with the addition of some machines and the most efficient work methods, he is physically unable to produce more than 100 a week. Frank decides to hire Bill George, a senior engineering student at State University, to work part-time while he is not going to school to help make the components. The two men's combined production is about 200 components a week.

A Turning Point

The demand is phenomenal; Frank feels that he could sell a thousand components a week if he could only manufacture that many. But he is not yet sufficiently confident of the long-run future of the product to quit his job and devote full-time to his small business. So he hires four more part-time people to work in his garage producing the components. Demand for the product continues to rise. Frank soon finds that coordinating the work schedule so that part-time people have full utilization of the machines, as well as keeping the garage clean enough to work in, keeping machines repaired, and making contact with the firms to which he is selling the components is taking entirely too much of his time. At some point he decides that he can now devote full-time to the component manufacturing business. He quits his job and begins a new career as president of Better Components, Inc. (BCI).

The demand for the product continues to grow. Frank finds that although he works 15 hours a day himself and the part-time people as much as possible, he is unable to keep up with the growing demand. By now, Bill George has graduated from the university, and Frank offers him a position as supervisor over the ten full-time employees and five part-time employees. Bill accepts. Frank has had to move the operation out of his garage and into a building better designed for this kind of work.

Over the next year, the demand continues to increase at an incredible pace. Frank continues to add employees and machines in an attempt to meet the demand, but he finds that more and more of his time is taken up with duties not directly related to turning out the product. He is spending a great deal of his time contacting potential buyers, purchasing the material from which to make the components, arranging transportation for the finished products to the buyers, hiring additional help, and dealing with problems of absenteeism, turnover, training, salary schedules, and so forth. Even more frustrating is the fact that Frank cannot find the time to sit down and do the kind of planning he feels is necessary to guide the development of the infant business.

What Now?

A year later, Bill George is directly supervising a work force of 75 people. Bill does his very best and he is good, but Frank realizes that he is somewhat overextended since no one short of superman would be able to successfully keep track of that many people and their problems. Frank decides some rational thought needs to go into the design of an organization to relieve these problems.

The organization he designs has people in special positions to help him with many of the administrative functions he can't find time to do on his own. For example, he hired a person with experience in the personnel area to negotiate with the employees, handle disciplinary problems, and design appropriate personnel procedures. He hired an accountant to keep the books for the operation and a sales manager to take over contacts with the customers. He hired three people as managers to help Bill George with supervising the actual production of the components, and things seemed to be running reasonably well for a while.

The Pressures of Size

Five years later Frank notices that as the size of his operation has increased and the complexity of the organization has increased, certain problems that didn't exist before have arisen. He finds that it is very

figure 1-2

ORGANIZATION OF BETTER COMPONENTS, INC.

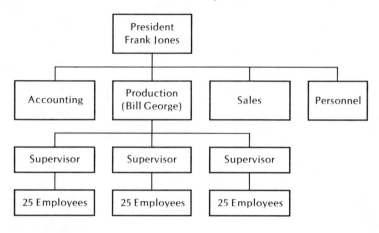

difficult to communicate with all his employees. Since everyone is essentially involved in doing his own job and since many of the jobs tend to overlap, more coordination is necessary than when it was possible to personally explain plans to everyone. Yet, formal mechanisms for coordinating the work of the different functional areas are currently lacking.

Frank also finds that the various functional areas (sales, accounting, personnel, production) seem to be vying with one another for influence in the decision-making process. He finds, too, that the vastness of the organization is presenting some control problems. Although he used to be able to keep track of the organization in his own head, he can no longer do that, and therefore a rather complex record keeping, reporting, and summarizing system has to be developed to control the finances of the operation.

Lessons from the Example of BCI

Frank Jones' situation illustrates rather graphically the need for organization as tasks grow in complexity and size. The need for organization is rooted in one very simple fact of human behavior: that Frank Jones or any one person cannot do all the work himself. If he could, there would be no need for an organization, but because he can't and because he needs more and more assistance to accomplish a task, he has no choice but to organize. Human limitations are the basis for the inevitable organization.

The BCI example shows how a business organization grew and evolved. It illustrates how increases in size led to the development of characteristics commonly found in many larger organizations. The example could just as well have been about a government agency or a hospital; the need for organization as the work load increases is the same.

An organization need not be large to be considered an organization. Smaller organizations, such as the corner drugstore or the city council, are just as much organizations as larger ones. Yet, the larger ones present some special difficulties and problems, and therefore much of our concern in this book will be primarily with the larger organizations.

As the organization in the example grew, it took on more of the characteristics of the typical larger organization. *Rationality* became more and more important. The effective pursuit of the goals of the organization required cooperation and clear understanding by its members. Major goals had to be broken into subgoals for each group, and specification of authority relationships involving who had the right to make decisions in which areas became necessary.

Furthermore, a hierarchical *structure* developed. This structure is, in one sense, a chain of formal authority running from the president to the next level of managers and on down the organization. It indicates who has what authority and where responsibility and reporting channels are located. The structure was based, at least in part, on specialization and division of labor.

Since the work load had gotten too big for one person, the work was divided up, and people with expertise in one area were assigned duties in that area. Labor was divided and specialists were used. The result of assigning these duties to different individuals was a functional organizational structure based upon specialization and division of labor.

Although it wasn't specifically mentioned in the example, another common result of an increase in size is an increase in the *formalization* inherent in the organization. As the organization grows, rules and formal mechanisms for coordination become necessary to keep everyone on a common track and working in the same direction. Furthermore, policies and procedures must be written after some point if everyone is to understand how the organization is supposed to operate. These examples of formalization show why guidelines to actions and interactions in the organization are commonly provided as size increases.

Another consequence of growth is likely to be an increase in the *complexity* of the operation, perhaps both internally and externally. This need not necessarily follow an increase in size, but it often does.

A HISTORY OF ORGANIZATIONS

The example just considered was a contemporary business organization, but the need for organizations is not at all new, nor do organizations have to have a for-profit motive to be worthy of study and consideration.

The history of organizations is as old as the history of mankind. From the earliest days people have needed to group together to accomplish certain goals. The goals may have been protection, food gathering, or the building of shelter; but even with these rather elementary tasks the need to organize activities to get the work done was very apparent.

The Egyptians

Some of the earliest written records currently available show man's awareness of the importance of organization. The organizing problems faced by the early Egyptians, for example, are very apparent if one considers the construction of the great pyramids. One pyramid, for example, required 100,000 men, working 20 years to complete. The pyramid covered 13 acres and measured 481 feet in height. It was constructed of about 2,300,000 stone blocks, each weighing an average of two and a half tons.[4] Just planning for and organizing the efforts of feeding and housing 100,000 men over a 20-year period are monumental efforts in themselves, regardless of the complex end product.

Translation of the written records maintained by the Egyptians supports the idea that their concepts of organization had reached a high level. Indeed, it is quite reasonable to assume without strong organizational abilities and understandings, the pyramids could not have been completed. Detailed written instructions were given to viziers (or managers) when they were appointed that defined their responsibility. The translation of parts of these instructions are presented and illustrate some of the Egyptian concerns for organizational problems and the practices they used to deal with them:

[On impartiality]
It's an abomination of the God to show partiality. This is the teaching: Thou shalt do the like, shalt regard him who is known to thee like him who is unknown to thee, and him who is near to . . . like him who is far . . . An official who does this then shall be flourished greatly in the place. [Don't show favoritism.]

[On responsibility]
The overseers of hundreds and the overseers of (word not translated) shall report to Him their affairs. ["Him" evidently refers to the top manager.]

[On reports]
Furthermore, He shall go in to take council on the affairs of the kind and there shall be reporting to him in the affairs of the Two Lands in his house everyday. [Daily reporting]

[On staff advice]
Let every office, from first to last proceed in the hall of the Vizier, to take council with Him.

[On authority]
It is He who appoints the overseers of the hundreds, in the hall of the king's house.[5]

A listing of organizational problems, concepts, and attempted solutions to them over time could be greatly extended. Needless to say, man has faced organizational problems since time began. The distillation of his experiences (good and bad) with differing organizational arrangements over time is, to a great extent, reflected in modern organization theory. This certainly does not argue that organizations as we view them today represent the last step in organizational evolution. On the contrary, many individuals who study or work in modern organizations argue that they have changed very little from the early organizational forms. In any event, organization *does* seem to be inevitable in human affairs.

THE EVOLUTION OF ORGANIZATIONS

Why have organizations evolved and taken the dominant position that they have in today's society? One point of view holds that it is basic human nature to organize to get work accomplished. To present this point of view, we will now consider *organizing* as a human phenomenon and conditions that surround and influence initial organizational formation, and later organizational growth.

An Overview of Organizing

Certain conditions must exist for an organization to form. For example, the potential for benefits to the members must exist. To be a member of an organization involves effort, compromise, and a restriction of behaviors. Therefore, there must be some positive benefit to offset these negative aspects of membership before individuals will voluntarily join an organization.

It has been suggested that there is a human "tendency toward organizing." Individuals living in small groups in prehistoric times probably did not enumerate reasons for forming these groups and then choose the benefits of group membership. But, rather, the combination of instinct and evolutionary growth and the need for protection may have ensured that those individuals having tendencies toward organizing experienced a greater survival rate, hence, perpetuating the characteristic.

Developing Collective Structure

Among higher level vertebrates, the social structure of an organization is easily observable in the form of a pecking order that consists of dominant and subordinate role behaviors. In a manner of speaking, this represents "authority" in its most primitive form. Authority, in whatever form, is necessary for any organization to function, since it is through authority that coordination of efforts is achieved.

Karl Weick has suggested that dissimilarities among individuals in an organization are in themselves one of the primary causes of structural alignment (which is usually associated with authority differences) in an organization.[6] He feels that people seem to like and interact with those most similar to themselves, and they seem to feel significant and unique when they are able to contrast themselves with others. It seems a logical outgrowth of this tendency that an individual entering a structural hierarchy will find his place in the structural pecking order of the organization by association with those groups toward which he feels an identity. As an individual's latent abilities and potentials become evident to the groups, he may (by promotion, for instance) become structurally aligned on a different hierarchical level.

Even though the organization is composed of different structural units, there exists a very real collective force that exhibits itself as "company policy" or "organizational thinking." Weick points out that:

> This leads to the point that once a structure is formed, people try to preserve it. They look for and provide one another with "structural assurances"; these are mutual indications that: (1) the structure can be counted on and will continue to operate, and (2) each will retain his place in it. . . .[7]

The relevant point about collective structure is that it is assumed to be a basic property of groups from which organizational properties derive.

Conditions for Organizing

We have discussed tendencies toward organizing on the personal level, but before an organization can form, certain things must exist in the society as a whole. More advanced societies tend to have better communications, more efficient methods of transferring resources, and therefore, the more advanced cultures tend to have more organizations since the environment is more conducive to organizational formation.

Organizations are not closed systems; that is, they must have inputs from the environment that they exchange for a portion of their outputs. Thus, if new organizations are to survive, they must find a societal need to fill so that they can obtain these inputs or resources. Furthermore, the new organization must develop links with existing organizations to exchange outputs. This "liability of newness" explains, in part, why so many new organizations fail.

To maintain itself, the organization must continue to interact with society to exchange outputs for needed inputs. Over the long run, it must be sufficiently flexible so it can adjust to environmental changes, or it runs the risk of no longer fulfilling a societal need and therefore becoming a social liability. This is the importance of the "open-systems" concept in learning about organizations. The interface between the organization and its environment must be studied and understood, since the extent to which the organization remains a viable part of the environment determines its survival. Obviously, the internal structure of the organization must also be maintained if the organization is to survive. We will now consider in more detail the process by which humans come to form organizations.

The Process of Organizing

Why do people form organizations in the first place? We suggested earlier that people organize if (and only if) they have some common purpose or goal. This purpose may not be explicitly stated or even consciously recognized. It may be something as simple as companionship or something as complex as a task environment in which self-actualization might be achieved. If some sort of commonality of interest or goals did not exist, each individual would very likely prefer to proceed on his own, since his goals would have nothing in common with those of other individuals.

In a sense, the initial process of organizing may be thought of as a decision by individuals to adhere to a set of rules to govern their behavior. The purpose of the rules is to guide the organization in the achievement of its goals. Even if a common purpose goal did exist, without rules the "organization" would simply be a group of individuals working independently and, perhaps, in random directions toward similar goals.

The rules to which the group decides to adhere may range from a simple "follow-the-leader" rule to a set of very specific rules derived through the rational and careful formulation of goals, objectives, activities, interactions, and operational procedures. In either case the concept is the same. In organizations the individual makes himself subject to a set of rules in hopes of more readily achieving a goal he has in common with other individuals. The goal, obviously, may be nothing more than to draw a paycheck and may thereby satisfy a monetary need. The process of organizing then includes the establishment of rules and adherence to those rules.

Weick on the Process of Organizing

Karl Weick feels that in the process of organizing all organizations attempt to stabilize themselves by removing uncertainty from their environment.[8] The very first thing an organization must do to remain a viable entity is to create a somewhat stable environment. This is done through the perceptions of the members of the organization. The perceptions of salient features in the environment "create" the environment to which the organization must adapt.

The removal of uncertainty from this "created" environment is viewed as a two-stage process. First, the uncertainty must be identified. Something that is unknown or unperceived cannot be dealt with. The second step is to actually remove the uncertainty. This is done by application of three organizational processes: enactment, selection, and retention. The process of *enactment* creates the information with which the organization must deal. The important distinction here again is that the human being creates the environment to which the system then adapts. This point is important, obviously, because the "real environment" and the enacted or perceived environment may be dissimilar, but organizations react to the enacted environment.

Next, the process of *selection* chooses the information bits or inputs from the environment that are consistent with the organization as it exists. This selection process removes the greatest share of uncertainty from the inputs by categorizing them on the basis of criteria established by past history and past experience. In effect, the selection process muddles through the variety present in inputs from the environment and orders the information.

The final process involved in organizing is *retention*. This process is suggested in selection. It can be thought of as retained historical information or experience. It serves as a criterion against which to check new information. These three processes, according to Weick, form a system the main purpose of which is to control the environment through the process of organizing.

Weick's contribution—the process of organizing—is concerned with "pure" organizing—the necessary processes that organizations develop, not the end product. The strength of his model is that it is unique. It focuses on the organization as it is *being formed* rather than as it currently exists and provides a link in our understanding between small groups and organizations. However, his model is essentially an information-processing one. His presentation is very abstract; yet nowhere else is the unique approach to the basic process of organizing spelled out. The process of organizing includes the occurrence of common goals, the acceptance of rules, and the development of enactment, selection, and retention mechanisms. The organization so formed is not necessarily like all other organizations, however. The societal conditions surrounding it have a great deal to do with its development and shape.

Societal Conditions

In understanding the evolution of organizations, it is of primary importance to understand the society surrounding the organizations since successful organizations must adapt themselves to this society.

An organization's history can be broken down in segments of all kinds. One can focus upon single member's activities in their jobs, or upon the activities involving a single function or geographic units, like the purchasing department or the European division. One can discuss social and intellectual domains, such as chemistry, supervision, or theology. One can attend to contiguous events, such as what happened during January of 1962.

Although prevalent, these analyses portray an organization as static, and do not reveal its developmental capabilities. Designing an organization to fit society's needs implies that it is less important to discover where an organization is than to understand how it got there, and where it can go tomorrow.[9]

It's been argued that the social structure affects the rate of formation of new organizations, particularly organizations of a new kind or those with a different structure.[10] Social conditions are thought to affect the motivation that people have to start new organizations as well as the likelihood that an organization will succeed. Stinchcombe has suggested that characteristics of individuals' motivation to organize are affected by the makeup of this social structure. The probability that a person or a group of persons will be motivated to start an organization is seen as dependent upon both the social structure and the positions that the founders occupied within it.

People form organizations under this rationale when:

1. They find or learn about alternative or better ways of doing things that are not being done within the existing social relationships or arrangements;

2. They believe that the future will be such that the organization will continue to be effective enough to warrant building it, and the investment of resources will be justified;

3. They, or some group with which they are identified, will receive some of the benefits of the better way of doing things;

4. They can lay hold of the resources of wealth, power, and legitimacy needed to build organizations; and

5. They can defeat or at least avoid being defeated by their opponents, whose interests are vested in the old way of doing things.[11]

An expansion of this idea suggests that various *combinations* of interests are an important basis for the establishment of organizations. As a number of people discover they have like or common interests, they are joined together to express these interests. Like interests exist when persons have similar goals, and the attainment of these goals by some persons does not necessarily diminish attainment by others.[12]

Time in History

Another interesting way in which social conditions or variables are thought to affect the formation of organizations has to do with the period of history during which a particular type of organization was invented. It has been suggested that this relates to the structure or appearance of that organization. Compare, for a moment, differences between modern economic society and medieval economic society. The organizations that exist (or existed) in each in the area of government, military, police, production-oriented organizations, religious organizations, etc., look quite different today than they did then.

Why? Perhaps an answer has to do with the conditions *surrounding* the organizations as well as the *knowledge* about organizing that exists at a given time. Stinchcombe suggests that organizations are more likely to form when the following historical conditions are present: (1) general literacy and special advanced schooling are available; (2) urbanization is present; (3) a money economy exists; (4) political revolutions can occur; and (5) greater richness of social/organizational life exists.[13]

The rationale behind the importance of these conditions is as follows. Societies of illiterates are seen as being quite different from societies of literates; practically every variable that encourages the formation of organizations is increased by *literacy* and schooling. In a society with small literate elite, organizations are much less likely to arise than in societies where literacy is widespread. They are likely to look quite different as well. *Urbanization* has basically the same effect that literacy does on the facilitation of organizational formation. "Innovators" are attracted to urban areas where they can exchange ideas, methods for organizing resources, etc. The existence of a *money economy* clearly increases the organizational capacity of a society by making resources easier to obtain, depersonalizing transactions, and allowing the development of mass markets. *Political revolution* can drastically shift relative advantages of vested interests, changing organizations and developing new ones in their wake. The *richness of the social/organizational life* of a group suggests that certain societies will have more resources to build new organizations. This is particularly true of organizations depending upon voluntary contribution of members' time. For example, compare the incidence of voluntary organizations in medieval times as we know it with the number of voluntary organizations existing in our society today.

Agricultural Development

Another characteristic that could have been added to Stinchcombe's list of five variables is that of agricultural sufficiency. Charles Harding makes note of the fact that agriculture is a prerequisite of industrial growth. Enough food must be produced to feed the full-time specialist of industry, because industry grows and survives best when it provides the tools that contribute to agricultural productivity.[14] A logical extension of the importance of agriculture argument is that geological, geographical, and ecological factors are important as well, since to some extent agricultural development and therefore industrial development depend upon these factors. This whole line of reasoning emphasizes the importance of the time in history and general development of a society in the development and design of organizations.

Other Conditions

Other societal conditions that have been suggested as important in the development of organizations are the rise of religious creeds and the type of economic system that has evolved. Max Weber noted that a relationship existed between the growth of Protestant religious beliefs in northern and western Europe and the rise of the industrial, commercial, and financial enterprise known as capitalism.[15]

Another factor that has been noted is the development of the corporate form of organization as a factor contributing to rapid industrial growth and development. This form of ownership, of course, provides the advantages of allowing business to be conducted with the liability for doing business spread more widely than was possible before. Furthermore, large amounts of capital that would not have otherwise been possible can be raised by corporations through the sale of securities. The corporation has a life of its own with its own identity and will not be necessarily dismantled by the death or retirement of its key members. This organizational form has undoubtedly contributed to the increase in the number of organizations.

Finally, it has been argued that increases in the technology available to a society ultimately result in more organizations. For example, Galbraith feels that technology requires specialized manpower and that the inevitable counterpart of specialization is organization.[16] Without organization, the work of the specialist would not result in a coherent end product. As the number of specialists increases, the effort of merely coodinating their work becomes a major task. Therefore, more organizations and subsystems of organizations must be developed to keep up with the increase in the number of specialists that result from an increase of technology in society.

Consider our earlier example of BCI. All of the above-mentioned conditions had to be present before the organization could be formed. The absence of literacy in the society, the absence of a money economy, or even the lack of the advantages of the corporate form would have probably scuttled the new organization or at least caused a very different-looking organization.

A Summary of Societal Conditions

It should be fairly apparent from this discussion that a number of factors influence the evolution of organizations. Many of these factors are contained in the societies in which the organizations are evolving. The unique forms that organizations take in different societies are dependent upon the social, political, religious, and philosophical milieu in which the neophyte organization is imbedded.

Furthermore, it should be obvious that organizations cannot take forms that have not been developed at that particular stage in history. For example, the matrix organizational form (which we will cover in detail later) was not a viable alternative to the bureaucratic form in the 1800s simply because it hadn't been invented yet. So, in addition to taking on the characteristics of the society around them, organizational forms are limited by the knowledge of alternative forms that are available at the point in history at which they are conceived.

ORGANIZATIONS AND THEIR "NICHE" IN SOCIETY

Kenneth Boulding suggests that organizations and the environment in which organizations exist are continually evolving.

> The organizations, institutions, ideas, and techniques of one period permit the rise of new organizations, institutions, ideas, and techniques which eventually may displace the former set almost entirely, and which, in turn, permit the rise of a still further succession. We thus see human history as structurally a continuation of the immense drama of evolution. Countries, businesses, unions, co-ops, churches, are the secessors in the immense process of ecological change. . . . Moreover, organizations of men at any one time form part of the whole ecosystem.[17]

A further explanation of Boulding's concept of ecological succession includes the idea that organizations must find their "niche" in society in order to survive. He suggests that if a new organization arises, there must either be a *new* niche created for it to fit into, or it must have the ability to fit into an already *existing* niche.

However, this is a very interdependent process. For example, it has been suggested that as manufacturing organizations have grown, so have the organizations peripheral to each specific industrial process—that is, those concerned with finance, marketing, communication, transportation, etc. These relationships are seen as being highly complex, but the history of a particular industry or the community or society as a whole cannot be understood without consideration of the relationships.[18] In such an example, the environment is seen as expanding to accommodate the growth of these new organizations, and new niches are being formed as a by-product, so the process is basically expansionary in its net effect. Unless an organization has found a niche that is expanding, growth is difficult. An organization's growth is an important topic for management since growth is generally taken as a sign of effectiveness or at least success. Growth is a topic in organization theory that has received more theoretical and empirical attention than the topics we have discussed to this point.

ORGANIZATIONAL GROWTH

It has been suggested by many theorists that all organizations follow similar patterns of growth; but organizational growth is difficult to measure. It is like the variable size in that they are both relative terms and that they are both meaningless except when they are used to describe another variable (such as percentage change in earnings per share or the growth in the number of employees in an organization).

Measurement of growth is essentially one measure of change, but growth has been handled in a number of different ways by a number of different authors. We will confine ourselves here to the contributions made by four different models to our understanding of change.

Models of Growth

New organizations face several simultaneous issues; they must be both able to get the task accomplished and at the same time build the structures that bring order to its key social and decisional processes. How well the organization survives is, of course, a function of how well the basic task is taken care of. Figure 1-3 shows the major states of social system growth and change according to one model.[19]

Figure 1-3 suggests that since an organization is especially concerned with task accomplishment in its formative and developmental years, an increase in output occurs. Then during the stable and dynamic equilibrium period in the middle stages of an organization's life cycle, output tends to stabilize. Then at some point, the organization will have to adjust or change to maintain its growth, or it will face decline and dissolution.

A variation on this theme is expounded by Gordon Lippitt.[20] He suggests that there are three developmental stages in an organization's life: birth, youth, and maturity. He argues, too, that some organizations succeed in reaching higher stages of development than others. Organizations usually go into decline only because management fails to notice the need for change or because of drastic changes in the external environment. Lippitt and Schmidt have identified critical concerns, key issues, and consequences associated with each of these stages of organizational growth (see Figure 1-4).[21]

A third approach to understanding the growth of organizations is suggested by Mason Haire.[22] Haire argues that we can talk of "lawful" processes involved in the growth of organizations just as we can talk about "laws of growth" for biological systems. He argues that these processes are grounded in the organization, its environment, and the interdependence of

figure 1-3

MAJOR STATES OF SOCIAL SYSTEMS' DEVELOPMENT AND CHANGE. *Source:*
R. E. Coffey, A. G. Athos, and E. A. Reynolds, *Behavior in Organizations*
(Englewood Cliffs, N.J.: Prentice-Hall, 1975), © 1968. Reprinted by permission of
Prentice-Hall, Inc., Englewood Cliffs, N.J.

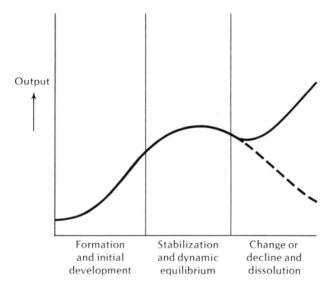

| Formation and initial development | Stabilization and dynamic equilibrium | Change or decline and dissolution |

organizational size, shape, and function. He feels that relatively simple
growth equations of the kinds used in population studies and other
biological disciplines can give us insight into the growth of organizations.

Haire says that the growth process in organizations is subject to natural
laws and that the discovery of these natural laws is the most reasonable
approach to understanding the process of organizational growth. He
especially focuses on the growth of the staff component in organizations.
For example, he feels the growth of staff functions in an organization
occurs because a structure is strongest where the "force tending to destroy
the structure is strongest. As organizations grow, the bracing material will
grow where the destructive forces are focused. The staff growth suggests
that this is in the area of coordination and control."[23]

Another useful model has been developed by Larry Greiner. He views a
work organization as moving through five distinct phases of development
as it grows. Each phase contains a relatively calm period that he calls an
evolutionary phase, which is ended by a management crisis marked by a
substantial amount of internal turmoil. This period of organizational crisis
is called a "revolution."[24] Greiner argues that since each phase is strongly
influenced by the previous one, a knowledge of the organization's history
can aid management in determining its future. He also believes that the

figure 1-4

STAGES OF ORGANIZATIONAL GROWTH

Developmental Stage	Critical Concern	Key Issue	Consequences if Concern Is Not Met
Birth	1. To create a new organization	What to risk	Frustration and inaction
	2. To survive as a viable system	What to sacrifice	Death of organization
			Further subsidy by "faith" capital
Youth	3. To gain stability	How to organize	Reactive, crisis-dominated organization
			Opportunistic rather than self-directing attitudes and policies
	4. To gain reputation and develop pride	How to review and evaluate	Difficulty in attracting good personnel and clients
			Inappropriate, overly aggressive, and distorted image building
Maturity	5. To achieve uniqueness and adaptability	Whether and how to change	Unnecessarily defensive or competitive attitudes, diffusion of energy
			Loss of most creative personnel
	6. To contribute to society	Whether and how to share	Possible lack of public respect and appreciation
			Bankruptcy or profit loss

Source: Gordon L. Lippitt and Warren H. Schmidt, "Crises in a Developing Organization," *Harvard Business Review,* vol. 45, no. 6, November–December, 1967, p. 103. Copyright © 1967 by the President and Fellows of Harvard College; all rights reserved.

figure 1-5

THE RELATIONSHIP BETWEEN SIZE, AGE, AND GROWTH RATES. *Source:*
L. Greiner, "Evolution and Revolution as Organizations Grow," *Harvard Business
Review* July–August, 1972, p. 41. Copyright © 1972 by the President and Fellows of
Harvard College; all rights reserved.

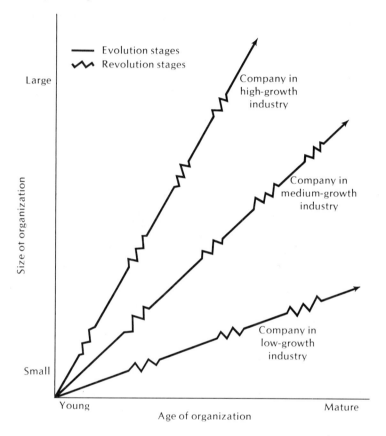

future of an organization is less determined by outside forces, such as
market conditions, than it is by past decisions.

   The key dimensions used in his model are size and age. The age of an
organization is critical because problems and decisions are rooted in time.
Historical studies can gather data from different time periods and make
comparisons to provide insight. The size of an organization is directly
related to problems and solutions of matters such as sales volume,
coordination, and communication. If the size remains fairly stable, it can
maintain the same management practices for lengthy periods. Figure 1-5
shows the relationship between size and age of organizations with different growth rates.

Greiner identifies a number of crises that occur at different stages in the growth of the organization. These are shown in Figure 1-6. First is the crisis of leadership. As the company grows in size and complexity and longer production runs become the rule, the need for greater efficiency cannot be achieved through informal channels of communication. New employees are not as dedicated to the product or the organization. Founders of the organization often find themselves playing the role of a manager, a role for which they might not be suited or may not be willing to handle. This crisis of leadership may lead to the founders relinquishing some of their power to a professional manager. This was demonstrated in the BCI example earlier in this chapter.

figure 1-6

SIZE, AGE, AND GROWTH RATES. *Source:* L. Greiner, "Evolution and Revolution as Organizations Grow," *Harvard Business Review* July–August, 1972, p. 41. Copyright © 1972 by the President and Fellows of Harvard College; all rights reserved.

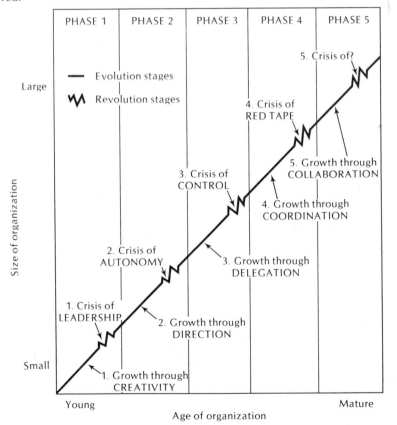

The second crisis is one of autonomy. Directive management techniques enable the organization to grow, but they may become ineffective as the organization becomes more complex and diverse. Lower level supervisors are more knowledgeable and demand more responsibility in decision-making powers. Resolution of this crisis may be through powerful top managers relinquishing some of their authority and a certain amount of power equalization.

The third crisis is the crisis of control. With decentralization of authority to managers, top executives may sense that they are losing control over a highly diversified operation. Field managers want to run their own shows without coordinating plans, money, technology, or manpower with the rest of the organization. Special coordination techniques are the resolution to this problem.

The next crisis is one of red tape. The new coordination systems prove useful for achieving growth and more coordinated efforts by line managers, but a lack of confidence builds between line and staff, between headquarters and field. Line becomes resentful of staff; staff complains about uncooperative and uninformed line managers; and everyone gets bogged down in the bureaucratic paper system. Procedure takes precedence over problem solving; the organization becomes too large and complex to be managed through formal programs and rigid systems. The solution to the red tape crisis is collaboration, which involves more flexible and behavioral approaches to the problems of managing a large organization.

Regardless of the different approaches taken by different growth models and the implications of each, growth clearly presents problems of adjustment for the organization. As organizations grow and evolve, they change; the problems of management change; and ultimately the organization's policies, procedures, structure, and so on, may have to change. Block 1-2 shows a case example.

Hospitals as organizations have undergone a tremendous amount of change in the last ten years. Block 1-2 documents the nature of many of the changes and growth pressures hospitals have recently faced. This provides an opportunity to view many of the interactions between growth in an organizational type and the social system of which it is a part and the resulting internal impact on the organization.

CONCLUSIONS

In this chapter we argued the value of a macro perspective in understanding organizations and what goes on in them. We suggested that organization was inevitable because of human limitations in being able to accomplish all the work necessary as work grows. The fact that organiza-

block 1-2

GROWTH AND CHANGE IN HOSPITALS

Until about ten years ago, hospitals were managed as a special kind of hotel. It was the administrator's responsibility to see that hospital rooms passed the white-glove test, that materials and supplies were used sparingly, and that daily operations buzzed along as usual. As nonprofit organizations, hospitals did not hold economic efficiency as a primary goal in the administration of services.

Financially, the hospital was usually well endowed. It was fashionable for the wealthy to donate or bequeath large sums to the hospital as a philanthropic deed or an expression of personal thanks. Payroll expenses were kept down by paying employees low wages. Balancing the hospital budget consisted primarily of satisfying the reporting requirements of third-party insurance groups that finance hospital services, such as Blue Cross, Medicare, and Medicaid. Reports completed for this purpose provided a sketchy and sometimes misleading picture of the hospital's financial situation. However, there was no pressure to prepare extra profit-and-loss-style reports for internal management use.

In those days, most doctors had offices outside the hospital. A doctor would typically make daily rounds of his hospitalized patients, delegating continuing on-site care to the nurses. Occasionally he taught medical students in the hospital in return for the privilege of admitting patients. Physicians played only a minor role in hospital management and decision making. The administration and nursing departments cooperatively managed the hospital.

The simultaneous emergence of two trends has disrupted this established system. First, the increasing complexity of the health-care system has called attention to the need for effective financial management. As error piled upon error, pressure from physicians and insurance agencies for more effective hospital management grew. Second, more doctors are now basing their practice within the hospital. These doctors are demanding a greater role in top-level decision making, breaking through the administrators' stronghold on hospital policy.

New developments in medical technology have increased the functions and changed the nature of hospitals, forcing them to expand and reorganize. Not only do hospitals house equipment and the personnel to operate it, but they also now function as a base for medical research and the education of young medical-care professionals. The total hospital today is an aggregation of new wings and buildings including research and educational facilities as well as patient-care areas. Rather than being integrated into the entire system, however, these new functions and services have simply been added on, both physically and administratively. The resulting system is organized neither for the convenience of its workers nor for the effectiveness of the patient-care process.

Meanwhile, as the financial needs of the hospital have increased, its economic situation has grown less healthy. Donations, once a major source of revenue, have decreased. More importantly, widespread unionization has forced hospital wages up. As the financial situation grows worse, both internal and external pressure for better management increases. Insurance groups are becoming more interested in finding out where their money is going and whether it is being spent effectively. Third parties are becoming more concerned with reviewing a hospital's costs, and soon they will require hospitals to prepare annual budgets. If such budgets are to be enforced, hospital rates will have to be set, requiring more skill in accounting than has yet been displayed.

Gayle E. Stone, "A History of Mismanagement." Reprinted with permission from the March, 1976 *MBA* magazine, p. 48. Copyright © 1976 by MBA Communications, Inc.

tions seem to have been around in fairly sophisticated form as far back as we can go in recorded history seems to bear out this view.

We saw that for organizations to evolve, certain processes must be developed and certain societal conditions must exist. Furthermore, the organization must find and fill a niche if it is to get the opportunity to grow and develop.

Organizational growth has been described as life cycles or growth stages and compared to biological systems. In an offshoot of this kind of reasoning internal crisis stages in the growth cycle of work organizations were described.

In the next chapter we turn to an important issue: How good is our knowledge of organizations? We chose this topic for the next chapter to make you a more sophisticated reader of the chapters that follow.

NOTES

[1]Chris Argyris, *The Applicability of Organizational Sociology* (Cambridge: Cambridge University Press, 1974), p. 118. Emphasis added.

[2]Ibid., p. 70.

[3]William B. Wolf, "Toward the Development of a General Theory of Management,"

Comparative Administrative Theory, ed. Preston B. LeBreton (Seattle, Washington: University of Washington Press, 1968), p. 180.

[4]William L. Westerman, *The Story of the Ancient Nations* (New York: D. Appleton, 1912), pp. 18–19.

[5]James Henry Breasted, *Ancient Records of Egypt,* vol. II, (Chicago: The University of Chicago Press, 1906), pp. 269–79.

[6]Karl Weick, *The Social Psychology of Organizing* (Reading, Mass.: Addison-Wesley, 1969).

[7]Ibid.

[8]Ibid.

[9]B. L. T. Hedberg, P. C. Nystrom, and W. H. Starbuck, "Camping on See-Saws: Prescriptions for a Self-Designing Organization." *Administrative Science Quarterly* 11 (March 1976): 41.

[10]Arthur L. Stinchcombe, "Social Structure and Organizations," *Handbook of Organizations,* ed. James G. March (Chicago: Rand McNally, 1965), p. 143.

[11]Ibid., p. 146.

[12]Lewis Kriesburg, "Internal Differentiation and the Establishment of Organizations," *Institutions and the Person,* ed. Howard S. Becker et al. (Chicago: Aldine, 1968).

[13]Stinchcombe, "Social Structure and Organizations," pp. 148–52.

[14]Charles F. Harding, III, "The Social Anthropology of American Industry," *Management and the Behavioral Sciences,* ed. Mameck S. Wadia (Boston: Allyn & Bacon, 1968).

[15]Ibid., p. 399.

[16]John Kenneth Galbraith, *The New Industrial State* (Boston: Houghton Mifflin, 1971).

[17]Kenneth Boulding, *The Organizational Revolution* (New York: Harper & Row, 1953), p. xxiii.

[18]Harding, "The Social Anthropology of American Industry," p. 398.

[19]R. E. Coffey, A. G. Athos, and E. A. Reynolds, *Behavior in Organizations* (Englewood Cliffs, N.J.: Prentice-Hall, 1975). p. 260.

[20]G. L. Lippitt, "Growth Stages of Organizations," *Organizational Renewal* (New York: Appleton-Century-Crofts, 1969), p. 28.

[21]G. L. Lippitt and W. H. Schmidt, "Crises in a Developing Organization," *Harvard Business Review* 45 (November-December 1967): 103.

[22]Mason Haire, "Biological Models and Empirical Histories of the Growth of Organizations," *Modern Organization Theory,* ed. M. Haire (New York: Wiley, 1959).

[23]Ibid., p. 305.

[24]Larry E. Greiner, "Evolution and Revolution as Organizations Grow," *Harvard Business Review* 50 (July/August 1972): 37.

SUGGESTIONS FOR FURTHER READING

ARGYRIS, CHRIS. *The Applicability of Organizational Sociology.* Cambridge: Cambridge University Press, 1974.

HALL, RICHARD H. *Organizations: Structure and Process,* 2nd ed. Englewood Cliffs, N.J.: Prentice-Hall, 1977.

PERROW, CHARLES. *Complex Organizations: A Critical Essay.* Glenview, Ill.: Scott, Foresman, 1972.

chapter two

LIMITS ON OUR KNOWLEDGE OF ORGANIZATIONS

It may seem to be of little value to spend time trying to understand the limitations of organizational research. But it is *important* to do so since understanding the limits of research influences the confidence that can be placed in its results. It helps define the limits of our knowledge about organizations. For example, if someone suggested to you that an opinion survey had shown that 95 percent of the population of the United States were registered members of the Greenback party your first reaction might be "I don't believe it. I would like to see the manner in which that study was done, so that I could determine whether or not it was accurate." Our information about organizations presents a very similar situation. We often may not believe the results of a study or may not agree with the conclusions reached. The purpose of this chapter is not to attempt to make you a sophisticated researcher but, rather, to make you a more educated consumer of the studies, theories, and conceptual schemes that appear in the organizational literature. Without a feel for the problem and pitfalls inherent in doing research on organization, one might be confused by some of the statements made or be overly accepting of conclusions reached. We feel that the state of the art in organization studies is such that the consumer of this and, indeed, any social science should recognize its limits.

KNOWLEDGE ABOUT ORGANIZATIONS

How do we come to know *what we know*? This question gets at the basic foundations of human knowledge. For most human beings, the accumulation of knowledge is a function of early childhood experiences that create frames of reference and interests that are later expanded and perhaps modified as individuals continue to grow and learn. These frames of reference and interests form the basis for organizing the world around us. They also serve as stimuli to explore certain areas and to ignore others. Our accumulated knowledge of organizations follows a very similar kind of pattern. Early frames of reference in the study of organizations were built on personal experience, through the observation of organizations by persons interested in understanding something about them. Many of these early observations were later made the subject of more rigorous testing and formal research.

Early Knowledge

As the study of organizations began to grow and develop, certain early ideas were expanded and others were rejected. A number of ideas about organizations seem to have been accepted basically on blind faith rather than on any carefully tested basis. The human being is made more aware of the *limits* of his knowledge by understanding how he acquired the knowledge, and the student of organization is made more aware of the limits of the knowledge we have about organizations by understanding how this knowledge has been accumulated. Ideas that have been taken as "fact" often are found to be untrue when subjected to the scrutiny of scientific testing.

Organizational study in the management area is but one subset of management knowledge. It has been suggested that much of management knowledge is based upon one of four approaches to knowledge:

> (1) Knowledge in the field of management can be acquired by listening to or reading the writings of men who have many years of practicing experience in a wide variety of managerial positions. (2) Knowledge in the field of management can be acquired by the study of cases which present in an abbreviated form a history of the experience of an individual manager, department, or firm. (3) Knowledge in the field of management can be acquired by learning a set of principles that are generally applicable to all organizations. (4) Knowledge in the field of management can be acquired by learning specific techniques from one or more of the underlying disciplines.[1]

Unfortunately, each of these bases of knowledge presents very special problems for the manager or administrator who wants to learn about organizations. One of the problems is that none of these methods allow the manager to view the "Big Picture" or the system as a whole. Neither do they allow him to make accurate judgments as to cause and effect.

Levels of Analysis

It was suggested earlier in the book that organizations can be studied on a number of different levels. The individual human being in the organization may serve as the unit of analysis or a level of study. Studying the organization at this micro level provides some very useful basic information for managers.

But we know that aggregations of individuals (such as small groups) may behave somewhat differently than these individuals would behave singly. Therefore, another useful level of analysis in the study of organizations is the group or interpersonal level, which can be thought of as "intermediate" level of analysis in studying organization. Work groups, friendship groups, cliques, and other multi-individual groupings in organizations provide additional useful information for understanding the organization and what is going on in it.

Yet, organizations exist as groupings of groups and display additional elements not found in the study of the intermediate or micro levels, such as formally designated organized structure, formal authority relationships, production technology, and so on. Furthermore, it has been argued that organizations are synergistic. Synergy is the idea that the organizational whole is more than simply a summation of its parts. Synergy suggests that a certain quality is added by grouping together in an organization a number of smaller groups. The macro level of organizational study views the organization itself as a unit of analysis.

These different perspectives for looking at organizational life—micro, intermediate, and macro—each has a big contribution to make to our knowledge of organizations. Our perspective here is, of course, the macro perspective. Proponents of each level of analysis sometimes view their own preferred perspective as the "only reasonable" way to gain knowledge about organizations.

However, each level has its *own special problems* relative to gaining valid knowledge about organizations. There are a number of problems that are somewhat unique to the macro level of analysis, and these special problems will be dealt with in this chapter.

With any level of analysis and in any scientific field of study, a basic approach or "philosophy" exists for determining which knowledge is "true." This philosophy of science forms the basis for the advancement made in man's pursuit of knowledge about organizations. Although using the organization itself as the unit of study leads to some very special problems, we feel it's important to briefly describe the philosophy of science that guides all scientific research, before looking at the specifics of organization study.

PHILOSOPHY OF SCIENCE

The social sciences (of which the study of organizations is a part) can be thought of as *applied* science. From theories social scientists derive operationally useful theorems that can be tested against fact. If the results of these tests don't contradict the operational hypotheses, part of the theory may be provisionally accepted as being true. Through this process, which will be elaborated later, social scientists search for the "objective truth;" they seek reality. Therefore, they are faced with a concern about what *objectivity* is and how scientists can attain and maintain objectivity while trying to discover facts and the relationships between facts.

Objectivity and Normativeness

Scientists are obviously affected by the earlier studies done in their fields, by the journals they have read while completing their education, and by their own perceptions of the world around them. These forces tend to "contaminate" pure objectivity with *normativeness*.

Psychologists tell us that the human being faces a large, unordered, blooming, buzzing confusion of stimuli from the environment and that these stimuli do not fall into a predetermined order by themselves. Human beings order them. Scientific observation would be impossible without some sort of ordering of stimuli. How could biologists study plants or animals meaningfully without ordering them into groupings of some sort— trees, grass, birds, mammals? But with this necessary ordering of the world come some problems of objectivity. Organizations are faced with this same problem and deal with it through creating an "enacted environment" as we suggested in chapter 1.

The problem of being able to view reality without prior preconceptions about that reality suggests that true objectivity is extremely difficult (if not impossible) in the social sciences. Only by concealing from themselves their a priori ideas about the world can ardent empiricists argue that their work in the social sciences is *totally* objective. Therefore, underlying every attempt to discover the "truth" about anything, including organizations, is a theory or at least an implicit ordering of information. Some determination *has* to be made as to the ordering of facts and their relationships in order to deal with information, thereby introducing normativeness.

It is important that the imperfection of all of the investigations done in the social sciences be clearly understood. It is also important that we understand that no study is ever the definitive work on an organizational phenomenon. Theories and perceptions change and evolve as new information is made available, and the study of organizations, like any subject matter in the social sciences, continues evolving as well.

Dealing with Normativeness

The basic tool for trying to deal with the effects of normativeness on the "facts" about organizations is the simple question, "Do you see what I see?" In following the logic suggested in this question, observations by one individual are replicated by another individual to see if similar results are obtained. Different conceptual schemes proposed by one scientist are tested and disputed by another. Through this process, greater agreement on what the facts *actually are* eventually emerges. The entire process can best be viewed as an ongoing stream or process, through which facts regarding organizations are honed, clarified, and examined in different contexts. Findings about some organizational variables may be viewed with more certainty simply because this process of honing is more advanced for them than for others. Indeed, there are undoubtedly a number of pertinent organizational variables that have not yet been discovered.

To advance our knowledge of organizations, two streams of research activities must come together. One is abstract reasoning and the other is experimentation. A research result that has been made available to other social scientists to view and test may be described as having met the requirements of the scientific method, but such is really nothing more than well-ordered empiricism. The full requirements of the system of examination that is the scientific method have not yet been met if the connection with theory has not been made.

Empiricism or empirical testing fits in well with the insistence on *confirmation* that has existed in the social sciences. For a number of reasons, hypothesis testing is currently the "in" method of confirmation; unfortunately, hypothesis testing can lead to charges that the research results are trivial, uninformative, or nongeneralizable. This occurs because the statement of a hypothesis requires a rather narrow definition of the phenomenon being viewed. Hypothesis testing or any other form of empirical confirmation must come together with the abstract logical world of theories for the process to be complete.

THE PROCESS OF SCIENTIFIC INQUIRY

Figure 2-1 shows a graphic representation of the scientific method in the social sciences. From having come in contact with the grey amorphous mass that we can label "reality," an observer gains exposure to a small portion of that reality. What he has viewed is then put in some sort of conceptual order in his mind. The observer has formed a "model" of reality from this conceptional ordering of the stimuli. He might even choose to make statements about the apparent relationships and call the statements a "theory."

Later, the individual might be interested in testing the model or exploring parts of it further, and perhaps some initial, exploratory empirical studies might be undertaken. As a result of these studies, the model might be revised. Then the revised model or theory can be subjected to some more specific tests, such as stating a formal hypothesis and then testing it.

figure 2-1

THE "SCIENTIFIC METHOD" OF THE SOCIAL SCIENCES

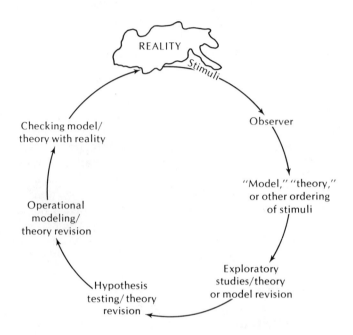

Hypotheses can occur as if/then statements about relationships existing in the theory. For example, if one turns the light switch to "off," *then* the room will be dark. This is a hypothesis that can be tested. Extensive hypothesis testing may lead to a feeling on the part of the observer that he understands reality sufficiently well that he can operationally model it. Simulations, computer models, mathematical models, and so forth might be undertaken at this point in the process. Obviously, a good bit of information about a phenomenon is necessary for this to be viable.

The final step in the process is one that unfortunately is sometimes neglected: a comparison of the model or theory with reality. Several important questions must be answered here. Does the theory still bear some resemblance to the reality? Can it predict reality? Does it help us understand reality? Obviously, if it doesn't, then the theory needs further revision or the incorporation of additional variables into it to remedy these failings; or perhaps the theory is of no value and should be scrapped.

Two basic research methods exist for studying organizations in either the exploratory or the hypothesis-testing stage. These are *field* methods and *laboratory experiment* methods.

figure 2-2

PROS AND CONS OF FIELD AND LABORATORY METHODS FOR STUDYING
ORGANIZATIONS

Field		Lab	
Pros	Cons	Pros	Cons
It is realistic— you have real people, real relationships, cliques, structures, goals, etc.	Control is very difficult.	Control is much easier than in the field.	It is artificial and relationships, tasks, goals, etc. have to be fabricated to approximate a real organization.
	It is hard to isolate the relationships among variables because of the complexity.	The study can be made simple and only one variable viewed if appropriate.	
It is complex—all the variables present in "reality" are there.	It is hard to find suitable organizations to study.		

RESEARCH METHODOLOGIES

When an organizational researcher wants to learn more about organizations, he is basically limited to one of two approaches. He can go out, find an organization, and study it in its natural environment, or he can try to duplicate one in the laboratory. These two methodologies are often referred to as field methods or laboratory methods.

Figure 2-2 summarizes the advantages and disadvantages of each. Basically the field method is more realistic and more complex; therefore, control is more difficult as is isolating the relationships among variables. Furthermore, it is hard to find suitable organizations to study. In the laboratory, control is much easier, and this methodology lends itself well to the study of a limited number of variables. However, it is somewhat artificial, and the relationships, tasks, and goals that would normally exist in a real organization have to be fabricated. To more fully acquaint you with each of these methods, we will now view each separately and more completely.

Field Methods

Field methods have been classified in a number of different ways, but for our purposes we will use the following classification: (1) the case or multiple case method, (2) the comparative method, (3) the natural experiment, (4) the field experiment.

Case Study

The case study or multiple case study generally entails an observation by the researcher of an organization or organizations and a written description of the researcher's overall impressions about the organization or of the specific organizational variables under consideration. This methodology may require the use of a "participant/observer" to gather the information. Observation is an especially useful method for the study of organizational *processes*, such as communication or change. Questionnaire research—another alternative—tends to provide data more effectively on such things as attitude, values, perceptions, and so on, but works less well on processes.

Case studies have provided us with a wealth of material on organizations; but they have been criticized for their lack of measurability and lack of objectivity thus making replication difficult. One also does not know if the results are an abnormal example based on a small sample of one or two. In many instances in newly developed theories or impressions about organizations, it's the only method that fits. For exploratory studies that lead to the development of theories, the case study or multiple case study may be among the most effective ways of gathering initial information.

Comparative Study

Another field method that is used commonly is the comparative study. Udy defines the comparative analysis of organizations as "seeking to establish general principles about organizations from the study of more than one organization at once."[2] This rather general definition allows almost any writer on the subject of organizations to adopt a label of "comparative" study. This perhaps is not of great importance but may be somewhat confusing.

The use of comparative methods is relatively widespread. They need not necessarily be confined strictly to empirically based research, although the common use of the term seems to imply that this is the case. Students of organization also should be warned that some researchers hold an overly rigid definition of comparative study. Some have placed exclusive claim on the use of the reference to an emerging body of *international* studies of organizations. The use of the term *comparative studies* is not used here solely to describe international or cross-cultural studies.

What sorts of things have been viewed in the comparative analysis of organizations? In 1967 Lawrence and Lorsch tried to determine what kind of organization is most successful in dealing with different environmental conditions.[3] Their study took place in three types of industries in the United States. Six firms in the plastics industry, two firms in the container industry, and two firms in the food industry were studied. The plastics industry was considered an "innovative" industry, the container industry a "stable" industry, and the food firms considered to be a "midrange" industry.

Among other useful findings that resulted from the comparative study of these firms was the suggestion that the different environments in which the organizations existed affected a number of organizational variables. Among these were *differentiation* (the extent to which organizations' departments were completely different from each other) and *integration* (the quality of the cooperation that existed among departments in the firms). The Lawrence and Lorsch study is probably one of the best examples of the comparative methodology. It will be examined in greater detail in a subsequent chapter.

One of the obvious difficulties with doing comparative study has to do with the matching of organizations. If one wishes to compare two or more organizations on a particular variable, one must be sure the organizations selected indeed have that variable in common. But even more importantly, the researcher must be sure that the observed variable indeed accounts for the observed differences. This is a common criticism that can apply to comparative studies.

Natural Experiment

A third kind of field study is the natural experiment. In this kind of experiment the researcher observes and perhaps takes measures on an organizational situation before a natural change takes place in the organization and then observes and/or measures the same variables after the change.

For example, let's suppose a researcher is interested in determining the effect of a change from a centralized organizational structure to a decentralized organizational structure on the number and direction of communications taking place in the organizational hierarchy. The researcher might measure the number and direction of communications taking place in the organization under the old system. Then when a reasonable period of time had passed after the change (so that the organization could return to some sort of equilibrium), he might again measure the number and direction of communications in the hierarchy and then make a comparison of the "pre" and "post" situations.

Field Experiment

The distinction between the natural experiment and the fourth kind of field study—the field experiment—basically centers on the role of the researcher. In the natural experiment the researcher merely takes advantage of a natural occurrence to study its effect on some dependent variable.

In the field experiment the researcher is instrumental in *causing* the manipulation of the independent variable.

For example, suppose a consultant is interested in determining the effect of a certain organizational development program on the level of coordination between departments in an organization. He might institute the program in one of his client organizations, and after having measured the level of coordination prior to the introduction of the change, again measure it after the change had been introduced. The distinction in this instance is that the *researcher* was the one who influenced or introduced the independent variable.

Any of the different field methods of study a researcher might choose to use has the advantages noted earlier; they are realistic and view organizations in their natural setting. But there are some overwhelming disadvantages as well in trying to do field research, including the difficulty of finding

---

block 2-1

A FIELD STUDY WITH PROBLEMS

An organizational researcher had gained entrance to a large business organization to study conditions surrounding interdepartmental cooperation. A great deal of time was spent becoming familiar with the organization and the people involved, gaining access to the necessary records, and carefully designing the study (which was to be a field experiment). Finally, the researcher made the necessary changes in the independent variable and sat back to watch and measure the effect on the dependent variable (interdepartmental cooperation).

But during this period of time a dip in the business cycle caused the organization's top management to make a decision about the reallocation of resources among the departments. A rather sizable cut in each department's budget was necessary. As a result, the departments involved were forced into the position of having to battle one another to try and minimize their losses in the reallocation of resources.

The net effect of this intervening variable on the research being conducted was to completely hide any effect the change in the communication channels might have had upon interdepartmental cooperation. The researcher wasted a good deal of time, effort, energy, and money and was unable to complete the research. This is not a totally isolated instance in the study of organizations, and these kinds of problems make studying organizations in the field a somewhat difficult process.

organizations to study, the difficulty of controlling variables that might influence the results, and the usually greater cost of a field experiment compared to a laboratory experiment.

A classic example of the difficulty of doing field research is illustrated by a research attempt with which the authors are familiar. See Block 2-1 for a brief case of study of an errant field study.

Laboratory Studies

An alternative to studying organizations in the field is to study at least portions of the organizational process in the laboratory. There are a number of advantages in doing this. For example, variables, such as the intervening variable in Block 2-1, can be much more carefully controlled. In a chapter in the *Handbook of Organizations* Karl Weick provides an excellent summary of the issues involved in doing laboratory research with organizations.[4] He notes that the increasing number of definitions of organizations that have been generated has provided many lists of organizational characteristics. This allows researchers to break organizations down into their component parts for study in the laboratory. Weick argues that this makes the laboratory study of organizations more attractive. However, the drawbacks and concerns of doing this must be dealt with.

Artificiality

One major concern about the usefulness of laboratory methods to study organizations has to do with artificiality. Weick feels that artificiality does not reduce the generalizability of the results of a laboratory study to the extent that many people think it does. He believes that critics often confuse problems of *novelty* (a situation is new to the subject) and problems of *control* (subjects make safe responses) with the general artificiality issue. Weick believes that "artificiality is a dangerous label to attach to experiments because it focuses attention on pseudo-issues and suggests self-defeating solutions."[5]

In conjunction with the artificiality problem, a novel question has been raised, "Can you really study an army in the laboratory?"[6] Zeldich argues that the purpose of experimentation is to construct and test theories, and since theories are abstract, the laboratory experiments associated with them *must be* of the same nature. He argues that researchers *do not* attempt to study armies in laboratories; rather, they try only to create those aspects of armies relevant to some theory and then study those in the laboratory.

Subjects

Another specific issue that deserves mention is the use of college students as experimental subjects when studying organizational phenomena. Various writers have argued that the behavior of college students may not be at all relevant for predicting the behavior of persons in real work organizations. However, college students are very often used as subjects in laboratory experiments simply because they are generally available to the academic researcher who also happens to be a teacher.

It has been suggested that in reporting study results methodological distinctions should be made between students *required* to participate in an experiment as part of their course work and those who *volunteer*. The argument is that this difference may be significant to the results obtained.[7] It has been further suggested that college students differ markedly from the noncollege population in age, social class, and learning ability.[8] These and other arguments about the use of college students as experimental subjects are not likely to be resolved immediately, but one should be aware of the arguments when viewing research done with college students. Of course, the major problem is associated with generalizing to other situations from such a sample.

We have seen that both field studies and laboratory studies have costs and benefits associated with them. Furthermore, in order to push back the frontiers of organizational knowledge, there is a pressing need to integrate laboratory and field study. As we suggested earlier in the discussion of Figure 2-1, the kind of methodology used depends somewhat on the nature of the problem being studied and upon the point in the development cycle of that particular theory or bit of knowledge.

Another major methodological problem deals with the fact that many studies have not been replicated in other kinds of organizations. We cannot currently control all variables that might affect an outcome in a given organization, so there is a real need for replication of experimental results in other settings. The outcome of this process is that the generalizability of the results can be enhanced. But regardless of whether the studies are conducted in laboratories or in the field, it is only through the continued study of organizations that our knowledge about them will be increased.

ORGANIZATIONAL TYPOLOGY

We stated earlier that we all order the world around us in one way or another. Ordering or classification schemes are a part of human knowledge that is very deeply ingrained and very basic. For example, all of us recognize a dog when we see one, even though there is a great deal of variance between a chihuahua and a Great Dane in terms of size, between a bulldog and a greyhound in terms of *physical conformation*, or a German shepherd and a basset hound in the *sound of their voices*. Yet, this is a scheme whereby animals are placed in a specific subclassification of Dog.

The same thing can be done on many different levels with organizations. Perhaps the most common is a classification based on size. We can classify the Department of Health, Education, and Welfare; AT&T; US Steel; and General Motors as *large* organizations, a classification based on size. We can classify the barber shop, the corner drug store, the beauty parlor, or the gift shop on the same criterion, as being *small* organizations. This classification scheme or "typology" is based upon the size of the organizational units involved. Other criteria might be used to classify these same organizations in other ways, such as with dogs.

Typologies can vary from rather concrete classifications, such as those based on size, to those based on very abstract criteria for classifying organizations. For example, Etzioni has classified organizations using "compliance with authority" as a major source of differences among organizations.[9] Etzioni suggests that organizations use either coercive, remunerative, or normative authority and that the kind of compliance that they receive from their employees is either alienative, utilitarian, or moral. This is a much more *abstract* way of creating an organizational classification scheme than simply using size as a criterion since "compliance" cannot be seen, touched, or tasted.

There are as many different typology or classification schemes as there are people who have thought or written about organizations. Given that fact, it is not at all unreasonable to state that the ultimate typology of organizations has not yet been created. Indeed, as we continue with our study of organizations in this book, a number of different models or typologies will be presented. Many of them deal with different variables or different aspects of the organization.

In viewing these typologies or models, it should be remembered that they represent someone's perception of organizational reality, perhaps based on some research that has been done in a limited area on a limited number of organizations. The fact that each typology seems to deal with only one part of the organizational existence sometimes causes those trying to learn about organizations to dismiss typologies as a useful approach to learning. However, it should be noted that they do provide useful tools for helping to understand some smaller portion of the phenomenon we call organization. The other caution is obviously not to look for all of the answers to organizational problems in any one model or typology.

In an excellent discussion of typologies Richard Hall suggests that:

> The essence of the typological effort really lies in the determination of the critical variable for differentiation of the phenomena under investigation. Since organizations are highly complex, classification schemes must represent this complexity. An adequate overall classification would have to take into account the array of external conditions, the total spectrum of actions and interactions within an organization and the outcome of organizational behavior.[10]

George B. Strother has reviewed a number of the very early "studies" that led to the development of an interest in scientifically viewing organizations.[11] Much of what follows is condensed from his review of the early history of organizational studies and provides a useful look at some of the earliest "studies" of organization upon which some of our current knowledge is based.

The first true bureaucratic form of administration evolved after the rise of the Roman Republic. The Roman Empire demanded the subordination of individuals to the organized state government. After Rome's decline, the early Christian church provided the only existing viable form of organization for many of the former Roman subjects. The early church reemphasized the worth of the individual relative to the organization, a concept that has received much attention in modern times.

Later, during the Renaissance one of the first writers on the subject of organization appeared. Machiavelli focused on the relationship between power and authority in his book *The Prince*. He was especially concerned with strong central government and tactics that could be used by an administrator to maintain power in that organization.

In 1689 Locke suggested an organizational concept that is still held today. He argued that the ultimate authority was contained in the citizens themselves and that the citizens had the right to remove their mandate to governmental rulers and to bring about a new government when it was appropriate. This idea of the "social contract" is still viable. In perhaps its most recent expression, Edgar H. Schein suggests in *Organizational Psychology* that the organization and its employees have a "psychological contract," which determines to some extent relations between the two.

In his observation of the Pin Factory Adam Smith commented on how the factory system achieved greater productivity by subdividing the skill of the craftsmen through specialization. This forms the basis for another current area of study and interest: specialization and its effect on the organization.

Early Management Studies
of Organization

Frederick W. Taylor studied organizations primarily by viewing first-level management and the employees. He worked with the organization of the work itself and supervisory techniques to provide greater efficiency. His work as well as that of Gantt, Gilbreth, and Emerson resulted in the human engineering movement and the infusion of "rationality" and efficiency into the design of organizations, which is continued to the present day.

Meanwhile, Henry Fayol, a successful executive, used the method of the participant/observer in summarizing his half-century experience as a successful executive. He argued that the organizational techniques of the successful manager could be abstracted, studied, and taught. His management process typology summarizes as planning, organizing, coordinating, and controlling and remains even today the basis for classic organizational administrative theory. These last writers form an important part of the stream of thought that can be labeled "a *management* approach to the study of organization."

Other Disciplines Study Organization

Around the same time, sociology and social psychology began to take an interest in organization. In a book published in 1921 sociologist Max Weber advanced a theory of bureaucracy that has proved to be a major point of departure for sociological approaches to the study of organization. More specific comments about bureaucracy and Weber's role in its study will be described in a later chapter, but a brief summary of the pertinent components of a bureaucratic organization according to Weber are as follows:

> The assignment of roles occurs on the basis of technical qualifications which are ascertained through formalized, impersonal procedures (e.g., examinations). Within the structure of hierarchically arranged authority, the activities of trained, salaried experts are governed by general, abstract, and clearly defined rules which preclude the necessity for the issuance of specific instructions for each specific case. . . . The pure type of Bureaucratic official is appointed . . .[12]

Social psychologists interested in organizations have tended to concentrate on either the small-group laboratory approach or the human relations approach to organization study. The human relations movement, of course (even though parts of it remain today), has been basically discredited for its normative assumptions about human behavior. Many of these normative assumptions have not withstood the close scrutiny of scientific evaluation.

Economists have contributed to the study of organizations to some extent. They have developed mathematical model building, which has become a rather major field for social theorists and is used in the study of organizations, too.

Until recently these different approaches to the studies of organization have gone essentially unnoticed by one another. In the past ten years there has been a good deal of lip service paid to the idea of interdisciplinary studies on a variety of subjects, including studies of organizations. For a number of reasons, this approach has never seemed to fulfill its promise.

However, in our study of organizations, we will attempt to draw from this diverse literature where appropriate and to bring in theories that help us understand organizations, regardless of their origins.

SPECIAL PROBLEMS IN STUDYING ORGANIZATIONS

As suggested in all the material that has gone before, the study of organizations carries with it its own special problems, problems over and above those normally encountered when doing research on individuals or groups. When we noted the different disciplines' contributions to knowledge about organizations, we implied that the problem is the difficulty in assimilating contributions from these diverse disciplines. An attempt will be made here to describe some of the other major difficulties in doing research when organizations are the unit of analysis.

Sample Size

Probably one of the primary difficulties for modern organization scholars stems from the nature of problems associated with sample size. Statistical treatment of data has provided us with a powerful tool for discovering relationships; but in order to treat a sample statistically, one must have drawn a sufficiently large sample so that one can make inferences about the population from which it was drawn. Many of the studies of organization have been case studies—that is, studies of one or two or perhaps as many as three organizations. This small sample size does not allow statistical treatment of differences among organizations in general, nor does it allow generalizations about specifics to the populations from which these samples were drawn. Such studies must be treated as case studies.

Furthermore, case studies have seemingly fallen into disrepute over the past several years. An examination of the better journals in organization theory reveals few case studies being reported. Some of this occurs because case studies are simply not being done, but they are not being done because they cannot be accepted for reporting in the better journals. As a result, someone wanting to do research on organizations is left with the problem of finding a rather large number of them to study. Of course, this presents some very special problems in terms of gaining entrance into that many organizations, finding enough organizations that are similar on the variable being studied, knowing something about each organization so that mistakes in designing the study can be avoided, and so forth.

An examination of a number of the studies on organization currently in the literature indicates a number of other problems. Many of the studies have used diverse samples, many different industries, and several different countries. This can be a real asset since it strengthens the conclusion if the results hold up in such a diverse sampling. But if differences among the studies are found, one can't be sure it wasn't due to the particular group selected.

Cause and Effect

Another major difficulty in the study of organizations has to do with determining cause and effect. When a change in one variable is accompanied by a change in another variable, it does not necessarily demonstrate that one change causes the other. For example, the fact that increases in the frequency of dysentery is accompanied by the tendency for tar to melt on the streets in the summer says nothing about causation. The relationship in this example is called a spurious relationship because the variables are not really related. The relationship is really due to a third factor, the increase in temperature which causes both to occur. If we were to control for the effect of temperature, we would find that the tar melting and dysentery both disappear when the temperature drops. However, to be able to do this, we must have determined variables that may be causing both and measure them.

Other Common Problems

Another problem has to do with common definitions and measurements. As long as every researcher continues to use his or her own measures and labels for the variables being used, it is very difficult to compare one study to another. Haas and Drabeck have suggested that there are three critical dimensions that characterize much of the variability in organization studies:

> (1) level of abstraction (analysis and data collected vary from highly descriptive and concrete to very abstract conceptualizations); (2) presence or absence of time (some studies reflect only one point in time, others are longitudinal); (3) the number of units selected for the study. Note that these three dimensions are clearly related. Thus, as one increases the number of units selected for the study there is of necessity an increase in the level of abstractness on which the analysis will be conducted.[13]

Another difficulty in determining cause and effect has to do with the time span over which the data were collected. Most studies are cross-sectional in nature; that is, the data are all collected at once. This is analogous to a "snapshot" of a situation at a given point in time.

Longitudinal studies are those in which the data are collected over a longer time span, which is more analogous to a film. Relationships unfold over time and can be viewed more completely than with a single point-in-time snapshot.

Determining what is causal for what is much more likely to occur when the study is longitudinal in nature. However, because of the difficulty associated with longitudinal studies, most information comes from cross-sectional studies.

This discussion is not meant to diminish the research efforts that have been made in the study of organizations. It is extremely difficult to do research at the macro organizational level as the relatively few efforts that have been made demonstrate. Few researchers have been willing to take up the challenge. A result of all the problems is that not enough has been done to demonstrate causality among macro level organizational variables. A number of relationships *have* been identified, however, and this allows consideration of some variables in building theories and downgrading the importance of others. It also gives a better idea of what to look for in future research efforts. A number of these variables will be dealt with in section three as things that have been found to have major impact on organization design.

The fact that research has only been able to account for 40 to 60 percent of the variance in predicting an organization's structure, for example, should limit our confidence that we understand all there is to know about the reality surrounding organization structure. It also means that not all the relevant variables that might affect structure have been discovered and that we probably need better measurement of the variables that have been studied. And so it goes with most organizational knowledge. These problems do not suggest there is no use in studying organizations. Rather, the knowledge we have is still developing and should be viewed as such.

Systems

Perhaps one of the useful concepts in understanding organizations that has come along recently is the idea that an organization is a system. The word *system* has become something of a buzz word, and unfortunately, the very simple, yet important, ramifications of exactly what the "systems perspective" is, have gotten lost in the rhetoric surrounding a "systems approach to this" and a "systems approach to that." The contribution of "a systems perspective" is simply that in an organization the various parts and processes are so interrelated that change in one necessarily implies change in the others as well. Or, put another way, the organization to be fully understood must be studied as a whole, taking into consideration the interrelationships among its parts. This is probably a big step toward understanding organizations, but it is also obviously a complication in studying organization systematically and in detail since the simple one-way relationships that are easy to test are probably inaccurate.

CONCLUSIONS

The purpose of this chapter was to introduce you to some of the issues and problems associated with how our knowledge of organizations is obtained. In discussing specific studies in subsequent chapters, we will call attention to some of these issues again.

We suggested that the basis for all scientific knowledge is the process of scientific inquiry. In the social sciences, of which the study of organizations is a part, the scientific process is beset by problems of normativeness. Replication of observations by others is one way in which attempts are made to overcome this problem.

Several different methods are available for studying organizations and can be grouped either as field methods or laboratory methods. Each has advantages and built-in disadvantages.

Organizational typologies are groupings of organizations or organizational characteristics on the basis of different criteria. They are quite useful in bringing some order to understanding organizations, but caution is urged to avoid the tendency to view any typology as "ultimate" or all-inclusive.

Organizations have been studied by a number of different disciplines over time. Each has had something to contribute, but until recently little effort has been made to bring together the contributions of the various disciplines.

Organizational study has its own special set of problems such as sample size, demonstrating cause and effect, and the difficulty of measuring systemic properties.

In the next chapter we begin our consideration of organizational structure. Structure, or the way an organization has chosen to divide up its activities and the arrangements it uses to coordinate and control those activities, is perhaps one of the most discussed and studied organizational variables.

NOTES

[1]Bernard D. Estafen, "Methods for Management Research in the 1970's: An Ecological Systems Approach," *Academy of Management Journal* 14 (March 1971): 53.

[2]S. H. Udy, Jr., "Comparative Analysis of Organizations," *The Handbook of Organizations*, ed. J. G. March (Chicago: Rand-McNally, 1965), p. 678.

[3]Paul R. Lawrence and Jay W. Lorsch, *Organization and Environment* (Cambridge, Mass.: Harvard University Press, 1967).

[4]Karl E. Weick, "Laboratory Experimentation with Organizations," *The Handbook of Organizations*, ed. James G. March (Chicago: Rand McNally, 1965), pp. 194, 260.

[5]Karl E. Weick, "Organizations in the Laboratory," *Methods of Organizational Research*, ed. Victor Broom (Pittsburgh, Pa.: University of Pittsburgh Press, 1967), pp. 1, 56.

[6]Morris Zeldich, "Can You Really Study an Army in the Laboratory," *A Psychological Reader on Complex Organizations*, ed. Amitai Etzioni (New York: Holt, Rinehart and Winston, 1969), pp. 528, 539.

[7]John Jung, "Current Practice Problems in the Use of College Students for Psychological Research," *Canadian Psychologist* 10 (1969): 280, 290.

8Reginald Smart, "Subject Selection Bias and Psychological Research," *Canadian Psychologist* 7 (1966): 115, 121.

9Amitai Etzioni, *A Comparative Analysis of Complex Organizations* (New York: The Free Press, 1961), p. 23.

10Richard H. Hall, *Organizations: Structure and Process* (Englewood Cliffs, N.J.: Prentice-Hall, 1972), p. 41.

11George B. Strother, "Problems in the Development of a Social Science of Organization," *The Social Science of Organization,* ed. H. Levitt (Englewood Cliffs, N.J.: Prentice-Hall, 1963), pp. 3, 37.

12Robert K. Merton, *Social Theories and Social Structure* (Glencoe, Ill.: The Free Press, 1957), p. 49.

13Eugene J. Haas and Thomas E. Drabeck, *Complex Organization: A Sociological Perspective* (New York: Macmillan, 1973), p. 375.

SUGGESTIONS FOR FURTHER READING

COOPER, WILLIAM W.; LEAVITT, HAROLD J.; and SHELLY, MAYNARD W., II. *New Perspectives in Organization Research.* New York: Wiley, 1964.

DUBIN, ROBERT. *Theory Building.* New York: The Free Press, 1969.

HAAS, EUGENE J., and DRABECK, THOMAS E. *Complex Organization: A Sociological Reader.* New York: Macmillan, 1973.

KERLINGER, F. N. *Foundations of Behavioral Research.* New York: Holt, Rinehart & Winston, 1964.

UDY, S. H., JR. "Comparative Analysis of Organizations." In *The Handbook of Organizations,* edited by J.G. March. Chicago: Rand McNally, 1965.

WEICK, KARL E. "Laboratory Experimentation with Organizations." In *The Handbook of Organizations,* edited by J.G. March. Chicago: Rand McNally, 1965.

section one   DIALOGUE

Over the last several years, as our interest in teaching macro organization theory has grown, several colleagues have remarked that this area of study seemed to be esoteric and impractical. They believed the literature was written for a relatively few management scholars and offered little that was of practical significance to managers. There may be some truth to these contentions, but whether they are any more true for macro organization theory than for the micro study of organizational behavior is still open to debate. In the two selections that accompany section one several themes speak to this issue.

Perrow traces the development of several schools of thought about organizations in the first selection. His historical perspective is helpful in realizing that no one school of thought has successfully captured a "complete understanding" of organizations. It also provides a counterpoint to the impracticality issue. One may wish to argue with several of his conclusions, but that is one of the purposes of the dialogue portion of this book.

Another purpose of dialogue is to enrich the text material with the original materials of a noted organization writer on a particular topic. Kurt Lewin is said to have originated the idea that nothing is so practical as a good theory. After reading Perrow's article, some readers may conclude that nothing is so impractical as a theory that purports to be useful but misleads the user.

In the second selection, Weick points out several of the pitfalls one may encounter in conducting organizational research. He argues that theories are built on regularities among events, people, and relationships. Some methods seem to be more powerful in discovering regularities, and as Weick indicates, some methods may provide little help in the search. The discovery of such regularities can be useful to managers if each organization is not unique. Most theories and research assume that each organization is not unique, and if that assumption is valid, Weick's article suggests which are the more powerful methods to discover the regularities.

THE SHORT AND GLORIOUS HISTORY
OF ORGANIZATIONAL THEORY

CHARLES PERROW

From the beginning, the forces of light and the forces of darkness have polarized the field of organizational analysis, and the struggle has been protracted and inconclusive. The forces of darkness have been represented by the mechanical school of organizational theory—those who treat the organization as a machine. This school characterizes organizations in terms of such things as: centralized authority, clear lines of authority, specialization and expertise, marked division of labor, rules and regulations, and clear separation of staff and line.

The forces of light, which by mid-20th century came to be characterized as the human relations school, emphasizes people rather than machines, accommodations rather than machinelike precision, and draws its inspiration from biological systems rather than engineering systems. It has emphasized such things as: delegation of authority, employee autonomy, trust and openness, concerns with the "whole person," and interpersonal dynamics.

THE RISE AND FALL OF SCIENTIFIC MANAGEMENT

The forces of darkness formulated their position first, starting in the early part of this century. They have been characterized as the scientific management or classical management school. This school started by parading simple-minded injunctions to plan ahead, keep records, write down policies, specialize, be decisive, and keep your span of control to about six people. These injunctions were needed as firms grew in size and complexity, since there were few models around beyond the railroads, the military, and the Catholic Church to guide organizations. And their injunctions worked. Executives began to delegate, reduce their span of control, keep records, and specialize. Planning ahead still is difficult, it seems, and the modern equivalent is Management by Objectives.

But many things intruded to make these simple-minded injunctions less relevant:

1. Labor became a more critical factor in the firm. As the technology increased in sophistication it took longer to train people, and more varied and specialized skills were needed. Thus, labor turnover cost more and recruitment became more selective. As a consequence, labor's power

Source: Reprinted by permission of the publisher from *Organizational Dynamics* (Summer 1973), copyright ©1973 by AMACOM, a division of American Management Associations.

increased. Unions and strikes appeared. Management adjusted by beginning to speak of a cooperative system of capital, management, and labor. The machine model began to lose its relevancy.

2. The increasing complexity of markets, variability of products, increasing number of branch plants, and changes in technology all required more adaptive organization. The scientific management school was ill-equipped to deal with rapid change. It had presumed that once the proper structure was achieved the firm could run forever without much tampering. By the late 1930s, people began writing about adaptation and change in industry from an organizational point of view and had to abandon some of the principles of scientific management.

3. Political, social, and cultural changes meant new expectations regarding the proper way to treat people. The dark, satanic mills needed at the least a whitewashing. Child labor and the brutality of supervision in many enterprises became no longer permissible. Even managers could not be expected to accept the authoritarian patterns of leadership that prevailed in the small firm run by the founding father.

4. As mergers and growth proceeded apace and the firm could no longer be viewed as the shadow of one man (the founding entrepreneur), a search for methods of selecting good leadership became a preoccupation. A good, clear, mechanical structure would no longer suffice. Instead, firms had to search for the qualities of leadership that could fill the large footsteps of the entrepreneur. They tacitly had to admit that something other than either "sound principles" or "dynamic leadership" was needed. The search for leadership traits implied that leaders were made, not just born, that the matter was complex, and that several skills were involved.

ENTER HUMAN RELATIONS

From the beginning, individual voices were raised against the implications of the scientific management school. "Bureaucracy" had always been a dirty word, and the job design efforts of Frederick Taylor were even the subject of a congressional investigation. But no effective counterforce developed until 1938, when a business executive with academic talents named Chester Barnard proposed the first new theory of organizations: Organizations are cooperative systems, not the products of mechanical engineering. He stressed natural groups within the organization, upward communication, authority from below rather than from above, and leaders who functioned as a cohesive force. With the spectre of labor unrest and the Great Depression upon him, Barnard's emphasis on the cooperative nature of organizations was well-timed. The year following the publication of his *Functions of the Executive* (1938) saw the publication of F. J. Roethlisberger and William Dickson's *Management and the Worker,* reporting on the first large-scale empirical investigation of productivity and social relations. The research, most of it conducted in the Hawthorne plant of the Western Electric Company during a period in which the workforce was reduced, highlighted the role of informal groups, work restriction norms, the value of decent, humane leadership, and the role of psychological manipulation of employees through the counseling system. World War II intervened, but after the war the human relations movement, building on the insights of Barnard and the Hawthorne studies, came into its own.

The first step was a search for the traits of good leadership. It went on furiously at university centers but at first failed to produce more than a list of Boy Scout maxims: A good leader was kind, courteous, loyal, courageous, etc. We suspected as much. However, the studies did turn up a distinction between "consideration," or employee-centered aspects of leadership, and job-centered, technical aspects labeled "initiating structure." Both were important, but the former received most of the attention and the latter went undeveloped. The former led directly to an examination of group processes, an investigation that has culminated in T-group programs and is moving forward still with encounter groups. Meanwhile, in England, the Tavistock Institute sensed the importance of the influence of the kind of task a group had to perform on the social relations within the group. The first important study, conducted among coal miners, showed that job simplification and specialization did not work under conditions of uncertainty and nonroutine tasks.

As this work flourished and spread, more adventurous theorists began to extend it beyond work groups to organizations as a whole. We now knew that there were a number of things that were bad for the morale and loyalty of groups—routine tasks, submission to authority, specialization of task, segregation of task sequence, ignorance of the goals of the firm, centralized decision making, and so on. If these were bad for groups, they were likely to be bad for groups of groups—i.e., for organizations. So people like Warren Bennis began talking about innovative, rapidly changing organizations that were made up of temporary leadership and role assignments, and democratic access to the goals of the firm. If rapidly changing technologies and unstable, turbulent environments were to characterize industry, then the structure of firms should be temporary and decentralized. The forces of light, of freedom, autonomy, change, humanity, creativity, and democracy were winning. Scientific management survived only in outdated text books. If the evangelizing of some of the human relations school theorists were excessive, and, if Likert's System 4, or MacGregor's Theory Y, or Blake's 9 × 9 evaded us, at least there was a rationale for the confusion, disorganization, scrambling, and stress: Systems should be temporary.

BUREAUCRACY'S COMEBACK

Meanwhile, in another part of the management forest, the mechanistic school was gathering its forces and preparing to outflank the forces of light.

First came the numbers men—the linear programmers, the budget experts, and the financial analysts—with their PERT systems and cost-benefit analyses. From another world, unburdened by most of the scientific management ideology and untouched by the human relations school, they began to parcel things out and give some meaning to those truisms, "plan ahead" and "keep records." Armed with emerging systems concepts, they carried the "mechanistic" analogy to its fullest—and it was very productive. Their work still goes on, largely untroubled by organizational theory; the theory, it seems clear, will have to adjust to them, rather than the other way around.

Then the words of Max Weber, first translated from the German in the 1940s—he wrote around 1910, incredibly—began to find their way into social science thought. At first, with his celebration of the efficiency of bureaucracy, he was received with only reluctant respect, and even with hostility. All writers were against bureaucracy. But it turned out, surprisingly, that managers were not. When asked, they acknowledge that they preferred clear lines of communication, clear specifications of authority and responsibility, and clear knowledge of whom they were responsible to. They were as wont to say "there ought to be a rule about this," as to say "there are too many rules around here," as wont to say "next week we've got to get organized," as to say "there is too much red tape." Gradually, studies began to show that bureaucratic organizations could change faster than nonbureaucratic ones, and that morale could be higher where there was clear evidence of bureaucracy.

What was this thing, then? Weber had showed us, for example, that bureaucracy was the most effective way of ridding organizations of favoritism, arbitrary authority, discrimination, payola, and kickbacks, and, yes, even incompetence. His model stressed expertise, and the favorite or the boss's nephew or the guy who burned up resources to make his performance look good was *not* the one with expertise. Rules could be changed; they could be dropped in exceptional circumstances; job security promoted more innovation. The sins of bureaucracy began to look like the sins of failing to follow its principles.

ENTER POWER, CONFLICT, AND DECISIONS

But another discipline began to intrude upon the confident work and increasingly elaborate models of the human relations theorists (largely social psychologists) and the uneasy toying with bureaucracy of the "structionalists" (largely sociologists). Both tended to study economic organizations. A few, like Philip Selznick, were noting conflict and differences in goals (perhaps because he was studying a public agency, the Tennessee Valley Authority), but most ignored conflict or treated it as a pathological manifestation of breakdowns in communication or the ego trips of unreconstructed managers.

But in the world of political parties, pressure groups, and legislative bodies, conflict was not only rampant, but to be expected—it was even functional. This was the domain of the political scientists. They kept talking about power, making it a legitimate concern for analysis. There was an open acknowledgment of "manipulation." These were political scientists who were "behaviorally" inclined—studying and recording behavior rather than constitutions and formal systems of government—and they came to a much more complex view of organized activity. It spilled over into the area of economic organizations, with the help of some economists like R. A. Gordon and some sociologists who were studying conflicting goals of treatment and custody in prisons and mental hospitals.

The presence of legitimately conflicting goals and techniques of preserving and using power did not, of course, sit well with a cooperative systems view of organizations. But it also puzzled the bureaucratic school (and what was left of the old scientific management school), for the impressive Weberian principles were designed to settle questions of power through organizational design and to keep conflict out through reliance on rational-legal authority and systems of careers, expertise, and hierarchy. But power was being overtly contested and exercised in covert ways, and conflict was bursting out all over, and even being creative.

Gradually, in the second half of the 1950s and in the next decade, the political-science view infiltrated both schools. Conflict could be healthy, even in a cooperative system, said the human relationists; it was the mode of resolution that counted, rather than prevention. Power became reconceptualized as "influence," and the distribution was less important, said Arnold Tannenbaum, than the total amount. For the bureaucratic school—never a clearly defined group of people, and largely without any clear ideology—it was easier to just absorb the new data and theories as something else to be thrown into the pot. That is to say, they floundered, writing books that went from topic to topic, without a clear view of organizations, or better yet, producing "readers" and leaving students to sort it all out.

Buried in the political-science viewpoint was a sleeper that only gradually began to undermine the dominant views. This was the idea, largely found in the work of Herbert Simon and James March, that because man was so limited—in intelligence, reasoning powers, information at his disposal, time available, and means of ordering his preferences clearly—he generally seized on the first acceptable alternative when deciding, rather than looking for the best; that he rarely changed things unless they really got bad, and even then he continued to try what had worked before; that he limited his search for solutions to well-worn paths and traditional sources of information and established ideas; that he was wont to remain preoccupied with routine, thus preventing innovation. They called these characteristics "cognitive limits on rationality" and spoke of "satisficing" rather than maximizing or optimizing. It is now called the "decision making" school, and is concerned with the basic question of how people make decisions.

This view had some rather unusual implications. It suggested that if managers were so limited, then they could be easily controlled. What was necessary was not to give direct orders (on the assumption that subordinates were idiots without expertise) or to leave them to their own devices (on the assumption that they were supermen who would somehow know what was best for the organization, how to coordinate with all other supermen, how to anticipate market changes, etc.). It was necessary to control only the *premises* of their decisions. Left to themselves, with those premises set, they could be predicted to rely on precedent, keep things stable and smooth, and respond to signals that reinforce the behavior desired of them.

To control the premises of decision making, March and Simon outline a variety of devices, all of which are familiar to you, but some of which you may not have seen before in quite this light. For example, organizations develop vocabularies, and this means that certain kinds of information are highlighted, and others are screened out—just as Eskimos (and skiers) distinguish many varieties of snow, while Londoners see only one. This is a form of attention-directing. Another is the reward system. Change the bonus for salesmen and you can shift them from volume selling to steady-account selling, or to selling quality products or new products. If you want to channel good people into a different function (because, for example, sales should no longer be the critical functions as the market changes, but engineering applications should), you may have to promote mediocre people in the unrewarded function in order to signal to the good people in the rewarded one that the game has changed. You cannot expect most people to make such decisions on their own because of the cognitive limits on their rationality, nor will you succeed by giving direct orders, because you yourself probably do not know whom to order where. You presume that once the signals are clear and the new sets of alternatives are manifest, they have enough ability to make the decision but you have had to change the premises for their decisions about their career lines.

It would take too long to go through the dozen or so devices, covering a range of decision areas (March and Simon are not that clear or systematic about them, themselves, so I have summarized them in my own book), but I think the message is clear.

It was becoming clear to the human relations school, and to the bureaucratic school. The human relationists had begun to speak of changing stimuli rather than changing personality. They had begun to see that the rewards that can change behavior can well be prestige, money, comfort, etc., rather than trust, openness, self-insight, and so on. The alternative to supportive relations need not be punishment, since behavior can best be changed by rewarding approved behavior rather than by punishing disapproved behavior. They were finding that although leadership may be centralized, it can function best through indirect and unobtrusive means such as changing the premises on which decisions are made, thus giving the impression that the subordinate is actually making a decision when he has only been switched to a different set of alternatives. The implications of this work were also beginning to filter into the human relations school, through an emphasis on behavioral psychology (the modern version of the much maligned stimulus-response school) that was supplanting personality theory (Freudian in its roots, and drawing heavily, in the human relations school, on Maslow).

For the bureaucratic school, this new line of thought reduced the heavy weight placed upon the bony structure of bureaucracy by highlighting the muscle and flesh that make these bones move. A single chain of command, precise division of labor, and clear lines of communication are simply not enough in themselves. Control can be achieved by using alternative communication channels, depending on the situation; by increasing or decreasing the static or "noise" in the system; by creating organizational myths and organizational vocabularies that allow only selective bits of information to enter the system; and through monitoring performance through indirect means rather than direct surveillance. Weber was all right for a starter, but organizations had changed vastly, and the leaders needed many more means of control and more subtle means of manipulation than they did at the turn of the century.

THE TECHNOLOGICAL QUALIFICATION

By now the forces of darkness and forces of light had moved respectively from midnight and noon to about 4 A.M. and 8 P.M. But any convergence or resolution would have to be on yet new terms, for soon after the political-science tradition had begun to infiltrate the established schools, another blow struck both of the major positions. Working quite independently of the Tavistock Group, with its emphasis on sociotechnical systems, and before the work of Burns and Stalker on mechanistic and organic firms, Joan Woodward was trying to see whether the classical scientific principles of organization made any sense in her survey of a hundred firms in South Essex. She tripped and stumbled over a piece of gold in the process. She picked up the gold, labeled it "technology," and made sense out of her otherwise hopeless data. Job-shop firms, mass-production firms, and continuous-process firms all had quite different structures because the type of tasks, or the "technology," was different. Somewhat later, researchers in America were coming to very similar conclusions based on studies of hospitals, juvenile correctional institutions, and industrial firms. Bureaucracy appeared to be the best form of organization for routine operations; temporary work groups, decentralization, and emphasis on interpersonel processes appeared to work best for nonroutine operations. A raft of studies appeared and are still appearing, all trying to show how the nature of the task affects the structure of the organization.

This severely complicated things for the human relations school, since it suggested that openness and trust, while good things in themselves, did not have much impact, or perhaps were not even possible in some kinds of work situations. The prescriptions that were being handed out would have to be drastically qualified. What might work for nonroutine, high-status, interesting, and challenging jobs performed by highly educated people might not be relevant or even beneficial for the vast majority of jobs and people.

It also forced the upholders of the revised bureaucratic theory to qualify their recommendations, since research and development units should obviously be run differently from mass-production units, and the difference between both of these and highly programmed and highly sophisticated continuous-process firms was obscure in terms of bureaucratic theory. But the bureaucratic school perhaps came out on top, because the forces of evil—authority, structure, division of labor, etc.—no longer looked evil, even if they were not applicable to a minority of industrial units.

The emphasis on technology raised other questions, however. A can company might be quite routine, and a plastics division nonroutine, but there were both routine and nonroutine units within each. How should they be integrated if the prescription were followed that, say, production should be bureaucratized and R&D not? James Thompson began spelling out different forms of interdependence among units in organizations, and Paul Lawrence and Jay Lorsch looked closely at the nature of integrating mechanisms. Lawrence and Lorsch found that firms performed best when the differences between units were *maximized* (in contrast to both the human relations and the bureaucratic school), as long as the integrating mechanisms stood half-way between the two—being neither strongly bureaucratic nor nonroutine. They also noted that attempts at participative management in routine situations were counterproductive, that the environments of some kinds of organizations were far from turbulent and customers did not want innovations and changes, that cost reduction, price and efficiency were trivial considerations in some firms, and so on. The technical insight was demolishing our comfortable truths right and left. They were also being questioned from another quarter.

ENTER GOALS, ENVIRONMENTS, AND SYSTEMS

The final seam was being mined by the sociologists while all this went on. This was the concern with organizational goals and the environment. Borrowing from the political scientists to some extent, but pushing ahead on their own, this "institutional school" came to see that goals were not fixed; conflicting goals could be pursued simultaneously, if there were enough slack resources, or sequentially (growth for the next four years, then cost-cutting and profit-taking for the next four); that goals were up for grabs in organizations, and units fought over them. Goals were, of course, not what they seemed to be, the important ones were quite unofficial; history played a big role; and assuming profit as the preeminent goal explained almost nothing about a firm's behavior.

They also did case studies that linked the organization to the web of influence of the environment; that showed how unique organizations were in many respects (so that, once again, there was no one best way to do things for all organizations); how organizations were embedded in their own history, making change difficult. Most striking of all, perhaps, the case studies revealed that the stated goals usually were not the real ones; the official leaders usually were not the real ones; the official leaders usually were not the powerful ones; claims of effectiveness and efficiency were deceptive or even untrue; the public interest was not being served; political influences were pervasive; favoritism, discrimination, and sheer corruption were commonplace. The accumulation of these studies presented quite a pill for either the forces of light or darkness to swallow, since it was hard to see how training sessions or interpersonal skills were relevant to these problems, and it was also clear that the vaunted efficiency of bureaucracy was hardly in evidence. What could they make of this wad of case studies?

We are still sorting it out. In one sense, the Weberian model is upheld because organizations are not, *by nature,* cooperative systems; top managers must exercise a great deal of effort to control them. But if organizations are tools in the hands of leaders, they may be very recalcitrant ones. Like the broom in the story of the sorcerer's apprentice, they occasionally get out of hand. If conflicting goals, bargaining, and unofficial leadership exists, where is the structure of Weberian bones and Simonian muscle? To what extent are organizations tools, and to what extent are they products of the varied interests and group strivings of their members? Does it vary by organization, in terms of some typological alchemy we have not discovered? We don't know. But at any rate, the bureaucratic model suffers again; it simply has not reckoned on the role of the environment. There are enormous sources of variations that the neat, though by now quite complex, neo-Weberian model could not account for.

The human relations model has also been badly-shaken by the findings of the institutional school, for it was wont to assume that goals were given and unproblematical, and that anything that promoted harmony and efficiency for an organization also was good for society. Human relationists assumed that the problems created by organizations were largely limited to the psychological consequences of poor interpersonal relations within them, rather than their impact on the environment. Could the organization really promote the psychological health of its members when by necessity it had to define psychological health in terms of the goals of the organization itself? The neo-Weberian model at least called manipulation "manipulation" and was skeptical of claims about autonomy and self-realization.

But on one thing all the varied schools of organizational analysis now seemed to be agreed: organizations are systems—indeed, they are open systems. As the growth of the field has forced ever more variables into our consciousness, flat claims of predictive power are beginning to decrease and research has become bewilderingly complex. Even consulting groups need more than one or two tools in their kit-bag as the software multiplies.

The systems view is intuitively simple. Everything is related to everything else, though in uneven degrees of tension and reciprocity. Every unit, organization, department, or work group takes in resources, transforms them, and sends them out, and thus interacts with the larger system. The psychological, sociological, and cultural aspects of units interact. The systems view was explicit in the institutional work, since they tried to study whole organizations; it became explicit in the human relations school, because they were so concerned with the interactions of people. The political science and technology viewpoints also had to come to this realization, since they deal with parts affecting each other (sales affecting production; technology affecting structure).

But as intuitively simple as it is, the systems view has been difficult to put into practical use. We still find ourselves ignoring the tenets of the open-systems view, possibly because of the cognitive limits on our rationality. General systems theory itself had not lived up to its heady predictions; it remains rather nebulous. But at least there is a model for calling us to account and for stretching our minds, our research tools, and our troubled nostrums.

SOME CONCLUSIONS

Where does all this leave us? We might summarize the prescriptions and proscriptions for management very roughly as follows:

1. A great deal of the "variance" in a firm's behavior depends on the environment. We have become more realistic about the limited range of change that can be induced through internal efforts. The goals of organizations, including those of profit and efficiency, vary greatly among industries and vary systematically by industries. This suggests that the impact of better management by itself will be limited, since so much will depend on market forces, competition, legislation, nature of the work force, available technologies and innovations, and so on. Another source of variation is, obviously, the history of the firm and its industry and its traditions.

2. A fair amount of variation in both firms and industries is due to the type of work done in the organization—the technology. We are now fairly confident in recommending that if work is predictable and routine, the necessary arrangement for getting the work done can be highly structured, and one can use a good deal of bureaucratic theory in accomplishing this. If it is not predictable, if it is nonroutine and there is a good deal of uncertainty as to how to do a job, then one had better utilize the theories that emphasize autonomy, temporary groups, multiple lines of authority and communications, and so on. We also know that this distinction is important when organizing different parts of an organization.

We are also getting a grasp on the question of what is the most critical function in different types of organizations. For some organizations, it is production; for others, marketing; for still others, development. Furthermore, firms go through phases whereby the initial development of a market or a product or manufacturing process or accounting scheme may require a nonbureaucratic structure, but once it comes on stream, the structure should change to reflect the changed character of the work.

3. In keeping with this, management should be advised that the attempt to produce change in an organization through managerial grids, sensitivity training, and even job enrichment and job enlargement is likely to be fairly ineffective for all but a few organizations. The critical reviews of research in all these fields show that there is no scientific evidence to support the claims of the proponents of these various methods; that research has told us a great deal about social psychology, but little about how to apply the highly complex findings to actual situations. The key word is *selectivity:* We have no broad-spectrum antibiotics for interpersonal relations. Of course, managers should be sensitive, decent, kind, courteous, and courageous, but we have known that for some time now, and beyond a minimal threshold level, the payoff is hard to measure. The various attempts to make work and interpersonal relations more humane and stimulating should be applauded, but we should not confuse this with solving problems of structure, or as the equivalent of decentralization or participatory democracy.

4. The burning cry in all organizations is for "good leadership," but we have learned that beyond a threshold level of adequacy it is extremely difficult to know what good leadership is. The hundreds of scientific studies of this phenomenon come to one general conclusion: Leadership is highly variable or "contingent" upon a large variety of important variables such as nature of task, size of the group, length of time the group has existed, type of personnel within the group and their relationships with each other, and amount of pressure the group is under. It does not seem likely that we'll be able to devise a way to select the best leader for a particular situation. Even if we could, that situation would probably change in a short time and thus would require a somewhat different type of leader.

Furthermore, we are beginning to realize that leadership involves more than smoothing the paths of human interaction. What has rarely been studied in this area is the wisdom or even the technical adequacy of a leader's decision. A leader does more than lead people; he also makes decisions about the allocation of resources, type of technology to be used, the nature of the market, and so on. This aspect of leadership remains very obscure, but it is obviously crucial.

5. If we cannot solve our problems through good human relations or through good leadership, what are we then left with? The literature suggests that changing the structures of organizations might be the most effective and certainly the quickest and cheapest method. However, we are now sophisticated enough to know that changing the formal structure by itself is not likely to produce the desired changes. In addition, one must be aware of a large range of subtle, unobtrusive, and even covert processes and change devices that exist. If inspection procedures are not working, we are now unlikely to rush in with sensitivity training, nor would we send down authoritative communications telling people to do a better job. We are more likely to find out where the authority really lies, whether the degree of specialization is adequate, what the rules and regulations are, and so on, but even this very likely will not be enough.

According to the neo-Weberian bureaucratic model, it has been influenced by work on decision making and behavioral psychology, we should find out how to manipulate the reward structure, change the premises of the decision makers through finer controls on the information received and the expectations generated, search for interdepartmental conflicts that prevent better inspection procedures from being followed, and after manipulating these variables, sit back and wait for two or three months for them to take hold. This is complicated and hardly as dramatic as many of the solutions currently being peddled, but I think the weight of organizational theory is in its favor.

We have probably learned more, over several decades of research and theory, about the things that do *not* work (even though some of them obviously *should* have worked) than we have about things that do work. On balance, this is an important gain and should not discourage us. As you know, organizations are extremely complicated. To have as much knowledge as we do have in a fledgling discipline that has had to borrow from the diverse tools and concepts of psychology, sociology, economics, engineering, biology, history, and even anthropology is not really so bad.

REFERENCES

This paper is an adaptation of the discussion to be found in Charles Perrow, *Complex Organizations: A Critical Essay*, Scott, Foresman, Glenview, Ill., 1972. All the points made in this paper are discussed thoroughly in that volume.

The best overview and discussion of classical management theory, and its changes over time is by Joseph Massie, "Management Theory" in the *Handbook of Organizations* edited by James March, Rand McNally, Chicago, 1965, pp. 387–422.

The best discussion of the changing justifications for managerial rule and worker obedience as they are related to changes in technology, etc., can be found in Reinhard Bendix's *Work and Authority in Industry*, Wiley, New York, 1956. See especially the chapter on the American experience.

Some of the leading lights of the classical view—F. W. Taylor, Col. Urwick, and Henry Fayol—are briefly discussed in *Writers on Organizations* by D. S. Pugh, D. J. Hickson, and C. R. Hinings, Penguin, 1971. This brief, readable, and useful book also contains selections from many other schools that I discuss, including Weber, Woodward, Cyert and March, Simon, the Hawthorne Investigations, and the Human Relations Movement as represented by Argyris, Herzberg, Likert, McGregor, and Blake and Mouton.

As good a place as any to start examining the human relations tradition is Rensis Likert, *The Human Organization*, McGraw-Hill, New York, 1967. See also his *New Patterns of Management*, McGraw-Hill, 1961.

The Buck Rogers school of organizational theory is best represented by Warren Bennis. See his *Changing Organizations*, McGraw-Hill, 1966, and his book with Philip Slater, *The Temporary Society*, Harper & Row, New York, 1968. Much of this work is linked into more general studies, e.g., Alvin Toffler's very popular paperback *Future Shock*, Random House, 1970, and Bantam Paperbacks; or Zibigniew Brzezinsky's *Between Two Ages: America's Role in the Technitronic Era*, Viking Press, New York, 1970. One of the first intimations of the new type of environment and firm and still perhaps the most perceptive is to be found in the volume by Tom Burns and G. Stalker, *The Management of Innovation*, Tavistock, London, 1961, where they distinguished between "organic" and "mechanistic" systems. The introduction, which is not very long, is an excellent and very tight summary of the book.

The political-science tradition came in through three important works. First, Herbert Simon's *Administrative Behavior*, Macmillan, New York, 1948, followed by the second half of James March and Herbert Simon's *Organizations*, Wiley, New York, 1958, then Richard M. Cyert and James March's *A Behavioral Theory of the Firm*, Prentice-Hall, Englewood Cliffs, N.J., 1963. All three of these books are fairly rough going, though chapters 1, 2, 3, and 6 of the last volume are fairly short and accessible. A quite interesting book in this tradition, though somewhat heavy-going, is Michael Crozier's *The Bureaucratic Phenomenon*, University of Chicago, and Tavistock Publications, 1964. This is a striking description of power in organizations, though there is a somewhat dubious attempt to link organization processes in France to the cultural traits of the French people.

The book by Joan Woodward, *Industrial Organisation: Theory and Practice*, Oxford University Press, London, 1965, is still very much worth reading. A fairly popular attempt to discuss the implications for this for management can be found in my own book *Organizational Analysis: A Sociological View,* Tavistock, 1970, chapters 2 and 3. The impact of technology on structure is still fairly controversial. A number of technical studies have found both support and nonsupport, largely because the concept is defined so differently, but there is general agreement that different structures and leadership techniques are needed for different situations. For studies that support and document this viewpoint see James Thompson, *Organizations in Action,* McGraw-Hill, 1967, and Paul Lawrence and Jay Lorsch, *Organizations and Environment,* Harvard University Press, Cambridge, Mass., 1967.

The best single work on the relation between the organization and the environment and one of the most readable books in the field is Philip Selznick's short volume *Leadership in Administration,* Row, Peterson, Evanston, Ill., 1957. But the large number of these studies are scattered about. I have summarized several in my *Complex Organizations: A Critical Essay.*

Lastly, the most elaborate and persuasive argument for a systems view of organizations is found in the first 100 pages of the book by Daniel Katz and Robert Kahn, *The Social Psychology of Organizations,* Wiley, 1966. It is not easy reading, however.

PROBLEMS IN CONTEMPORARY
ORGANIZATION THEORY

KARL WEICK

There are several concepts, assumptions, and practices in current organization theory that seem to stifle the expansion and testing of theories. These impediments must be recognized and removed if a robust theory of organizations is to result. The following sections discuss pitfalls that the reader would be wise to avoid.

ANECDOTAL EVIDENCE AS THE EMPIRICAL BASE

Any discipline will rise or fall depending on the reliability and validity of the observations on which its theories are based. Few fields have made so much of so little as has organization theory. The large number of theories, concepts, and prescriptions in this field far outdistances the empirical findings on which they are supposed to be grounded. For instance, considerable use has been made of anecdotal case studies. Even though case studies have a richness of detail, they have at least four drawbacks: they are (1) situation-specific, (2) ahistorical, (3) tacitly prescriptive, and (4) one-sided. These four items are drawbacks because of their effect on theory construction.

Any organizational environment is turbulent and contains several barriers to survival and growth of the individual. Organizations are demanding and not everyone can survive these demands, at least not without sizable cost. A goodly number of organizational case studies describe ways of "making out" or getting by in a basically alien environment (e.g., Bass, 1967b). They imply that if the reader took seriously the author's remarks, he could do a "better" job threading his way through the intricacies of the organization. The problem comes when we try to build theory from a case study. We can learn from it what to do and not do to survive in that particular environment, but we learn much less about the environment itself and why those particular adjustments are the best ones. Even if we get some idea of what it is in the environment that makes the author's remarks accurate, we still don't know what will happen if the environment changes and if the capacities of persons within the organization shift. This is what we mean when we say that case studies are situation-specific. In essence, we are forced into a more static view of the organization by the simple fact that mechanisms associated with processes, change, development, restructuring, and fluidity are not highlighted.

Source: Karl E. Weick, *The Social Psychology of Organizing* (Reading, Mass.: Addison-Wesley, 1969).

Now it is true that many case studies involve organizations undergoing stress or change (e.g., Barnes, 1960; Lawrence, 1958; O'Connell, 1968; Whyte and Hamilton, 1964). In fact, the bulk of case studies deal with circumstances where a problem exists and there is a great deal of unease among the members. These descriptions supply a vivid slice of life in organizations and depict what it feels like to be immersed in big trouble which must be handled by cumbersome organizational mechanisms. But this type of information isn't very helpful in theory construction. Theories are built on regularities among events, people, and relationships, not on sporadic, infrequent, explosive episodes. The point is that there are repetitive behaviors and events that constitute order in an organization whether they are reported in the case study or not. Getting into trouble can be just as orderly and repetitious as getting out. It is these regularities which theory attempts to capture, and it is precisely these regularities which are absent from many case studies. We are not arguing that repetition is more important than novelty or uniqueness. Instead, we are saying that the bulk of action is repetitive rather than nonrepetitive. The warrant for this assumption can be argued in terms of psychoanalytic theory (LaBarre, 1968), evolutionary theory (Campbell, 1965b), learning theory (Skinner, 1963), role theory (Kahn *et al.*, 1964), or cybernetic theory (MacKay, 1968). What we are saying here is that case studies are ahistorical. It is difficult to tell what the group being described has done in the past that is being *repeated* in the present, and it is even harder to discover what it is about the environment that produces this repetition. Precisely this information is needed if lawful relationships are to be stated.

The usefulness of a theory is *not* determined by its usability in the everyday business of running an organization or "making out" in one. Theoretical usefulness is not defined in terms of pragmatics. Most case studies, however, are pragmatically based or can be read pragmatically. This means that a case study will tell us what works and what doesn't work in a particular organization. It will often provide a tacit "prescription" for getting along in the organization. But we do not know the conditions under which that pragmatic recommendation or prescription holds. Consider, for example, a case study that describes a set of circumstances in which a problem eventually was solved when members participated more fully in the decisions that affected them. This has a "lesson." The lesson is: if you want better decisions, let those who will be affected by them make them. We are tempted to state this in terms of a "law": as participation increases, the acceptability of a decision will increase. But a statement like this actually *hinders* theory construction. What we know is that participation affects decision acceptance. But we are left with the question: under what conditions? It is *not* a universal law that every time there is a change in participation, there is a corresponding change in decision acceptance. Sometimes yes, sometimes no. What we have to discover and build into a theory are precisely those elements that condition this relationship. That information is seldom available in a case study.

Most case studies do not describe any circumstances where the author's prescription *did not* work. They are one-sided; that is, the author does not provide us with a meaningful comparison so that we can see what it is that produces the regularity he sees. We can determine the causative factors only if we have a set of circumstances in which his observed regularity fails to occur. By comparing the circumstances at the time of failure with the circumstances at the time of success, we can determine what is common and what is different between the two. It is this information that enables us to construct a theory about organizations which will contain a realistic set of lawful relationships.

The inadequacy of organization theory's empirical base cannot be blamed solely on case studies. Field experiments on organizational problems also are culpable, as was demonstrated recently by Carey's (1967) extensive criticism of the most venerable set of field experiments in organization theory, the Hawthorne studies (Roethlisberger and Dickson, 1939). Carey makes it abundantly clear that these studies, which many theorists use as a point of departure, are replete with erroneous interpretations and do not demonstrate what everyone thought they did. For example, Carey refutes the conclusion, drawn from these studies, that relaxed and friendly supervision causes higher productivity. On closer inspection, the Hawthorne studies actually reveal the opposite relationship—because of higher productivity, the managers became more relaxed. Furthermore, the increase in productivity was caused by a simple change of personnel in the work group. Two recalcitrant workers were dismissed halfway through the study and were replaced by two women who needed jobs in order to handle their financial problems. Their efforts and prodding led to an increase in the group's output, and it was only *after* this output increase that the management relaxed the coercive style of supervision they had used previously. The fact that higher productivity causes managers to become more considerate has been recently demonstrated in the laboratory by Lowin and Craig (1968).

These findings are of great importance because so much organization theory and practice has assumed all along that the style of supervision affects productivity. The fact that the reverse direction of causation is just as likely demonstrates clearly the necessity for greater care and precision in experimentation and theory construction. Premature application of dubious findings is fatal both for practice and theory. Actually, it is not surprising that managers in business organizations are often disappointed by the results and recommendations produced by behavioral scientists. The problem is not that the theories are too abstract to be applied. Managers have sufficient intelligence to understand that a scientist's job is to develop theories that eventually may address practical issues *if* they are developed consistently and are tested with precision (e.g., Lundberg, 1968). The real problem is that current methods of theory construction and data collection drive a wedge between the world portrayed in the theories and the real world. The reinterpretation of the Hawthorne studies demonstrates this point. When these results were originally published, managers interested in improving output understandably latched onto them, as did organization theorists. But they did so without close scrutiny of what actually had been demonstrated.

The implications of this analysis should be clear. Reliable data are needed for generating and testing useful theories. The data have to be unambiguous, and the only way we can generate unambiguous data is by using techniques that resolve ambiguity. To accomplish this, we typically need multiple methods, or techniques which are imperfect in *different* ways. When multiple methods are applied, the imperfections in each method tend to cancel one another, and the resulting data are less ambiguous. As we have said over and over, the likelihood that clear data will be produced depends on the number and kinds of comparisons that are made. The experimental method, whether applied in field experiments (e.g., Scott, 1965; Seashore, 1966), controlled naturalistic observation (e.g., Weick, 1968), contrived laboratory experiments (e.g., Weick, 1965, 1967), or simulated environments (e.g., Abt Associates, 1965; Drabek and Haas, 1967; Guetzkow, 1962, 1968) is the principal tactic by which more durable and useful data can be obtained. The several variations that are possible within the experimental method permit the canceling of imperfections. There are techniques available that, if applied with sufficient concern for detail, can provide the data which case studies seldom do. And they can provide these data with more frequency than even the best case studies can. It is routine for an experimental method to produce useful data. It is exceptional when case studies do so.

CONSIDERING MANAGEMENT PROBLEMS IN MANAGEMENT TERMS

Organization theory has often been stifled because it has worked on problems that managers thought were problems and has studied them using managerial concepts rather than psychological or sociological ones. The only way in which understanding can be advanced is if the symbols used by practitioners are removed, and the phenomena recast into language that has psychological or sociological meaning. For example, managers talk about line-staff relationships, span of control, the size of departments, cost-efficiency ratios, etc. This is managerial talk and it helps managers get on with their work of managing. But managerial talk carves up the world of the organization in a particular way. It isolates certain phenomena and certain implications. If a psychologist decides to develop empirical laws about "line-staff relationships" he already is at a disadvantage. He tacitly accepts the manager's definition of the problem *and* the relevant components. He takes the phenomenon that the manager points to and his way of pointing to it as the principal arena in which the search for relationships should be conducted. There is little chance that he can gain an understanding of the phenomenon psychologically, or build this understanding into a framework that will have broader relevance. All he can do is tack on selected psychological concepts to a problem with little psychological relevance. For example, a manager might observe that whenever his department contains more than 25 people, morale drops sharply. If a theorist takes this observation at face value, and then proceeds to develop a theory of the effects of size on morale, he is not likely to tell us anything of theoretical importance. The problem has been phrased in managerial, not psychological, terms. If instead of looking at gross changes in size, the investigator were to study the more basic psychological questions, such as what happens to people when they feel crowded, ignored, anonymous, on display, or unmonitored, then the chance of understanding the effects of size would improve. Linkages between size and morale would become more apparent because the psychologist would be exploring psychological states that mediate this effect; the resulting theory would be applicable to a wider variety of settings than those in which the manager operates (e.g., the psychologist could predict what would happen in husband-wife dyads when the husband felt crowded); and the psychologist would be in a better position to link his theory with other theories and move toward unification of knowledge (e.g., the theory might suggest that crowding is an instance of the more general phenomenon of approach-avoidance gradients; Schneirla, 1959). Note that all of these latter benefits can be realized only if the scientist remains faithful to and exploits his discipline's strengths. After all, he is equipped to do what the average layman cannot, namely, to conduct psychological or sociological analyses of everyday phenomena. He abandons most of his tools for doing such analyses if he accepts managerial problems phrased in managerial terms.

An interesting paradox arises. Most scientists want the knowledge they have obtained to be accepted by other people, to make a difference in their lives, and to improve the human condition in some way. They have every right to want this, because they may know something with greater certainty than anyone else does. But generating something acceptable and true is possible only if the scientist first *ignores* the everyday labels with which the phenomenon comes to him, and replaces these labels with symbols he can work with. Only if he does this can he discover truths that deserve acceptance. If the scientist is concerned with acceptability from the start, then the chance that he will produce anything acceptable in the long run is reduced. You have to destroy acceptability in order to produce it.

BIBLIOGRAPHY

ABT ASSOCIATES (1965), *Survey of the State of the Art: Social, Political and Economic Models and Simulations.* Cambridge, Mass.: Abt Associates Inc.

BARNES, L. B. (1960), *Organizational Systems and Engineering Groups.* Cambridge, Mass.: Harvard University Press.

Bass, B. M. (1967b), *How to Succeed in Business According to Business Students and Managers.* Technical Report 15. Management Research Center, University of Pittsburgh.

Campbell, D. T. (1965b), "Variation and Selective Retention in Socio-Cultural Evolution." In H. R. Barringer, G. E. Blanksten, and R. Mack (Eds.), *Social Change in Developing Areas.* Cambridge, Mass.: Schenkman. Pp. 19–49.

Carey, A. (1967), "The Hawthorne Studies: A Radical Criticism." *American Sociological Review,* 32, 403–16.

Drabek, T. E., and J. E. Haas (1967), "Realism in Laboratory Simulation: Myth or Method?" *Social Forces,* 45, 337–46.

Guetzkow, H. (1962), "Joining Field and Laboratory Work in Disaster Research." In G. W. Baker and D. W. Chapman (Eds.), *Man and Society in Disaster.* New York: Basic Books. Pp. 337–55.

Guetzkow, H. (1968), "Some Correspondences Between Simulations and 'Realities' in International Relations." In M. Kaplan (Ed.), *New Approaches to International Relations.* New York: St. Martin's Press.

Kahn, R. L.; D. M. Wolfe; R. P. Quinn; J. D. Snoek; and R. A. Rosenthal (1964), *Organizational Stress.* New York: Wiley.

LaBarre, W. (1968), "Personality from a Psychoanalytic Viewpoint." In E. Norbeck, D. Price-Williams, and W. McCord (Eds.), *The Study of Personality.* New York: Holt, Rinehart & Winston. Pp. 65–87.

Lawrence, P. R. (1958), *The Changing of Organizational Behavior Patterns.* Cambridge, Mass.: Harvard University Press.

Lowin, A., and J. R. Craig (1968), "The Influence of Level of Performance on Managerial Style: An Experimental Object-Lesson in the Ambiguity of Correlational Data." *Organizational Behavior and Human Performance,* 3, 440–58.

Lundberg, C. C. (1968), "Toward Understanding Behavioral Science by Administrators." In D. R. Hampton (Ed.), *Behavioral Concepts in Management.* Belmont, Calif.: Dickenson. Pp. 69–83.

MacKay, D. M. (1968), "Toward an Information-Flow Model of Human Behavior." In W. R. Buckley (Ed.), *Modern Systems Research for the Behavioral Scientist.* Chicago: Aldine. Pp. 359–68.

O'Connell, J. J. (1968), *Managing Organizational Innovation.* Homewood, Ill.: Irwin.

Roethlisberger, F. J., and W. Dickson (1939), *Management and the Worker.* Cambridge: Harvard University Press.

Schneirla, T. C. (1959), "An Evolutionary and Developmental Theory of Biphasic Processes Underlying Approach and Withdrawal." In M. R. Jones (Ed.), *Nebraska Symposium on Motivation,* 1959. Lincoln: Univ. of Nebraska Press. Pp. 1–42.

Scott, W. R. (1965), "Field Methods in the Study of Organizations." In J. G. March (Ed.), *Handbook of Organizations.* Chicago: Rand McNally. Pp. 261–304.

Seashore, S. E. (1966), "Field Experiments with Formal Organizations." In R. Bowers (Ed.), *Studies on Behavior in Organizations.* Athens, Ga.: Univ. of Georgia Press. Pp. 87–100.

Skinner, B. F. (1963), "Behaviorism at Fifty." *Science*, 140, 951-58.

Weick, K. E. (1965), "Laboratory Experimentation with Organizations." In J. G. March (Ed.), *Handbook of Organizations*. Chicago: Rand McNally. Pp. 194–260.

Weick, K. E. (1967), "Organizations in the Laboratory." In V. H. Vroom (Ed.), *Methods of Organizational Research*. Pittsburgh: Univ. of Pittsburgh Press. Pp. 1–56.

Weick, K. E. (1968), "Systematic Observational Methods." In G. Lindzey and E. Aronson (Eds.), *The Handbook of Social Psychology* (2nd ed.). Vol. 2. Reading, Mass.: Addison-Wesley.

Whyte, W. F., and Edith L. Hamilton (1964). *Action Research for Management*. Homewood, Ill.: Irwin-Dorsey.

section two

This section is designed to deal with the issues surrounding how one might build an organization. Structure has long been the focus of organization studies, perhaps because it is the most visible part of an organization other than physical aspects such as the buildings and grounds. The groupings of jobs, departments, divisions, and so on, are usually reflected on an organization chart and constitute what is commonly thought of when organizational structure is discussed. We will see in this section that although this description is essentially correct, much more is involved.

Chapter 3 looks at what was initially developed to be guidelines for the "ideal" organizational structure—bureaucracy. Then we turn to current empirical studies to help define the dimensions of organizational structure.

Chapter 4 examines two of the very basic "How to do it" issues involved in designing an organization's structure—how will the task be divided into jobs and how will the resulting jobs be combined into departments? In addition, issues surrounding job design and redesign are covered.

Chapter 5 considers "patterns in business organization design," one way of describing the next level of aggregation that is the combination of departments, divisions, etc., into organizational wholes. Like Chapter 4, this chapter takes the practitioners' pragmatic perspective.

The objectives for section two are to answer the general questions:

1. What "should" organizations look like?
2. How are organizations usually built?

THE MANAGEMENT
OF ORGANIZATIONAL
DESIGN

chapter 3

BUREAUCRACY
AND STRUCTURE

A businessman gets the "runaround" when trying to determine if he should file a certain report with a government agency. A customer receives an account closure notice and gets no satisfaction from the clerk who explains "that is our rule." Both are angry and blame the "bureaucracy." To most people, bureaucracy is that aspect of any organization responsible for the red tape, "buck passing," and impersonal treatment they encounter. This description may be accurate enough for the laymen, but it is not adequate for those who wish to understand organizations. In this analysis bureaucracy refers to a special type of organization, and it is used as a point of departure for a discussion of the structural aspects of organizations.

Bureaucracy was the first set of ideas that was proposed as a design for the organization as a whole, and it spawned interest in the study of organizations by academicians. The purpose of this chapter is to help you become familiar with bureaucracy and the related concept of organization structure, how they have developed, and how they are studied and viewed today. First, we will consider bureaucracy.

MAX WEBER AND BUREAUCRACY

Max Weber originated the concept of bureaucracy as a model to be used in his analysis of organized industrial society. Later writers were to use his model as an "ideal" standard to which the existing structure of an organization could be compared. To fully understand his concept and put its uses and criticisms into perspective, one must know his purposes as well as the characteristics of the model.

Weber was a German scholar trained in law, economics, history, and philosophy. He had traveled widely in Europe and the United States and was interested in labor problems, political management, voluntary associations, and industrial psychology.[1] In developing his ideal organization concept Weber was attempting a representation of a social phenomenon. He was not interested in representing the whole of organizational reality or in depicting the "average" organization.

Weber was concerned with the role bureaucracy plays in allowing certain people to dominate other people. He believed that in order to legitimately dominate a large number of people, the followers must *feel obligated* to obey the orders of the leader, and the leader must believe he has the *right* to order the followers. In addition, the leader needs a tool with which to administer his orders to large numbers of members. That tool is the "administrative method" used by the leader.

Weber combined these beliefs about the legitimized exercise of power and the administrative method to characterize three methods of exercising domination.[2]

1. *Charismatic domination* occurs when a leader can command followers because of his exceptional performance and because his followers believe in him personally. Followers are administered to through the most "faithful" in a loosely organized way. Examples might be the leadership of Jesus Christ or Charles Manson.

2. *Traditional domination* occurs when the leader commands because of inherited position. The followers believe this is his right since affairs have always been conducted this way. Followers are administered to by officials who are personal dependents of the leader or allies who administer the domain by contract. Examples might be found in feudal societies with kings and serfs.

3. *Legal domination* occurs when the leader can command because he has obtained his position through a legal procedure that the followers consider "right and correct." Followers obey because they accept the law and procedure. The administrative method in this case is the bureaucracy. An example might be the military officer or the corporation president as leaders.

Rationality

In contrast with the first two methods of domination, Weber saw legal domination and its associated administrative method, bureaucracy, as the most efficient and ideal form of organization. Compared to the charismatic and traditional forms, the legal/bureaucratic form was *rational;* that is, impersonal rules replaced blind faith and arbitrary personal judgment.

He saw the bureaucratic type of organization emerging as the dominant form in Western society during the Industrial Revolution and saw it as the most efficient form yet devised to dominate man. But in its use and development Weber recognized possible threats to democracy and individual freedom.

Weber's Model

Weber attempted to construct a model of a perfectly rational organization: one that performed its job with maximum efficiency. The model of bureaucracy he constructed was his organizational design for achieving perfect rationality and efficiency.

Basing his model on reasoning rather than empirical evidence, he described the characteristics of this ideal administrative framework. It was composed of these features:

1. *Impersonal and formal conduct.* Personality and emotionally based relationships interfere with rationality. Therefore, nepotism and favoritism on a nonperformance-related basis should be eliminated.

2. *Employment and promotion on the basis of technical competence and performance.* These criteria are the real basis for legitimization of authority. Following them ensures that the best qualified people will pursue a career in the organization and remain loyal to it.

3. *Systematic specialization of labor and specification of responsibilities.* All the work necessary to accomplish the tasks of the organization should be divided into specific areas of competence. Each employee and supervisor would have authority over his functions and would not interfere with the conduct of others' jobs.

4. *Well-ordered system of rules and procedures that regulate the conduct of work.* Rules serve several purposes:
   a. They standardize operations and decisions.
   b. They serve as receptacles of past learning.
   c. They protect incumbents and ensure equality of treatment.
The learning of rules represents much of the technical competence of incumbents because they tell them what decision to make and when to make it.

5. *Hierarchy of positions such that every position is controlled by a higher one.* The hierarchy of authority is impersonal, based on rules, and the superior position is held by one having greater expertise. Thus, compliance with rules and coordination is systematically ensured.

6. *Complete separation of the property and affairs of the organization from the personal property and affairs of the incumbents.* This serves to prevent the demands and interests of personal affairs from interfering with the rational impersonal conduct of the organizational business.

This characterization does not capture all of Weber's description of the ideal bureaucracy, but it does provide the main characteristics of his model. He did not intend it to be a theory of organizational reality or a theory of organizations. But it has become the basis for much influential thought and investigation on organizations.

Post-Weber Criticism

Since Weber's initial formulations, bureaucracy has also become the subject of much debate and criticism. Some criticisms hinge on whether his model was an adequate theoretical representation of the way organizations are actually structured, whereas others focus on the inadequacies of bureaucracy as a way to effectively conduct the affairs of an organization. These latter criticisms have been numerous, and a sample of the more significant ones will be provided at other points in the book.

Most investigations of bureaucracy since Weber have focused primarily on the *internal* workings of organizations. Early studies were mostly case studies of a relatively few organizations. Many of the results focused on the unintended consequences of using the bureaucratic model. Several noted sociologists were occupied with studying the dysfunctions of rules and goal displacement, while organizational psychologists were concerned about the impact of a bureaucratic organization on people in the organization.

The Sociologists

Robert Merton was one of the first to see the unintended consequences of bureaucracy.[3] He saw control and coordination by rules as an aid to the organization's rationality because rules promote predictability of behavior. But they also make the bureaucrat's behavior less flexible. An emphasis on rules develops in bureaucracies, and eventually the rules are adopted by members as personal goals. The rules are no longer merely ways to achieve organizational goals but become personal goals in themselves. This "displacement" of organizational goals by personal goals then leads to organizational ineffectiveness.

Like Merton, Philip Selznick believed that means can become ends through goal displacement.[4] In his view displacement arises from the need to delegate powers to subunits in the organization. As the organization becomes larger and gains more departmental subunits, it becomes necessary to delegate operational decision-making authority to the subunits, an argument much like we developed in chapter 1.

These separate departments then develop goals of their own. For example, maximum sales may become the goal of a marketing department or long production runs the goal of the production department. Priorities shift from the organizational goal of overall profit to specific goals for individual subunits, which may not equal the organizational goal when added together. This situation leads to a necessity for *recentralization* of control by top management in an attempt to reintegrate efforts toward the major organizational goals.

In Alvin Gouldner's work the theme of unintended consequence of control through rules reappears.[5] He argues that rules define *minimum acceptable behavior* and performance requirements as well as desired behavior and performance. When the organizational goals are not adopted by employees as their own (i.e., internalized) the consequence is performance at the minimal levels specified by the rules. This situation leads to increased effort on the part of management to further control behavior.

However, two other sociologists, Blau and Scott did not see goal displacement as inevitable.[6] They found that when organizations or subunits are not threatened and are secure in their relationships, the result can be a "succession" of goals. As units succeed in meeting their initial goals, they adopt more advanced subsequent goals. But if proper conditions are not present and the organizational unit fails in its goal attempts, it may focus its efforts toward survival as a goal.

Several emphases are apparent in the work of these sociologists. Unlike Weber, their concern was with the internal workings of the organization. Weber was concerned with the role of bureaucracy in *society*, whereas these critics emphasized how well the bureaucratic model worked in the real world and indicated some of the unintended consequences of using bureaucratic rules to control behavior in organizations.

One sociologist who did not confine his interest to the internal workings of the organization was James D. Thompson.[7] Thompson saw the organization's environment playing a key role in the determination of its behavior. He criticized the bureaucratic model for ignoring environment. For Thompson the major criticism of Weber's model was that it treated the organization as though it were a closed system not affected by the uncertainties of the environment. He suggests that environmental uncertainties make it difficult to predict the future and thus limit the ability of any organization to preplan or determine all its actions. Since planning is the essence of rationality and the ability of an organization to plan is limited by the environment, the bureaucratic model was founded on an inappropriate assumption, according to Thompson.

By examining Weber's model relative to real organizations, the sociologists raised certain cautions about assuming it is representative of actual organizations. Their analyses also cause one to be cautious in proposing that bureaucracy is a universal organizational model.

The Organizational Psychologists

A pioneering criticism from organizational psychology comes from Warren Bennis. He sees the model as overly *mechanical* and no longer useful.[8] It fails to provide executives with the means to deal with a modern organizational environment that is characterized by change rather than by stability. The flaws and dysfunctions of the bureaucratic model as it exists in present organizations according to Bennis are extensive. A partial listing would include that:

1. It is inhumane and denies man's needs.
2. It is incompatible with the development of a mature personality.

block 3-1

LIKERT'S ORGANIZATION SYSTEMS

The Survey Research Center at the University of Michigan has been the home of numerous studies concerned with the internal workings of organizations. Rensis Likert, building on the efforts of many of its members, described the characteristics of what he believed to be an effective organization as well as what he thought were less effective ones.

Likert argued that organizations can be characterized by using eight dimensions. These dimensions ignore structural characteristics to emphasize *processes* although the degree of centralization (a structural variable) seems to be implicitly dealt with in several of the dimensions. He developed an extensive questionnaire to measure the character of: (1) leadership processes, (2) motivational processes, (3) communication processes, (4) interpersonal interactions, (5) decision-making processes, (6) goal-setting processes, (7) control processes, and (8) performance goals and training.

These dimensions were used to describe four general types of organizational management systems. System I provides an exploitive and authoritarian environment where there is low motivation, little interpersonal support and participation, only downward communication and authoritarian control. System II provided a benevolent and authoritarian environment. It is similar to System I but is more paternalistic. System III is described as a consultative environment having upward and downward communication, supportive leadership, a certain degree of self-regulation and consultative goal setting. System IV provides a participative environment with more emphasis on self-regulation and mutual support, openness, and trust, high performance goals, and more involved participation at all levels.

Likert believes that as an organization moves from a System I toward a System IV, it becomes more adaptable, improves performances, employee satisfaction and involvement through greater utilization of peoples' knowledge, ability, and potential. Most organizations are thought to be Systems II or III, but members would prefer the organization to be more like System IV.

Although Likert's approach emphasizes processes rather than structural dimensions, it is similar to Weber's ideal bureaucracy. System IV is seen as the one best way for the organization to conduct its affairs. Its character seems different from Weber's model, but it is conceivable that a participative system could still have most of the characteristics of a Weberian bureaucracy. Likert's approach is also similar in that all the characteristics are somewhat tied together. That is, they are not seen as mutually independent; it is unlikely one would utilize participative goal setting and decision making while practicing authoritarian leadership processes.

Based on Rensis Likert, *The Human Organization* (New York: McGraw-Hill, 1967).

3. It promotes conformity.

4. It does not consider the informal organization and interpersonal difficulties.

5. The hierarchy interferes with communication.

6. Innovation and new knowledge are stifled.

7. It is ineffective in a turbulent environment.

These criticisms are representative of the organizational psychology view of bureaucracy. Members of this school of thought tend to focus on individual and group behavior in organizations. Rensis Likert (See Block 3-1) is also representative of these organizational scholars in his emphasis on the *processes* involved with people working together. He sees certain changes as leading to more effective organizations: greater participation, less regulation of members' behavior, more open, authentic behavior between members, and greater appeal to the "real" motivations of people. At one time Bennis predicted the death of bureaucracy as an organizational form; however, in a recent interview he reversed his prediction and concluded that they may be inevitable.[9]

The thrust of these criticisms is that the bureaucratic model makes inadequate assumptions about the "real" nature of man and does not address itself to the interaction of people within the organization. Although one may agree with some of these criticisms, this book will not dwell on them nor their attempts to modify the administrative apparatus of organizations.

USING TYPOLOGIES TO UNDERSTAND ORGANIZATIONS

From the review thus far you can see that not all organizations fit the bureaucratic ideal. Furthermore, organizations are different from one another. If the bureaucratic model of an "ideal" organization can't help us classify organizations as to their structural differences, what can help our understanding of these differences? In chapter 2 we introduced organizational typology or classification as a possible method for doing this.

Although organizations do differ, they are also similar; not every organization is completely unique. To the extent they are similar, the application of effective management practice in one may be transferable to others. To the extent they are different, the same management practice may lead to ineffectiveness and inefficiency in different situations. For example, a bureaucratic organizational system may work well under stable conditions employing a simple routine technology, but it might be inappropriate under the opposite conditions.[10] The classification of organizations by relevant variables allows categorization of organizations into *types* so that generalization about these organizational types can help determine when a variable or practice may be useful, hence, the word *typology*.

We suggested earlier that classifications are useful in facilitating the screening out of many nonrelevant data so one can concentrate on what is relevant to one's specific purposes. The human mind uses classification in perception and the thinking processes to handle the great number of stimuli it receives.[11] Thus, by classifying, humans are better able to comprehend and manage information.

Classification schemes have been developed that use different criteria in their construction. The better known are those in which the developer has deduced the criteria he considers most important and from these dimensions constructed a classification scheme. Figure 3-1 presents six such typologies. It should be noted that any of these classifications might include bureaucratic or nonbureaucratic forms.

A different approach can be taken. Two groups of researchers measured a number of different organizational dimensions. The results were analyzed and found to form clusters of similar organizations based on the dimensions measured. Figure 3-2 presents two examples of this approach. Notice that the Pugh, Hickson, and Hindings study differentiates among different kinds of bureaucracy.

This approach represents initial attempts toward classification based on actual situations. However, empirically derived approaches may pose barriers to the usefulness of such knowledge to practitioners since it requires them to measure their own situation before they can decide if a piece of knowledge may be applicable.

Haas and Drabek have concluded that "future taxonomic work is an essential ingredient in the enterprise of a science of organizations.[12] The development of an adequate typology is important to both the science of organizations and the management of organizations. However, the typologies developed to date have failed to be sufficiently discriminatory. Organizations can often be placed in more than one category.

One extensive review of typology development concludes that, "these schemes simply do not place organizations into categories that are sufficiently differentiated from each other in terms of important organizational characteristics."[13] Perhaps none of the existing typologies are completely satisfactory. When all the variables relevant to understanding organizations have been identified and measured in a variety of organizations and when it has been determined which ones possess which characteristics and to what degree, an adequate typology will be available.

The important point to be made is that classification of organizations as bureaucratic or nonbureaucratic is a very simplistic typology that adds

figure 3-1

THEORETICAL TYPOLOGIES OF ORGANIZATIONS

Author	Dimensions	Example
Hughes[14]	Philanthropic	Miami University
	Family business	Percy's Carmel Corn Shop
	Corporate	Armco Steel
	Military	U.S. Air Force Academy
	Voluntary	Academy of Management
Parsons[15]	Pattern maintenance	Churches
	Economic production	Businesses
	Integrative relations	Hospitals
	Political goals	Armies
Katz and Kahn[16] (first order)	Production	Railroads
	Maintenance	Schools
	Adaptation	Universities
	Managerial or political	Governmental agencies
Katz and Kahn[16] (second order)	Through-put	People or objects
	Maintenance process	Use of intrinsic or instrumental rewards
	Bureaucratic structure	Elaborateness and ease of membership
	Equilibrium	Status quo or growth
Etzioni[17]	Congruent types:	
	Coercive	Prisons
	Utilitarian	Manufacturing
	Normative	Fraternal
Blau and Scott[18]	Mutual benefit	United Automobile Workers
	Service	Schools
	Commonwealth	National Labor Relations Board
	Business	Prentice-Hall

figure 3-2

EMPIRICALLY BASED TYPOLOGIES OF ORGANIZATION

Author	Dimensions	Example
Haas, Hall, and Johnson[19]	Class I	Motel, bank
	Class II	Hotel, bank
	Class III	State penal institution
	Class IV	Airport
	Class V	Private hospitals
	Class VI	State hospitals
	Class VII	Private welfare agency
	Class VIII	State penal institution
	Class IX	County political party
	Class X	Railroad
Pugh, Hickson, and Hinings[20]	Full bureaucracy	Government department
	Nascent full bureaucracy	Civil engineering firm
	Workflow bureaucracy	Food manufacturer
	Nascent workflow bureaucracy	Brewery
	Preworkflow bureaucracy	Food manufacturer
	Personnel bureaucracy	Food manufacturer
	Implicitly structured bureaucracy	Department store

very little to our knowledge of managing organizations. This typology describes an organization and its structure in relatively black or white terms. Even the Pugh, Hickson, and Hinings typology of bureaucracies in Figure 3-2 does not provide us with a complete classification of organization structural types. Indeed, in our opinion the ultimate structural typology has not yet been devised, and we do not propose to develop one here. Instead, our study of organizations now focuses on what *is* known about the structures of organizations without a complete typology (as helpful as it might be) to guide our explorations.

ORGANIZATIONAL STRUCTURE

What is the best method of organizing to get work done? How can we make the organization of work more efficient? What is the relationship between different parts of the organization? In the following chapters we will deal with how practitioners and academicians have approached these questions and others. But in the remainder of this chapter we deal with how present-day researchers have studied the internal *structures* of organizations. Structure in one sense is the arrangement of duties used for organizing the work to be done. The introduction of more sophisticated views of structure will follow.

The bureaucratic model treats organizations as closed-rational systems that do not recognize the environment as a force affecting the internal organization structure or skeleton. The model assumes that resources enter the organization at a constant rate as it needs them and that the environment does not intrude into the organization. If one assumes, as this model does, that the organization can close off its internal affairs from its environment and can remove itself from the major source of uncertainty and if organizations can control internal operations so that everything is predictable, the primary conditions for bureaucratic rationality have been achieved. It has achieved the status of a closed system.

Today, most theorists recognize that organizations are not closed systems, but they would *like to be* because of the desirability of rational behavior. Most organizations are open systems, since they receive inputs from their environment and must export products and services to the environment. These contacts with the environment necessarily influence the structures and internal operations of an organization.

Different Approaches to Structure

Child has pointed out various schools of thought that focus on causes of differences in organizational structure.[21] Some believe that certain factors, such as size, environment, or technology, *determine* organization structure. They argue that such factors impose economic or other constraints on organizations that *force* them to choose certain structures over others. Each school argues that its particular factor is the primary determinant of structure. Because advocates of each contextual factor have taken the position that their factor *dictates* to the organization what its structure must be, this approach has been called the imperative school of thought on organizational structure. Each of these imperatives will be examined in detail in coming chapters.

Child sees the manager or administrator as the missing link in these theories. Situational factors are forces that are considered by these executives, but perhaps they are not interpreted accurately, or simply ignored. Child's view is represented by Figure 3-3. He criticizes the imperative approach for ignoring the role played by executives in making conscious choices about the organization's structure and their attempts to manipulate the situational factors.

figure 3-3

CHILD'S RECONSTRUCTION OF THE IMPERATIVE APPROACHES

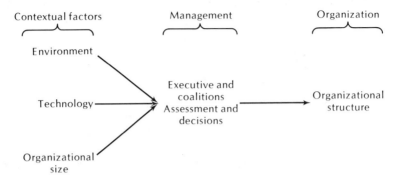

For example, an executive may refuse to diversify in order to grow in the United States because of threats of antitrust action. Instead he may choose to confront the threat directly by keeping the organization's present character in the United States and expanding its foreign operations.

There is a school of thought, represented by Chandler[22] and a business policy group at the Harvard Business School,[23] that sees such strategic choice by management as the most important variable in understanding an organization's structure. In this view, changes in goals and strategic decisions become the starting point for understanding structure, although they are not usually treated as imperatives.

By now you have probably guessed that there is no consensus as to what "causes" organization structure. Furthermore, although the open-system nature of organizations receives a great deal of verbal attention, most empirical work has been concerned instead with the internal operations of the organization and what causes it. Only in some theoretical works, such as those of Thompson,[24] Katz and Kahn[25] and Kast and Rozenweig,[26] have management theorists treated organizations as an open system in any comprehensive way, and dealt with the ramifications of an open system on the resulting structural arrangements.

Before turning our attention to how different factors influence structure, we need to concern ourselves with a more complete definition of structure than has been given to this point. What is organization structure?

A More Sophisticated Definition of Structure

To the casual observer, structure may be represented by a document called the "organization chart," or by the hierarchy of authority and reporting relationships. Certainly these are partially correct. Everyone seems to have some understanding of what is meant by the term, but it is not always easy to find a consensus on a definition. It is common to find authors writing about structure and what variables compose it without defining it, the definition being implied by the variables they discuss.[27]

March and Simon define structure as consisting ". . . simply of those aspects of the pattern of behavior in the organization that are relatively stable and that change only slowly."[28] The behaviors they see as stable are programs that permit adaptation to stable parts of an environment and those that control the process of adaptation. Katz and Kahn say, ". . . structure is to be found in an interrelated set of events which return to complete and renew a cycle of activities."[29]

Thompson refers to the division of major components into departments and the establishments of connections between them. He says, "It is the internal differentiation and patterning of relationships that we will refer to as structure."[30] He goes on to refer to structure as the primary means by which the organization sets limits and boundaries for efficient performance by its members, "by delimiting responsibilities, control over resources, and other matters. . . ."[31]

The variety of definitions implies the lack of consensus. It also implies that writers tend to use definitions best suited to their own purposes. However, there is some commonality among them. They either state or suggest that structure is something that is a relatively continuous pattern of parts that are interrelated. For our purposes we will modify a definition offered by Child.[32] *Organizational structure is defined as the relatively enduring allocation of work roles and administrative mechanisms that creates a pattern of interrelated work activities and allows the organization to conduct, coordinate, and control its work activities.*

As we saw in chapter 1, organizations exist because a few people cannot produce a product—for example, steel—as efficiently as many people. Each of the few would have to perform many jobs. As an enterprise grows larger and contains many different jobs, this would virtually be impossible. The tasks must be divided up. Thus, specialization is employed; the benefits of increased knowledge and skill relative to a task accrue; and a higher individual level of skill develops, resulting in more effective and efficient performance of jobs.

As departments and jobs become more differentiated and distinctly separate in their functions, more effort must be devoted to coordination of these separated roles to ensure that they come together. This leads to the development of administrative mechanisms designed to control and integrate activities. On the one hand, differentiation among jobs resulting from specialization leads to effective and efficient performance. On the other hand, it leads to somewhat increased costs by requiring greater integrative efforts. If the benefits of increased differentiation do not offset the increased costs of integration or coordinating the diversity, the organization will become more inefficient. The organization must continually struggle to balance these forces as it evolves. The variables selected by researchers to measure or define structure are those they believe reveal the organization's efforts to deal with this struggle—that is, its attempts at differentiation and integration.

STRUCTURAL DIMENSIONS

The dilemma just presented is more easily stated than measured. A number of variables have been proposed to measure the organization's efforts at differentiation and integration, and researchers have measured and studied some of these. But definition and measurement of structural variables is often inconsistent across studies, making comparison difficult. The practical problems of conducting organizational research, including variation in the investigator's frame of reference and differences in approach to the problems, all have contributed to the inconsistencies in the studies in this area.

Champion has examined the literature on formal organization structure and has catalogued variables according to their *frequency of use* in key trade journals and textbooks.[33] His list includes:

1. Organization size
2. Complexity or differentiation
3. Formalization
4. Control
5. Administrative component
6. Bureaucratization
7. Centralization
8. Levels of authority

[handwritten margin note: Different aspects of Structure]

It is apparent that many different aspects of structure have been viewed as being important. Definitions for these factors have often varied across reports. To some extent, this represents disagreement about the precise meaning of a particular concept (such as centralization), and to a degree, it represents differences of opinion as to how the concept should be interpreted and measured.

Determining Structural Dimensions

Most of the studies of structure have begun with Weber's central characteristics of bureaucracy, which were discussed earlier. There are at least two ways one could examine an organization's structure using this model. We could ask, "Is this structure bureaucratic or not?" Using this question, an investigator might simply make a checklist using Weber's characteristics. Going through the list, the researcher could ask, for example, "Does the organization have a well-defined hierarchy of authority?" If each such a question has an affirmative answer, the researcher could conclude the organization is a genuine bureaucracy.

But what could we say if we obtained one or two negative answers? Would the conclusion be that it is not a bureaucratic structure because it is not 100 percent pure? The authors know of one firm in which many bureaucratic characteristics can be found, but one would find it difficult to confirm the impersonality of interpersonal relations (a bureaucratic characteristic) since business meetings tend toward beer parties. How should this organization be classified? How many rules and procedures does an organization have to have to be classified as a bureaucracy? Is the mere absence of any one of the characteristics enough to classify the structure as nonbureaucratic? Most investigators today would say it is not. Rather, they would ask the question, "To what degree is the structure bureaucratic?" This represents the second approach—continua of structural variables.

There is some disagreement as to whether all the bureaucratic dimensions vary together—for example, whether an organization having a great number of rules and procedures will also have extensive decentralization.[34] The usual approach is to assume that each of the dimensions of structure can vary independently. This is helpful in that dimensions can be studied individually and in relationship with other dimensions. Blau and Schoenherr, for instance, have argued that their research showed the employment of more formalized organization procedures actually allows the use of more decentralized authority.[35] This approach is useful in allowing us to be more precise in determining the effects of structural determinants or in investigating what aspects of structure may be associated with effective performance. Lawrence and Lorsch, for example, argue that to be effective a firm should match its structure to its environment.[36] Perhaps the principal disadvantage is that we now have *many* types of structures to deal with rather than a simple typology. Let's examine some of the most important studies on which our current knowledge of structural dimensions is based.

Empirical Studies of Structural Dimensions

Richard Hall was one of the first to demonstrate that an organization could be very bureaucratic in one characteristic and much less bureaucratic in another characteristic.[37] For example, there was little relationship found between the use of division of labor and the use of rules. Later, other investigators employed more extensive measures and studied the phenomenon in many more organizations. For a study in which the effect of bureaucracy on professionals was measured see Block 3-2.

block 3-2

PROFESSIONALS AND BUREAUCRACY

Richard Hall reports a study concerned with bureaucracy and professionals. The impact of organizations on professionals and vice versa has been a concern of analysts since professionalization seems to be increasing and professionals are increasingly employed by organizations.

In this study Hall examines a member of occupational professions such as physicians, accountants, teachers, lawyers, social workers, personnel, and engineers. He wanted to know the relationship between professionalization and degree of bureaucratization. The degree of professionalization was measured in two ways: The occupations were categorized by the extent to which "the occupation follows a given sequence of professionalization steps" (Hall, p. 97). For example, an occupation that has created a full-time occupation, established a training school, formed a professional association, and developed a code of ethics would have advanced further than one that only became a full-time occupation and established a training school at an affiliated university.

Professionals can also be characterized by their attitudes so Hall used attitudinal measures. He determined the degree to which each professional: (1) used a professional organization as a source of ideas and judgments, (2) believed the profession served and benefitted the public, (3) believed that fellow professionals should regulate and judge their work, (4) felt a sense of dedication to the work and willingness to do it for less external reward, and (5) felt each practitioner should make his own decisions without external pressure.

To measure bureaucratization, each professional was asked the degree to which his organization possessed the bureaucratic characteristic of: (1) division of labor, (2) rules, (3) procedures, (4) impersonality, (5) selection and promotion on technical competence, and (6) hierarchy of authority. These variables were examined in three organizational settings. The first setting, called autonomous, was where the professional is not subject to either outside or administrative jurisdiction, e.g., a law firm. A heteronomous setting was such as a public school where outsiders may determine the structure. The third setting was where professionals formed a department in a larger organization such as engineering in a manufacturing firm. In total, 542 professionals from 11 different occupations in 27 different organizations took part in the study.

The findings from this research let Hall make several conclusions. In general:

1. The attributes of a profession do not necessarily correspond to the attitudes of its professionals. Some more advanced groups (more professional attributes) held weak professional attitudes, and some less advanced groups held strong attitudes.

2. Autonomous organizations tend to be less bureaucratic than the other two types of organizations. Heteronomous organizations tended to have more rules, procedures, and impersonality. Departments tend to have greater hierarchy of authority and division of labor. With respect to the use of technical competence for selection and promotion, the departments were less bureaucratic than the other two.

3. Stronger professional attitudes go with lower perceptions of bureaucratic characteristics. The major exception to this pattern was the positive relationship between emphasis on technical competence and stronger professional attitudes.

4. There is not necessarily an inherent conflict between the professional and his organization.

Based on Richard H. Hall, "Professionalization and Bureaucratization," *American Sociological Review* 33 (February 1968): 92–104.

Aston Group Studies

A group of investigators in the Industrial Administration Research Unit at the University of Aston in Birmingham, England conducted research that was to become one of the most influential research programs in the field of organization theory. The work of this group is often referred to as the "Aston studies." The methods they developed for measuring structural dimensions are as close as the field has come to a common procedure.

The Aston group studied 46 work organizations in the Birmingham area. The organizations represented a diverse cross section of work organizations.[38] They included family-dominated firms, governmental departments, manufacturing firms making automobiles and glass, and food processors as well as service organizations, such as public water and public education departments. All of the organizational units employed more than 250 employees, and 14 employed over 2000. The researchers interviewed chief executives and several department heads and examined documents whenever possible. They attempted to establish what officials expected and what they permitted to be done.

From the literature on organizations this group derived six primary dimensions of structure. The primary dimensions the group defined and with which they began their research indicate the structural dimension they expected to find. They were:

1. *Specialization*—"the division of labor within the organization, the distribution of official duties among a number of positions."[39] They measured the number of different specialties performed and the extent to which there were specialized roles within each specialty.

2. *Standardization*—any procedure that occurs regularly, is legitimitized by the organization, has rules that cover circumstances, and applies invariably. The executives were presented with a list of possible procedures they might employ, and they indicated the ones they had available. The list included possible procedures for such activities as financial, people operations, stock, and quality control.

3. *Formalization*—"denotes the extent to which rules, procedures, instructions, and communications are written."[40] From an extensive list of possible documents the group determined the different purposes for which they were used.

4. *Centralization*—where is the authority to make legitimate decisions that affect the organization located? The researchers wanted to know where the last person who had to give his consent was located in the hierarchy. The location of the assenting executive for each of 37 recurring decisions was determined.

5. *Configuration*—"is the shape of the role structure."[41] It is analogous to a very complete organization chart. The group measured a number of aspects of organizational shape. To determine width, they used such measures as the number of persons who directly report to the chief executive and the number of workers who report to a first-level supervisor. To determine height, they counted the number of jobs from the lowest worker to the chief executive. They also counted the number of (1) employees not involved in producing the output, (2) supervisors directly responsible for the output, and (3) clerks.

6. *Traditionalism*—is the extent to which procedures are standardized but unwritten; that is, there is a customary way of doing things that is verbally communicated. This was determined from the difference between ten standardization items and ten equivalent formalization items.

They found that many of the dimensions were highly related; "in other words, an organization with many specialists tends also to have more standard routines, more documentation, and a larger supportive hierarchy."[42] However, organizations that had high scores on specialization, standardization, and formalization tended to be low on centralization. The usual interpretation of this finding has been that once an organization has structured the activities of its members through specialization, work procedures, and documents, it can allow decisions to be made at lower levels in the organization.

The goal was to find the basic dimensions of an organization's structure.

The a priori dimensions proved to be related to each other, which suggested that some of them may really be measuring the same thing. They continued their search by using a statistical technique called factor analysis. This procedure allows an investigator to find out what measures or scales go together and are also independent of other scales. Using this procedure, dimensions of structure that seem to be measuring similar things were combined into factors that were independent and different from other factors. The net result was four fundamental dimensions of structure based on *actual organizational activities*.

The fundamental dimensions of structure revealed by this analysis of the Aston group's works were:

1. *Structuring of activities.* This dimension was composed of the variables specialization, standardization, formalization, and vertical span of control.

2. *Concentration of authority.* This dimension is the extent to which authority to make decisions is located at higher levels in the hierarchy and to what extent outside units (e.g., headquarters) control the decisions affecting the organization. To a lesser extent it also encompassed the percent of supervisors responsible for producing the organization's output and standardization of selection procedures.

3. *Line control of workflow.* This dimension defines the extent to which the flow of work is controlled by the line personnel themselves rather than through impersonal procedures. An organization high in this factor would have a high percentage of supervisors responsible for producing the output, a low ratio of direct workers to first-line supervisors, a low amount of formal job performance records, and a high amount of procedures for controlling personnel. Later, the group concluded that the more the organization's output involved a service or nonstandard product, the more the organization relied on personal rather than impersonal control of the workflow.[43]

4. *Supportive component.* This dimension is concerned with the relative size of the auxiliary and supportive activities. These are activities not involved in controlling work flow, but assist, supplement, and support the organization. It is composed of such variables as the percentage of clerks and nonworkflow personnel.

The Aston group's work established fundamental dimensions of structure that were mutually independent of each other. Like Hall, they had shown that each characteristic could vary along an independent dimension. They concluded, "It is demonstrated here that bureaucracy is not unitary, but that organizations may be bureaucratic in any number of ways."[44]

The results of this study are extremely useful. It questioned the efficacy of a model of a "pure bureaucratic" type of organization. It provided investigators with measures of structure based on empirical reality, which allow investigation of differences between organization structures and the possible causes for these differences.

Seldom are researchers able to conduct studies that are above the criticism of their peers, and the Aston studies are no exception. There were several possible weaknesses as well as alternative interpretations of their results. But this work spawned much additional research into possible determinants of structural patterns as well as attempts to replicate their results.

The National Study

Child replicated the Aston study using the same measurements and procedures that had been used.[45] The primary difference between the two studies was in the selection of the organizations studied. Child called his sample the national sample because he selected firms from all the industrial areas of England and Scotland. Firms from six industries: electronics, pharmaceuticals, chocolate, newspapers, advertising, and insurance were included. These were chosen to provide representation in manufacturing and service-related industries and variability in technical and product environments. All the organizations were business firms and ranged in average size from 150 to 6350 employees. His sample included 82 firms and differed from the Aston study in that it was almost totally composed of units that were autonomous; that is, they were not branches or departments of parent organizations. In the Aston study 20 of the 46 organizations were branches.

Child analyzed his results in much the same manner as the Aston group but with slightly different results. The close relationship between specialization, standardization, formalization, and vertical span of control in the Aston group's first dimension *(structuring of activities)* was replicated. But Child found a much stronger negative relationship between centralization of decision making and structuring of activities. This relationship became even stronger when only manufacturing firms were considered. The relationship was negative, indicating that firms with high structuring of activities tended to be relatively low in centralization and vice versa.

In the Aston study centralization was so weakly related to the structuring-of-activities factor that it was considered to be independent of it and became a part of their second factor, and in the national sample centralization did not emerge in a separate independent dimension either. The other two dimensions of structure found by the Aston group were essentially confirmed by Child (see Figure 3-4).

The Reimann Study

Reimann also investigated the basic dimensions of structure. He studied 19 manufacturing firms in Ohio using an abbreviated set of the measures developed by the Aston group as well as eight other aspects of structure.[46] Many of these additional aspects were very similar to the ones used in the two other studies. Reimann factor analyzed his data and found several

figure 3-4

COMPARISON OF THREE STUDIES OF THE FUNDAMENTAL DIMENSIONS OF ORGANIZATION STRUCTURE

Aston Group	Child	Reimann

1. Structuring of activities
  a. Specialization
  b. Standardization
  c. Formalization
  d. Vertical span of control
	1. Administrative controls
	  a. Specialization
	  b. Standardization
	  c. Formalization
	  d. Vertical span of control
	  e. Centralization (negative)
		1. Specialization
		
		2. Formalization

2. Concentration of authority
  a. Centralization
  b. Autonomy
	Centralization is a part of factor above.	3. Decentralization

3. Line control of work flow	2. Unnamed but compares to Aston's third factor	No comparable factor
4. Supportive component	3. Unnamed but compares to Aston's fourth factor	4. Supportive component

independent dimensions. Three dimensions of structure emerged: (1) decentralization, (2) specialization, and (3) formalization. He also found a fourth dimension—supportive component—but argued for dropping it.

In Figure 3-4 the dimensions of structure found by each of these studies is summarized and compared to the results of the others. One can see that there is considerable agreement in the three studies as to the dimensions of structure present in organizations. But these studies did not produce *exactly* the same results.

Comparison of the Studies

In the Aston study specialization and formalization were both part of the *structuring of activities* factor. In Child's study *centralization* was also part of that dimension. Thus, Reimann's results differ from both of those studies since he found three dimensions that described essentially the same aspects of structure as Child's one and the Aston study's two. He had also produced a fourth dimension, which was like the supportive component dimension found by the Aston study and confirmed by Child, but he abandoned it because it had not been confirmed by further analysis.

One of the reasons offered by Reimann to explain the differences among these studies was the samples of firms studied. Both his study and the Aston group's contained branch organizations, whereas Child's firms were more autonomous. Although this explanation is appealing, a later re-analysis of the data of two studies that controlled for organizational autonomy gives reason to believe that this approach may not explain away the differences.[47]

Reimann also suggested that British organizations may be more conservative in their attempts at organization than are American firms. Citing results obtained on manufacturing firms in India he concludes, "the bureaucratic structure space may be a function, among other things, of the sociocultural environment of the organization he studied."[48] This argument, however, does not explain the difference between the Child and Aston studies.

Reimann later reasoned that the structural dimensions obtained may depend on the types of organizations studied as well as their autonomy and environment.[49] In a different analysis of apparently the same 19 manufacturing plants, he discovered that the dimensions of structure that went together independent of others changed according to organizational performance. He divided the firms into ten high-performing and nine low-performing organizations and analyzed the results separately. The high-performing firms had distinct structural dimensions like those just reported for his first study. The low-performing firms seemed to have only one mixed dimension. One must be cautious in interpreting this result since there is a question about much real difference there was in the firm's performance. In addition, the association does not show that one caused the other. However, one explanation may be that effective firms do a better job of contingently matching their structures to the demands of their situation.[50]

Convergence of the Studies

Attempts to empirically discover the basic dimensions of organization structure have obviously produced mixed results, but there is some agreement on the variables that compose structure. Many of these come from operational interpretations of Weber's original model, and some incorporate variables suggested by other writers on organizations. The relative weight of each variable as it contributes to organizational effectiveness and efficiency has not yet been determined. We can speculate that future research will show that several of these variables can be combined in different ways as a means of improving organization performance where structural redesign is a problem.

There is further agreement among the studies since they have all produced similar independent basic dimensions of structure. There are clearly several different fundamental dimensions to an organization's structure such that changing any one factor does not necessarily lead to a corresponding change in another factor. We should be cautious in describing an organization structure as being either bureaucratic or nonbureaucratic. Building arguments about management practice that depend on a simple dichotomy such as bureaucratic versus nonbureaucratic organizations is tenuous at best.

CONCLUSIONS ON BUREAUCRACY AND STRUCTURE

The structure of organizations obviously does differ and the basic dimensions may change according to several factors. This discussion of structure has suggested that autonomy from control by other organizations, sociocultural influences in the environment, and the organization's performance may affect the variables that compose the basic relevant structural dimensions. The discussion on typologies suggested that the goals of the organization, the functions it performs for society, and the authority form it uses may have an impact. Other factors, such as size, technology, environment, and strategic choice, have been suggested as being determinants of structure and, in turn, may cause some variables to change together.

The studies discussed here have somewhat reduced the number of dimensions that one has to use to understand and study organizational structure. Instead of many variables, we now can use a few dimensions to describe an organization's structure, and we can be confident that we have accounted for much of it, although additional variables may be important for a specific study.

However, this does not mean that the field no longer needs to continue attempts to determine the fundamental dimensions of structure. Efforts such as those described here have been major advances, but continual refinement is necessary. There is not yet a solid consensus about the definition of variables nor how they should be measured. Such standardization is desirable for comparison of results and building on other researchers' efforts.

At the same time, a healthy skepticism is desirable. Too often, premature closure on a discovery has hurt the credability of organizational scholars with students, managers, and other scholars. For example, in the micro study of organizational behavior increased worker satisfaction was at one time thought to lead to increased productivity. Efforts to improve worker satisfaction became the "snake oil" of the field. We now know the relationship is not such a simple one.[51]

But researchers and practitioners cannot always wait for a final determination; they must proceed on as sound a basis as possible, and the studies reported here have provided a foundation upon which to proceed.

Although the study of organization structure has reduced the number of fundamental dimensions (see Figure 3-4), it has also complicated our understanding by showing that each dimension is relatively independent of the others. From trying to understand bureaucratic and nonbureaucratic structures, we have come to trying to understand all the possible combinations of four or more fundamental factors. The study of organizations does seem complex.

In the next chapter some of the "how-to-do-it" issues of designing organization structures for business organizations will be explored. Grouping activities together to form jobs and some of the options available in job design as well as departmentation are considered. This is the second of three chapters dealing with the important issues surrounding structure.

NOTES

[1]Max Weber, *From Max Weber: Essays in Sociology,* trans. and ed. H. H. Gerth and C. Wright Mills (New York: Oxford University Press, 1958), pp. 196–204.

[2]Nicos P. Mouzelis, *Organization and Bureaucracy: An Analysis of Modern Theories* (Chicago: Aldine, 1968).

[3]Robert K. Merton, "Bureaucratic Structure and Personality," *Social Forces,* 18 (1940):560–68.

[4]Philip Selznick, *TVA and the Grass Roots* (Berkeley: University of California Press, 1969).

[5]Alvin W. Gouldner, *Patterns of Industrial Bureaucracy* (New York: The Free Press, 1954).

[6]Peter M. Blau and William R. Scott, *Formal Organizations* (San Francisco: Chandler, 1962).

[7]James D. Thompson, *Organizations in Action* (New York: McGraw-Hill, 1967).

[8]Warren G. Bennis, *Changing Organizations* (New York: McGraw-Hill, 1966).

[9]"Conversation: An Interview with Warren Bennis," *Organizational Dynamics* 2 (Winter 1974):50–66.

[10]Tom Burns and G. W. Stalker, *The Management of Innovation* (London: Tavistock, 1961) and Charles Perrow, *Organizational Analysis: A Sociological View* (Belmont, Calif.: Wadsworth, 1970).

[11]Jerome S. Bruner, "Social Psychology and Perception," *Readings in Social Psychology,* 3rd ed., ed. Eleanor E. Maccoby, Theodore M. Newcomb, and Eugene L. Hartley (New York: Holt, Rinehart & Winston, 1958), pp. 85–94.

[12]J. Eugene Haas and Thomas E. Drabek, *Complex Organizations: A Sociological Perspective* (New York: Macmillan, 1973), p. 374.

[13]Hall, *Organizations,* 62.

[14]E. C. Hughes, "The Sociological Study of Work," *American Journal of Sociology* 57 (1952):423-26.

[15]Talcott Parsons, *Structure and Process in Modern Society* (New York: The Free Press, 1960).

[16]Daniel Katz and Robert L. Kahn, *The Social Psychology of Organizations* (New York: Wiley, 1966).

[17]Amitai Etzioni, *A Comparative Analysis of Complex Organizations,* rev. ed. (New York: The Free Press, 1975).

[18]Blau and Scott, *Formal Organizations.*

[19]Richard H. Hall, *Organizations: Structure and Process* (Englewood Cliffs, N.J.: Prentice-Hall, 1972).

[20]D. R. Pugh, D. J. Hickson, and C. R. Hinings, "An Empirical Taxonomy of Structures of Work Organizations," *Administrative Science Quarterly* 14 (1969):115-26.

[21]John Child, "Organizational Structure, Environment and Performance: The Role of Strategic Choice," *Sociology* 6 (1972):1–22.

[22]Alfred D. Chandler, Jr., *Strategy and Structure* (Cambridge, Mass.: M.I.T. Press, 1962).

[23]Edmund P. Learned and Audrey T. Sproat, *Organization Theory and Policy* (Homewood, Ill.: Irwin, 1966).

[24]Thompson, *Organizations in Action.*

[25]Katz and Kahn, *Social Psychology of Organizations.*

[26]Fremont E. Kast and James E. Rosenzweig, *Contingency Views of Management* (Chicago: Science Research Associates, 1973).

[27]Dean J. Champion, *The Sociology of Organizations* (New York: McGraw-Hill, 1975); Hall, *Organizations;* Roger Mansfield, "Bureaucracy and Centralization: An Examination of Organizational Structure," *Administrative Science Quarterly* 18 (1973):477–88.

[28]James G. March and Herbert A. Simon, *Organizations* (New York: Wiley, 1958), p. 170.

[29]Katz and Kahn, *Social Psychology of Organizations,* p. 21.

[30]Thompson, *Organizations in Action,* p. 51.

[31]Ibid., p. 54.

[32]Child, "Organizational Structure, Environment and Performance."

[33]Champion, *The Sociology of Organizations.*

[34]John Child, "Organization Structure and Strategies of Control: A Replication of the Aston Study," *Administrative Science Quarterly* 17 (1972):163–76; and Roger Mansfield, "Bureaucracy and Centralization: An Examination of Organizational Structure," *Administrative Science Quarterly* 18 (1973):477–88.

[35]Peter M. Blau and Richard A. Schoenherr, *The Structure of Organizations* (New York: Basic Books, 1971).

[36]Paul R. Lawrence and Jay W. Lorsch, *Organization and Environment* (Cambridge, Mass.: Harvard University Press, 1967).

[37]Richard H. Hall, "The Concept of Bureaucracy: An Empirical Assessment," *American Journal of Sociology* 69 (1963):32–40.

[38]D. S. Pugh, D. J. Hickson, C. R. Hinings, and C. Turner, "Dimensions of Organization Structure," *Administrative Science Quarterly* 13 (1968):65–105.

[39]Ibid., pp. 72–73.

[40]Ibid., p. 75.

[41]Ibid., p. 78.

[42]Ibid., p. 82.

[43]D. S. Pugh, D. J. Hickson, C. R. Hinings, and C. Turner, "The Context of Organization Structures," *Administrative Science Quarterly* 14 (1969):91–114.

[44]Pugh et al., "Dimensions of Organization Structure," p. 88.

[45]Child, "Organization Structure and Strategies of Control."

[46]Bernard C. Reimann, "On the Dimensions of Bureaucratic Structure: An Empirical Reappraisal," *Administrative Science Quarterly* 18 (1973):462–76.

[47]Lex Donaldson, John Child, and Howard Aldrich, "The Aston Findings on Centralization: Further Discussion," *Administrative Science Quarterly* 20 (1975):453–60.

[48]Reimann, "On the Dimensions of Bureaucratic Structure," p. 470.

[49]Bernard C. Reimann, "Dimensions of Structure in Effective Organizations: Some Empirical Evidence," *Academy of Management Journal* 17 (1974):693–708.

[50]Lawrence and Lorsch, *Organization and Environment;* and Gary Dessler, *Organization and Management: A Contingency Approach* (Englewood Cliffs, N.J.: Prentice-Hall, 1976).

[51]Edward E. Lawler, III, *Motivation in Work Organizations* (Monterey, Calif.: Brooks/Cole, 1973); and Donald P. Schwab and Larry L. Cummings, "Theories of Performance and Satisfaction: A Review," *Industrial Relations* 9 (1970):408–30.

SUGGESTIONS FOR FURTHER READING

BENNIS, WARREN G. *Changing Organizations.* New York: McGraw-Hill, 1966.

KATZ, DANIEL and KAHN, ROBERT L. *The Social Psychology of Organizations.* New York: Wiley, 1966.

MARCH, JAMES G., and SIMON, HERBERT A. *Organizations.* New York: Wiley, 1958.

MOUZELIS, NICOS P. *Organization and Bureaucracy: An Analysis of Modern Theories.* Chicago: Aldine, 1968.

THOMPSON, JAMES D. *Organizations in Action.* New York: McGraw-Hill, 1967.

WEBER, MAX. *The Theory of Social and Economic Organization,* translated by A. M. Henderson and Talcott Parsons. New York: The Free Press, 1947.

chapter 4

BASIC PROCESSES IN BUSINESS ORGANIZATION DESIGN

In this chapter we will address the basic processes used for designing of jobs and departments in an organization. Particular attention will be paid to the criteria used to group activities into jobs and jobs into departments. This subject has been almost the exclusive province of management writers rather than organization theorists or researchers. From an analysis of the differences in goal orientation between practitioner and scholar, the discussion will proceed to traditionally suggested steps in organizational design. Since the central focus of traditional organization design has been how to group activities into jobs and departments, the major focus of this chapter will be upon these issues. The *patterns* that result from the grouping of departments will be discussed in chapter 5 that follows, to complete the three-chapter sequence on the important organizational variable of *structure*.

DIFFERENCES IN GOAL ORIENTATION
BETWEEN PRACTITIONER AND SCHOLAR

In chapter 3 the emphasis was on how scholars have approached organization structure. In this chapter we will turn our attention to the perspective of those who actually design organizational structures. There are similarities among the dimensions used by both scholars and practitioners. Indeed, it would be surprising if there were not, since most scholarly work is based on observation and research in real organizations. But there are differences as well. The scholar's objectives are often grounded in science—that is, the desire to understand, describe, and predict. The manager or executive's goal is to build an organization that will facilitate the accomplishment of both the organization's and the dominant coalition's objectives.

Such differences are not incompatible since the end result of both is predictability and thus the ability to control. The manager is concerned primarily with his own organization. The scholar is interested in all organizations or some special subset of organizations and searches for dimensions along which to compare these organizations. The manager looks for what will work for his organization given its special situation. The executive cannot wait for science; he must proceed.

One result of these two different approaches is that practitioners have developed a different language for the dimensions of organization. For example, *specialization* is roughly comparable to the *responsibilities* of a job in practitioners' terms. Scholars' terms, such as *standardization* and *formalization*, in practice become *policies, procedures, budgets, programs, schedules*, and so on.

Concepts about organizations may be grouped in a way that makes translation and comparability difficult. For example, the patterns of groupings in a business organization often lead to descriptive terms for the whole structure, such as *functional, divisional,* or *matrix*. The dimensions of structure described in chapter 3 are not comparable, although they could be used to describe any of these three. In this chapter the primary objective will be to describe how the manager has approached the structuring of organizations.

TRADITIONAL ORGANIZATION APPROACHES

Weber's writing on bureaucracy is considered a classic in organization theory, but it was not translated and generally available to managers until the late 1940s. During this time, however, there was hardly a vacuum in the management literature about how to organize.

Practitioners had their own ideas and writings that formed the basis for what has been called the classical theory of organization and management.[1] This literature generally refers to management thought on organizing that resulted from the personal experience of practitioners and consultants. As professional schools for administrators and managers developed, scholars began contributing to this stream of writing. This entire literature has been extensively reviewed and criticized.[2] We will provide a discussion of the literature to show how business organizations have approached organizational design.

Most of the writings connected with this school of thought did not confine their attention solely to organization. They were concerned with all elements of administration. In these writings attempts were made to provide practitioners with a simple framework for understanding the management process. The classical writers were actually developing a "theory of management" rather than a "theory of organizations." In addition to the organization of an enterprise, they were interested in such topics as planning, command, coordination, and control.[3] Focus was on practice; that is, what should a manager do with a given problem?

Early Writers

The early writers, such as Taylor, Fayol, and Mooney and Reiley were business executives and focused on what they saw from that perspective. This characteristic is still true today of much of the management literature. The emphasis is on the prescriptive means for achieving some goal. The approach tends to be "how we did it at XYZ Corporation" if by an executive, and "how you can or should do it at XYZ Corporation" if by a consultant. In any event, the purpose is to tell practicing managers what to do.

We will not completely review the development of classical literature and its attempts to provide a theory of management practice, but we will describe the dimensions and patterns that practitioners have used in designing organization structure. You are referred to extensive reviews and criticisms provided by other authors, if you are interested in pursuing classical management thought.[4] The approach will be an eclectic one in that we have selected concepts and references believed to be representative of the way practitioners have viewed design. The discussion begins with an overview of procedures that have been suggested as the steps to follow in designing an entire organization.

Suggested Processes for Designing Organization

Peterson, Plowman, and Trickett have argued for a uniform method for designing an organization structure, and they suggested a formula that they believed captured the process used by organizations to design structure.[5] The formula consists of five steps:

1. Determine the specific objectives of the company and each subunit.
2. For each objective determine the action necessary to achieve it.
3. "Combine and separate these activities into logical, cohesive, functional groups."
4. Draw a chart of these groupings and examine for overlaps and inconsistency.
5. Make up an organization chart detailing positions and establishing a position responsible for each functional grouping.[6]

Louis Allen, a consultant and management writer, proposed that the best approach to design involved:

1. Identify objectives.

2. Identify the major work to meet objectives.

3. Start at the bottom and organize the end activities first.

4. Determine what management positions are needed to manage the end activities and the management positions.

5. Group related work and positions together in terms of desired results.

6. Make sure the groupings form balanced packages with appropriate organizational status.

7. Establish an appropriate number of subordinates for each manager.[7]

A more current discussion of the process by Peter Drucker describes a similar approach. Drucker says, "Organizing has to start out with the desired results."[8] Next, a manager determines the key activities necessary to obtain the objectives by determining where excellence is needed and where performance failure would hinder results. The third step is to determine which activities should be grouped together and which should not be. The manager should group activities together that make the same kind of contribution. Drucker sees four basic kinds of activities based on the kind of contribution they make:

1. Activities that produce results relating to revenues generation such as sales and treasury, those that contribute to revenue generation such as production and purchasing, and those that supply information to revenue and cost centers.

2. Activities that support the result producing activities with their outputs.

3. Activities that provide for the "hygiene and housekeeping"[9] such as the cafeteria.

4. Top management activities dealing with issues such as strategy, structure, growth, size, change, and diversification.[10]

The fourth step is to affix the responsibility and authority for decisions to be made. To do so properly, the character of the decision must be considered. Here, a manager must consider:

1. At what level in the organization will a manager have the knowledge and experience to decide.

2. At what level will all the activities and objectives affected by the decision be given adequate consideration.

3. Which managers need to help make the decision as well as which of them need to be informed.

4. What the relationships between managers are. Which other managers must contribute to, and receive contributions from, a given manager to carry out their responsibilities? Drucker's guide is "to impose . . . the smallest possible number of relationships."[11]

Each of these guides to organizational design shares certain common concerns. In each it is emphasized that structuring must begin with the *objectives* and desired *results*. The structure should be directed toward the goals one wishes to achieve. There is agreement that division of work is necessary, and a manager can determine what activities are required if objectives are clearly specified. In addition, separate activities should be grouped together on the basis of similarity, although there is some difference of opinion as to how they should be similar. Finally, an executive should assign the responsibility for the groupings to a specific manager by determining what and how much authority each manager should have to make decisions.

The central focus of those concerned with implementing organizational design has been the proper grouping of activities and the allocation of responsibility and authority to achieve organizational objectives. In the remainder of this chapter the discussion will center around these concerns.

Activity Grouping

It is clear from the previous discussion that designing an organizational structure begins with specification of objectives. From here a designer proceeds to the determination of the activities necessary to achieve objectives and later to grouping of the activities. This is, of course, more easily stated than carried out. Authorities on the subject are never very specific about how one determines what activities are required to meet objectives. As Thompson has indicated, "Administrative management also assumes . . . tasks are known . . ."[12] It is common to skip this step and proceed to the bases one should use to group the activities together.[13] If any attention is given to this step, it usually only involves a general statement as to the nature of the business the organization is in, such as manufacturing or merchandising.[14] Perhaps this lack of attention occurs because it is difficult to generalize to all firms or because the units most people deal with are already organized and the problem to be addressed is really one of reorganization.

We have noted that there is a distinct void in the literature as to how one should first determine the required activities. The void, however, is a conceptual one. Managers in organizations somehow decide what must be done to reach their objectives. They may observe other similar firms, and they can clearly learn from their own past experience. Certainly mistakes are made, but the designers either have organizing experience or will soon acquire it. As a result, they develop their own cause-and-effect beliefs about which activities and groupings are required and beneficial. This cause/effect belief, based on experience, fills the void in the formal literature on grouping activities together.

Means/End Chain

Litterer suggests a process called "means/end chain."[15] This concept is useful in understanding the relationship between organizational goals and specific activities. In this process every goal or end requires a decision about the means by which it will be attained. These means then become subgoals for someone else, which, in turn, require decisions about their means of attainment. Through this process, one can elaborate a chain of goals and contributing activities. This process is continued ". . . with progressively more specific decisions being made until an existing means for accomplishing an end could have been used."[16] Existing means are products, programs, procedures, or skills that are available and can be used to perform a task or solve a problem. See Figure 4-1 for an illustration of a means/end hierarchy or chain.

There are several implications that can be drawn from this process: (1) the process outlined is a top-down process, (2) the development of the

figure 4-1

A MEANS/END HIERARCHY

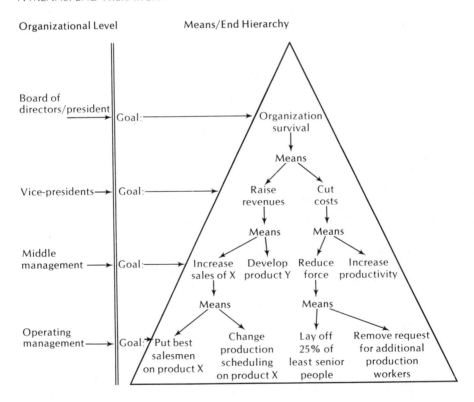

chain generates a specification of strategy and technology for achieving objectives, and (3) each activity (means) should contribute to the achievement of the ends sought (goals).

There appears to be some disagreement in the field as to whether an organization is really built from the top down or the bottom up. Actually the process seems to proceed in both directions.[17] Activities are combined into jobs; jobs are assigned positions relative to other jobs and then grouped together into departments and so on. Managers do divide up their own and their subordinates' work load by creating new jobs; this is part of the means/end chain process in operation.

An argument regarding building organizations that is both interesting and controversial is related to what determines an organization's structure. Is it primarily *objectives* as is implied by this chapter and many practicing managers, or is it *technology* or *environment* or *size* as implied by some scholars of the "imperative" school of thought? The imperative argument suggests that these other factors will *dictate* the structure an organization will use. In section three this issue will be reviewed because of its importance and centrality to organization theory. Technology will be covered in chapter 6, size in chapter 7, and environment in chapter 8.

Another related issue seems to be a matter of rational efficiency. Only activities that contribute to goal fulfillment need be defined and organized. Any other activities are wasteful of resources. "The first test of the legitimacy and adequacy of each subgoal must be resolved in terms of the ultimate goal."[18] This *does* provide an ultimate decision point as to the appropriateness of some organizational activities.

The model linking means to ends in a continuous chain is useful in conceptualizing the process. It is not very concrete for suggesting what activities should be selected. That determination is a matter of specific situational needs and knowledge. If one contemplates the designing of a major corporation's structure all at once using the model, the task is overwhelming. But a large organization is seldom built overnight. It usually grows from a small, less elaborate and less differentiated form or by the combination of several smaller ones.

As an organization grows, new tasks and people are added, and new strategies are adopted. Most commonly, the organizational design task is one of reassessment and reorganization and is usually done one subunit at a time. S. M. Davis has provided a description of the development of business corporations in which he argues that entrepreneurs, such as Henry Ford, were not organization builders.[19] He saw the leaders that *followed* these men as the real developers of the organization. "Organization structures were specifically devised to help administrators implement new growth strategies."[20] The genius of many organizational founders was not in organizational design but in engineering, sales, or something related.

Professional managers and administrators often had to supply some rationality of design to the organization at a later time.

Job Design

Essential to this part of our discussion of organizations has been the concept of designing jobs by grouping together activities to be done in those jobs. Division of labor has often been seen as a crucial characteristic of job design in organizations. It is implied in the definition of organization structure and in the processes recommended for designing structures. It refers to the divisions of tasks to be performed and their assignment to different roles and individuals.

One result of division of labor is specialization. That is, if X and Y decide to dig ditches and divide the labor so that X digs and Y hauls the dirt away, the work X performs is different from the work Y performs; each is a specialist. This has been going on for centuries in families and societies as well as organizations. "Social organizations move toward the multiplication and elaboration of roles with greater specialization of function."[21] The societies that contain many complex organizations recognize this when they provide for the selection and training of individuals for occupations. Individuals are ". . . taught to fashion careers, either within an occupation or in some combination of them."[22]

Why does this occur? Two reasons have been suggested. First, there is the limited capacity of individuals. For example, the physical task of building a bridge is beyond the capacity of one person. A rancher may be able to construct a small bridge across a small creek, but to build a bridge across the Ohio River becomes physically impossible for one person. It is also virtually impossible due to lack of knowledge. Even at higher managerial levels, it is difficult for a manager to have all the knowledge and skills required to manufacture and market both light bulbs and turbines as does General Electric. Second, "It is a far more efficient way of accomplishing a purpose."[24] Greater uniformity of product or service should result from specialization, and it is also expected that output per person will increase as people become better at their single task.

Specialization

The literature on the relative advantages and disadvantages of specialization is vast, and we cannot hope to review it all here. To summarize some of its important points, the advantages mentioned above are seen to accrue because:

1. The specialist performs fewer tasks. He concerns himself with fewer operations that can be readily learned because he continually repeats them, and proficiency is supposed to increase.

2. The time to learn the task is lessened; a specialist can reach maximum proficiency sooner, and the costs of training are reduced.

3. Better matching of skills, abilities, and knowledge is possible between the job and the occupant, because the variety required is lessened.

4. The dependency on any particular worker or job is lessened. Jobs can be so designed that workers can easily be replaced. Occupants can be treated as interchangeable parts.

The relationship between specialization and performance, because of such advantages, has been documented by a number of researchers.[25] The advantages have also become part of the cause/effect belief system of those who design jobs. The goal is to design simple, low-skilled, short-cycle, and repetitive jobs, particularly at the lower hierarchical levels. A job is viewed as a part in the organization "machine," and it is desirable to design the jobs so that the parts and the energy inputs (people) may be easily replaced. This orientation is seen in a study by Davis and Canter.[26] They reported on the criteria that job designers actually used in assigning tasks to jobs. These were:

1. Break the job into the smallest components possible to reduce skill requirements.

2. Make the content of the job as repetitive as possible.

3. Minimize internal transportation and handling time.

4. Provide suitable working conditions.

5. Obtain greater specialization.

6. Stabilize production and reduce job shifts to a minimum.

7. Have engineering departments, whenever possible, take an active part in assigning tasks and jobs.

Furthermore, the job designers' comments about the relationship between job content and productivity indicate they believe productivity is increased by the extent to which jobs are made simpler, lower skilled, shorter cycled and repetitive—that is, more specialized.

Disadvantages of Specialization

The disadvantages associated with specialization seem to result from carrying it too far. Most managers and scholars agree with the need for some specialization, but many believe it can be carried far beyond the point of diminishing returns. Some believe the cost to individuals, organizations, and our society now outweighs its benefits.

It is often said that people don't like their work, that jobs are not interesting, or that the challenge has been automated out of most jobs. This conclusion has been determined by a special report, *Work in America,* done by a task force for the Department of Health, Education, and Welfare as well as by the popularizers of the "job enrichment" movement.[27] In fact, the topic became so popular that NBC did a special on work alienation "Bored Stiff With Your Work?" Of all the popularization of worker discontent or alienation perhaps none has received as much attention as the worker rebellion against repetitive, meaningless work at the Chevrolet Vega plant at Lordstown, Ohio. Articles citing worker sabotage against the dehumanizing effects of highly specialized mass assembly operations have been reported in *Business Week, Harper's, Playboy, Time, Newsweek,* and most major newspapers across the country.

Job Enrichment: A Special Case of Job Design

In response to this worker discontent, many have advocated the job enrichment (JE) procedure as a means of producing positive industrial mental health among today's workers. Job enrichment is one approach to redesigning jobs. The general argument for this position is that, as people continue to grow academically through the educational system, they wish to perform in jobs that challenge their abilities and provide a means for satisfying higher level human needs. Furthermore, the nation may be seeing the development of a work force that sees work as less of a means to an end and more of an end in itself. It may be that society has reached a point at which work is no longer a means of providing for basic human satisfactions, such as food and housing, but is now seen by a much larger segment of the population as a way to self-fulfillment of higher level needs on the job.

Management, workers, public officials, college professors, and the popular press all seem to be distressed by employee attitudes about the current quality of life at work. Accompanying this discontent has been a declining output per man-hour rate, which may or may not be related to poor job design.

In the process of designing jobs to promote specialization, designers have created counter pressures, which through their effect on motivation may have led to problems with absenteeism, turnover, productivity, quality, and satisfaction. When specialization is carried too far in jobs where the cooperation and motivation of the worker is important, it may eventually lead to more inefficiency than efficiency. Such concerns have led to argument for a specific kind of job redesign—job enrichment. Job enrichment proponents hold that specialization should be reversed by increasing the variety of skills required on a job, by increasing the significance of the tasks performed, by increasing the job holders' autonomy from management in performing the job, and by providing the job holder greater identity with the job and greater feedback from the job

block 4-1

EXTENT OF JOB ENRICHMENT PRACTICE

In order to determine the current status of job enrichment, Luthans and Reif conducted a mailed questionnaire survey of a random sample of 300 of the top 1000 *Fortune* industrials. Of the 132 firms that responded, 37 were using a job enrichment program on a formal or informal basis. They reported that the primary problems associated with job enrichment was the reluctance of employees currently in enriched jobs to accept added authority and responsibility, their inability to adapt to change, suspicion of management's motives in instituting job enrichment, their impractical expectations, their concern about adjusting to self-control, and their fear of failure. In addition, they report questionable acceptance of job enrichment on the part of supervisors as well as employees. Luthans and Reif suggest that the response that best summarizes the attitude toward job enrichment was the following:

> As an applied concept job enrichment is probably here to stay. As a formalized program I view it as a passing fancy created by unions for purposes of disruption and feather-bedding, by consultants to create more clients, and by publishers and educators as a current fad to talk and write about. If properly used, a good social improvement. But we still need the ability to design, make, and sell widgets for profit or there won't be any jobs left to enrich.

Based on F. Luthans and W. E. Reif, "Job Enrichment: Long on Theory and Short on Practice," *Organizational Dynamics* 3 (1974):30–48.

itself.[28] Such job characteristics are expected to increase the worker's motivation to work and reverse the problems just mentioned. Job enrichment essentially involves redesigning jobs to incorporate the characteristics mentioned.

Factors in the Success of Job Enrichment

The list of companies that have attempted this redesign approach is long and impressive including AT&T, Polaroid, General Foods, Texas Instruments, Proctor and Gamble, IBM, ICI, Syntex, and Bankers Trust. These companies have frequently reported increases in productivity, quality, and morale, with decreases in turnover and absenteeism as a result of redesigning jobs. Why then has job enrichment not been universally accepted and implemented? The reason for this failure may be found in a lack of understanding about the limitations of job design in general and job enrichment in particular.

There are several factors that seem to be important in job redesign success. A thorough diagnosis of specific situations for these factors may be the key to successful applications. Examining job redesign programs reveals a discernible set of factors that tend to go with successful programs, some factors having more importance for the job redesign success than others. Figure 4-2 provides a summary of job redesign success factors.[29]

Individual Considerations

Many of the factors that influence the success of job redesign are found in the *individual characteristics of the work force.* These include age, cultural background, education, job skills, work experience, work values, individual needs, motives or expectations, role clarity, and worker self-confidence.

The first of these factors, age, has consistently been used to show that younger workers tend to be less satisfied with their work and react more positively to job enrichment. Cultural factors influence the effectiveness of job enrichment in that workers with rural backgrounds respond more favorably than those who have grown up in urban environments.

Higher education levels seem to be associated with the willingness to accept increased autonomy, responsibility, and the challenge of enriched jobs. More highly skilled workers and managers tend to be concerned with using their skills on the job, developing abilities, and meeting self-esteem and self-actualization needs. Previous work experience also seems to influence the reaction to job redesign by indicating that employees who have had nonroutine experiences in the recent past but presently perform routine, repetitive jobs are dissatisfied and react more favorably to job redesign.

Workers who value independence and autonomy in their relationships with their managers seem to be more willing to accept the additional responsibility of redesigned jobs. They also participate more readily in the redesign and management of their jobs and get more satisfaction from the job. Employees who do well in enriched jobs prefer working on individual problems independent of others, changing ambiguous job settings, and solving complex mental problems. Employees with high growth needs (the desire to fully use present skills and develop new ones) respond to jobs that offer variety, autonomy, task identity, and feedback on their job performance. The satisfaction and personal involvement of these employees increases and absenteeism declines. Studies have also shown that rural workers have stronger personal growth needs than urban workers. In

figure 4-2

JOB REDESIGN

	Success Factor Chart
Factor	Characteristics
Individual	1. Young 2. Rural background 3. Values hard work and involvement 4. Higher education level 5. Higher skill level 6. Nonroutine work experience 7. Presently dissatisfied with job 8. Values independence and autonomy 9. High growth needs 10. Confidence in ability to learn new tasks
Job and technological	1. Low task certainty 2. High task flexibility 3. R.O.I. for present setup vs. R.O.I. for redesigned work place 4. Dynamic and changing market 5. Continuous process or unit production
Managerial	1. Low formality of organizational structure and processes 2. Participative and considerate leadership style 3. Long-range perspective 4. Expertise in implementing job enrichment available 5. Favorable union relations

addition, workers who desire some definition of the job and its objectives (role clarity), but who also want some freedom in how the job is to be performed, find job enrichment highly satisfying.

Some workers frequently resist redesign efforts because they do not have the self-confidence that they can learn the new task. Employees with high self-esteem and confidence appear to be motivated more readily to participate in the redesign.

In sum, the *individual* factors that influence the success of job redesign are:

1. Worker age
2. Worker cultural background
3. Worker educational level
4. Worker job skill level

5. Previous work experience
6. Work values
7. Worker needs and motives
8. Role clarity
9. Worker self-confidence

Job and Technological Considerations

Some job situations are not readily applicable to redesign efforts; thus, most companies who use job redesign do not attempt to change all of their organization's jobs. However, many jobs do respond well to enrichment. Some considerations in selecting appropriate jobs for redesign are:

1. Task certainty
2. Task flexibility
3. Capital invested in the job
4. Stability of markets and technology
5. Technological type

The greater the certainty of the task performed in terms of fixed procedures, the less autonomous and independent work behavior can be and, thus, the less appropriate job enrichment as a specific job redesign tool would be. Job certainty can be measured by examining the clarity of information about performing the job, its programmability, and the time required for performance feedback. In the flexibility of jobs there are four dimensions that should be built into a job if job redesign is to achieve best results. The more flexible a job is for incorporating these four factors, the better the chances are for success. First, task variety allows workers to use a number of different skills and abilities. Second, job autonomy permits self-determination of work methods, sequence, and speed. Third, being able to identify with the task usually permits a whole piece of work, and the worker can perceive that he has contributed to something of consequence (psychological closure). Fourth, feedback permits the worker to see what has been accomplished.

One obstacle to redesigning in heavy assembly industries is the large investment in capital equipment per worker. The efficiencies of an organization's technology may offset the costs of turnover, absenteeism, sabotage, and quality. Return on investment with present setups must be compared to the possible returns from a redesign. The optimal time to consider redesign is when new plants and facilities are contemplated. Government write-off policies may eventually help to encourage changes in equipment when the purpose is for job enrichment.

The degree of specialization is often determined by another factor, the relative stability of the market and technological environments. A dy-

JOB ENRICHMENT AT IMPERIAL CHEMICAL INDUSTRIES

Paul, Robertson, and Herzberg conducted successful job enrichment programs in Imperial Chemical Industries, Limited and four other British companies. This study is discussed in detail because of the care taken with experimental design. Experiment and control groups were used, and care was taken to eliminate the influence of interfering variables. Effort was made to minimize the Hawthorne effect by keeping participants and their supervisors informed on all aspects of the program.

The one study dealt with the sales representatives of a wholesale and retail outlet. The situation presented by the authors was one in which the company in question had a healthy share of the market but was in a static growth period, and its position was being threatened by competition. The critical factor in this situation was determined to be the sales representatives' efforts. The conditions of employment for these individuals compared favorably with the rest of the industry, and a job reaction survey indicated general job satisfaction. A program of job enrichment was undertaken with the objective of regaining the initiative in the sales area.

The primary theme of the program was to "build the sales representative's job so that it became more complete in its own right." First, in the area of responsibilities, the sales representatives began to determine their own frequency for calling on customers and maintaining their own records on their calls. Reports by the sales representatives were filed according to their discretion. The sales representatives were granted the authority to settle customer complaints up to $250 on their own signature, to buy back faulty material or excess material and decide on its disposal, and to set their own price on their products within a range of ±10 percent of the company norm. Finally, technical services were provided to the sales representatives "on demand," on a first priority basis, and without prior paperwork; communication was by direct contact. Results of the program included: (1) a 19 percent increase in sales (sales representatives not on the program experienced a 5 percent decrease in sales); (2) an improvement in sales over the rest of the industry by 6 to 7 percent; (3) an increase in dollar revenues over other sales representatives; (4) more favorable job reaction survey results.

The other studies cited by Paul et al. produced similar results using essentially the same philosophy (i.e., redesigning jobs to provide more latitude in decisions, a larger voice in company policy, and greater authority and responsibility in general). There was one exception to the generality of the findings involving the factory foremen. Of two experimental groups, one improved on its job reaction survey and the other did not. The conclusions from these studies are as follows:

1. Positive results of job enrichment can be obtained under differing circumstances for people doing different jobs at different levels.

2. Meaningful results can be obtained for "real-life" situations very far from the "experimental ideal."

3. Jobs can be enriched without inevitably facing demands for higher pay or better conditions to match new responsibilities.

4. Enriching the jobs of subordinates results in more time for meaningful responsibilities for supervisors—their jobs are not "impoverished," but are also enriched.

5. The gains from job enrichment seem to relate more to performance than to satisfaction, at least in the short term; "attitudes do not change overnight. Satisfaction is the result of performance, not vice versa."

6. Participation is not a substitute for job enrichment but, rather, an important part of it if it is "participation in the act of management" and not a "consultative exercise" designed to give employees a "sense" of involvement.

7. Job enrichment changes should be made nonselectively—without regard to individual differences—as long as the changes are "opportunities rather than demands"; in this way, there is no reason to fear adverse reactions and although poor performers may remain poor, good performers will get better—". . . the existence of individual differences is no bar to investigating the possibilities of job enrichment."

Based on W. J. Paul, Jr., K. B. Robertson, and F. Herzberg, "Job Enrichment Pays Off," *Harvard Business Review* 47 (1969):61–78.

namic, changing environment usually affords the opportunity for job redesign as it tends to foster production flexibility. Types of technology also influence job enrichment decisions by providing feelings of satisfaction, autonomy, and control over the work place, which tend to vary according to the production technology employed. Technological flexibility as to job redesign is the highest in continuous-process industries—for example, petroleum—and lowest in mass production technologies with unit- or job-order production technologies in between. Thus, technology constitutes an automation continuum, and as there is movement in either direction from the middle-level technologies (that is, mass production) feelings of worker satisfaction with the content of jobs can be increased. Therefore, jobs should be designed as near to either end of the continuum as the technology permits. As one moves toward either end, job enrichment becomes easier and increases the chances of success.

Managerial Considerations

Why would management be interested in job redesign? Essentially to improve the organization's ratio of inputs to outputs or to increase efficiency and effectiveness, yet this improvement or increase is not automatic when jobs are redesigned. From management's standpoint there are five important considerations that would presumably influence an organization's effectiveness with job redesign. These include organizational formality, leadership style, the firm's long-range prognosis for itself, the managerial expertise found in the organization, and the status of unionization.

The formality of an organization's structures and processes—for example, rules and procedures, measurement and evaluation practices, and so on—can be characterized as falling on a continuum from high formality and rigidness to low formality and flexibility. Not only can this affect workers' attitudes directly, but it can provide a set of forces that counter job redesign efforts. Increasing the job enrichment factors usually requires a decrease in formality. Furthermore, the leadership style of the organization's supervisors should be compatible with the goals of job enrichment if it is to work. It is difficult to increase the core dimensions of a job when supervisors are concerned with exercising unilateral control over subordinates. Success of the effort is aided by using managers who are comfortable with a participative leadership style. This may require a redesign of their role prescriptions, too, since some supervisors see job enrichment as a threat because vertical enlargement of subordinates' jobs encroaches on the supervisor's job. So a redesign or different emphasis is called for in the supervisor's job as well.

Another alternative is to shift supervisors so that their style is compatible with the design of their job and so that only supervisors who welcome the challenge of working in a newly conceived role are placed in charge of the redesigned work place. The long-range outlook of the organization is also important. Job redesign efforts require a long-range perspective; they usually require one to three years to be successful. If a company tends to focus on the short run or if managers are highly mobile, the chances of success are not good. Otherwise the company managers may consider it not worthwhile to get involved since it can be a time consuming process with little immediate and obvious payoff. Continuous and enthusiastic support from a top management that believes in its worth adds to the chances of success.

The managerial expertise in the organization must be considered. There is often a general lack of knowledge among managers on how to implement the principles of job enrichment. In addition, the manager may lack the confidence to be flexible enough to deviate from the standard methods of job enrichment. Not all programs have required internal or external experts, but it helps to ensure success if the employer has one of its own people trained to serve as a consultant to the redesign team.

Finally, the organization's union status must be recognized. Companies with good union relations have had less resistance to job redesign efforts. However, it is not unusual for unions to see enriching the paycheck as the way to enrich jobs. Those complicated job classifications and work rules in the contract must be renegotiated, or they will serve as limitations on what can be done. However, union opposition can be overcome and their cooperation attained as experiences at AT&T, Texas Instruments, and Maytag show.

Job redesign is not a panacea; it has many limitations. However, with a careful diagnosis of situational factors like those mentioned here, it may lead to decreases in absenteeism, in turnover, and in quality costs. It may also increase worker job satisfaction and production flexibility.

Departmentalization

Not only must tasks be grouped into jobs, but jobs must be combined into some meaningful groups. The major question is: What provides a reasonable basis for making this combination? These groups of related jobs are usually called departments and are under the direction of one manager.

The need to departmentalize arises primarily from:

1. Specialization. The advantages cited for job specialization apply to departments as well.

2. Span of control. A manager is limited in the number of people he can effectively manage. Once the number of subordinates exceeds this limit, he must find a way to multiply his efforts. He can do this by grouping some of the jobs together, placing a manager in charge, and dealing primarily with only persons in charge of specific areas of work rather than all the individual job holders.

3. Coordination requirements. All the individual job efforts need to be brought together to achieve a particular goal. One way to do this is to put all the work needed to achieve an objective together. This facilitates decision making, communication, and control.

The basis for grouping activities seems to be widely known and discussed in most principles-of-management textbooks. It has been suggested that Luther Gulick was the first to comprehensively discuss the subject.[30] Gulick saw four useful logical bases for combination: (1) purpose, (2) process, (3) the person to be served or the thing to be dealt with, and (4) the location of activities.[31] Similar activities were placed together apart from dissimilar ones, and the same base should be used at any particular level in the organization. Gulick's categories have been elaborated on and added to, but his original listing remains a part of subsequent attempts.

Criteria for Grouping Jobs

A number of bases have been used for grouping jobs together into departments. Many different criteria may be used within the same organization. The location, product, and function criteria seem to be the most frequently used bases at the first level below the president, but they are also frequently used at all levels in the organization. A comprehensive listing of criteria for departmentation would include:

1. *Numbers.* A given number of workers are assigned to a worker crew or manager. It seems to be used primarily when little specialized skill is required and task completion depends on manpower. In large organizations sections of labor gangs and yard crews often follow this pattern, and it is assumed that each member can do the job assigned.

2. *Time.* This usually refers to shifts within a department. A given department assignment may require manpower assignment beyond the normal work day or around the clock. It is often used when a facility or process must run continuously. To make maximum use of a computer facility, attendants may be required around the clock. Many manufacturing processes, such as the making of steel, cannot be shut down readily as furnaces and ovens are only shut down for maintenance. In such cases a crew of specialists is assigned to a shift and is overseen by a "turn foreman." This base is usually coupled with another grouping base, such as process.

3. *Process or equipment.* This base has to do with the equipment required to produce a product or the sequence of steps necessary to transform an input into an output. To avoid duplication of equipment, all of certain machines may be located together; that is, all milling machines may be located together even though every product produced is milled or every other department in the plant may have to use the milling department's services. By locating all milling operations in one department, the firm can fully utilize the expensive machines—for example only five machines may be required instead of six. In other cases the equipment required may be so expensive and so large it is not practical to duplicate. Steel plants have most of their operating departments organized in this fashion. Each process department may contain a number of heterogeneous specialties the major task of which is to operate and maintain the process facility.

4. *Customers or clientele.* This base is used when there are differences among the customers being served, and the organization must differentiate between the product or service provided or to provide emphasis to the cultivation of a specific customer market. It is quite common to find the marketing or sales function separating departments in this fashion. Industrial customers may be separated from retail customers because of differences in sales techniques and demands made on the seller. The former may buy on the basis of the seller developing products to their specifications and the latter on the basis of brand name.

5. *Market channel.* Koontz and O'Donnell described the use of this base as "one of building divisions and departments around markets and the channels by which they are reached."[32] It seems to be prevalent in firms that are marketing centered as opposed to product or technology centered. Several products may be sold through one channel, or a single product may be sold through several channels. The methods employed for sales, advertising, and promotion and service can, and do, vary according to marketing channel rather than the product or customer. Thus, it is not unusual to find a product, such as antifreeze, produced by one division and being marketed by another division. Some firms have consumer product groups to market rather diverse products because they are moved to the markets through the same or similar channels.

6. *Location.* This base is essentially geographical or territorial in nature. All the firm's activities that are performed in a given location are grouped. It has fairly common use in sales activities, but it is also used to group any company activities. Geographical dispersion and the need to coordinate and control activities at a more local level are important considerations in its use.

7. *Function.* "The functional structure is the building block of organization. It is the module from which other forms are built."[33] Although it is seen by most authors as the predominately used base for grouping activities, there seems to be no definition that readily distinguishes it from other bases. Authors have seen it as being "basic activities,"[34] "principal activities,"[35] or activities "specialized in character."[36] Almost all authorities on organization see specialty of work as characteristic of such groupings—that is, finance, sales, production, and personnel. Perhaps it should be seen as grouping based on occupational specialty. All jobs having to do with a similar or related occupational work are grouped together—for example, all jobs of a production nature are under the direction of a common superior. It is believed that most business firms begin and sustain their early growth through the use of this approach because it tends to follow naturally from division of labor and the original occupational specialties required to operate a business. This is an organizational base on which we elaborate in the next chapter.

8. *Product.* Products or product lines can form the base for groupings in multiproduct firms. At the whole-firm level, all the activities required to develop, produce, and market a product may be grouped together. It may also be used as a base at lower levels. A manufacturing firm, for example, may group its equipment according to the different products it produces. B. F. Goodrich Chemical has its product development center grouped by product lines. Many of the largest corporations are organized at upper levels along product lines—for example, General Electric, General Motors, DuPont, and Westinghouse. There has been a tendency to associate the use of product grouping with large size, but a more crucial factor may be product diversity.[37] We will have more to say about this base in the next chapter too.

Obviously, the firm that sets out to design its grouping of jobs has quite a choice. Each basis for making the grouping has its relative advantages and disadvantages. Much will depend on each firm's unique situation. Of particular importance will be its objectives, strategy for reaching these objectives, and the relative effectiveness and efficiency of each alternative in contributing to goal attainment. Many firms will employ several of the above some place within the organization or combine them in some fashion in designing the structure to be used.

Thompson's Criteria

In referring to departmentation criteria James D. Thompson argues that the real question organizations face is not which basis for departmentalization to use, "but rather in which priority are the several criteria to be exercised. That priority, we suggest is determined by the nature and location of the interdependency . . ."[38] He argued that both technology and environment would determine the type of interdependence, and, in turn, each type of interdependence calls for certain types of coordination if costs are to be minimized. In chapter 6 we discuss the relationship between technology and types of interdependence. Figure 4-3 shows the "appropriate" coordination technique and its relative costs for each type of interdependence according to Thompson.

In grouping positions into departments jobs should be placed together to achieve greatest interdependence and minimize costs. According to Thompson, departments are set up first to handle *reciprocal* interdependence. Any jobs in which the output of any one job becomes the input for another and vice versa (reciprocal interdependence) are confined to one unit and made relatively autonomous from other groups—for example, a research and development team. If none of the positions require reciprocal interdependence, then positions that require *sequential* interdependence (where the output of any one position is dependent on the output of the position that precedes it in the work sequence, such as assembly line operation) are grouped to be confined and relatively autonomous. When neither of these more costly types of coordination are required, the organization should group similar positions together—for example, all

figure 4-3

THOMPSON'S TECHNOLOGY, INTERDEPENDENCE, AND COORDINATION TYPES

Technology	Interdependence	Coordination	Cost
Mediating	Pooled	Standardization	Lowest
Long-linked	Sequential	Plans	Medium
Intensive	Reciprocal	Mutual adjustment	Highest

figure 4-4

THOMPSON'S MODEL OF THE DETERMINATION OF ACTIVITY GROUPING

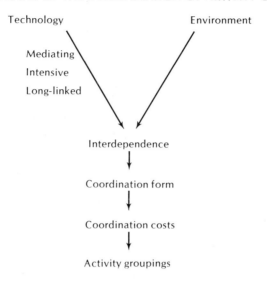

accounting together—so it may use standardization to coordinate them. This is called pooled interdependence.

In a similar fashion the location and autonomy of departments is determined by the nature of the required interdependence among them. In this approach, coordination costs determine what positions will be grouped into departments. But costs also derive from the type of coordination technique used. The coordination technique that is appropriate depends on the nature of interdependence the unit requires, which, in turn, is a function of its technology and the environment. This causal sequence of how departmentalization occurs is shown in Figure 4-4. In several of the previously presented schemes, similar activities are grouped together. In contrast, Thompson argues that this occurs only after interdependence of activities is provided for in departmentalization. His scheme seems to provide a rationale for understanding why such a wide variety of criteria other than merely similarity of jobs have been used in forming departments.

CONCLUSIONS

In this chapter the *practitioner's* approach to the design of organizations has been described. From this literature it is clear that managers consider goal achievement as the prime factor in the determination of organizational structure. This point will assume greater importance in later chapters when we discuss other major variables that researchers consider structural determinants. In the present review of the manager's perspective, one finds little mention of such variables as environment, technology, or size as major considerations in the design of the organization.

In this chapter the major focus has been on the design of jobs and departments. For job design we viewed the major consideration as the extent to which specialization should be pursued. It was argued that the organization can go too far with specialization and may need to redesign jobs to maximize human output. In the design of departments we saw that the organization has a number of criteria it can employ in grouping jobs, all of which may be reasonable depending on the organization's situation. However, the ultimate criterion may be the relative cost of coordination. In the next chapter, the final one in this section on organization structure, we consider organization structural patterns. These patterns result from the way organizations choose to put their jobs together into departments and the way the departments are put together to form the organization itself.

NOTES

[1]Ernest Dale, *Management: Theory and Practice* (New York: McGraw-Hill, 1965).

[2]Joseph L. Massie, "Management Theory," *Handbook of Organization,* ed. James G. March (Chicago: Rand McNally, 1965), pp. 387–422.

[3]Henrie Fayol, *General and Industrial Management,* trans. Constance Storrs (London: Pitman, 1949).

[4]Massie, "Management Theory"; Dale, *Management;* James G. March and Herbert A. Simon, *Organizations* (New York: Wiley, 1958); William G. Scott, "Organization Theory: An Overview and Appraisal," *Journal of the Academy of Management* 4 (1961):7–28; and Gary Dessler, *Organization and Management* (Englewood Cliffs, N.J.: Prentice-Hall, 1976).

[5]Elmore E. Peterson, Grosvenor Plowman, and Joseph M. Trickett, *Business Organization and Management,* 5th ed. (Homewood, Ill.: Irwin, 1962).

[6]Ibid., p. 54.

[7]Louis Allen, *Management and Organization* (New York: McGraw-Hill, 1958), pp. 72–77.

[8]Peter F. Drucker, *Management: Tasks, Responsibilities, Practices* (New York: Harper & Row, 1974), p. 530.

[9]Ibid., p. 539.

[10]Ibid., p. 603.

[11]Ibid., p. 545.

[12]James D. Thompson, *Organization in Action* (New York: McGraw-Hill, 1967).

[13]Ernest Dale, *Planning and Developing the Company Organization Structure* (New York: American Management Association, 1952).

[14]Ibid.

[15]Joseph A. Litterer, *The Analysis of Organizations,* 2nd ed. (New York: Wiley, 1973).

[16]Ibid., p. 324.

[17]Allen, *Management and Organization.*

[18]James H. Donnelly, Jr., James L. Gibson, and John M. Ivancevich, *Fundamentals of Management* (Austin, Texas: Business Publications, 1971), p. 63.

[19]S. M. Davis, "U.S. Versus Latin American Business and Culture," *Harvard Business Review* 47 (1969):88–98.

[20]Ibid., p. 93.

[21]Daniel Katz and Robert L. Kahn, *The Social Psychology of Organization* (New York: Wiley, 1966).

22Thompson, *Organizations in Action*, p. 104.

23Litterer, *The Analysis of Organizations.*

24Ibid., p. 351.

25Ernest R. Hilgard, *Introduction to Psychology* (New York: Harcourt, Brace, and World, 1962).

26Louis E. Davis and Ralph Canter, "Current Job Design Criteria," *Journal of Industrial Engineering* 6 (1955):6.

27Special Task Force to the Secretary of Health, Education, and Welfare, *Work in America* (Cambridge, Mass.: M.I.T. Press, 1972).

28Richard J. Hackman and Gregory R. Oldham, "Development of the Job Diagnostic Survey," *Journal of Applied Psychology* 60 (1975):159–70; and William E. Rosenbach, "An Evaluation of Participative Work Redesign: A Longitudinal Field Experiment," unpublished doctoral dissertation, University of Colorado, Boulder, 1977.

29This discussion is based on an extensive review of the literature summarized in Cyril P. Morgan and Richard W. Beatty, "Organizational Considerations in Applying Job Enrichment," *Colorado Business Review*, vol. 47, no. 9 (September 1974):2–4.

30Massie, "Management Theory."

31Ibid., p. 400.

32Harold Koontz and Cyril O'Donnell, *Management: A Systems and Contingency Analysis of Managerial Functions* (New York: McGraw-Hill, 1976), p. 316.

33Allen, *Management and Organization*, p. 78.

34Koontz and O'Donnell, *Management*, p. 300.

35Dale, *Company Organization Structure*, p. 25.

36Peterson et al., *Business Organization and Management*, p. 160.

37Allen, *Management and Organization.*

38Thompson, *Organizations in Action*, p. 57.

SUGGESTIONS FOR FURTHER READING

ALLEN, LOUIS. *Management and Organization.* New York: McGraw-Hill, 1958.

DRUCKER, PETER F. *Management: Tasks, Responsibilities, Practices.* New York: Harper & Row, 1974.

MASSIE, JOSEPH L. "Management Theory." In *The Handbook of Organizations*, edited by J.G. March. Chicago: Rand McNally, 1965.

chapter 5

PATTERNS
OF BUSINESS ORGANIZATION
DESIGN

The way an organization chooses to group its jobs together results in departments. Likewise, departmentalization provides patterns of the over-all structure of activities. It is this pattern of departments, often shown in organization charts, that at least partially defines a firm's structure. It is perhaps most comparable to what was termed "configuration" in chapter 3, but it also contains some aspects of structuring of activities, supportive component, and decentralization. These patterns represent the overall plan the firm uses for its design.

A firm may be organized around several of the criteria discussed in chapter 4, but generally a more limited number will be used as the foundation for the overall company pattern. The pattern of structure tends to assume one of two forms: functional or divisional.[1] In addition, there may be several other patterns used as an overlay to these forms: matrix organizations, committees, project and temporary groups, and line and staff groups.

THE FUNCTIONAL ORGANIZATION STRUCTURE

The essential feature of a functional structure is that all similar and related occupational specialties are grouped together. It brings together under one executive the related occupational skills. Figure 5-1 shows a functional organization structure.

All personnel, manufacturing, sales, and other functions report to, and are controlled by, the executive in charge of the respective area. A purchasing agent may be located in a manufacturing plant hundreds of miles away from the manufacturing vice-president, but the primary reporting relationship is to that vice-president. However, in practice, the plant manager may share supervision and control, and the vice-president coordinates such work throughout the company.

figure 5-1

A FUNCTIONAL ORGANIZATION STRUCTURE
AT THE TOP MANAGEMENT LEVEL

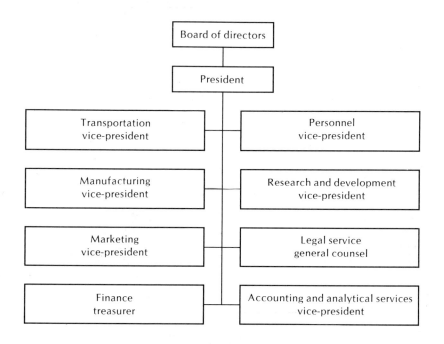

The term *functional* comes from the idea that these are the functions or activities the organization must perform if it is to carry on its business. It seems natural that an organization begins its operations by emphasizing the kind of work it must do to meet its objectives. As it grows and division of labor leads to specialization, the organization has more work to do; it adds new specialties and further divides its presently employed specialties. For example, recall from chapter 1 that when the volume of work expanded and the difficulties of supervising several functions and numerous workers increased at BCI, Frank Jones found it desirable to employ several managers. Each manager may initially supervise several specialties. For example, personnel and purchasing may both report to the plant manager because these specialties in this company spend most of their time servicing the manufacturing function.

As work expands, a further subdivision may take place within the personnel department. The personnel generalist becomes a manager with subordinates who specialize in employment, records and fringe benefits, training, and industrial relations. The response to growth is to create new jobs in the functional areas where the work has increased. The general pattern is to add jobs at the bottom of each department. But in some cases specialty departments may become so large or important that departments are separated to become a complete independent functional department. In our example, personnel, purchasing, and product development may be "spun-off" to provide greater emphasis to their activities, or they may need to further specialize. Personnel may decide the demands made on it require that the employment office be divided among specialists who concentrate on professional/managerial and factory/clerical employment. Purchasing may split its specialists among classes of materials purchased. After such continued elaboration, the firm's overall pattern may look like the one pictured in Figure 5-2.

Characteristic Advantages of the Functional Structure

The functional structural form has certain potential advantages and disadvantages. Whether or not the advantages are realized depends on the specific firm's situation. For example, a large divisionalized firm, such as General Motors, has such large *product* divisions, each division can employ more specialists than most smaller functional firms. Thus, for the purposes of discussing the relative strengths and weaknesses of functionalization, we will assume that everything else is equal, even though this is hardly ever the case. The relative advantages of the functional structure will be classified as specialization, economy, and coordination and control.

Functional Specialization

One thing the functional form does very well is to promote the development of specialization. The functional executive and his subordinates can concentrate their efforts on one kind of work. By grouping all related work together, the firm can employ specialists—for example, in testing and training. In contrast, personnel people in a divisionalized organization would have to remain generalists since they must do all the personnel work for their respective divisions. Thus, the firm can employ a greater variety of skills.

If all the same kind of work is located together, a specialist has a clear career path to pursue. As one advances, the specialist can learn more and more about his work. This also means that a supervisor will be knowledgeable about subordinates' work and can provide technical assistance and adequate evaluation. Furthermore, a specialist feels at home and comfortable in his surroundings. His colleagues understand him, speak his language, and share similar perspectives. All this makes the department attractive to those with a professional orientation.

figure 5-2

FUNCTIONAL ORGANIZATION STRUCTURE AFTER ELABORATION

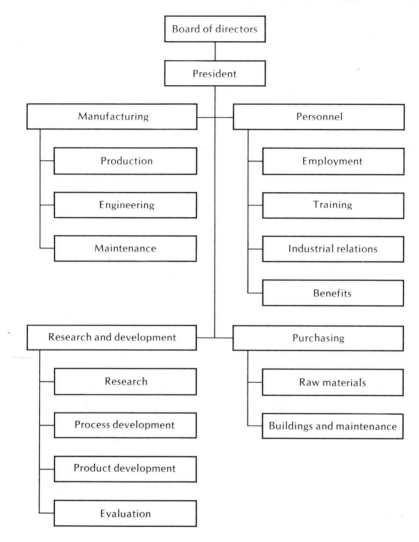

Economy of Resources

A main source of economy with the functional form is the tendency to fully use resources by avoiding the duplication that sometimes occurs in divisionalized structures. In a divisional organization equipment or a position may be added because it is needed by a division even though its full capacity is not to be utilized and other divisions have under-used equipment. In other cases there may be enough work in one division to require a new piece of equipment but not enough to justify more capable equipment that would increase tolerances and quality. In a functional structure this capacity could be used because all the manufacturing work is consolidated; duplication and unused capacities can be controlled and evaluated more closely. Similarly, the skills of specialists can be more fully used.

Such advantages are closely related to another advantage suggested by Allen, in that there "is the ease of decreasing or expanding the size of the function without sacrificing its resources of skill and experience."[2] Economic flexibility is gained because the firm can add or subtract specialists at the bottom of the function and still retain its key people. Similarly, as it grows in volume of work that is common to the whole company, it can do so by adding smaller units of capacity. A firm with several divisions may have to add capacity in multiples determined by its number of divisions.

Control and Coordination

Because all work of one kind is under one manager or executive, the work within the function can be more carefully controlled and coordinated. The ultimate responsibility for all work of one kind is concentrated in one person. There is a clear chain of command for communication and authoritative decisions.

Such features make it possible to see that innovative ideas are shared within the function and that they will receive a fair hearing by top management. There is a common point at which all ideas and decisions come together. Innovations from one department can be passed on to others. Having a representative in the first tier of executives allows policies and programs to be heard at the top, but it also ensures that they will be tested and filtered first by other specialists in the area of work. Of course, this may depend on the influence and status of the top person in the function.

The functional structure tends to force decisions about exceptions to policy and new policies and programs upward until a person or position of sufficient breadth to see all the ramifications is reached. It also tends to force similar decisions that cut across functional areas upward. As a result, it can promote centralized control of a function and decisions pertaining to several functions. This allows for uniformity and coordination of policies, programs, and standards of performance. It also allows outstanding leaders to project their personality, knowledge, and decision-making abilities. To the extent that they are omniscient, the results can be good.

One function may often have been most important in a firm's development and in its continued growth and success. Centralized control and coordination can facilitate the promotion of this function especially if the company president is drawn from this area.

These potential advantages are very powerful ones. They probably account for the popularity of functionalization as a structural form. It is the more prevalent pattern among business firms and especially smaller nondiversified organizations. Even among divisionalized firms, it is a prevalent pattern within divisions.

Characteristic Disadvantages of the Functional Structure

Some of the limitations of the functional form are associated with organizational size.[3] The argument is that as the size of the firm increases, the disadvantages accumulate more rapidly until they outweigh the advantages. However, many of the very largest firms continued to use a basic functional pattern even when they became very large. Goodyear Tire and Rubber, General Motors, Armco Steel, and Atlantic Richfield are examples of firms that grew very large with this form. This is not to say they did not make modifications in the pure form. Indeed, they did employ other bases for groupings and in addition used committees and project groups. But the basic functional pattern was used successfully for a very long time. Even firms that eventually moved to a divisional pattern may have divisions, such as Chevrolet division of General Motors, that themselves use the functional form and are larger than most other divisionalized companies.

Size is one important complicating factor, but it is not the only one. Increases in geographical dispersion, product and marketing diversity and the corresponding diversity in technology used, environments encountered, and strategies employed may be even more significant.

The astute reader has already concluded that the relative advantages are like two-edged swords; they can cut both ways. In some circumstances, they can lead to disadvantages. Specialization may lead to parochialism and goal displacement, or control and coordination can lead to overload for an executive. The characteristics that make a person a great weight lifter serve him poorly in becoming a great long distance runner, but a combination of the two may make a great wrestler. So it is with the functional organization, which is designed primarily to promote specialization in types of occupational work, which can lead to relative disadvantages in other areas.

Responsibility for Performance

The end result of the specialist's work should be the firm's product or service, the output. But no one functional department is totally responsible for the product or service. Each department focuses on its contribution to the product, but not the entire product. Research develops it, manufacturing produces it, and marketing sells it. Only at the very top—the president or executive committee—is anyone responsible for pulling everything together.

Not only does this place the burden of coordination and control for operations at the top, where the emphasis should be on longer range problems, but it makes judging the performance of each department difficult. The departments' work is interdependent in producing a product, but no one unit is completely responsible. The marketing executive cannot be completely responsible for sales volume if the product does not measure up to competition. Manufacturing can hold down costs but not increase sales volume. Only the president has control over both costs and revenue. When this situation is multiplied by numerous products, the control problems become compounded. In addition, because all the firm's products are made by one manufacturing department and sold by one marketing department, many of the costs are allocated to a "common pot." Unless the firm has a very sophisticated cost accounting system, it is often difficult to know the total costs of developing, producing, and marketing each product.

Closely connected with this functional form difficulty is another. It fails to provide a fertile training ground to develop managers for the top spot. There are no positions in which a manager can learn to handle the total of the president's job. The functional managers tend to see only one side of the product and one type of work, such as sales, finance, or production. Managers may be exposed to other areas and may even be asked to manage areas outside their specialty, but they do not deal with it all at once until they get the top spot. Thus, one does not know for certain if he can handle the top job until he has it. Even at the head of each specialty, it may be desirable to have a person who has a broad perspective about the firm as well as his own specialty. It is not easy to obtain such people and still retain the advantages of specialization.

Coordination and Control

Although the functional form has real advantages for coordination within functions, it has disadvantages in coordinating between functions. As we just discussed, responsibility for the total picture tends to be forced upward. As firms become more specialized, the departments tend to become more isolated from departments in other functional units. With isolation and increased specialization, the departments may become parochial. There is no corresponding decrease in the importance of the dependency among the functions as to developing, producing, and marketing the product. The need for coordination is just as great, but the difficulties in doing so are increased.

Lawrence and Lorsch found that functional departments develop different orientations as to time perspective, goals, structure, and interpersonal affairs.[4] Such orientations also lead to difficulties in coordination and conflict among departments.

Closely allied with these difficulties are the delays in decision making and the increased costs for integrative efforts. Increased numbers of levels and new coordination difficulties mean problems must travel farther for a decision and new coordinating mechanisms must be developed.[5] New rules, policies, positions, committees, and departments whose purpose is coordinating or control start to increase.

As these problems multiply, the need for top executives to share their responsibility and authority for operating the organization increases. One way to do this is to push the authority to make decisions to lower levels in the organization or decentralize. But as we already noted, the characteristics of the form tend to push decision making upward. As a result, it is difficult to decentralize decisions that will affect other functions. For example, in a firm that has several plants having all personnel decisions coordinated through one department would be very slow. We can locate a personnel person (or a purchasing or scheduling person) in each plant. But then to whom are they accountable? If it is the plant manager, the personnel executive begins to lose some of the advantages that accrue to him through the functional form. In reality the personnel man will have two bosses and a situation that has the potential for conflicting orders and other associated problems.

Diversification

The functional pattern works best with a limited product range.[6] It can retain its advantages when it can "keep its primary effort focused on one or a very few closely related products."[7] The disadvantages of the functional form are compounded when a firm starts to diversify. The lack of emphasis on the end product or service mentioned earlier is not as critical when the firm has only a few similar products, and it can use the same specialist skills on all of them. Each functional area person is not only a specialist in his work but is also a limited product specialist. At General Electric an electrical engineer can concentrate his talent on light bulbs or appliances or hydroturbines. He can know his occupational specialty and his product thoroughly because GE is organized into a product division form.

When a firm starts adding new products, the occupational specialist must spread his talent, and the likelihood is that he will not know each of the products as well as he knew the one before. The same idea applies to other specialists as well. If the volume of business becomes great enough, the firm can employ specialists who also know the new product well. But it is difficult to ask the electrical engineer to know everything within his occupation that applies to light bulbs, electric generators, and stereo systems.

The example given applied to a technical specialty at a lower organizational level. But now let us consider the manufacturing vice-president who must oversee the production of a diversified product line. His difficulties are the result of product lines times specialties. His required detailed knowledge is less at this level, but still the demands made on him are multiplied by the different product lines as well as specialties. For the marketing department, the demands are increased by new product knowledge required as well, and also by the fact that different customers and marketing channels may be involved.

The greater the diversification in terms of the technical and marketing demands the more difficulty the functional organizational form has in adjusting. Diversification limits the advantages and accentuates the disadvantages. In addition, because the emphasis is on the *kind of work,* some products may not get the attention required for them to develop into major ones for the firm. Building the coalition of specialties working on one product to push it is complicated by the structure. Firms have responded to these problems by developing modifications in the structure to get product emphasis. We will discuss them after divisionalization.

**THE DIVISIONAL ORGANIZATION
STRUCTURE**

The second basic structural form employed by organizations is the divisional structure. In this form the organization is divided into several fairly autonomous units. Each unit is relatively self-contained in that it has the resources to operate independently of other divisions. Each unit is headed by an executive who is responsible for the company's investment in facilities, capital, and people as well as for the unit's development and performance. It is similar to dividing a firm into several smaller companies, but it is not *quite* the same, since each "smaller company" is not completely independent. Each unit is *not* a separate legal entity; it is still part of the company and has no stock of its own. Each division is still directly accountable to the corporation. General Motors, AT&T, General Foods, and Caterpillar Tractor are examples of firms using this form.

Figure 5-3 shows charts of a company whose basic structure is divisional. This firm, like most, uses *product* divisions. A few firms employ *geographic* divisions. In 1969 about 76 percent of the 500 largest firms in the United States were organized on a product division basis, whereas only 1.5 percent used the geographic division form. In 1949 approximately 63 percent of the largest 500 firms were organized along functional lines, but by 1969 about 11 percent used this form.[8] Among the *largest* firms, the *product division form* of organization seems to be prevalent.

The tendency to change from a functional structure to a divisional one can partly be explained by the increase in firms adopting a diversification

figure 5-3

A PRODUCT DIVISION ORGANIZATIONAL STRUCTURE

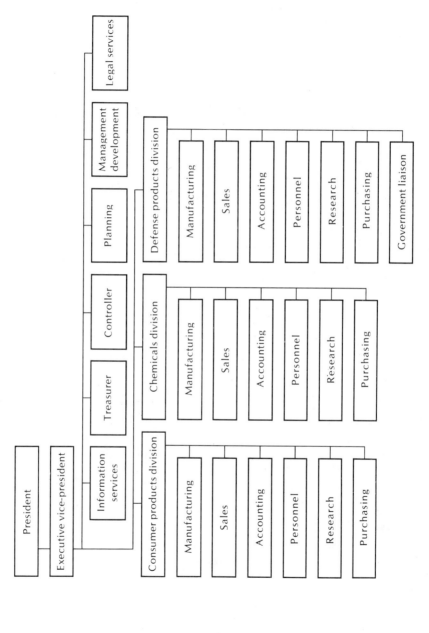

strategy. Rumelt has found this to be partially true especially during the 1950s.[9] Allen has also suggested diversification as a primary reason for the change and suggested that product divisionalization often occurs in relatively smaller firms.[10] However, it has been shown that many firms have adopted this form when not employing such a strategy, and others who have followed such a strategy have not divisionalized.[11] So although diversification may be responsible for divisionalization in some situations, it clearly is not always the case. See Block 5-1 for a study in which this was not the reason for divisionalization.

The essential feature of the divisional structure is self-containment. Each division is like a self-contained functional organization. It has all its own occupational specialties to develop, produce, and market its particular product. Once the firm has created its "little companies," each division is typically organized along functional lines again. The firm can retain many of the advantages of the functional pattern and minimize many of its disadvantages.

The way organizations operate under this form varies. Central corporate offices usually exist that assist the president in performance of his job and often provide assistance to the divisions. They help the president oversee, control, and coordinate the divisions. They do long-range planning for the whole company. They deal with finance and tax matters. They monitor the performance of the divisions and help the corporate executives evaluate proposals for capital outlays by the divisions. The division manager does have the responsibility and authority for the performance of his division, but it is often subject to some degree of evaluation and control by the corporation. Each firm must work out the practical questions surrounding exactly what the division manager can decide on his own and how far he can go independent of the firm's policies. Usually financial matters such as capital investment are rather closely controlled, and proposals over a given limit must be reviewed and approval given by the corporation. The degree of divisional autonomy will vary considerably from firm to firm.

Characteristic Advantages
of the Divisional Structure

Dividing a firm into several semiautonomous divisions allows the firm many of the advantages of the functional organization. It also makes available certain additional potential advantages. Whether or not the potential is met will be determined by the relative strengths and the weaknesses and the firm's provisions for making the transition and adjusting the concept to its particular business. For example, General Electric ran into trouble when it divisionalized its General Electric Credit Corporation because it used the same pattern it had used for its other

block 5-1

DIVISIONAL ORGANIZATIONS IN EUROPE

Lawrence G. Franko has studied the change in organizational structure occurring in the largest European companies and provides some insight into reasons for the changes in structure that have occurred there. Prior to about 1960 most European firms employed the basic functional pattern described in this chapter. By 1972 about 70 percent of the 127 firms he studied had changed to the divisional structure. Many of these firms had not fully adopted the American practice of corporate executives who manage the total organizational performance, but the new structures were essentially the same divisional pattern employed in America.

In America, it has been argued, the move to a divisional structure was an accompaniment of an adoption of a product diversification strategy. Franko cites evidence that a similar phenomenon can be found in Europe. But he also argues it is not always the case, and product diversification has not in itself been responsible for the changes.

Franko cites evidence and argues that the changes in structure may be the response to a less negotiable environment. In Europe for many years there was little antitrust legislation or enforcement of it. The firms had more opportunity to coordinate with competitors. Firms were also able to erect more barriers to trade such as tariffs and quotas. Because of such conditions, European firms could effectively negotiate their environments. However, since World War II and especially since the creation of the European Economic Community, the ability of the firms to negotiate their environment has declined. Tariff barriers have declined and competition, both with European firms and outside firms, has increased. The enforcement of antitrust regulations has also increased. Such changes mean a less negotiable environment. Franko argues that in industries where the environment has become less negotiable, the movement toward divisional structures has been strongest. He also argues that where the environment is still negotiable there is little structural change even in diversified firms.

Franko's evidence is associative, and he does not show cause and effect, but it is persuasive in its suggestion that product diversification may not be the only strategy that leads to multidivisional organization patterns.

Based on Lawrence G. Franko, "The Move Toward a Multidivisional Structure in European Organizations," *Administrative Science Quarterly* 19 (December 1974):493-506.

divisions.[12] However, in general, firms with a product divisionalized form of organization show superior financial performance.[13] The relative advantages of the divisional structure are classified for discussion under the topics of emphasis on the product, control and appraisal, and motivation and management development.

Emphasis on the Product

The product or service is the output the organization has to contribute to society and its success will determine the firm's "bottom-line." Many of a firm's major objectives are centered on what it hopes to achieve with its products. When a firm sets up divisions, Peter Drucker says it starts with the question, "What results do we aim for?"[14] The focus is on the end result, or goal. In a functionally organized firm, the focus is on the work required to produce the results rather than the results themselves.

The divisional organizational form points all the specialists toward the end result of their work. As the firm diversifies in a functional organization, no one person is responsible for coordinating and controlling all the work that goes into any one product or group of products. By gathering all the work together into one unit the mission of which is to develop, produce, and market the product, we encourage specialists to focus on their product. It prevents some products from being neglected and others from being overemphasized. It also promotes a clarity of purpose because people can emphasize and coordinate their work toward a known desired end result. Because the division head has almost total responsibility for a product, it can reduce provincial thinking at this level.

Control and Appraisal

Theoretically since each division has all the resources it needs to achieve its mission, it is easier to control and coordinate. Decision makers can be held responsible for the total results. If their product is not successful, it is the division manager who is responsible.

The division management can be held accountable for the consequences of its actions because results and responsibility can be identified. The revenue contribution and costs can be more easily determined by product or product group. If all products are made by the same manufacturing unit, the costs are not so easy to separate. This way one can know how much it costs to make and sell a Chevrolet or a Buick. One can have revenue statements for each division. Business performance and results can be known earlier and action taken without neglecting other areas of the company's business.

A similar asset is that the division manager and his subordinates can focus their attention on a smaller information set. They do not have to worry about the general money market; top corporate management provides that service to them. They only have to focus on the environment, technology, and market for their own product; they do not have to know all about light bulbs as well as refrigerators and generators. This reduces the amount of uncertainty, distractions and information to which attention must be given. Thus, it allows them to concentrate their efforts and better understand and appraise their situation. Similarly, corporate management can be removed from the operating details. Buffered from such details, they can concentrate on total company matters. Long-range planning and strategy can be given proper attention.

Motivation and Development of Management

Several authors believe that this advantage is primary.[15] People understand what the organization is trying to do and what their part is in it; they can see the consequences of their actions. From this feedback they can learn and take corrective action; they can direct themselves. Feedback, completeness, and autonomy are aspects of jobs that job enrichment proponents have found to be motivating, and they are built into the division manager's job. There are more managers in this form who have total responsibility for some aspect of a product. There are several sales, manufacturing, and division managers instead of one in each area, since each division has its own set of functional executives focused on each product line.

Not only are managers more likely to be highly motivated, they also receive broader experience. Each division manager is learning how to run a total business, not just one functional aspect of an organization. Several persons are being prepared to head the firm, and people are trained and tested for their ability to handle total responsibility.

Characteristic Disadvantages of the Divisional Structure

As with the functional organization, the divisional design has characteristics that can be dysfunctional. With the divisional form these include executive development, economy, and coordination.

Executive Development

For each semiautonomous division a firm creates, it needs more management talent, since each division must compete in its own sphere. Although divisions help to develop managers with total top management perspectives, it also creates a need for them. This can be particularly acute when the firm first changes to this structure, because it has had few places in which to train them. If the company has not prepared such managers well in advance, it may be forced to seek outside talent. In time this problem may disappear, but in the short run it can be costly.

Executive career development is another problem because it is harder to shift people between divisions. Each division is fairly autonomous; it is up to its management to hire and develop people, and division management may resist the transfer of good people out of the operation. A person may have a career limited by the size and scope of his own division. If there is no central personnel office to coordinate career development or little contact between divisions, a person can easily miss out on opportunities for advancement and new experiences.

At the top of a division, the managers get well-rounded experience but only in their division's work. The head of Westinghouse's Defense Product Group may learn little about running the total corporate operation because the two are so different. Most presidents receive a substantial exposure to the financial side of a business before assuming the presidency. But finance is one of the last areas to be decentralized, so the division manager may receive little training in this area as well. The divisionalized company does provide more training grounds for its people, but these may have limitations.

Economy

When divisions are created, each requires the talent and resources to compete in the market place. Each needs its own facilities, capital, managers, and specialties, which can lead to duplication of resources and, perhaps, to acquisition of more in total than the firm needs. Each division will now need its own marketing and manufacturing managers as well as other functional managers and, therefore, will need more higher priced talent in the total organization. A company that needed only five milling machines before may now need eight so each division can do its own work. If this requirement is carried to the level of complete plants, offices, and staffs, the cost of duplication can be enormous. It may not be possible to completely divide up company resources so each division has what it needs to operate and be autonomous, and some firms do limit this practice.

Each functional area in a division may not be able to specialize to the extent it could within a larger functional organization. For example, a firm that has 20 personnel specialists in one group can allow some to concentrate on employment and others on training and so on. But if these 20 are spread over ten divisions, each must become more a generalist. The organization can no longer afford to let one concentrate only on developing testing programs. If the company wants to retain all its specialized skills, it must greatly increase its employment and either duplicate or concentrate some of the specialties in the home office. The result can be duplication or too many staff people.

A qualifying factor here is the scale of operations. If each division is sufficiently large, it may still achieve the economies of scale. In fact, it may gain through losing the diseconomies of an overly large scale of operations.

The eventual economies to be gained must offset the initial investments if the form is to be more economical.

In addition, the technology the firm employs may not lend itself to being economically divided up into divisions. The steel business cannot afford to duplicate blast furnaces, coke ovens, rolling mills, and annealing ovens in order to have separate product divisions because most of their flat products are made in the same general way. Armco Steel has a building-and-drainage products division, but it cannot afford to let this division have its own steel-making facilities. Technology often determines how far a firm can go in creating autonomous divisions.

Coordination

Coordination of all the work required to develop, produce, and market a product may be facilitated by divisionalization, but other kinds of coordination may be hindered. We have already mentioned the difficulties in coordinating career development, but there are other problems as well. Divisions are concerned primarily with their own operations and objectives, and each division manager is often in competition with his counterparts. Divisions may have little real incentive to cooperate with other divisions. Pontiac may compete with Oldsmobile for customers and for resources, and the firm may have great need to coordinate certain parts of the relationship between the divisions. For example, General Motors can achieve great savings by coordinating body styles and component parts. The company can realize great cost savings if the same part can be used in building Pontiacs and Chevrolets.

When a company sets up divisions, it also must decentralize some control and authority, which may make it difficult to see that policies are adopted and followed uniformly. A manager who is being held accountable for results may resent having to conform to a uniform policy imposed from "headquarters."

A firm may choose a policy that requires internal buying; that is, whenever possible a division must give preferential purchase of its materials to a sister division. If a division can purchase the same material cheaper outside the firm, it is difficult to hold that division responsible for its results in the market place. As a result, the firm often has to establish elaborate home office staff groups to develop and coordinate companywide policies and procedures. These groups may help the chief executive officer control the divisions and do long-range planning and coordinate their efforts, but they also add to indirect costs.

Finally, autonomy among the divisions may make coordination of customer relations and product development difficult. One division may develop a new product idea that has potential but fail to develop it further because it does not quite fit its own product mix. At the same time, another division might successfully develop it if that division were aware of it.

Relations with customers and the public can be more difficult to monitor. Moore cites the example of American Machine and Foundry Company,[16] in which one of their divisions was about to sue a supplier who was a major customer of two other divisions. In other cases different divisions may share the same customers leading to multiple sales calls and sometimes unwarranted competition.

Multiple divisions can lead to multiple reputations with the public and government as well as with customers. Although the firm may have several divisions, for official purposes it is one legal entity, and any of the divisions can get the firm into legal difficulties. If one of the divisions is cited for OSHA, EPA, or EEO violations, the whole firm is answerable. If Ford Motor's taconite mining operation gets a bad reputation, it can spread to the whole firm's image.

Because of such problems, a division's autonomy is often more apparent than real. The division manager's authority may be quite restricted by policies, review of programs, budgets, and objectives. Since divisions tend to focus on operating results and "their business," the long-range viewpoint can be neglected in favor of making "their business" look good relative to others. Corporate management obviously must develop appropriate objectives and criteria and the means for appraisal and review of division performance to ensure total company performance.[17]

OVERLAYS:
MODIFICATION OF THE BASIC
STRUCTURES

The functional and divisional forms are the primary patterns of organization commonly employed. However, there are other patterns that can be identified and that are often used in conjunction with the primary patterns. In a sense they are reflections of management attempts to modify the basic patterns to overcome disadvantages and make them work more efficiently and effectively. For example, a firm employing a functional pattern may find it useful to create a product-line group composed of specialists from each relevant department who are assigned to the group part time. The group has the mission of coordinating the efforts required to develop, produce, and market a new product. In this way the firm can overcome some of the weaknesses of their basic pattern. The group may continue to oversee the product permanently, or it may be disbanded after the product becomes established.

Usually every organization develops a unique combination of modifications. Some are created to fill specialized roles that require greater emphasis, and others are attempts to differentiate areas of responsibility, avoid conflicts, and clarify authority. Other arrangements might be designed to promote coordination at lower levels in the organization. We will discuss several of the more prominent modification patterns that have been used. We have called them "overlays" because they are imposed on the basic functional or divisional pattern. For the purpose of our analysis, we will discuss three major overlays separately: line and staff, lateral relations, and the matrix organization.

Line and Staff

The concept of line and staff has been present in management literature for many years, but its longevity has not increased the clarity of the concepts.[18] Many authors believe it is possible to identify a line-and-staff pattern within an organization, although there is some confusion about the appropriate criteria for distinguishing one from the other. There is even a question in some quarters whether enough difference exists to usefully distinguish between the line and staff of an organization. Nevertheless, the concept has been an important one in management literature.

The concept has to do with the pattern of relationships that results from the assignment of roles to individuals and departments. The differences in the roles are concerned with objectives and the authority to make decisions. As a firm grows, executives must find ways to share their work load. Some of the increased load results from work directly related to accomplishing the primary objectives of the firm, such as the need to produce greater quantity of the product. Additional work load is related to performing the administrative or managerial function, such as planning for expansion or controlling the quality of new hires. As the firm grows, it finds that certain work performs a service to all departments, such as planning for expansion or hiring, but is not directly involved in producing the product or service. BCI in chapter 1 is a good example.

Line units are those that are responsible and accountable for the accomplishment of the firm's *primary objectives*—producing the product or service. The role of staff units usually is to provide advice and service to line people in carrying out their work.[19] They support and provide auxiliary service to both executives and line units. According to this line of reasoning, one could examine the objectives of a firm and from them determine its line units. If a firm's primary objective is to develop, produce, and sell a product, then research and development and manufacturing and marketing would be seen as its line units; everything else would be staff. In hospitals, public accounting firms, or city government, the line units would consist of different kinds of specialties.

Line and staff are also distinguished by their decision-making authority. Since line executives are accountable for accomplishing the primary objectives, they are supposed to have the final authority to make decisions. Line managers are not superior to, nor do they command, staff positions that do not report to them. Similarly, line positions do not report to a staff manager. Staff managers suggest and advise. Line managers listen and decide. In describing the relationship, Allen says the decisive factor is that "in case of disagreement, the line manager has the right to make final operating decisions."[20] Maintaining the final decision-making authority in line positions is thought to keep authority in those positions accountable for results. It is also thought to preserve a clear, unbroken chain of command from top to bottom.

In practice, the employment of line and staff may lead to a confusing picture. There are different kinds of staff and differences in the authority delegated to staff across organizations. As a result, the differences in prescribed roles are not nearly as clear as we have described, and several problems are encountered in making the line/staff concept work.

Staff Authority

Several authors distinguish between types of authority that staff may have with respect to line.[21] These authority types seem to be constrained, but increasing levels of influence over the line's decision-making discretion.

The first type we might call *normal staff advice.* It corresponds to the description of staff's role just given. In essence, staff's role is to provide advice, information, or service. The staff person may recommend an action or try to sell his plan. The operating manager decides whether to follow or ignore the staff's ideas. If the operating manager accepts staff's advice, the plan becomes that manager's plan, and he is accountable to his line superiors for it.

Compulsory staff consultation is a slight escalation of staff's influence. The only change in the line/staff relationship is that the line manager must consult and listen to staff's advice. The goal is to specify when an expert should be consulted but not to limit the discretion of an executive.

Concurrent authority is an important escalation of staff's authority, in which the line manager's discretion is limited. This requires that staff must be consulted and staff's agreement obtained before action can be taken. When it is used, the firm usually wants to be sure the staff's expertise is a part of any decision. For example, an organization may want to be sure any contract is approved by legal counsel so all contracts must be reviewed by the legal department; or it may want to be sure that all personnel actions are reviewed by its Affirmative Action officer.

Functional authority is considered the greatest limitation of the operating manager's discretion. This type permits a staff person to give orders to an operating manager. The orders are to carry the same weight as those of line superiors. The order may be rescinded by a superior executive, but until then it stands. This staff discretion is usually limited to specific aspects of the job about which the staff has a particular expertise. The plant safety engineer may be permitted to stop any operation in the plant until unsafe conditions are corrected, for example.

Although staff authority under normal conditions seems to be greatly constrained, the actual influence is often much greater than the formal limitations would imply. In most cases staff relies more on informed persuasion and informal influence with line managers to accomplish their goals. Since they are experts in their respective areas, staff people can withhold valuable advice or slow down service to pressure a manager to heed their influence attempts. A cooperative staff can be an important asset, but because staff people are experts in areas in which line managers are not, they can sometimes overwhelm the line manager with their specialized knowledge. They may have more influence with higher levels of line management because these managers depend on them to provide information about line performance. If information is power, staff is powerful, since it is often staff's job to gather, assemble, and interpret information for the organization.

Uses and Types of Staff

As an executive looks for ways to share his work load, he may turn first to his immediate subordinates. These line managers do serve as staff to some extent, since they can provide advice, information, and help within the capabilities of their knowledge. But this assistance is limited since they have their own work that needs their concentrated attention. Furthermore, they may not possess the specialized skills required by their superior. Eventually, specialized personnel are needed for more specialized roles.

Often specialized assistance is needed by many of the line managers themselves. For example, locating, hiring, and training new employees or instituting an office services department to provide secretarial and printing services can benefit many departments. In both cases, the firm can gain economies by using a single department to service all other departments and add a higher level of professional expertise by specializing.

There may be a need for a staff member to aid executives in the planning and control activities of their jobs. In the first instance, the firm may create a marketing research or economic forecasting unit to help determine appropriate plans and strategies for future action. In the latter instance, it may create units to monitor the internal activities that are presently being conducted, such as an internal auditor. A credit, wage and salary, or quality control department can use the technical skills, concentrated attention, and objectivity needed to provide the information required for executives to monitor activities and take corrective action.

In addition, the firm may need units to aid line managers in improving operations and dealing with special problems. Line people may have difficulty finding the time to devote to certain problems and not have the required skills to handle them as well as an expert. Operations research or organizational development units are examples of such staff use.

These examples of the possible uses of staff can help us identify several types of staff found in organizations. One type of staff is referred to as *personal staff*.[22] The personal staff provides assistance to one manager. This is the manager's personal aide who takes over part of the manager's duties and assists the manager in meeting his responsibilities. This person would serve only that manager and have only the duties and authority the manager assigns. Allen distinguishes between two types of personal staff.[23] The *staff assistant* assists the manager in specific phases of the superior's job and usually only in administrative details rather than supervisory aspects. People in this type of position are called administrative assistants, staff assistants, or assistants. The *line assistant* also helps the manager fulfill responsibilities but acts more as a subordinate manager. He may help the manager in all aspects of his superior's job. He may be used in several ways; in some cases the assistant may be assigned part of the manager's responsibilities to carry out on his own. The assistant may oversee and monitor the daily operations and take over when the superior is absent. He may also act as his superior's agent. In such cases, it is hard to distinguish the assistant from a normal line subordinate. This type of position frequently carries the title assistant manager, associate director, or something similar. A proliferation of personal staff positions is often taken as an indication of the need to redesign the assignment of responsibilities and authority.

The most commonly recognized type of staff is the *specialized staff*. These are units or persons who serve as staff to all the other line and staff departments. Most of our previous discussion of line-and-staff relations applied to these units and persons. One point does require further note; in functional structures the functional departments all provide specialized staff assistance. When the firm has several plants or operating locations, it may become difficult to supply staff assistance to operating managers. Similarly, when a firm divisionalizes, it creates separated, semi-autonomous managers who need staff assistance. Both processes highlight the need to properly locate staff.

Two criteria seem to be important in locating staff assistance: proximity to need and economy. Often, trade-offs must be made between the two. The organization chart in Figure 5-4 shows how a firm might locate its staff units.

At the executive level the company has staff departments to assist top management in planning and running the total company affairs. They may develop company policies, monitor division performance, assist division staff units and help top management plan for the future. In some cases they

figure 5-4

A DIVISIONAL ORGANIZATION STRUCTURE
SHOWING PLACEMENT OF STAFF

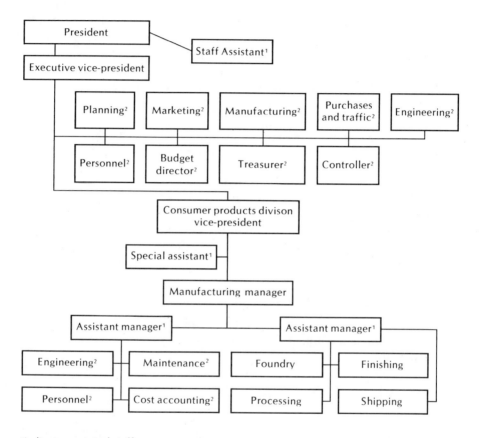

[1]indicates personal staff
[2]indicates specialized staff

may provide a service to all company units because it is more economical—for example, legal services.

The staff that managers need to run their operations are located at the division and plant level. Particular attention will be devoted to the staff that is used on a relatively continuous basis. Generally, these staff people will report primarily to the division or the plant manager. In some cases the corporate staff will exercise some measure of authority over these units.

Problems in the Operation of Staff

Both the concept and the practice of achieving coordination and cooperation between line and staff have been criticized. That problems and limitations do exist is well reported, and there seems to be considerable conflict between line-and-staff officials.[24] Some of these difficulties stem from the concept itself and others from the way the relationship is used in practice. The principle that line always has the final say seems to lead both line and staff to view staff as less important and even inferior.[25]

Newman[26] cites several common problems that arise in using a line-and-staff pattern.

1. Vague definitions of duties and authority. Misunderstanding about the staff role leaves much room for role expectations to be violated or go unfulfilled.

2. Scarcity of good staff men. A staff person needs more than technical expertise. He must have the personal skills needed to work in a subordinate advisory capacity.

3. Mixing staff and operating duties. It may be very difficult to be both an advisor and an action-oriented decision maker.

4. Disregard of staff by the boss himself. Some line managers see staff as undermining their position and authority. Others do not maintain enough contact with staff to use their expertise. Both can lead to underuse of staff.

However, although the line/staff concept seems to be characterized by potential problems, it is perhaps the most often used overlay to the basic organization forms.

Lateral Relations Mechanisms

A majority of organizations employ some form of lateral relations mechanism that involves the creation of a group. A possible rationale has been suggested by Galbraith.[27] As the typical bureaucratic approaches can no longer handle the amount of information that must be processed, the organization must find ways to increase its capacity to handle information. One way to do this is to follow a strategy of creating better lateral relations.

The essential idea is to let decisions be made at the level in the organization where the information exists. The typical bureaucratic procedure is to allow information and decisions to flow up the hierarchy until an executive is found who has the proper perspective, information, and authority to make a decision. Different lateral relations strategies attempt to gain perspective by bringing together all persons who have the necessary information. The effect is often to create groups that can focus on problems, projects, or products that the basic patterns find difficult to do. It allows the organization to cut across departmental lines and to decentralize decision making.

Lateral relations take many different forms, ranging from two department managers who get together to solve joint problems and share information to the much talked-about informal organization. We will concentrate on three of the more commonly used formal forms.

Committees

From a broad perspective committees can be viewed as encompassing all formal lateral relations. The primary factor that differentiates them from the two other forms is *purpose*. A committee can be formed for any purpose, but product and project groups are formed specifically to manage certain products or projects. Committees can be used for (1) gathering and sharing information, (2) studying issues to recommend action, and (3) developing ideas. Just about any issue about which several people must be informed, their views or cooperation solicited, or their efforts coordinated has been the object of committee formation.

Usually committees have a limited membership, a designated leader, and a specific goal. A committee may report to a manager at the next hierarchical level above that of the membership. Its leader is expected to run the meetings but usually has no direct formal authority over the members. In addition, the committee rarely supervises the work of others.

Some committees are "standing committees" with relatively stable membership. The committee meets regularly to deal with problems that involve the membership's departments. At top levels in the organization these may be policy-making groups or general management committees. In other cases members may meet to review progress and share information as to problems and work load. In the former the group makes decisions; in the latter the shared information is expected to improve coordination.

Other committees are of a more temporary nature. Membership consists of those who share in the current problems or are assigned to deal with them, and the committee continues only as long as the problem exists. The assignment may be to study an issue and make a recommendation for a new wage-and-salary package, or it may be to facilitate scheduling problems during a strike. In this case the committee is a temporary measure that bypasses the existing organization structure until the need disappears.

Committees have been criticized for wasting time, encouraging compromise, and violating the chain of command among other things. They have been praised for developing cooperation and creativity. As a result, much of the applied group literature has focused on making groups like committees more effective. The writing on this topic is prolific, and much of it is quite normative. Some of the prescriptions have been verified, but many have not. It is beyond the scope of our treatment to go into it here, but you are referred to several examples. [28]

Project Groups

When a company decides to build a new plant, to whom does it assign the job? Probably no functional department or division is in charge of building new plants. Possibly the work could be divided, assigning each part to regular departments, but such a task is usually not handled successfully as a part-time job. Either regular duties or the project is likely to suffer. Most organizations find it better to set up a temporary organization. In some industries, such as construction or aerospace, project organizations may resemble the previously described division organizational form.

Project management allows the main organization to proceed normally while giving concentrated attention to a new, unfamiliar, and involved project. Stewart[29] has indicated that project organization is a viable form when the undertaking is:

1. A one-time task with specifically definable results
2. Large in scope
3. Unfamiliar or lacks precedent
4. Calls for a high degree of interdependence among the tasks
5. A high stake in the successful completion of the project

Project groups are made up of a team of specialists. In some cases the members may be drawn from the firm's functional departments to which they return when the project ends. A few may remain to help operate such an undertaking as a new plant, or the members may be hired from the outside and go to work for another firm when their project job ends. In the construction and government contracting industries, many craftsmen and engineers travel from project to project. In either case the members are temporary, and the size of the group may change with the different phases of the work.

The project is usually under the direction of a project manager who has the responsibility for controlling activities in terms of time and budget, detailed planning, gathering resources, and coordinating efforts. He may have little direct authority over team members, so he has to work through normal department managers, or the project may be set up so that they report directly to him. The project manager's relationships with the parent organization's department managers may be filled with ambiguity and uncertainty and thus have the potential for conflict. The manager must find a way to cope with these and find integrative solutions; often without formal authority or guidelines.

Product Groups

Like project groups, product groups are a means of obtaining concentrated attention on an undertaking that needs tight coordination. In a large multiproduct firm it is easy for individual products and product lines to get lost unless they have a "champion." This problem was addressed earlier when comparing functional and divisional patterns, but even in a large division with many products the problem can be manifest. One solution is to appoint a formal product champion, the product manager. The product manager is expected to guide product development from its early inception to market maturity and see that it receives the attention it requires to become and remain a successful product. In marketing-oriented industries where product life cycles are limited, this overlay is an important pattern in the firm's structure.

Product management's operation varies. It is similar to project management in that the project is the development of a product for the product manager. A product requires a high degree of interdependence among departments to develop it. The manager may have a team of specialists to aid him. These persons, however, often give only part-time attention to it since the rest of their time is spent in their respective departments. Like the project manager, the product manager is expected to obtain resources internally, plan programs, and serve as a focal point in communication and in coordinating efforts. The manager often has somewhat limited authority to make decisions, to supervise the team, and to see that departments cooperate. There are also other important differences with project management: there is no definite termination point; the task may continue indefinitely; and the task is usually not unique in that there are other product groups, and the firm has undertaken such tasks before. As in project management, a significant issue is to define the relationship between the product unit and the basic functional departments. How much responsibility, authority and discretion each unit will have must be worked out. But unlike project management there is some precedent or experience upon which to resolve these issues.

Product management has been used for some time by such firms as Proctor and Gamble and General Foods. In these cases the unit is primarily marketing oriented with concern for market planning and research, sales, pricing, packaging, and so on. However, in recent years some interesting variations have developed that emphasize more complete product management.

One variation has stressed the entrepreneurial aspects of new-product management. In this case, the scientist who developed the product in research becomes the product manager. The scientist is expected to take "his" product and guide its development through the various stages to market maturity. The firm supplies the scientist with advice and resources, but he must compete and champion it in the firm's internal marketplace.

This approach is believed to provide important motivational benefits that promote product development. It allows the originator of an idea to follow "his" idea through to completion. Thus, the originator can become an entrepreneur and stay with the product; or, if he chooses, he can turn it over to another product manager.

B. F. Goodrich Chemical Company has used another variation. When a potential new product is identified, the organization forms a small business team. The team usually consists of managers from research, development (product and process), marketing, and manufacturing. The chairman usually is determined by the stage of development of the product with the marketing person eventually expected to take over. The team operates as a business within a business. It coordinates the product's development, process development, manufacture, and marketing but does so through the firm's regular operating departments. Team members report to several layers of councils or committees who oversee, coordinate, and financially control the numerous small business teams. The members of the team also have major responsibilities in their respective departments, and, in some cases, they may be members of several small business teams. Their principal performance evaluation is tied more to their work in their departments than to the product's success. This approach is very similar to the matrix organization but, in essence, is a functional structure with the extensive use of product group overlays.

Matrix Organization

The term *matrix organization* has sometimes been used to describe all organizations that make more than minimal use of project teams or product groups. However, in our view the term should be reserved for describing such organizations as TRW Systems, where matrix organization has acquired the status of a basic organizational pattern.

The pattern that results is mixed since it combines project management and functional departmentalization. It represents an attempt to retain the advantages of functional specialization while adding the project management advantage of improved coordination.[30] Figure 5-5 shows a chart of a matrix organization.

The matrix organization grew out of organizations responding to changes in their environment. In the United States, NASA and the Department of Defense initiated contracting practices that required contractors to use project management.[31] For each particular project, a firm had to develop a project organization.

In order to (1) maintain the advantages of specialization and resource conservation, (2) meet government requirements, and (3) obtain the coordination advantages of project management, the firms with several projects devised a full-time matrix structure. The structure contains both project

figure 5-5

A MATRIX ORGANIZATION STRUCTURE

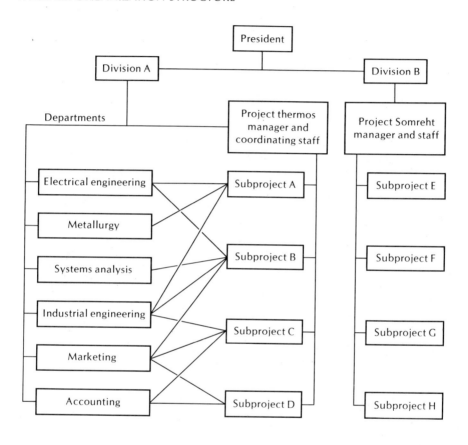

groups and functional departments. Many of the firm's employees will have dual assignments. A mechanical engineer, for example, may be assigned to both project A and to the engineering department. If project A is completed, the engineer would go back to his engineering department to work and perhaps be assigned to a new project. He has a home base, but he works full-time on the project. The reporting relationship is dual; he reports to both project and department manager. The functional departments may carry out much of the operational work for several of the projects. Scheduling and priorities must be worked out with the functional departments and with other projects.

As we indicated earlier, a basic problem is determining the responsibility and authority relationships between functional and project managers. The problem is magnified in the matrix organization simply because

153

many projects are involved. As a result, there are many more demands for resources and priorities. Friedlander has indicated that there is commonly a lack of jurisdictional clarity.[32] The dual reporting relationship and assignments can cause role ambiguity, concerns for career development, and the weakening of ties with professional reference groups for employees. Because of such problems, some observers believe organization development techniques are required to make it work well.[33]

CONCLUSIONS

In this chapter we examined two basic organizational structures and a number of modifications to these basic patterns. The approach has been primarily descriptive, although a number of antedotal and logical observations have been made. This is primarily because there has been little formal or systematic research conducted in this area.

We have argued that both practitioner and scholar have the same end objective—improving the effectiveness of organizations. The first step toward that goal is understanding the phenomenon. It is obvious when one compares the scholar's approach (chapter 3) with the practitioner's approach (chapters 4 and 5) that the two have taken different directions in their efforts to understand organizational structure. In chapter 4 we discussed some of the reasons why scholars and practitioners have chosen different routes to the same goal. These different approaches may eventually be merged into a common understanding, but at present it often seems that the two speak a different language. The scholar is seen as being esoteric and the practitioner as being nonscientific.

Organization theory is long overdue for attempts to study organizations as management understands them and attempts to integrate the scholar's and practitioner's viewpoints. Perhaps the new generation of students who understand the points of view of both will provide this integration.

In this section (especially chapters 4 and 5) we have been concerned with the province of the organizational designer, the practitioner. The next section (chapters 6, 7, 8, and 9) deals with topics that have been the main focus of the organizational scholar. There is more research available on these topics than on anything we have discussed to this point. As a result, the material will be more scholarly and presented in a somewhat different manner, as we strive to make the research findings clear.

NOTES

[1]Franklin G. Moore, *Management: Organization and Practice* (New York: Harper & Row, 1964); Allan C. Filley, Robert J. House, and Steven Kerr, *Managerial Process and Organization Behavior,* 2nd ed. (Glenview, Ill.: Scott, Foresman, 1976); and Louis Allen, *Management and Organization* (New York: McGraw-Hill, 1958). In developing this we owe a particular debt to Louis Allen's work. His book is a summary of his findings in the study of over 230 companies; it is particularly rich in examples.
[2]Allen, *Management and Organization,* p. 83.

[3]Rolf E. Rogers, *Organization Theory* (Boston: Allyn & Bacon, 1975).

[4]Paul R. Lawrence, and Jay W. Lorsch, *Organization and Environment* (Cambridge, Mass.: Harvard University Press, 1967).

[5]For an excellent discussion of strategies to use in modifying structures to deal with these problems see Jay Galbraith, *Designing Complex Organizations* (Reading, Mass.: Addison-Wesley, 1973).

[6]Peter F. Drucker, *Management: Tasks, Responsibilities, Practices* (New York: Harper & Row, 1974), p. 530.

[7]Allen, *Management and Organization*, p. 82.

[8]Richard P. Rumelt, *Strategy, Structure and Economic Performance* (Cambridge, Mass.: Harvard University Press, 1974).

[9]Ibid.

[10]Allen, *Management and Organization*.

[11]Rumelt, *Strategy*.

[12]Drucker, *Management*.

[13]Rumelt, *Strategy*.

[14]Drucker, *Management*.

[15]Ibid.; Moore, *Management*; and William H. Newman, Charles E. Summer, and E. Kirby Warren, *The Process of Management: Concepts, Behavior, and Practice*, 3rd ed. (Englewood Cliffs, N.J.: Prentice-Hall, 1972).

[16]Moore, *Management*.

[17]David S. Solomons, *Divisional Performance: Measurement and Control* (New York: Financial Executives Research Foundation, 1965).

[18]Phillip J. Browne, and Robert T. Golembiewski, "The Line-Staff Concept Revisited: An Empirical Study of Organizational Images," *Academy of Management Journal* 17 (1974):406–17.

[19]Allen, *Management and Organization*.

[20]Ibid., p. 206.

[21]Ibid.; Newman et al., *Process of Management*; and Filley et al., *Managerial Process*.

[22]Some authors classify staff with slightly different categories. See Dessler, *Organization and Management*; and Newman et al., *Process of Management*.

[23]Allen, *Management and Organization*.

[24]See Browne, *Line-Staff Concept Revisited*, for example.

[25]Ibid.

[26]Newman, *Process of Management*.

[27]Galbraith, *Designing Complex Organizations*.

[28]Ibid.; Robert T. Golembiewski, "Small Groups and Large Organizations," *Handbook of Organizations*, ed. James G. March (Chicago: Rand McNally, 1965); Chris Argyris, *Interpersonal Competence and Organizational Effectiveness* (Homewood, Ill.: The Dorsey Press, 1962).

[29]John M. Stewart, "Making Project Management Work," *Business Horizons* 8 (Fall 1965):54–68.

[30]Donald Ralph Kingdon, *Matrix Organization* (London: Tavistock, 1973).

[31]Ibid.

[32]Frank Friedlander, "The Relationship of Task and Human Conditions to Effective Organization Structure," *Managing for Accomplishment*, ed. B. M. Bass, R. Cooper, and J. A. Haas (Lexington, Mass.: Heath, 1970).

[33]"Teamwork Through Conflict," *Business Week* (March 20, 1971), pp. 44–50.

SUGGESTIONS FOR FURTHER READING

ALLEN, LOUIS. *Management and Organization*. New York: McGraw-Hill, 1958.

CHANDLER, ALFRED D. *Strategy and Structure*. Cambridge, Mass.: M.I.T. Press, 1962.

NEWMAN, WILLIAM H., and WARREN, E. KIRBY. *The Process of Management: Concepts, Behavior and Practice*, 4th ed. Englewood Cliffs, N.J.: Prentice-Hall, 1977.

section two   DIALOGUE

In the 1960s the complex projects required to begin space exploration forced aerospace firms to realign their organization structures both to make use of specialized skills and to achieve better coordination of several projects. The result of these efforts was one of the "overlays" we presented in this section—the matrix organization, a combination of functional and project forms of organization. The use of this new form has been growing outside the aerospace industry as more firms face similar problems.

Using an information processing point of view, Jay Galbraith provides an indepth look at the matrix organization, at the variety and types of matrix designs, as well as at the considerations of which a designer should be aware in choosing an appropriate structure. The matrix organization is not for every firm, but this article should help decision makers decide to what degree to pursue a matrix design.

MATRIX ORGANIZATION DESIGNS
How to Combine Functional and Project Forms

JAY R. GALBRAITH

Each form of organizational design has its own set of advantages and disadvantages. If, for example, the functional structure is adopted, projects fall behind; if project organization is chosen, technologies are less well-developed. The matrix design attempts to achieve the benefits of both forms. The history of The Standard Products Co. illustrates the change from the functional form to a pure matrix form. Measures were taken that allowed Standard to achieve high levels of technical sophistication necessary to innovate products and simultaneously get these products to the market quickly to maintain competitive position. Since not all organizations need a pure matrix organization, the author describes the alternatives and lists some factors that help determine the choices.

Each era of management evolves new forms of organization as new problems are encountered. Earlier generations of managers invented the centralized functional form, the line-staff form, and the decentralized product division structure as a response to increasing size and complexity of tasks. The current generation of management has developed two new forms as a response to high technology. The first is the free-form conglomerate; the other is the matrix organization, which was developed primarily in the aerospace industry.

The matrix organization grows out of the organizational choice between project and functional forms, although it is not limited to those bases of the authority structure.[1] Research in the behavioral sciences now permits a detailing of the choices among the alternate intermediate forms between the project and functional extremes. Detailing such a choice is necessary since many businessmen see their organizations facing situations in the 1970's that are similar to those faced by the aerospace firms in the 1960's. As a result, a great many unanswered questions arise concerning the use of the matrix organization. For example, what are the various kinds of matrix designs, what is the difference between the designs, how do they work, and how do I choose a design that is appropriate for my organization?

The problem of designing organizations arises from the choices available among alternative bases of the authority structure. The most common alternatives are to group together activities which bear on a common product, common customer, common geographic area, common business

Jay R. Galbraith, *Business Horizons* 14 (February 1971):pp 29-40 Copyright 1971 by the foundation for the School of Business at Indiana University. Reprinted by permission.

function (marketing, engineering, manufacturing, and so on), or common process (forging, stamping, machining, and so on). Each of these bases has various costs and economies associated with it. For example, the functional structure facilitates the acquisition of specialized inputs. It permits the hiring of an electromechanical and an electronics engineer rather than two electrical engineers. It minimizes the number necessary by pooling specialized resources and time sharing them across products or projects. It provides career paths for specialists. Therefore, the organization can hire, utilize, and retain specialists.

These capabilities are necessary if the organization is going to develop high technology products. However, the tasks that the organization must perform require varying amounts of the specialized resources applied in varying sequences. The problem of simultaneously completing all tasks on time, with appropriate quality and while fully utilizing all specialist resources, is all but impossible in the functional structure. It requires either fantastic amounts of information or long lead times for task completion.

The product or project form of organization has exactly the opposite set of benefits and costs. It facilitates coordination among specialties to achieve on-time completion and to meet budget targets. It allows a quick reaction capability to tackle problems that develop in one specialty, thereby reducing the impact on other specialties. However, if the organization has two projects, each requiring one half-time electronics engineer and one half-time electromechanical engineer, the pure project organization must either hire two electrical engineers—and reduce specialization—or hire four engineers (two electronics and two electromechanical)—and incur duplication costs. In addition, no one is responsible for long-run technical development of the specialties. Thus, each form of organization has its own set of advantages and disadvantages. A similar analysis could be applied to geographically or client-based structures.

The problem is that when one basis of organization is chosen, the benefits of the others are surrendered. If the functional structure is adopted, the technologies are developed but the projects fall behind schedule. If the project organization is chosen, there is better cost and schedule performance but the technologies are not developed as well. In the past, managers made a judgment as to whether technical development or schedule completion was more important and chose the appropriate form.

However, in the 1960's with a space race and missile gap, the aerospace firms were faced with a situation where both technical performance and coordination were important. The result was the matrix design, which attempts to achieve the benefits of both forms. However, the matrix carries some costs of its own. A study of the development of a matrix design is contained in the history of The Standard Products Co., a hypothetical company that has changed its form of organization from a functional structure to a matrix.

The Standard Products Co. has competed effectively for a number of years by offering a varied line of products that were sold to other organizations. Standard produced and sold its products through a functional organization like the one represented in Figure 1. A moderate number of changes in the product line and production processes were made each year. Therefore, a major management problem was to coordinate the flow of work from engineering through marketing. The coordination was achieved through several integrating mechanisms:

Rules and procedures—One of the ways to constrain behavior in order to achieve an integrated pattern is to specify rules and procedures. If all personnel follow the rules, the resultant behavior is integrated without having to maintain on-going communication. Rules are used for the most predictable and repetitive activities.

Planning process—For less repetitive activities, Standard does not specify the procedure to be used but specifies a goal or target to be achieved, and lets the individual choose the procedure appropriate to the goal. Therefore, processes are undertaken to elaborate schedules and budgets. The usefulness of plans and rules is that they reduce the need for on-going communication between specialized subunits.

Hierarchical referral—When situations are encountered for which there are no rules or when problems cause the goals to be exceeded, these situations are referred upward in the hierarchy for resolution. This is the standard management-by-exception principle. This resolves the nonroutine and unpredictable events that all organizations encounter.

Direct contact—In order to prevent top executives from becoming overloaded with problems, as many problems as possible are resolved by the affected managers at low levels by informal contacts. These remove small problems from the upward referral process.

Liaison departments—In some cases, where there is a large volume of contacts between two departments, a liaison department evolves to handle the transactions. This typically occurs between engineering and manufacturing in order to handle engineering changes and design problems.[2]

The Standard Products Co. utilized these mechanisms to integrate the functionally organized specialties. They were effective in the sense that Standard could respond to changes in the market with new products on a timely basis, the new products were completed on schedule and within budget, and the executives had sufficient time to devote to long-range planning.

Matrix Begins Evolution

A few years ago, a significant change occurred in the market for one of Standard's major product lines. A competitor came out with a new design utilizing an entirely new raw material. The initial success caused Standard to

figure 1

STANDARD'S FUNCTIONAL ORGANIZATION

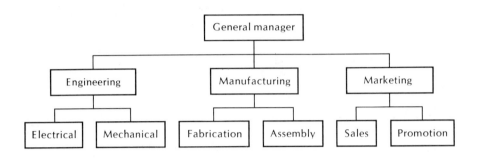

react by developing one of their own incorporating the new material. They hired some specialists in the area and began their normal new product introduction activities. However, this time the product began to fall behind schedule, and it appeared that the product would arrive on the market at a time later than planned. In response, the general manager called a meeting to analyze the situation.

Task Force. After a briefing, it was obvious to the general manager and the directors of the three functions what was happening. Standard's lack of experience with the new material had caused them to underestimate the number and kinds of problems. The uncertainty led to a deterioration in usefulness of plans and schedules. The problems affected all functions, which meant that informal contacts and liaison processes were cumbersome; therefore, the majority of the problems were referred upward. This led to overloads on the directors of the functions and the general manager, which in turn added to the delays. Thus, the new situation required more decision making and more information processing than the current organization could provide.

The directors of engineering and manufacturing suggested that the cause of the problem was an overly ambitious schedule. More time should have been allowed for the new product; if realistic schedules were set, the current coordination processes would be adequate. They proposed that the schedules be adjusted by adding three to six months to the current due dates, which would allow more time to make the necessary decisions.

The director of marketing objected, reporting that the company would lose a good percentage of the market if the introduction was delayed. A number of big customers were waiting for Standard's version of the new product, and a delay would cost the company some of these customers. The general manager agreed with the marketing director. He proposed that they

160

should not change the schedule to fit their current coordination processes, but that they should introduce some new coordination mechanisms to meet the scheduled due dates.

The group agreed with the general manager's position and began to search for alternative solutions. One of the solution requirements suggested was to reduce the distance between the sources of information and the points of decision. At this point the manufacturing director cautioned them about decentralizing decisions. He reminded them of previous experiences when decisions were made at low levels of the engineering organization. The data the decision makers had were current but they were also local in scope; severe problems in the manufacturing process resulted. When these decisions were centralized, the global perspective prevented these problems from developing. Therefore, they had to increase decision-making power at lower levels without losing the inputs of all affected units. The alternative that met both requirements was a group with representation from all the major departments to enter into joint decisions.

The group was appointed and named the "new product task force." It was to last as long as cross-functional problems occurred on the new product introduction. The group was to meet and solve joint problems within the budget limits set by the general manager and the directors; problems requiring more budget went to the top management group. The purpose was to make as many decisions as possible at low levels with the people most knowledgeable. This should reduce the delays and yet ensure that all the· information inputs were considered.

The task force consisted of nine people; three, one from each function, were full-time and the others were part-time. They met at least every other day to discuss and resolve joint problems. Several difficulties caused them to shift membership. First, the engineering representatives were too high in the organization and, therefore, not knowledgeable about the technical alternatives and consequences. They were replaced with lower level people. The opposite occurred with respect to the manufacturing representatives. Quite often they did not have either information or the authority to commit the production organization to joint decisions made by the task force. They were replaced by higher level people. Eventually, the group had both the information and the authority to make good group decisions. The result was effective coordination: coordination = f (authority × information).

Creation of the task force was the correct solution. Decision delays were reduced, and collective action was achieved by the joint decisions. The product arrived on time, and the task force members returned to their regular duties.

Teams. No sooner had the product been introduced than salesmen began to bring back stories about new competitors. One was introducing a second-generation design based on improvements in the raw material. Since the customers were excited by its potential and the technical people thought it was feasible, Standard started a second-generation redesign across all its product lines. This time, they set up the task force structure in advance and committed themselves to an ambitious schedule.

Again the general manager became concerned. This time the product was not falling behind schedule, but in order to meet target dates the top management was drawn into day-to-day decisions on a continual basis. This was leaving very little time to think about the third-generation product line. Already Standard had to respond twice to changes initiated by others. It was time for a thorough strategy formulation. Indeed, the more rapid the change in technology and markets, the greater the amount of strategic decision making that is necessary. However, these are the same changes that pull top management into day-to-day decisions. The general manager again called a meeting to discuss and resolve the problem.

The solution requirements to the problem were the same as before. They had to find a way to push a greater number of decisions down to lower levels. At the same time, they had to guarantee that all interdependent subunits would be considered in the decision so that coordination would be maintained. The result was a more extensive use of joint decision making and shared responsibility.

The joint decision making was to take place through a team structure. The teams consisted of representatives of all functions and were formed around major product lines. There were two levels of teams, one at lower levels and another at the middle-management level. Each level had defined discretionary limits; problems that the lower level could not solve were referred to the middle-level team. If the middle level could not solve the problem, it went to top management. A greater number of day-to-day operating problems were thereby solved at lower levels of the hierarchy, freeing top management for long-range decisions.

The teams, unlike the task force, were permanent. New products were regarded as a fact of life, and the teams met on a continual basis to solve recurring interfunctional problems. Task forces were still used to solve temporary problems. In fact, all the coordination mechanisms of rules, plans, upward referral, direct contact, liaison men, and task forces were used, in addition to the teams.

Product Managers. The team structure achieved interfunctional coordination and permitted top management to step out of day-to-day decision making. However, the teams were not uniformly effective. Standard's strategy required the addition of highly skilled, highly educated technical people to continue to innovate and compete in the high technology industry. Sometimes these specialists would dominate a team because of their superior technical knowledge. That is, the team could not distinguish

between providing technical information and supplying managerial judgment after all the facts were identified. In addition, the specialists' personalities were different from the personalities of the other team members,
which made the problem of conflict resolution much more difficult.[3]

Reports of these problems began to reach the general manager, who
realized that a great number of decisions of consequence were being made
at lower and middle levels of management. He also knew that they should be
made with a general manager's perspective. This depends on having the
necessary information and a reasonable balance of power among the joint
decision makers. Now the technical people were upsetting the power
balance because others could not challenge them on technical matters. As a
result, the general manager chose three technically qualified men and made
them product managers in charge of the three major product lines.[4] They
were to act as chairmen of the product team meetings and generally
facilitate the interfunctional decision making.

Since these men had no formal authority, they had to resort to their
technical competence and their interpersonal skills in order to be effective.
The fact that they reported to the general manager gave them some
additional power. These men were successful in bringing the global, general
manager perspective lower in the organization to improve the joint decision-making process.

The need for this role was necessitated by the increasing differences in
attitudes and goals among the technical, production, and marketing team
participants. These differences are necessary for successful subtask performance but interfere with team collaboration. The product manager allows
collaboration without reducing these necessary differences. The cost is the
additional overhead for the product management salaries.

Product Management Departments. Standard Products was now successfully following a strategy of new product innovation and introduction. It
was leading the industry in changes in technology and products. As the
number of new products increased, so did the amount of decision making
around product considerations. The frequent needs for trade-offs across
engineering, production, and marketing lines increased the influence of the
product managers. It was not that the functional managers lost influence;
rather, it was the increase in decisions relating to products.

The increase in the influence of the product managers was revealed in
several ways. First, their salaries became substantial. Second, they began to
have a greater voice in the budgeting process, starting with approval of
functional budgets relating to their products. The next change was an
accumulation of staff around the products, which became product departments with considerable influence.

At Standard this came about with the increase in new product introduc-
tions. A lack of information developed concerning product costs and

revenues for addition, deletion, modification, and pricing decisions. The general manager instituted a new information system that reported costs and revenues by product as well as by function. This gave product managers the need for a staff and a basis for more effective interfunctional collaboration.

In establishing the product departments, the general manager resisted requests from the product managers to reorganize around product divisions. While he agreed with their analysis that better coordination was needed across functions and for more effective product decision making, he was unwilling to take the chance that this move might reduce specialization in the technical areas or perhaps lose the economies of scale in production. He felt that a modification of the information system to report on a product and a functional basis along with a product staff group would provide the means for more coordination. He still needed the effective technical group to drive the innovative process. The general manager also maintained a climate where collaboration across product lines and functions was encouraged and rewarded.

The Matrix Completed

By now Standard Products was a high technology company; its products were undergoing constant change. The uncertainty brought about by the new technology and the new products required an enormous amount of decision making to plan-replan all the schedules, budgets, designs, and so on. As a result, the number of decisions and the number of consequential decisions made at low levels increased considerably. This brought on two concerns for the general manager and top management.

The first was the old concern for the quality of decisions made at low levels of the organization. The product managers helped solve this at middle and top levels, but their influence did not reach low into the organization where a considerable number of decisions were made jointly. They were not always made in the best interest of the firm as a whole. The product managers again recommended a move to product divisions to give these low-level decisions the proper product orientation.

The director of engineering objected, using the second problem to back up his objection. He said the move to product divisions would reduce the influence of the technical people at a time when they were having morale and turnover problems with these employees. The increase in joint decisions at low levels meant that these technical people were spending a lot of time in meetings. Their technical input was not always needed, and they preferred to work on technical problems, not product problems. Their dissatisfaction would only be aggravated by a change to product divisions.

The top management group recognized both of these problems. They needed more product orientation at low levels, and they needed to improve the morale of the technical people whose inputs were needed for product innovations. Their solution involved the creation of a new role—that of subproduct manager.[5] The subproduct manager would be chosen from the functional organization and would represent the product line within the function. He would report to both the functional manager and the product manager, thereby creating a dual authority structure. The addition of a reporting relation on the product side increases the amount of product influence at lower levels.

The addition of the subproduct manager was intended to solve the morale problem also. Because he would participate in the product team meetings, the technical people did not need to be present. The subproduct manager would participate on the teams but would call on the technical experts within his department as they were needed. This permitted the functional department to be represented by the subproduct manager, and the technical people to concentrate on strictly technical matters.

Standard Products has now moved to a pure matrix organization as indicated in Figure 2. The pure matrix organization is distinguished from the previous cross-functional forms by two features. *First,* the pure matrix has a dual authority relationship somewhere in the organization. *Second,* there is a power balance between the product management and functional sides. While equal power is an unachievable razor's edge, a reasonable balance can be obtained through enforced collaboration on budgets, salaries, dual information and reporting systems, and dual authority relations. Such a balance is required because the problems that the organization faces are uncertain and must be solved on their own merits—not on any predetermined power structure.

Thus over a period of time, the Standard Products Co. has changed from a functional organization to a pure matrix organization using dual authority relationships, product management departments, product teams at several levels, and temporary task forces. These additional decision-making mechanisms were added to cope with the change in products and technologies. The changes caused a good deal of uncertainty concerning resource allocations, budgets, and schedules. In the process of task execution, more was learned about the problem causing a need for rescheduling and rebudgeting. This required the processing of information and the making of decisions.

In order to increase its capacity to make product relevant decisions, Standard lowered the level at which decisions were made. Coordination was achieved by making joint decisions across functions. Product managers and subproduct managers were added to bring a general manager's perspective to bear on the joint decision-making processes. In addition, the information and reporting system was changed in order to provide reports by function and by product. Combined, these measures allowed Standard to achieve the high levels of technical sophistication necessary to innovate products and

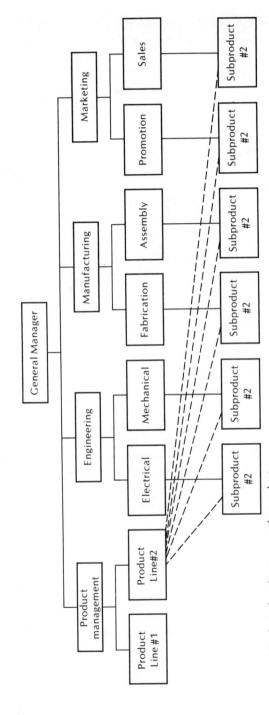

--- Technical authority over the product

— Formal authority over the product (in product organization, these relationships may be reversed)

figure 2

STANDARD'S PURE MATRIX ORGANIZATION

simultaneously to get these products to the market quickly to maintain competitive position.

HOW DO I CHOOSE A DESIGN?

Not all organizations need a pure matrix organization with a dual authority relationship. Many, however, can benefit from some cross-functional forms to relieve top decision makers from day-to-day operations. If this is so, how does one choose the degree to which his organization should pursue these lateral forms? To begin to answer this question, let us first lay out the alternatives, then list the choice determining factors.

The choice, shown in Figure 3, is indicated by the wide range of alternatives between a pure functional organization and a pure product organization with the matrix being half-way between. The Standard Products Co. could have evolved into a matrix from a product organization by adding functional teams and managers. Thus there is a continuum of organization designs between the functional and product forms. The design is specified by the choice among the authority structure; integrating mechanisms such as task forces, teams and so on; and by the formal

figure 3

THE RANGE OF ALTERNATIVES

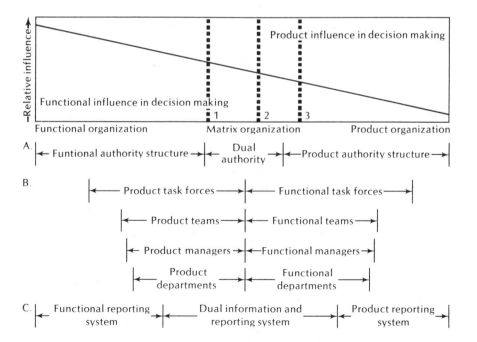

information system. The way these are combined is illustrated in Figure 3. These design variables will help to regulate the relative distribution of influence between the product and functional considerations in the firm's operations.

The remaining factors determining influence are such things as roles in budget approvals, design changes, location and size of offices, salary, and so on. Thus there is a choice of integrating devices, authority structure, information system, and influence distribution. The factors that determine choice are diversity of the product line, the rate of change of the product line, interdependencies among subunits, level of technology, presence of economies of scale, and organization size.

Product Lines

The greater the diversity among product lines and the greater the rate of change of products in the line the greater the pressure to move toward product structures.[6] When product lines become diverse, it becomes difficult for general managers and functional managers to maintain knowledge in all areas; the amount of information they must handle exceeds their capacity to absorb it. Similarly, the faster the rate of new product introduction, the more unfamiliar are the tasks being performed.

Managers are, therefore, less able to make precise estimates concerning resource allocations, schedules, and priorities. During the process of new product introduction, these same decisions are made repeatedly. The decisions concern trade-offs among engineering, manufacturing, and marketing. This means there must be greater product influence in the decision process. The effect of diversity and change is to create a force to locate the organization farther to the right in Figure 3.

Interdependence

The functional division of labor in organizations creates interdependencies among the specialized subunits. That is, a problem of action in one unit has a direct impact on the goal accomplishment of the other units. Organizations usually devise mechanisms that uncouple the subunits, such as in-process-inventory and order backlogs. The degree to which inventories and backlogs develop is a function of how tight the schedule is. If there is a little slack in the schedule, then the functional departments can resolve their own problems. However, if rapid response to market changes is a basis of competition, then schedules are squeezed and activities run in parallel rather than series.[7] This means that problems in one unit directly affect another. The effect is a greater number of joint decisions involving engineering, manufacturing, and production. A greater need for product influence in these decisions arises due to the tight schedule. Thus the tighter the schedule, the greater the force to move to the right in Figure 3.

Although the tightness of the schedule is the most obvious source of interdependence, tight couplings can arise from reliability requirements and other design specifications. If the specifications require a more precise fit and operation of parts, then the groups designing and manufacturing the parts must also "fit and operate" more closely. This requires more coordination in the form of communication and decision making.

Level of Technology

If tight schedules and new products were the only forces operating, every organization would be organized around product lines. The level of technology or degree to which new technology is being used is a counteracting force. The use of new technologies requires expertise in the technical specialties in engineering, in production engineering, in manufacturing, and market research in marketing. Some of the expertise may be purchased outside the organization.

However, if the expertise is critical to competitive effectiveness, the organization must acquire it internally. If the organization is to make effective use of the expertise, the functional form of organization is superior, as described earlier in the article. Therefore the greater the need for expertise, the greater the force to move to the left in Figure 3.

Economies of Scale and Size

The other factor favoring a functional form is the degree to which expensive equipment in manufacturing, test facilities in engineering, and warehousing facilities in marketing are used in producing and selling the product. (Warehousing introduces another dimension of organization structure, for example, geographical divisions. For our purposes, we will be concerned only with product and function dimensions.) It is usually more expensive to buy small facilities for product divisions than a few large ones for functional departments. The greater the economies of scale, the greater the force to move to the left in Figure 3. Mixed structures are always possible. That is, the capital intensive fabrication operation can organize along functional process lines, and the labor intensive assembly operation can organize along product lines.

The size of the organization is important in that it modifies the effect of expertise and economies of scale. That is, the greater the size of the organization the smaller the costs of lost specialization and lost economies of scale when the product form is adopted. Thus while size by itself has little effect on organization structure, it does moderate the effects of the previously mentioned factors.

The Choice

While research on organizations has not achieved a sophistication that would allow us to compute the results of the above factors and locate a point in Figure 3, we can still make our subjective weightings. In addition, we can locate our present position and make changes in the appropriate directions as product lines, schedules, technologies, and size change during the normal course of business. The framework provides some basis for planning the organization along with planning the strategy and resource allocations.

If the organization's present structure is on the left side of the figure, many of the symptoms occurring in the Standard Products example signal a need for change. To what degree are communication overloads occurring? Are top executives being drawn into day-to-day decisions to the detriment of strategy development? How long does it take to get top level decisions made in order to continue work on new products? If the answers to these questions indicate an overload, then some movement toward a matrix is appropriate. Probably a sequence of moves until the bottlenecks disappear is the best strategy; this will allow for the proper attitudinal and behavioral changes to keep pace.

If the organization is product organized, then movements to the left toward a matrix are more subtle. They must be triggered by monitoring the respective technological environments.

An example from the aerospace industry may help. In the late fifties and early sixties the environment was characterized by the space race and missile gap. In this environment, technical performance and technology development were primary, and most firms adopted organizations characterized by the dotted line at "1" in Figure 3. The functional departments had the greatest influence on the decision-making process. During the McNamara era, they moved to point "2." The environment shifted to incentive contracts, PERT-cost systems, and increased importance of cost and schedule considerations.

Currently, the shift has continued toward point "3." Now the environment is characterized by tight budgets, a cost overrun on the C-5 project, and Proxmire hearings in the Senate. The result is greater influence by the project managers. All these have taken place in response to the changing character of the market. A few firms recently moved back toward point "2" in response to the decreasing size of some firms. The reduction in defense spending has resulted in cutbacks in projects and employment. In order to maintain technical capabilities with reduced size, these firms have formed functional departments under functional managers with line responsibility. These changes show how changes in need for expertise, goals, and size affect the organization design choice.

Many organizations are experiencing pressures that force them to consider various forms of matrix designs. The most common pressure is increased volume of new products. Organizations facing this situation must either adopt some form of matrix organization, change to product forms of organization, or increase the time between start and introduction of the new product process.

For most organizations, the matrix design is the most effective alternative. Managers must be aware of the different kinds of matrix designs and develop some basis for choosing among them.

NOTES

[1]See Jon F. Mee, "Matrix Organization," *Business Horizons* (Summer 1964), p. 70.

[2]For a more detailed explanation, see Jay R. Galbraith, *Organization Design* (Reading, Mass.: Addison-Wesley Publishing Co., Inc., 1971).

[3]See Paul R. Lawrence and Jay Lorsch, "Differentiation and Integration in Complex Organizations," *Administrative Science Quarterly* (June, 1967).

[4]Paul R. Lawrence and Jay Lorsch, "New Management Job: the Integration," *Harvard Business Review* (November-December, 1967).

[5]Jay Lorsch, "Matrix Organization and Technical Innovations" in Jay Galbraith, ed., *Matrix Organizations: Organization Design for High Technology* (Cambridge, Mass.: The M.I.T. Press, 1971).

[6]For product line diversity, see Alfred Chandler, *Strategy and Structure* (Cambridge, Mass.: The M.I.T. Press, 1962); for product change rate, see Tom Burns and G. M. Stalker, *Management and Innovation* (London: Tavistock Publications, 1958).

[7]For a case study of this effect, see Jay Galbraith, "Environmental and Technological Determinants of Organization Design" in Jay Lorsch and Paul R. Lawrence, eds., *Studies in Organization Design* (Homewood, Ill.: Richard D. Irwin, Inc., 1970).

section three

This section deals with dimensions of organizations that have each been considered at some point as an "imperative" for organizations. Each of the topics *is* important for really understanding organizations, their structures, and, to some extent, their actions. However, we point out as we discuss each variable that the "compelling" or imperative nature of each on the organization is subject to some debate.

For example, technology and its impact on the organization is discussed in chapter 6. There are those who argue that technological differences *force* the organization to adapt a particular structure to match a particular technology. In dealing with this and other similar arguments for the other imperatives, we carefully review the empirical and theoretical literature to see if this imperative is indeed a demonstrated fact.

Chapter 7 deals with another important variable: organizational size. Large organizations seem to be different from small organizations to most people. How does a difference in size really manifest itself in organizational structures?

Chapter 8 deals with the impact of the environment in which the organization exists on the organization and its actions. We further consider a very special kind of environmental influence—interorganizational relations, how other organizations in the environment influence a given organization.

Chapter 9 deals with internal or intraorganizational issues. It was not our intention to cover all possible internal organizational phenomena since that could infringe on the study of organizational behavior but, rather, to look at three important internal variables that have at times been considered imperatives. We discuss power, control, and rules as three of the most important intraorganizational phenomena for understanding organizations.

The objective for section three is to answer the general question: What things about organizations have been found to be keys to understanding them?

THE IMPERATIVES:

Critical Dimensions for Understanding Organizations

chapter 6

TECHNOLOGY:

Its Impact
on the Organization

We have used the word *technology* before. What exactly is technology? The techniques and technical processes an organization uses to change inputs, such as materials, knowledge, energy, and capital, into outputs, such as products and services, is its *technology*. Regardless of whether the organization is an accounting firm, a welfare agency, or a newspaper, it will use a technology of some sort in order to produce its product or service.

Although all work organizations have in common the fact that they do employ a technology, they differ as to which technologies they use and the variety and combinations they use. This basic fact of organizational life has made technology an important variable in organizational analysis.

In this book technology will be treated as a variable to be studied as a part of analyzing an organization. Most analysts agree that technology is an important variable. They may differ, however, on whether it is the variable that holds the ultimate passkey to understanding organization structure, processes, problems, and success. This debate is nowhere more vividly seen than in the development of the belief that technology is an "imperative" to organizations.

THE TECHNOLOGICAL IMPERATIVE

In the technological imperative school of thought, the technology employed to accomplish the organization's task is believed to be the *primary determinate* of its structure and processes. The degree to which technology is seen to *cause* structure has varied, but this central theme has been present in the literature for some time. Figure 6-1 shows the generally hypothesized relationship.

175

figure 6-1

RELATIONSHIP OF TECHNOLOGY TO ORGANIZATION STRUCTURE
AND PROCESSES

Early Views

The early scientific management approach was characterized by work study to improve the techniques of task accomplishment. Later, work process sequencing and flow was emphasized. The main thrust was to improve work techniques. Social factors, such as individuals and groups, were to be adapted to the existing technology. Later some social scientists saw the importance of social structure in the organization.[1] With this discovery came the development of the human relations school of thought. The emphasis was on people performing in organizations as members of a social group, and for many analysts, technology was dropped out of the picture.

The 1950s saw the resurrection of technology as an important variable in the study of social organizations. A classic study of the coal-getting process by Trist and Bamforth depicted the interrelationship between the technical and social systems of an organization by pointing out the disruption of the social structure in an organization as a result of a technological change—that is, a new way to extract coal.[2] The mine had changed its method of coal-getting from a manual to a machine-assisted method. There was greater specialization of work with no means of coordinating efforts or communicating between miners. Productivity and morale suffered and absenteeism increased as a result of the technological change; consequently, both the social and technical system suffered. This and other studies led to the "sociotechnical system" view of organizations, which saw technology and the social organization as interrelated.[3] Other social scientists saw organization variables and outcomes stemming from technology, too. For example, Whyte saw such behavioral variables as interaction, activity, and sentiments flowing in part from the technology of organizations.[4]

Chapple and Sayles introduced a concept whereby the flow of raw materials through an organization and the operations performed on those raw materials—that is, the technology—directly result in specific interaction patterns, supervisory spans of control, group development, and organization structure.[5] In contrast to the human relations perspective,

Sayles developed a typology of work groups resulting from the impact of technology rather than from group processes. Walker and Guest analyzed the effects on workers' social interaction resulting from the routine, repetitive work of the assembly line.[6] They assumed that people require variety and challenge on the job and were able to document the stifling and unsatisfying nature of assembly-line work.

These early views illustrate that technology has been the subject of study as a crucial variable in understanding organizations, but it was not until the studies by Joan Woodward that it emerged as an "imperative" in organizational study.

The Imperative Develops: Woodward's Studies

The origin of the view that technology *determines* organization is usually assigned to a study of manufacturing firms in southeast Essex, England, although Joan Woodward herself did *not* claim a causal relationship. Woodward and a team of researchers from Southeast Essex Technical College conducted a study of the extent to which management principles were used in Britain.[7] The study began in the mid-1950s, but reanalysis continued into the late 1960s.[8] Ninety-one percent of the firms in the area with more than 100 employees were studied. The majority of the firms included were relatively small with only 17 having over 1000 employees and about 35 having less than 250 employees. The group covered diverse types of production, but electronic, chemical, and engineering firms were prominent.

The researchers conducted interviews, examined company records, and observed firm operations until they had the information they wanted. The information gathered included:

1. The success of the firm based on such factors as share of the market, fiscal data, and judgment of industry executives
2. The technology of the firm—that is, the type of manufacturing process employed
3. The extent to which there was a formalization and specification of tasks and responsibilities—that is, style of management
4. The form and shape of the organization structure as indicated by such factors as spans of control, number of levels, and administrative component

Woodward found considerable variation in the organizational patterns among the firms and concluded that there was no *common* application of management principles. But she was also interested in whether *business success* was in any way associated with organizational practice. After dividing the firms into above-average, average, and below-average success categories, she looked for differences among these groups of firms. Again, no common pattern was found, and there was no relationship with success. At this point, the researchers turned to technology as a possible explanation of the variation in organizational practices.

Almost accidentally, Woodward discovered that the differences among the firms could be associated with the production processes (technology) they employed. Originally, Woodward classified the firms into ten categories, but in her analysis she emphasized three major types of production processes.[9] She saw these categories as constituting "a scale of technical complexity. This term is used here to mean the extent to which the production process is controllable and its results predictable."[10] Her three major categories were:

1. *Unit or small-batch production*—for example, job shop, assembly of one-by-one, or manufacture of lots requiring less than a week
2. *Large-batch and mass-production*—for example, lots requiring over a week to produce or assembly lines
3. *Process production*—for example, long or continuous runs through standardized, repetitive procedures for such items as gases and chemicals

Woodward believed that technical complexity increased as one moves from unit to mass to process production. Thus, in process production the manufacturing process would be more controllable and results more predictable than in unit or small-batch production.

The production process employed grows out of the nature of the firm's business. Unit and small-batch firms are geared to products that must be changed to customer specifications or product variability, such as custom cabinets. The product becomes more standardized as we move up the scale, so the firm can standardize the production process and achieve smoother production runs.

Using her classifications of technical complexity, Woodward found a number of associations with organizational characteristics:

1. As technical complexity increased so did the span of control of the chief executive, proportion of graduates among production supervisors, number of management levels, ratio of managers to employment, ratio of clerks, etc., to direct labor.
2. There was an inverse (U-shaped) relationship between technical complexity and the span of control of first-line supervisors and the style of management. Unit and process production were similar in that both had smaller spans of control and an organic management style. In mass production the span of control was larger and employed a more formal, rigid mechanistic style of management.
3. Within the particular technology categories the more successful firms had

similar characteristics. The less successful firms had organizational characteristics that deviated the most from the median.

4. There was no relationship between size of the firm (number of employees)
and technical complexity and organizational characteristics.

Woodward's research stimulated a number of efforts to replicate her
findings. It also stimulated a number of criticisms of the emphasis on
technology, methodology, and scales of measurement she used. However,
her findings provide much of the support for technology as a significant
determinant of other organizational variables. It was not until the late
1960s that reports of studies began to reinforce and/or dispute Woodward's emphasis on technology as an imperative. Woodward had demonstrated that different production systems impose different constraints that
set limits on the range of viable practices for organizations. Most of the
later studies of technology's impact on structure are built on her categories
and thesis.

Research Support of Woodward

One of the first to confirm Woodward's findings was Edward Harvey.[11]
Harvey argued that "it is not only important to take into account the form
of technology, as Woodward has done, but also to consider the amount of
change within a given form."[12] He argued that the frequency of problems
that call for innovation decreases as one moves from unit to mass to
process production. He pointed out the comparability of his approach to
Woodward's, but he preferred the precision of his own measure. His
measure was a continuum from "diffuseness" to "specificity." A technically diffuse firm would be one with a great many product changes in the
preceding ten years. Technical specificity was present when few changes
had occurred.

Although Harvey studied fewer aspects of the organizations than
Woodward had done, his findings reaffirm hers. In 43 industrial organizations he found that as the technical diffuseness *decreased* (less product
change over time) there was an *increase* in structural variables such as:

1. The number of specialized subunits
2. The number of levels of authority
3. The ratio of management to total personnel
4. The extent of program specification as to roles, communication, and steps
in material conversion

In addition he found no relationship between technology and size or
between size and structure. Nor did he find any evidence that location,

environment, form of ownership and control, or historical factors altered these findings.

Soon after, Zwerman repeated Woodward's study in the Minneapolis–St. Paul area with 55 firms.[13] With a few exceptions his findings repeated Woodward's. But in contrast to Woodward, he found that size (number of employees) was positively related to the span of control of the chief executive, to success of the firm, and to the number of management levels in the firm. In addition, he did not find technology to be related to the span of control of first-line supervisors as Woodward had. He found that firms in which management and ownership had been separated had more levels of management, a larger span of control at the top, and lower labor costs. Finally, he found technology to be associated with the ratio of nonmanagement supervisors to managers and dependent on a local market for its customers. His study both replicated and strongly confirmed Woodward's.

Woodward had found that successful firms had structures like those of the average firm in the same production process category. This suggested that a particular production process imposes economic constraints on management such that, in the long run, they must adapt their organization structure to their technology. When structure is not matched to technology, additional costs are incurred leading to a lack of success. Thus, technology was seen as dictating to an organization what its structure must be.

This rationale is important to the viewpoint that technology is an imperative. But the findings also indicate there was considerable difference in structures within each production process category. This variation indicates that not all firms were *compelled* to match their structure to their technology. They may have made an inefficient choice, but the fact that they did make a different choice indicates that technology *does not* dictate. Management awareness and choices stand between technological pressures and organizational structures.

All these major studies tended to confirm the fact that technology is important in understanding organizations. It is no wonder that some scholars in the field began to see technology as the single most important variable in understanding why organizations take a particular form. Both Perrow[14] and Thompson[15] developed models that tried to explain how technology affected organizational structure. Their models went beyond categories of production systems, and they provided frameworks that could be applied to nonmanufacturing systems. But the promise of technology as *the* explanatory variable seemed to be premature as the studies that we report on now soon showed.

The Doubtful Imperative: Aston Studies

In chapter 3, we described the efforts of the Aston group to establish the fundamental dimensions of structure. This was only the beginning of their studies. They also developed ways to measure technology using data from the same organizations described earlier.[16]

As a part of their analysis they measured a number of factors that might be important "in influencing the structure and functioning of an organization."[17] Their approach allowed them to investigate the relationship between technology and structure and, at the same time, to take into account the impact of other factors, such as size and location.

In one of their reports the Aston group attempted to determine how far technology determines the form taken by the structure of an organization.[18] The group built a classification of technology concepts, constructed scales to measure one kind of technology, and also classified their sample of organizations according to Woodward's scheme.

Their classification of technology was threefold:

1. *Operations technology*—defined as "equipping and sequencing of activities in the workflow." (Workflow is the production and distribution of output.)

2. *Materials technology*—characteristics of the materials used in the workflow, such as the uniformity and stability of the "raw material."

3. *Knowledge technology*—characteristics of the knowledge used in the workflow, such as Perrow's "number of exceptional cases encountered in the work," technology and technical complexity.

Originally, the Aston group believed there were five basic dimensions to operations technology.[19] But after having measured the five hypothesized variables, they found that they were highly related and seem to be measuring aspects of the same thing. They then put all the measures together to form an overall variable called *workflow integration*. Workflow integration contained such elements as the extent to which the workflow was automated, interdependent, measurable, and adaptable to other purposes. They had developed a scale of operations technology that could be applied to all types of work organizations, not just manufacturing organizations as Woodward's classification seemed to do.

Using this measure of technology (workflow integration) the group found technology to be moderately related to the basic dimensions of structure:

1. Structuring of activities
2. Concentration of authority
3. Line control of workflow
4. Supportive component

Technology was also related to subordinate/supervisor ratio and the percentage of certain employees to total employees. More importantly, their analysis showed that other factors could explain more of the variation in structure than technology.[20] Technology was able to explain *very little* additional variation. They concluded there was no substantial relationship between technology and structure, and its effects were over-whelmed by the size of the organization.

The group then attempted to replicate Woodward's research. They used her original ten-point classifications to form a scale of "production continuity" and placed their own sample firms along it. They seem to have been successful in their classification, although Woodward's reports of her criteria are vague, and it is difficult to say if she would have rated the firms in exactly the same way. This analysis revealed fewer relationships, but some moderate relationship between technology and structure did remain. However, when the size of the organization was held constant, all the technology/structure relationships *disappeared*.

The results of the Aston study were almost completely inconsistent with those of Woodward. They rejected the sweeping "technological imperative" that technology *dictates* structure.[21] But they attempted to reconcile their findings with earlier research by stating:

> variables of operations technology will be related only to those structural variables that are centered on the workflow. The smaller the organization, the wider the structural effects of technology; the larger the organization, the more such effects are confined to particular variables, and size and dependence and similar factors make the greater overall impact.[22]

In larger organizations the authors speculate that managers are buffered from the effect of the technology by the specialists, paper work, and standard procedures that go with size. As a result, the basic activities and structural framework of management is probably not affected much by the particular technology in which the organization is engaged.

So, the technological imperative thesis became doubtful. Furthermore, scales had been developed to measure technology that were also usable in nonmanufacturing organizations. These scales measured several aspects of technology and were not dependent on a classification based on the dominant production process. The Aston group also had suggested that size mediated or intervened in any effect technology might have on the organization. Their findings suggest that technology's greatest impact would probably be in small manufacturing organizations. Finally, their work stimulated other researchers to reinvestigate the role of technology.

Criticisms of the Aston Studies

Aldrich was one of the first to find fault with the Aston study.[23] This most significant criticism was concerned with the theoretical implications drawn from their analysis. He argued these researchers did not investigate all the plausible explanations for their technology-size-structure results.

He then outlined a model of organizational development and tested several possible causal models using the statistics reported by the Aston studies.

From his reexamination, Aldrich proposed a developmental sequence for organizational components. In his model workflow integration (technology) plays a central role in determining structure. Size is seen as resulting from operating variability, workflow integration (technology), and structuring of activities. Technology is thought to have a major impact on the structuring of activities, concentration of authority, and size. In their reply to Aldrich, Pugh and Hickson of the Aston group agreed that his model "seems likely in some instances," but that in other cases size may precede structure.[24]

The dialogue surrounding the Aston studies is illustrative of several of the major problems suggested in chapter 2 regarding organizational research. First, virtually all of the studies fail to allow one to make conclusions as to *what* causes *what*. The data were gathered on all variables at about the same time, and with everything occurring simultaneously we cannot definitely state that a change in one variable *causes* a change in another. For example, do increases in size lead to increases in structuring of activities? When studies are done that measure the changes over time (longitudinal studies), we may be able to arrive at more definite conclusions. Related to this need for studies over a period of time is the question of whether structuring of activities may allow for increased size, but growth may then promote increased structuring of activities.

Another problem is whether organizations as open systems can be considered to be in a "steady state." It may be that they are more dynamic than we have assumed, and if such is the case, a change in the system may be initiated by any one of its variables. Furthermore, the cause/effect beliefs of executives may determine upon which variable they choose to focus their manipulation attempts.

An organization may attempt to achieve success by maintaining flexibility in its operations technology, or it may attempt to maximize efficiency by increasing the scale of its operations. Increased output may be achieved by adding more employees and equipment to the same process or changing the production process, perhaps by substituting capital for labor or moving from a small- to a large-batch system. If there are many paths to the same goal, we will need more powerful study designs than have been used in the past to really feel confident in conclusions made from studies of organizations.

Since the findings of the Aston group, several studies have added to the mounting evidence that technology is neither the sole nor primary determinate of the structural aspects of an organization. Although none have answered the causality questions, they have contributed to, and perhaps complicated, our understanding of how technology is related to structure.

The Doubtful Imperative:
The National Study

In chapter 3 we reported Child's attempts to replicate the Aston studies in his national study. He replicated the studies that tried to predict organization structure as well as made several new analyses.[25] Child and Mansfield investigated the relationship between technology, size, and structure using the Aston workflow integration measure and their own version of Woodward's measure. Workflow integration was found to be modestly associated with components of specialization and standardization, but their relationship with size was stronger. When the size of the organization was held constant, the associations with workflow integration decreased. Futhermore, when only manufacturing firms were considered, the relationship between technology and structure decreased while the structure/size relationship became stronger.

When using Woodward's scale, Child and Mansfield found a different pattern but reached the same conclusion as the Aston group did.[26] They conclude that the results as a whole support the finding that "size has a much closer relationship to the aspects of structure measured than does technology."[27]

In the National study, size has a stronger association with structure than does technology, but technology is related even when size is held constant. Technology was most strongly associated with the supportive activities that are closely tied to the workflow and has its strongest tie to structure in smaller firms. This agrees with the Aston research, but it differed in that Child and Mansfield found that the individual subscales of workflow integration related differently to structure; that is, some related to one dimension of structure but not to others.

The Aston and National studies are probably the most rigorous and comprehensive studies of the relationship between dimensions of structure and different aspects of an organization's context. In general, these two studies tend to confirm each other, although there are several exceptions. Perhaps this similarity occurs because they have used the same measures of organizational properties, but it is from such consistent patterns that theories and models can be constructed.

A Midpoint Summary: Child's Model

After reviewing the similarity between the results of his study, the Aston group's, and one by Blau and Schoenherr, Child hypothesizes the model shown in Figure 6-2.[28] As we indicated in chapter 3, every complex organization deals with two issues in its structural design: differentiation and integration. Child proposes the same issues but calls the former *complexity*—that is, role and functional specialization and levels of required expertise. The latter he calls *control*—that is, formalization and decentralization.

figure 6-2

CHILD'S MODEL OF RELATIONSHIPS BETWEEN CONTEXTUAL VARIABLES AND ORGANIZATIONAL STRUCTURE. *Source:* John Child, "Predicting and Understanding Organization Structure," *Administrative Science Quarterly* 18 (June 1973):183.

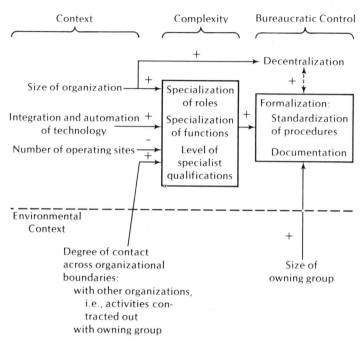

In Child's model increased size, workflow integration, and contact with outside groups leads to increased complexity in organizations. On the other hand, increases in the number of operating sites (geographical decentralization) tends to lower complexity. As complexity increases, it leads to increases in formalization. Size also leads to pressure on top executives to decentralize authority. Decentralization and formalization are associated with each other in a complementary way, reinforcing each other. Increases in formalization are also encouraged by increases in the size of the owning group. As he himself indicates, Child's model must be treated as hypothetical, but it is one of the first to show how several variables might affect an organization's structure.

The model is based on data from actual studies in numerous organizations. It shows that no one variable such as technology should be considered an imperative by itself. But it is tentative, and much work must follow before a conclusive model of what causes structure can be derived with a high degree of confidence. It is likely that researchers will continue

Negandhi and Reimann studied 30 manufacturing firms representing a variety of industries in India. They tried to predict the extent of decentralization in these firms. They measured size, dependence of the firm on the parent company, suppliers and customers, technology (Woodward's three classes), market competition, and organizational concern (interest in such groups as consumers, employees, stockholders, and government).

Organizational concern, size, and dependence were related to decentralization. Organizational concern was the best predictor of decentralization followed by dependence. The dependence finding supports a similar finding by the Aston group and Child's earlier report. The finding that technology was *unrelated* seems in conflict with these studies but is not because Woodward's measure was also unrelated in these two studies. The failure of size to help predict decentralization is in conflict, but this is probably because size and organizational concern were strongly associated with each other as well as with decentralization.

Based on Anant R. Negandhi and Bernard C. Reimann, "Correlates of Decentralization: Closed and Open Systems Perspectives," *Academy of Management Journal* 16 (December 1973):570–82.

to discover aspects of an organization that influence organization structure and processes. It is also likely that new studies will produce evidence that is in conflict with previous work.

SUBSEQUENT STUDIES OF TECHNOLOGY

Negandhi and Reimann studied the effect of technology and several other contextual variables on decentralization.[29] See Block 6-1 for details. In general, their research does not contradict Child's model, but it does add another variable to be considered in developing a comprehensive model of how structure is derived. An organization's concern for its various publics as well as several aspects of dependence are both concerned with environmental relations. In chapter 8 we will deal specifically with the environment.

Khandwalla reported a study that focuses on the integration aspect[30] of organizational tendencies. He criticizes previous research for not having been guided by an explicit model of how technology might affect structure. He then proposes a model that hypothesizes how mass output technology leads eventually to decentralization and the use of sophisticated controls. Block 6-2 provides a report of this study.

When Khandwalla's results are compared to Child's model, we find little conflict. Technology related only to vertical integration (not included by Child), although Child saw it as promoting complexity. In his revised model Khandwalla also sees it directly and indirectly promoting complexity. Size was shown to be related to decentralization, as in the Child model. The decentralization/controls relationship also confirms Child's model. In general, these results tend to support the previous findings of the Aston and National studies, but the variables of "mass output orientation" and "use of controls" are not directly comparable. Khandwalla did not include the extensive list of variables measured by Child and the Aston group; however, the results are quite supportive of these previous results.

Peter Blau and others investigated the impact of technology and size on a number of structural dimensions in manufacturing firms.[31] In addition to the Woodward and Aston measures of technology, they looked at the effect the use of the computer had on structure. These authors report results that generally support the findings reported earlier from the Aston and national studies. Block 6-3 summarizes that study.

They found that the proportion of workers in jobs involved in direct production, the span of control of managers, and the extent of decentralization differed according to the production system employed (Woodward's small-batch, mass, and process production types). A problem in comparing this study with previous studies is that automation via computer introduces a new measure of technology for which there is no comparison in the previous studies. Their findings about the impact of the computer do not conflict with the Child model but probably should be added to it. Here, technology is shown to have a differential effect on complexity according to production type and a negative relationship with decentralization. This both conflicts with parts of the model and clutters its simplicity. Despite these findings, the authors state that their overall conclusion supports that of the Aston group in that the effects of size are pervasive and stronger than technology and that the structure of organizations "depends greatly on their size."[32]

The studies reviewed here use a consistent view of technology. They have all focused their attention on operations technology. Recall that operations technology is "the equipping and sequencing of activities in the workflow."[33] It is concerned with producing and distributing a good or service. All work organizations have an operations technology of one kind or another.

In the studies we have reviewed the predominant operations technology under study was that of the manufacturing function. Woodward's scale

block 6-2

MASS OUTPUT TECHNOLOGY AND BUREAUCRATIC CONTROL

Khandwalla sent a questionnaire to the presidents of firms in a number of carefully chosen industries. Seventy-nine firms participated. The presidents were asked to provide ratings of several variables:

1. Mass output orientation of their technology. They were asked to rate the extent to which their firm used each of five technologies in the production of their products. The five were selected from Woodward's classifications: custom, small-batch, large-batch, mass production and continuous process. The more mass output oriented firms would be those using continuous process.

2. Vertical integration. The extent to which the firm engaged in activities that allowed it to control the inputs (factors of production) and outputs (channels of distribution).

3. Delegation of authority. The extent to which decision-making authority in nine key areas had been decentralized to the chief executive's subordinates.

4. Use of sophisticated controls. The extent to which the firm used each of nine different control techniques. The techniques included such controls as performance audits, statistical quality control, flexible or activity budgeting, and standard costing.

He also measured each firm's size and its average rate of profit on net worth.

Khandwalla's analysis revealed that his measure of technology was related to vertical integration but no other study variable. Size was related to all the other variables except profitability, which related to none of the variables. His model was generally supported in that technology predicted vertical integration, which in turn predicted decentralization, and decentralization predicted the use of sophisticated controls. When the firms were divided into high- and low-profit groups the model received even stronger support. Again, size by itself helped predict the organizational aspects. The influence of size in his analysis prompted him to revise his model to include size.

Based on Pradip N. Khandwalla, "Mass Output Orientation of Operations Technology and Organization Structure," *Administrative Science Quarterly* 19 (March 1974): 74–97.

block 6-3

TECHNOLOGY AND ORGANIZATION IN MANUFACTURING

Peter Blau et al, studied a diverse cross-section of 110 manufacturing organizations in New Jersey. The average organization had 497 employees, but size ranged from less than 100 to more than 4000. The investigators were interested in the relationship between size, several measures of technology, and several aspects of structure. They looked at three aspects of technology: (1) mechanization or automaticity—the degree to which the plant used automatic machines, (2) a shortened version of Woodward's scales, and (3) a new variable—the use of computers. They were interested in the number of different functions for which the computer was used, both on-site and off-site. To measure structure they looked at a number of managerial levels, number of departments and specialization, percentages of workers in different categories, and spans of control.

They found that the degree of mechanization was unrelated to structural dimensions except for the proportion of workers in indirect production (such as maintenance). Woodward's scale produced essentially the same pattern. The Aston group had suggested technology may have its strongest effect on variables directly linked to production and in smaller organizations. Blau et al, found little evidence to support this belief. However, some dimensions of structure did vary according to the type of production system used in the Woodward, Aston, and national studies. Blau found that mass production differed most from process production and small-batch plants were somewhere in between both as to proportion of workers in direct production and span of control. They summarized their finding by stating:

> advances in production technology do not have linear, but do have curvilinear, relationships with various aspects of plant structure. As one moves from small-batch to mass production, the nature of manufacturing tasks becomes more uniform, which is reflected in an increase in routine work, a lower skill level of the labor force, and reductions in support components. The data indicate that these trends are reversed in advance production technologies. Thus, production jobs are least standardized in process plants, since they generally involve maintenance of complex equipment or responsible monitoring functions there.[34]

An aspect of technology considered here, but not included in previous studies, was automation via the computer. It was found that the computer was used very little, in directly controlling manufacturing equipment, but had wide use in the administrative support of production, marketing, and distribution. The use of a computer to perform different functions was positively, but modestly, related to most of their measures of differentiation, percentages of nonproduction employees, and spans of control. All of these tend to increase as the computer is used in more and more functions.

The authors also found that technology had some important relationships with decentralization of key operating decisions and authority over personnel matters. As one moves from small-batch to mass production to process production (increase in mechanization), it becomes more and more likely that the key production and marketing decisions will be made at levels in the firm above the plant manager—at corporate headquarters. Authority over personnel matters are most decentralized in mass production plants followed by small-batch and then process plants. In addition, the location of the computer makes the difference. An inhouse computer promoted decentralization to the plant-manager level but not below.

Based on Peter Blau, Cecilia McHugh Falbe, William McKinley, and Phelps K. Tracy, "Technology and Organization in Manufacturing," *Administrative Science Quarterly* 21 (March 1976):20–40.

was used exclusively to measure the predominate manufacturing process. The Aston scales could be used in other types of organizations, and some service firms were studied. The Blau measure of computer use also can be used in nonproduction functions. However, the emphasis in the scales and their use in studies has been where mechanization can be substituted for human labor. Other theoreticians, notably Perrow and Thompson, have argued for broader meanings of technology.

TOWARD A BROADER MEANING
FOR TECHNOLOGY: PERROW

Noting the difficulties of building a general organization theory with the limited view of technology as automation, Perrow proposed a more general definition. It was his idea that technology could be thought of as:

the actions that an individual performs upon an object, with or without the aid of tools or mechanical devices, in order to make some change in that object. The object or "raw material" may be a living being, human or otherwise, a symbol or an inanimate object.[35]

This view of technology concentrates on problem-solving activities, whether they be mechanical or not, and characteristics of the raw material used; thus, it can apply to all types of organizations.

Beside offering the general problem-solving definition of technology noted above, Perrow has subscribed somewhat to the technological imperative by advancing a classification of organizations based on technology. The technological variables Perrow uses are the characteristics of the "search behavior" of the person who works on raw materials (Is much or little search for solutions required in order to solve problems?) and how many exceptions to familiar problem-solving techniques the raw material presents (Are there few or many exceptions or novel situations presented?). With these dimensions of technology, Perrow develops a fourfold classification of organizations: craft, nonroutine, engineering, and routine organizations. Figure 6-3 shows the degree of search required, and the number of exceptions to normal problem-solving characteristics of each type.

He argues that firms in each of the categories face different problems and thus must employ different technologies and different organization structures. For example, firms that have few exceptions to their familiar problem-solving processes and know what processes and procedures to use (for example, the county license-plate operation) will use routine technologies and employ bureaucratic structures. He also argues that firms will "attempt to maximize the congruence between their technology and their structure."[36] Perrow has not yet validated his scheme, but others have used it or some part of it.

Very little empirical research has been done using Perrow's model despite the attractiveness of its universality and the implications for structure that are built upon it. This is probably because it is difficult to transform his scheme into measures that can be used in doing field research.[37]

figure 6-3

PERROW'S TECHNOLOGY CLASSIFICATION

Type of Organization	Characteristics	
	Search	Exceptions
1. Craft	Much	Few
2. Nonroutine	Much	Many
3. Routine	Little	Few
4. Engineering	Little	Many

Two studies have attempted to verify the classification capabilities of his model. Lynch, and Van De Ven and Delbecq have provided support for the model in that they were able to classify subunits of a larger organization using measures derived from the model.[38] However, these studies only show that one can use it to characterize technologies. They do not show that there are associations or cause/effect relationships between technology and structure. Moreover, there are no complete tests of Perrow's model as it relates to several dimensions of structure; that is, there are no studies that are in any way comparable to the scope of the studies growing out of the work of Woodward.

Partial Tests of Perrow

However, some studies that indirectly apply have been made. Hage and Aiken studied 13 health and welfare agencies.[39] They were interested in the relationship between the routineness of individual jobs and the goals and social structure of the agencies. The routineness measure dealt with the amount of variety people experienced in their jobs and may be considered similar to the Perrow dimension of the number of exceptions; more routine work requires fewer exceptions. The individuals' ratings of their job were combined to form a score for the agency. They found that as routineness of the jobs increased, the following increased as well:

1. Centralization of policies
2. Presence of a rules manual
3. Presence of job descriptions
4. Job specifications
5. Emphasis on efficiency and quantity of output versus quality of service and morale

However, they also found that professional training decreased, and there was no relationship with the psychological and social distance between supervisor and subordinates, hierarchy of authority or discretion over work decisions, and goal innovativeness. This study does provide some support for part of Perrow's model.

Mohr looked at the manageability of tasks and materials of individual jobs in 144 groups from 13 health departments.[40] Manageability was composed of uniformity, complexity, and analyzability: dimensions that are similar to those used by Perrow. He found little relationship between the extent to which a given management style was appropriate to a given technology (a Perrow hypothesis) and effectiveness of the group.

Grimes and Klein used a scheme essentially the same as Perrow's to study the relationship between technology and the autonomy of management.[41] They concluded that the technology of the whole organization plays little part in affecting the management autonomy. They suggested that "the impact of technology on autonomy structure would seem to become more diffuse as one moves further from the task itself. . . ."[42]

Taken together, these studies seem to provide very limited support for the conclusions Perrow derives from his model, especially with regard to concentration of authority. The limited tests using this model do not conflict with the evidence accumulated using the operations technology concept. Again, the impact of technology on an organization seems to be limited, or at least specific, and does not justify it being considered an imperative.

**TOWARD A BROADER MEANING
FOR TECHNOLOGY: THOMPSON**

In an extremely influential book, James D. Thompson developed a set of propositions about organizations in which technology is a major determinant of structure.[43] In Thompson's view, organizations are intentionally rational. To be rational, they must plan; and to be able to plan, they must be able to predict. Uncertainty is the enemy of prediction; so if an organization is to be able to predict, it must limit uncertainty.

Uncertainty in the environment cannot be controlled as well as that within the firm itself. The firm attempts to protect or "buffer" its "technical core" from the uncertainty of its environment. If the firm is to be rational, it must do so at least with its technical core—that is, with those parts and processes it uses to transform the materials it alters as its primary function. Three basic types of technologies are discussed by Thompson: mediating (for example, used by a bank as it mediates between its customers and the services it provides), intensive (for example, used by a hospital as it performs all of the necessary functions for the care of its patients), and long linked (for example, used by a factory as various operations are linked in a sequence). These were discussed in chapter 4 in connection with determining coordination types that might be used. See figure 4-3 and 4-4 for review. Each of these technologies requires that certain harmonious forms of interdependence and coordination be used among organizational units in order for the organization to operate efficiently.

There are costs connected with coordination efforts so organizations are under economic constraints to adjust their coordinative efforts; for example, mutual adjustment is more costly to use than planning. In this way technology determines the type of coordination and control structures the organization will employ.

In Thompson's model both environment and technology are important determinants of structure, but their impacts are different. The primary impact of technology is upon efforts to coordinate and control the "buffered" or closed internal part of the organization—its "technical core." The environment has its primary impact on the organization's structuring attempts to protect and adapt to the uncertainty that exists in the environment. To do this, units are created to monitor and survey what is happening in the environment, plan responses to it, and develop a structure that is appropriate for the degree of uncertainty present in the environment.

Pieces of Thompson's model have been tested and validated in various ways, but most of the attention of researchers has been focused on the environment. These will be addressed in chapter 8. The technology portion of his model has received very little direct attention. Khandwalla used the model implicitly in his research on the use of sophisticated controls.[44] He did show the relationship between mass output technology and vertical integration and less directly to decentralization and the use of sophisticated controls, but he used Woodward's measures of technology in his study.

Mahoney and Frost used Thompson's classification of technologies to investigate the association of different effectiveness criteria with the types of technologies.[45] They studied 386 organizational units in 17 business firms. Thompson had related his classifications to the technologies of entire firms, but these authors applied his types to subunits within firms. They reasoned that types could be distinguished by the degree of discretion the technology allows to decision makers.

In their operationalized measure, as one moves from long-linked to mediating to intensive technology the degree of discretion increases. Their results seem to support the hypothesis proposed by Thompson that the kind of criterion used to judge effectiveness changes with the type of technology employed. Long-linked and mediating technologies were closely associated with the use of standardization, rules, and advanced planning. Intensive technologies related more to relationships with other units (mutual adjustment) and the quality of staff.

Although the research is supportive of parts of Thompson's model, it did not investigate it all. It associated the technology of subunits with the type of criterion the unit used in judging effectiveness. This procedure leaves out the linkage between technology, interdependence, coordination, and structural adjustment. The relationships between technology and effectiveness may have been stronger (or weaker) if these intervening steps were accounted for in the study.

In a study of the relationship between organization climate and effectiveness of organizational subunits. Hitt found that technology of the subunit was an important factor in determining which climate dimensions were related to effectiveness.[46] Hitt and Morgan had found that dimensions of organizational climate such as identity, warmth, and rewards were related to the effectiveness of a subunit.[47] Hitt then classified the subunits according to Thompson's technologies and found that the dimensions of climate that were most associated with effectiveness varied according to the technology used by the unit.[48] Technology served to moderate the relationship.

Montanari investigated the ability of several contextual variables to predict selected structural variables.[49] He included technology, size, and environment as well as strategic choice and position power of executives in attempting to predict most of the structural variables discussed here. Examples provided by Thompson and Mahoney and Frost were used to classify industries according to their predominate technologies, and Montanari selected his sample of 210 firms from these. He found no direct relationship between technology and many structural dimensions. However, he did find that technology may influence which of the other measures (size, environment, strategic choice, and position power) were directly related to structure. Montanari deals with this on pages 286–98.

In the studies using Thompson's framework there seems to be little support for a technological imperative, but there is support for the moderating effect of technology; that is, technology alters the relationship between other variables, such as size or environment, and structure.

CONCLUSIONS

In the study of organizations the belief that the technology employed can explain differences among the organizations has been an important and persistent concept. One can hardly look at human history and deny the importance of technology. But do the technical processes used to convert inputs to outputs *directly determine* an organization's structure and processes? A prudent response would have to be a qualified "no."

Technology, as it has been presented here, does seem to be associated with some aspects of organization structure, especially configuration. It has also been linked to different variables such as complexity, control, and decentralization, in different studies. But the impact of technology does not seem to be all pervasive. There is little support for treating technology as an *imperative*; it does not seem to *dictate* structure. Technology's impact seems to be selective in that it does not relate to all dimensions and is often not related to any. This is not the pattern one would expect if technology were a pervasive determinant.

There is some support to indicate that technology at the subunit level may have a more powerful influence than it does at the total organization level. Many of the studies we have reported concentrated on the extent of mechanization or automation of the *predominate production process*. Yet, organizations may employ more than one technology. This is especially clear if the Perrow or Thompson concepts are considered. By concentrating on the predominate technology or on only mechanization, one may obscure much of the importance of technology. Several of the studies have indicated that it may be more fruitful to pursue technological impact at the organizational subunit level.

There is also some support for viewing technology as a moderator; that is, technology by itself may have little direct impact, but it alters the relationship between other variables and structure. Several reports indicate that workflow integration has less impact in manufacturing firms than in service firms when the impact of size increases. It may be, then, that once a fair degree of mechanization is present, technology is no longer important, and other variables, such as size, assume greater importance. Similarly, we may find that the technological categories of Woodward and Thompson are qualitatively different and not points on a continuum. The impact of variables, such as size, autonomy, and so on, might be shown to differ according to the technology employed, whereas structure is not the direct result of the technology.

Another point regarding technology as an imperative is raised by the number of studies that show other variables to be more strongly related to structure. Several of the studies supporting the technology imperative did not include these other variables; as a result, we do not know if their findings could be better explained by such factors.

Aldrich has argued that theoretically one can build a stronger case for technology determining structure than one can for size as the determinant, since he feels that a firm's technology will be chosen *before* it designs a structure and prior to achieving growth. So, if technology precedes size and size follows structure, only technology could logically cause structure. Of course, his argument holds only if this is the true sequence of events. However, we *do not know* the actual sequence of events, and so the argument remains. Which comes first, size or technology?

Since most organizations evolve, grow, decline, and change over time, the argument may often be irrelevant. The choice of product, competition, anticipated demand, resources available, and so on, may all influence the scale of operations and the technology, even perhaps simultaneously. Later in its existence, a firm may find that a change in strategy is called for by similar factors, and it may decide to increase its scale of operations, specialize its product line, and move to a more rigid technology. In our studies we have little data to suggest how tightly managers are constrained in their choices by such factors as technology. This is a key argument in the technology/imperative perspective. If managers have a considerable range of choice *regardless* of technology, then there is little basis for the imperative argument.

Ironically, the most theoretically developed models have been those of Perrow and Thompson, but they have been the least subject to empirical testing. Much of the research available has not been guided by an explicit model of how and why technology affects structure. Although Perrow and Thompson both attempted this, little direct evidence of the validity of their models could be cited. It is hard to decide whether technology has more theoretical or empirical support. To us the support for the importance of technology is more theoretical than empirical.

We have tried to make comparisons among the major studies. However, this is not always accurate because of the differences in definitions, measurements, sample of organizations, and ways the information was analyzed.

There is disagreement on the definition of technology among the researchers, but there is even more disagreement about how to measure it. This makes comparison of studies difficult. A researcher may believe his own measure is similar to what another has used, but we do not know if this is true until we have compared them. Seldom is this done.

In addition, the studies have employed somewhat diverse samples, although manufacturing firms have been predominate. It may be more accurate to conclude that the technological imperative has received little support among manufacturing firms.

Another point is that firms may employ several technologies. We have made this point in the previous section, but it bears reemphasis. Most studies have placed the total organization on a technology continuum indicating the extent of some technological dimension. The real differences in technology may be qualitative differences of degree, and classifying the whole organization by the predominate technology may neglect the impact that other aspects could have on structure.

Finally, several authors have suggested that there are really several dimensions to technology, and they may relate to structure in different ways. Child and Mansfield found that separate dimensions of workflow integration were related in different ways to structural dimensions.[50] Because of these and other such problems, not only is comparison difficult, but we also must be cautious in dismissing technology as an important structural determinant. We should continue to investigate it with these possibilities in mind.

The fact that research has only been able to account for 40 to 60 percent of the variance in organization structure should limit our confidence. It also means not all the relevant variables that might affect structure have been discovered and that we need better measurement of the variables. If the debate about technology is to be settled, we must use research designs that permit us to track changes over time as they occur in an organization's development and that allow one to document the effect when an organization deliberately changes its technology. We expect that this will be a long time in coming and the debate about the relative importance of technology will continue.

In the next chapter we deal with another variable that has achieved "imperative" status in some circles. We have already been introduced to the concept, and there is no doubt that this *is* an important variable in understanding organizations. The variable is SIZE.

NOTES

1Elton Mayo, *The Human Problems of an Industrial Civilization* (New York: Macmillan, 1933).

2E. L. Trist and K. W. Bamforth, "Some Social and Psychological Consequences of the Long-Wall Method of Coal Getting." *Human Relations* 4 (February 1951):3–38.

3See, for example, E. J. Miller and A. K. Rice, *Systems in Organization: The Control of Task and Sentient Boundaries* (London: Tavistock, 1963).

4William F. Whyte cited by David Silverman, *Theory of Organizations* (New York: Basic Books, 1970).

5Eliot O. Chapple and Leonard R. Sayles, *The Measure of Management* (New York: Macmillan, 1954).

6Charles R. Walker and Robert H. Guest, *The Man on the Assembly Line* (Cambridge, Mass.: Harvard University Press, 1952).

7Joan Woodward, *Management and Technology: Problems of Progress in Industry Series No. 3* (London: Her Majesty's Stationery Office, 1958).

8Joan Woodward, *Industrial Organization: Theory and Practice* (London: Oxford University Press, 1965); and Joan Woodward, ed., *Industrial Organization: Behavior and Control* (London: Oxford University Press, 1970).

9Woodward, *Management and Technology*, p. 11.

10Ibid., p. 12.

11Edward Harvey, "Technology and the Structure of Organizations," *American Sociological Review* 33 (1968):247–59.

12Ibid., p. 249.

13William L. Zwerman, *New Perspectives on Organization Theory* (Westport, Conn.: Greenwood Publishing, 1970).

14Charles Perrow, "A Framework for the Comparative Analysis of Organizations," *American Sociological Review* 32 (1967):194–208.

15James D. Thompson, *Organizations in Action* (New York: McGraw-Hill, 1967).

16David J. Hickson, D. S. Pugh, and Diana C. Pheysey, "Operations Technology and Organization Structure: An Empirical Reappraisal," *Administrative Science Quarterly* 14 (1969):378–98.

17D. S. Pugh, D. J. Hickson, C. R. Hinings, and C. Turner, "The Context of Organization Structures," *Administrative Science Quarterly* 14 (1969):91.

18Hickson et al., "Operations Technology," 1969, p. 378.

19Ibid., pp. 382–83.

20Pugh et al., "Context of Organization."

21Hickson et al., "Operations Technology," p. 393.

22Ibid., p. 395.

23Howard E. Aldrich, "Technology and Organizational Structure: A Reexamination of the Findings of the Aston Group," *Administrative Science Quarterly* 17 (1972):26–43.

24D. S. Pugh and D. J. Hickson, "Causal Inference and the Aston Studies," *Administrative Science Quarterly* 17 (1972):275.

25John Child and Roger Mansfield, "Technology, Size and Organization Structure," *Sociology* 6 (1972):369–93; John Child, "Organization Structure and Strategies of Control: A Replication of the Aston Study," *Administrative Science Quarterly* 17 (1972):163–77; and John Child, "Predicting and Understanding Organization Structure," *Administrative Science Quarterly* 18 (1973):168–85.

26Child and Mansfield, "Technology, Size and Organization Structure."

27Ibid., p. 383.

28Child, "Predicting and Understanding Organization Structure."

29Anant R. Negandhi and Bernard C. Reimann, "Correlates of Decentralization: Closed and Open Systems Perspective," *Academy of Management Journal* 16 (1973): 570–82.

[30]Pradip N. Khandwalla, "Mass Output Orientation of Operations Technology and Organization Structure," *Administrative Science Quarterly* 19 (1974):74–97.

[31]Peter M. Blau, Cecilia McHugh Falbe, William McKinley, and Phelps K. Tracy, "Technology and Organization in Manufacturing," *Administrative Science Quarterly* 21 (1976): 20–30.

[32]Ibid., p. 26.

[33]Hickson et al. "Operations Technology," p. 380.

[34]Blau et al., "Technology and Organization in Manufacturing," p. 30.

[35]Charles Perrow, "A Framework for a Comparative Analysis of Organizations," *American Sociological Review* 32 (April 1967): 195.

[36]Charles Perrow, *Organizational Analysis: A Sociological Perspective.* (Belmont, Calif.: Wadsworth, 1970), p. 80.

[37]Beverly P. Lynch, "An Empirical Assessment of Perrow's Technology Construct," *Administrative Science Quarterly* 19 (September 1974): 338–56.

[38]Lynch, "An Empirical Assessment"; and Andrew H. Van De Ven And André L. Delbecq, "Design Variations within Organizations," *Academy of Management Proceedings, 33rd Annual Meeting,* Boston, August, 1973, 483–89.

[39]Jerald Hage and Michael Aiken, "Routine Technology, Social Structure, and Organizational Goals," *Administrative Science Quarterly* 14 (September 1969): 366–76.

[40]Lawrence Mohr, "Operations Technology and Organizational Structure," *Administrative Science Quarterly* 16 (December 1971): 444–59.

[41]A. J. Grimes and S. M. Klein, "The Technological Imperative: The Relative Impact of Task Unit, Modal Technology, and Hierarchy on Structure," *Academy of Management Journal* 16 (December 1973): 583–97.

[42]Ibid., p. 596.

[43]Thompson, *Organizations in Action.*

[44]Khandwalla, "Mass Output Orientation."

[45]Thomas A. Mahoney and Peter J. Frost, "The Role of Technology in Models of Organizational Effectiveness," *Organizational Behavior and Human Performance* 11 (1974): 122–38.

[46]Michael A. Hitt, "Technology: An Intervening Variable in the Relationship Between Organizational Climate and Work-Unit Effectiveness," *Proceedings Academy of Management, 35th Annual Meeting,* New Orleans, August 1975.

[47]Michael A. Hitt and Cyril P. Morgan, "The Relationship of Organizational Climate to Dimensions of Work-Unit Effectiveness," (Stillwater: Oklahoma State University, March, 1975), unpublished working paper.

[48]Hitt, "Technology."

[49]John R. Montanari, "An Expanded Theory of Structural Determination: An Empirical Investigation of the Impact of Managerial Discretion on Organizational Structure," unpublished doctoral dissertation, University of Colorado, Boulder, 1976.

[50]Child and Mansfield, "Technology, Size and Organization Structure."

SUGGESTIONS FOR FURTHER READING

CHILD, JOHN, and MANSFIELD, ROGER. "Technology, Size and Organization Structure." *Sociology* 6 (1972):369–93.

PERROW, CHARLES. *Organizational Analysis: A Sociological Perspective.* Belmont, Calif.: Wadsworth, 1970.

THOMPSON, JAMES D. *Organizations in Action.* New York: McGraw-Hill, 1967.

WOODWARD, JOAN, ed. *Industrial Organization: Behavior and Control.* London: Oxford University Press, 1970.

chapter 7

ORGANIZATION SIZE

Since the time of Max Weber, organizational size has been seen as a significant variable in organizational analysis. More recently, a growing body of empirical research has tried to determine the effect of organizational size on several dimensions of organizational structure. Exactly how size is related to other organizational variables remains a controversial issue. Organizational size has been shown to be associated with complexity (horizontal and vertical differentiation), formalization, the administrative component, and decentralization as well as variables such as salaries, satisfaction, and motivation.

Although these variables have been shown to be associated with size, there is little to prove that increases in size actually *cause* the changes in the other variables. Even so some theorists have been inclined to elevate the status of size to that of an *imperative* where size is seen to dictate certain structural dimensions.[1] Blau and Schoenherr conclude "that size is the most important condition affecting the structure of organizations. . ."[2] Pugh, Hickson, Hinings, and Turner conclude from the Aston studies that size is the primary causal variable for certain structural variables.[3] On the other hand, Haas, Hall, and Johnson believe that size may not be relevant in determining structure.[4] After reviewing the literature on size, Hall takes the position that "size, while related to some important characteristics, is not as important as other factors in understanding the form organizations take."[5] In his re-examination of the Aston study, Aldrich takes a similar position.[6] Clearly, a major issue remains as to how important size is in determining structure. The positions taken range from "size is the primary factor that determines structure" to "size is irrelevant."

This controversy is quite similar to the one that surrounds the impact of technology. In this chapter we will review the research literature that investigates the relationship between size and organization structure with

200

particular emphasis on studies that include a number of structural variables. Many of these studies were discussed in the technology chapter and you may wish to refer back to that discussion for some of the background on the particular study. The status of organization size as a determinant of the various structural dimensions will be analyzed, and the literature on the administrative component will be evaluated. Finally, a model of hypothesized relationships is offered.

The Size/Structure Argument

Generally the argument that size *determines* organization structure assumes the following form.[7] As an organization increases in size, it is able to obtain benefits from increasing specialization and become more differentiated. The number of subunits increases, and these subunits are grouped around functional specialties, which are alike within themselves but different in function from other subunits. The differences among subunits increases the difficulty of coordinating them. In response to the need for improved coordination and control, the executives attempt to achieve integration with certain structural changes. More formalized and standardized rules and procedures increase formalization, which reduces the demand on executives for routine decisions and sets the limits for discretion at lower levels. Authority is decentralized to allow decisions to be made at lower levels. Decentralization and formalization reinforce each other. Formalization permits decentralization, but the need to decentralize encourages more formalization. More levels are created in the hierarchy to coordinate the diverse subunits. Finally, the numbers of administrative, professional, and clerical personnel are increased because they are required to institute and operate the new system of controls. All these tactics allow the organization to grow without losing control. Thus, a more impersonal system of controls is substituted for direct personal supervision of operations. We will now review some of the studies that are relevant to these arguments.

ORGANIZATION SIZE AS AN IMPERATIVE

The status of organization size as a determinant of structure can be traced back to Weber, but it is only in more recent times that this relationship has been subjected to closer scrutiny. As a number of studies appeared that investigated the relationship between size and the administrative component, size began to assume a central position as a possible predictor of structure. Most of these studies examined only one or two structural dimensions in a limited sample of organizations, but later studies of a more comprehensive nature began to appear.

Preimperative Studies

Several of the studies that are pertinent here have been reported in chapter 6. These will not be extensively reviewed here, but the conclusions that are relevant to the size imperative will be emphasized.

Woodward and Affirmations

One of the first comprehensive studies was that by Woodward.[8] Woodward concluded that size had no significant effect on organizational characteristics nor was it related to her measure of technology. Instead, she concluded that it was the production system employed (technology) by a firm that was most related to organizational characteristics. Later, others suggested that the range of size in her sample of manufacturing firms was restricted and that consequently she had studied only small manufacturing firms.[9] This would, in effect, restrict the role that size could play in affecting structure and emphasize the role that technology might play. Her results were later confirmed by several other studies. Harvey found that technological diffuseness was related to structure but that size was not.[10] Like Woodward he also found that size was not related to technology.

Several other studies, while supporting the same general conclusion as those just reported, suggested that size may be related to certain specific aspects of structure. Zwerman replicated Woodward's research in the United States.[11] His findings strongly supported Woodward's conclusions, but there were several exceptions. He reported a positive relationship between the organization's size and the span of control of the chief executive, the success of the firm, and the number of management levels in the firm.

Hall, Haas, and Johnson

Hall, Haas, and Johnson examined the relationship between size and complexity and formalization in 75 diverse types of organizations.[12] They argued that if size is an important determinant of organization structure its importance could be demonstrated in a large number of different kinds of organizations. The group of organizations they studied included manufacturing, governmental, religious, penal, educational, and commercial organizations that ranged in size from six to over 9000 employees. From tape-recorded interviews and examination of organizational documents, they were able to construct measurements of several aspects of complexity and formalization. They state that as a general conclusion, "the most immediate implication of these findings is that neither complexity nor formalization can be implied from knowledge of organization size."[13] Later they conclude, "These findings suggest that size may be rather irrelevant as a factor in determining organizational structure."[14] But an examination of their findings, although supporting the conclusion that all aspects of structure cannot be predicted from size, may allow one to question their conclusion that size is irrelevant, at least for several *dimensions* of structure.

With respect to complexity, six of the eleven measures were significantly related to size. Location of physical facilities and personnel, the number of levels in the deepest division and the average number of levels in the organization, and the division of labor within departments were all related to size. With respect to formalization they found that "relatively strong relationships exist between size and the formalization of the authority structure, the stipulation of penalties for rule violation in writing, and orientation and inservice training procedures."[15] Unlike the Harvey and Woodward studies, Zwerman and Hall et al. had reported evidence that indicated size might be an important variable in understanding organization structure.

The Imperative Arrives

The argument that organization size is a primary determinant of organization structure was rather late in arriving. First to appear, and in several ways the most influential, were reports from the Aston studies. They were influential because they had measured a number of variables that might affect organization structure including technology. Because they had included a number of variables in the context of an organization's situation, their argument that size was the most important factor affecting an organization's structure carried added weight.

Aston Studies

As part of their analysis of organizations, the Aston group attempted to determine the relative importance of a number of variables in predicting structure.[16] In particular, they were interested in the influence of an organization's *context* on its structure. For the purpose of their study, they assumed that organization structure would depend on certain factors of the firm's situation. From the literature on organizations they distilled a number of factors that could be used to describe the situation that surrounded an organization's structure—its context. The seven dimensions of context chosen were:

1. Origin and history
2. Ownership and control
3. Size
4. Charter
5. Technology
6. Location
7. Dependence

These dimensions of context were correlated with the measures of organization structure that they had developed.[17]

It was found that a number of these contextual variables *were* significantly related to several dimensions of structure. More importantly, because the authors had measured a number of aspects of the context, they were able to see which ones could best predict organization structure. They were able to control for the impact of each factor while examining the ability of each to predict organization structure. Strictly speaking, this approach does not establish that one variable is more important than another in determining structure, but it does establish which will do a better job of predicting structure as well as which combination of variables does the best job of predicting structure.

Figure 7-1 shows the combination of contextual factors that did the best job of predicting organizational structure in the Aston study. For the structural dimension—structuring of activities—organization size predicted best. It was followed by their measure of technology—workflow integration—but this dimension did not increase the prediction a great deal. They concluded, "Given information about how many employees an organization has, and an outline of its technology in terms of how integrated and automated the work process is, its structuring of activities can be estimated within fairly close limits."[18]

For concentration of authority, the dependence of the organization on other organizations and the dispersion of its operating sites contributed the most to prediction. Operating variability—the manufacture of nonstan-

figure 7-1

THE COMBINATION OF CONTEXTUAL DIMENSIONS PREDICTING
ORGANIZATION STRUCTURE IN THE ASTON STUDY

Structural Dimensions	Contextual Dimensions
1. Structuring of activities	1. Organization size
	2. Workflow integration
	3. Size of parent organization
2. Concentration of authority	1. Dependence
	2. Number of operating sites
	3. Age of organization
	4. Operating diversity
	5. Workflow integration
	6. Size of parent organization
3. Line control of workflow	1. Operating variability
	2. Workflow integration
	3. Number of operating sites

dardized goods for producers rather than standard goods for the con- sumer—was the best predictor of line control of workflow.

The results of the Aston studies were important for our purposes in this chapter because they placed size in a much more central role as a determinant of structure especially when compared to technology. Its association with specialization, standardization, formalization, and cen- tralization of decisions was consistently stronger.[19] As a result, the authors rejected the technological imperative and argued that size and dependence had the greater overall impact on structure.

In an attempt to reconcile their findings with those of Woodward, the authors concluded that size modified the impact that technology had on structure. They reasoned that in smaller organizations technology does have a greater impact on structure because more activities are centered around the workflow. But as the organization grows, the impact is lessened by the growth of specialized departments, standardized procedures, and formalized paper work, and only in activities tied closely to the technology itself does technology play a major role in determining structure. In effect, they were arguing that size and dependence were more important in determining organization structure.

Although the Aston study does argue for a central role for size, it does not establish size as the only variable predicting structure. Dependence along with several other variables seemed to be more important in predicting concentration of authority. Size contributed nothing to the prediction of both concentration of authority and line control of workflow. In both cases other factors played a greater role in predicting these structural dimensions. So, although size had been reestablished as a significant variable for the understanding of organization structure, it could not be seen as an imperative for *all* dimensions of structure. A more cautious position would be to conclude that different contextual variables probably influence different structural variables.

Blau and Schoenherr

Peter Blau and his associates at the University of Chicago were engaged in a very large project to study organizational characteristics at about the same time the Aston group was conducting its study, but it was not pub- lished until after the Aston work began to appear.[20] They sought to understand why organizations developed a number of structural charac- teristics and how these attributes related to one another. See Block 7-1.

The Blau study, appearing soon after the Aston study, reinforced the importance of organization size as a possible structural determinant. Like the Aston group, they concluded that size was more important than technology in predicting organization structure, but they went further in their support of size. They believed the effects of size to be pervasive, affecting such major variables as decentralization as well. More than any other study, it argued for the importance of size as the central, if not the only, variable in understanding structure.

In addition, they made an important theoretical contribution by proposing the first theory of how size affects organization structure. They provided a series of propositions that stated the relationship between size and several dimensions of structure. The theory was confined to dimensions of differentiation and requirements for managerial manpower, but it provided a theory that could be tested by others. It not only stated that there were strong relationships between size and aspects of differentiation, but it also defined the relationship by indicating the impact of increasing size decreases as larger sizes are obtained. Unlike those in the Aston study, Blau's organizations demonstrated little variation in technology. The organizations were service organizations that made little use of mechanization (the electric typewriter being about the most advanced mechanized form). They cannot be compared to the variety of industrial and service organizations studied by the Aston group, some of which made extensive use of mechanization. In effect, the limited range of mechanization may have controlled for this aspect of technology and made it impossible for it to affect structure. One is left with the conclusion that in organizations in which technology (mechanization) is not used organizational size may assume a dominant role in influencing structure.

The National Study

Child's efforts to replicate the Aston studies and his assessment of technology as a structural determinant have been reported earlier. Reported here are his findings as to effect of size on structure.[22] His results indicate that organizational size was positively related to specialization (both role and function), standardization, formalization, and vertical span and negatively related to centralization. These relationships were even stronger when only manufacturing organizations were considered. The relationships were stronger than those for technology and remained when technology was held constant.

Organizational size was not nearly so important in predicting configuration variables—that is, the percent of total employment accounted for by different categories of employees. With configuration variables the relationships were few and generally weak when the whole sample of firms was considered. However, in manufacturing firms there were more and stronger relationships. Technology demonstrated stronger relationships with configuration variables than size, except in the smallest firms. But size was the best predictor of the main structural variables. The national study was a strong confirmation of the results reported by both the Aston group and Blau and Schoenherr.

Later, Child compared the national study results with results from the Aston study, the Blau and Schoenherr study, and two studies conducted in labor unions and engineering firms using identical measures.[23] He was able to compare the results from these five studies to better determine the role that organizational size plays in predicting organizational structure. Figure

figure 7-2

PRODUCT-MOMENT CORRELATIONS OF SELECTED STRUCTURAL VARIABLES WITH SIZE OF ORGANIZATION (LOG. NUMBER EMPLOYED)

Structural Variables (Blau & Schoenherr in Parentheses)	National study		Aston study			Labor Unions† (N = 7)	U.S. Employment Security Agencies‡ (N = 53)
	Total Sample (N = 82)	Manufacturing Orgs. (N = 40)	Total Sample (N = 46)	Manufacturing Orgs. (N = 31)	Manufacturing Orgs.* (N = 9)		
Functional specialization (Number of divisions)	.61	.65	.67	.75	.84	.73	.55
Overall role specialization (Division of labor)	.72	.90	.74	.83	.87	not available	.82
Overall standardization (Extent of regulations)	.63	.76	.56	.65	.84	.82	.41
Overall documentation (No equivalent measure)	.58	.69	.55	.67	.83	.70	—
Overall centralization 1. Delegation personnel 2. Delegation budget 3. Decentralization: influence	−.58	−.74	−.39	−.47	−.64	−.62	1. −.27§ 2. −.21§ 3. −.35§
Vertical span (Number of hierarchical levels)	.65	.63	.67	.77	.82	.74	.73

*Hinings and Lee (1971). ‡Blau and Schoenherr (1971). †Warner and Donaldson, unpublished data. §Signs reversed.

Source: John Child, "Predicting and Understanding Organization Structure," *Administrative Science Quarterly* 18 (June 1973):170 reproduced with permission of the publisher.

7-2 reproduces his comparison of the relationships found between size and major structural variables in the five studies.

The results from these studies indicate that "larger organizations are more specialized, have more rules, more documentation, more extended hierarchies, and a greater decentralization of decision making further down such hierarchies."[24] He was also able to determine that the relationship between size and structure was curvilinear. This means that as size increased specialization, formalization and vertical span also increased but at a declining rate. Centralization decreased but at a declining rate as size increased.

Knowing such relationships allows one to predict what changes in structure may occur as organization size increases. However, Child knew from his own and other studies that other variables also were related to structure. By using several such variables one might be able to predict structure with greater confidence and also determine which ones did the best job of predicting which structural variables. This is what Child did. His analysis and resulting model were reported in chapter 6. Child hypothesized a model in which organizational size was seen as playing a dominant, but not an exclusive role, in the prediction of complexity and decentralization. Formalization was primarily dependent on the level of complexity. The complete model can be seen in chapter 6 (Figure 6-2).

Khandwalla

Khandwalla studied the relationship of technology and size (annual sales) with decentralization and the use of sophisticated controls.[25] (See Block 6-2, chapter 6.) His results provide support for Child's findings as to the ability of organizational size to predict the level of bureaucratic control and decentralization. Both size and decentralization were good predictors of the use of sophisticated controls (formalization). Complexity was not included in this study although Khandwalla hypothesized that it was through complexity that size exercised its influence on bureaucratic control. In Child's report workflow integration was a negative predictor of decentralization, but in this study there was no direct relationship. However, this measure of technology did predict vertical integration, which, in turn, helped to predict decentralization.

Blau, Falbe, McKinley, and Tracy

Blau et al. studied the relationship between size, technology, differentiation, the size of various personnel components, supervisory spans of control, and decentralization.[26] (See Block 6-3, chapter 6.) They found a substantial relationship between size and differentiation (comparable to complexity), size of the various personnel components, and spans of control. The relationship between size and decentralization was not reported. This study provides support for the effect of size on complexity.

It also supports a relationship between technology and complexity and technology and decentralization although the relationship is not a simple linear one.

The use and location of the computer was also shown to affect complexity and decentralization. This study provides partial support for Child's model, but it also argues for further refinement particularly as to the positive relationship between the use of the computer and complexity, the negative relationship between technology and decentralization, and the relationship between the location of the computer and decentralization.

Size and Organization Structure in Summary

The relationship between organization size and structure has been the subject of much study and conjecture. This review has only sampled the large number of studies that have been conducted.[27] Size has been rather consistently related to structure in most of these studies, but its exact role in determining structural characteristics is still controversial. It is evident that no consensus exists as to these issues.

The case for size as an imperative is easier to evaluate. In balance, the effects of size seem to be more pervasive, and its relationships with structural variables are often stronger than those of technology. This would seem to make a stronger case for organization size as an imperative than for technology. However, there are still some reasons for not concluding that size is an imperative to structure. In the first place, its effects do not seem to be all pervasive, and some structural variables, such as decentralization, are often better predictors of other structural variables. Thus, one cannot view size as determining all structural dimensions. Its effects are not complete. Even where size is the best predictor of a structural characteristic, it does not determine all the variation present. Taken as a whole, size may be the most important contextual variable in predicting some dimensions of structure, but it is difficult to conclude that it dictates all of an organization's structure. Although its status as a structural imperative is in doubt, there is little doubt that it should be seen as a very important codeterminant with other factors.

Theoretical Considerations

Other than Blau's theory of how increases in size cause greater differentiation, the literature provides little theory development. There is some evidence to support Blau's theory as to the relationship between size and complexity. There is also evidence to dispute portions of it. This theory confines itself to three variables—size, complexity, and administrative component—and it is evident from the present review that other variables may affect complexity as well as other structural dimensions.

It is apparent that the field has not been ready to advance a theory of structural determination. Child's model of relationships among his study variables, which has been discussed here, may be an important aid in suggesting variables and directions upon which to build a theory.

Definition and Measurement of Size

In reviewing the studies incorporating organization size as a variable, the authors have ignored its definition. There has been little attention paid to defining size. Most investigators have operationally defined organization size as the number of full-time or full-time equivalent members of the organization. Unlike the problems encountered in measuring and defining technology, size studies show remarkable agreement and consistency. With the exception of Khandwalla, all the studies reported here have defined and measured size in this way. These studies use the actual number of employees, categorical ranges of employees, or a logarithm of the number of employees in the analysis of relationships.

There are several ways of measuring size. Aldrich has pointed out that many theorists mean by size the magnitude of an organization's output.[28] In financial fields the magnitude of assets, deposits, or resources controlled are used as indicators of size. Examples of other conceivable indicators of size are number of sites, sales volume, customers, volume of products, and budgets. Why, then, has full-time employment been the measure most used?

One reason for the common use of numbers of employees as a size measure is that it has been found to be related to the measures of structure. That there are controversial interpretations of these findings has only led to further research using numbers of employees to resolve the issues. A second reason for its use is the often cited finding that different measures of size are highly related. Pugh et al. used the logarithm of the number of employees and the net assets employed by the organization to measure size because they expected assets to reveal relationships that numbers of employees would not.[29] The use of net assets was abandoned when it was found to have a high correlation with number of personnel. Child reported relationships among several measures of size.[30] Total numbers employed correlated less dramatically in this study with number of operating sites, net assets, and sales turnover.

Although the size of the samples are not large, it does appear that the degree of association between different indicators of size is affected by the nature of the sample. It may be that the relationships between sales volume, assets, and numbers of employees are strong enough to be substituted for one another. However, there is not sufficient evidence to conclude this is possible in all industries or in all organizations. A more conservative position would be to conclude that numbers of employees have been shown to be associated with several dimensions of organizational structure.

When one is concerned with the possible effect of increasing numbers of employees on organization structure, then employment is an appropriate measure. If one is investigating structure and technology, then assets, sales, and net plant may be worth including in the study. Similarly, if one is concerned with the effect of environment then size measures should also include sales and assets. Greater market power can lead to entry barriers and higher industry concentration ratios.

Size in terms of sales and assets may lead to less environmental uncertainty. Firms with greater market power may have greater assurance of capital acquisition and less variability in operating return through less outside threat and less uncertainty.

Aldrich has criticized the use of employment as a causal variable on theoretical grounds. He argued that it is more plausible that decisions as to the organizations' technology, certain structural aspects, and desired scale of operations are made prior to increases in the size of the work force. Khandwalla has argued that forecasted sales are the starting point for planning, budgeting, and structural modifications. One can argue that changes in plans and desired scale of operations are what lead to increases in employment.

Finally, we can observe that the samples of organizations used in these studies are quite homogeneous as to the function they perform for society. Researchers have largely studied one type of organization at a time. Blau's theory was primarily based on data from one type of organization in which mechanization was relatively unimportant. In other samples technology, autonomy, and so on, have become significant and the effect of size less pervasive. When the distinction between organization types and its possible implications are ignored or unrecognized, one may be unwittingly controlling other important variables. On the other hand, the use of heterogeneous samples may obscure or make it impossible to find regularities that are true for some types of organizations. One must face this dilemma and be cautious in attempts to generalize findings to all organization types.

In the next part of this chapter we will focus our attention on the studies that do *not* include several structural dimensions. In these studies organization size has been investigated as the major predictor of one structural dimension—the administrative component.

Perhaps more studies on the relative size of the administrative component have been carried out than on any other structural variable.[31] The pragmatic justification for such studies has usually been grounded in the economic rationale of the need for efficient use of resources. Since human resources constitute the chief resources of most organizations, the staffing and use of human inputs can be an important source of efficiency. If an organization uses too many people to accomplish its objectives, it is being inefficient, but it can also be inefficient if it uses them in the wrong combinations.

The proper combination of indirect or supportive personnel to workers directly involved in producing the organization's product or service has been the main focus of studies on the use of human resources in organization theory. Generally, the rationale is that the smaller the amount of human resources allocated to indirect or supportive activities in relation to the amount allocated to direct production efforts, the more efficient is the organization's conversion process. In addition, it is assumed that as an organization grows in scale of operations economies of scale should allow it to decrease the proportion of personnel allocated to indirect activities and thereby achieve contributions to greater efficiency. This rationale seems to ignore the contributions that administrators, professionals, and clerical personnel may provide to those directly involved in achieving the organization's goals. Their presence is only seen in terms of increased overhead costs and their contributions are somewhat suspect in terms of achieving objectives and in lowering the costs of production. If one subscribes to the hypothesis that increased numbers of personnel in the administrative component result from "empire building," then this rationale is justified. However, if an increase in the administrative component is thought to result from creating staff positions to take over specialized portions of managers' jobs, providing for coordination of direct production functions, and improving methods to increase the effectiveness and efficiency of conversion efforts, then the issue becomes whether these allocations contribute more than their cost. The basic assumption of economies of scale has itself not been tested. As several authors have observed the existence of economies of scale is still an open empirical question awaiting verification.[32]

The attentions of researchers have been focused on two questions: (1) What variables can best predict changes in the administrative component? (2) What is the real relationship between such predictors and the administrative component? The latter question has received the most attention because of the early discovery that organization size predicts changes in the administrative component and perhaps because organization size is relatively easy to measure.

Organization Size and the Administrative Component

The earliest hypothesis about the relationship between organization size and the administrative component was that as size increases the proportion of employees in the administrative component also increases. This relationship received support from a study by Terrien and Mills of 428 California school districts where they found that the percentage of employees holding jobs such as superintendent, assistants and staff, principals and business managers, increased as the size of the school district increased.[33] Later, Hinings,[34] in a study of labor unions, found results that support this hypothesis. The basic explanation for this finding is that administrators and staff are responsible for coordination and integration and that as the number of employees increases the problem of coordination becomes more difficult; thus, the organization must allocate more resources (personnel) to the task of providing coordination and integration.

Many of the studies on the relationship between organization size and the administrative component have produced results that are the opposite of the ones cited above. In contrast, they show the relationship to be negative or curvilinear. Note that this is not to say the absolute number of employees in the administrative component does not rise but only that as the size of the organization increases the proportion of employees allocated to the administrative component decreases. The inverse relationship between organizational size and the proportion of employees in the administrative component has been reported in industrial organizations, hospitals, educational systems, and government employment security agencies. Because of the number of studies supporting this relationship, it is tempting to conclude that increases in organization size lead to a decrease in the relative size of the supportive component. But this conclusion is more simplistic than the studies warrant.

Administrative Component and Complexity

Several studies have shown that increased size is accompanied by increases in complexity (greater role specialization, functional specialization, and levels of expertise as well as greater numbers of levels in the hierarchy). Several of these studies were reported earlier in the chapter. Other studies have found that increases in complexity are accompanied by increases in the administrative component. Here we see the first indication that organization size is not the only variable affecting the administrative component.

In Blau and Schoenherr's resolution of these conflicting effects organization size causes increases in complexity, which, in turn, causes increases in the administrative component, but increases in organization size also produce economies of scale, which allows the administrative component to decrease relative to size.[35] Thus, size has both a direct and an indirect effect with the former causing decreases and the latter causing increases. In most organizations the result is that the effects of economies of scale exceed the effects of complexity, causing the relative size of the administrative component to be less in large organizations than in small organizations. Blau and Schoenherr cite two studies, one in employment security agencies and one in government finance offices, that support their conclusions.

Goldman tested the theory in a study of 124 department stores.[36] The results supported the theory in that size was directly related to complexity and that size and complexity had opposing effects on the administrative component. In his conclusions, Goldman states: "The effects of size do stimulate an economy of scale in management near the bottom of the hierarchy, but have little impact at middle levels, except insofar as they encourage differentiation."[37]

Coates and Updegraff argued that the presence of economies of scale was still an open question.[38] Furthermore, administrators may divide their time between administrative duties and direct input duties, and a simple count of the personnel present would not detect this fact. In their study of banks, they related administrative time (time spent by administrators on various duties) to size to evaluate whether economies of scale are obtained as size increases. They suggest that economies of scale do not change as organization size changes. This study indicates that the increasing size of organizations does not lead to economies of scale; thus, this variable does not explain the negative relationship between size and the administrative component. Murphy criticized the study by Coates and Updegraff and cites three studies in the banking industry that were consistent with the hypothesis that economies of scale may be responsible for the negative relationship.[39]

The Effect of Growth and Decline

Is the relationship between organization size and the administrative component the same when the size of the organization is declining as it is when the organization is growing? One could argue that administrative employees are harder to locate and train and that management would thus be reluctant to lay them off or fire them. Conversely, one could argue that the contribution of administrative component personnel is less valuable and that the organization can do without their services more easily than the services of those directly involved in producing goods or services.

What the organization will do probably depends on the reasons for the decline. If the company is divesting itself of part of its business, is in need of severe cost cutting, or expects the decline in demand for its products or services to be long lasting, then one may expect proportionate cuts in the administrative component. If the reasons for the decline in direct-production employees are not expected to cause a prolonged reduction, then one might expect to find very few employees in the administrative component being let go.

Until recently the effect of organizational decline on the administrative component received little attention, particularly in business organizations. It was assumed that the process of decline in organizations would produce the opposite effect of what occurs during a period of growth. Several studies have suggested that these assumptions may not be completely warranted.

Tsouderos studied the effect of growth and decline on administrative office employees in volunteer associations.[40] In this longitudinal study, the office employees staff grew as size increased, but in periods of decline there was a negative relationship with size. Holdaway and Blowers used seven different measures of the administrative component in their study of 41 Canadian school systems.[41] They found that there was a negative relationship between size and the administrative component in only three of the seven measures. The negative relationship was not supported in their longitudinal analysis, but they were concerned primarily with growing systems. Hendershot and James studied 299 school districts over a seven-year period.[42] Their results support the general negative relationship so often reported, but they also report that the growth rate itself, independent of size, was negatively related to the administrative component. They conclude that the size-to-administrative-component relationship may be confused because of varying growth rates.

Freeman and Hannan studied the effect of changing school enrollments on the number of teachers employed (direct component) and the number of professional staff, nonprofessional staff, and administrators (administrative component) in 769 California school districts.[43] The authors equate changes in enrollments with demand for school services and hypothesize from their results that:

> when demand is increasing, the size of the direct component increases as does the supportive component. But when demand declines, the loss in direct component is not matched by loss in the supportive component. That is, the supportive component tends to increase on the upswings but decreases less on the downswings.[44]

From these studies one can see some indication that the administrative component relationship with size behaves differently during growth than during decline. There is also some reason to question a negative relationship during periods of growth. In addition, the relationship between size and the administrative component may be different for the separate subcomponents of the administrative component.

Subcomponents of the Administrative Component

In this review of studies on the administrative component we find that the concept itself has not been uniformly defined and measured by researchers. For example, Blau and Schoenherr excluded direct (line) managers; Holdaway and Blowers excluded managers of the direct component and professional staff, and Tsouderos included only a clerical group.

This raises two serious questions for the study of the administrative component. The first question is whether the numerous studies can really be compared. The second question is whether all the subcomponents behave in the same way. In the Aston, National, and Blau et al. studies reviewed earlier in the chapter it was shown that organization size did not relate similarly to all components of configuration. These findings will not be repeated here although they are relevant to the issue and support a closer examination of the question.

In one of the first efforts to desegregate the administrative component DeSpelder compared the ratio of staff to line personnel to organization size in the metallic automobile parts manufacturing industry.[45] Managers in line and in staff groups were included with their respective role assignments. In most of the relationships studied some subcomponent of staff is related to the total number of direct production employees. The ratio for total staff to total line personnel indicates that the ratios increase rapidly at first but then remain constant with an eventual tendency to decline. This relationship was also found for a number of subcomponents of staff such as accounting, purchasing, maintenance, engineering, and sales. In other staff functional areas, such as inspection, personnel, and product and materials handling, the actual number of staff to line increased at a constant positive rate, although the ratio increased rapidly at first then leveled off to remain constant. In a few cases there was an inverse relationship with direct production personnel—for example, total management personnel.

Rushing related the size of manufacturing industries (measured by the number of production personnel) to several subcomponents of the administrative component.[46] Earlier he had found that there were at least five heterogeneous subcomponents and that they were not all related with each other nor to size in the same way.[47] However, in this study of 41 industries it was found that the ratios of managerial personnel, professional personnel, and clerical personnel to production personnel were each consistently negatively related to size. Each of these subcomponents were positively related to increasing division of labor (an aspect of complexity). Although the effects of size and division of labor were opposite and independent of each other, these two variables did interact in their effect on the administrative component.

Child studied the relationship of the administrative component to a number of possible contextual predictors.[48] His sample was 54 manufacturing organizations drawn from the national study. He called the administrative component "nonworkflow employment" in the Aston terminology and excluded the managers of production employees from it. He also used the numbers of employees in each subcomponent instead of the ratio of these numbers to total employment. He found a strong positive relationship between total employment and the total nonworkflow employment, total line managers, and the total of line managers and nonworkflow employees added. Other variables, such as technology, complexity, and the number of operating sites, also were related.

Child also gathered data on the number of employees in 16 different nonworkflow functions. The different subcomponents differed considerably in their relationship with each other and in their relationship with size. After further analysis, he concludes "that the supportive component is not a homogeneous category," and that "what is true of the whole supportive component may not be true of its separate parts."[49]

Taken together, these studies argue strongly for desegregating the administrative component into its subcomponents. The use of the term *administrative component* obscures the relationship of its subcomponents to organization size and leads to conclusions that are not always true for its subcomponents.

The Administrative Component and Other Variables

The relationship between complexity and the administrative component has been repeatedly shown in this review. Are organization size and complexity the only variables that are associated with the administrative component? Although the size/administrative component relationship has received the most attention, several researchers have pointed out the significance of other variables in determining the relative size of the administrative component and its subcomponents.

Using census data similar to that used by Rushing, Pondy found that the proportion of employees in the administrative component was negatively related to size and positively related to functional complexity.[50] He also found that form of ownership played an important part. Not only did the relative size of the administrative component increase with increasing separation of ownership from management, but the relationship between size and the administrative component also grew stronger as this separation was held constant. He argues that when the owners are also the management, they allow the administrative component to increase only to the degree doing so will increase profits and not weaken their personal control over the organization. He concludes that the administrative component is "strongly influenced by managerial motivations and patterns of ownership."[51]

After an extensive review of previous studies, Child hypothesized that organization size, complexity, number of operating sites, several measures of technology, concentration of control in the hands of the owners, and the organization belonging to a larger organization would all be related to the administrative component independent of their relationship with each other.[52] In addition, they would relate differently to the several subcomponents of the administrative component.

Child found a strong positive relationship between the number of employees in the administrative component and the total employment (organization size). This relationship was so strong that it obscured the relationship between the administrative component and the other variables, but when the effect of size was controlled, the relationships with other variables became clearer. He also found that the proportion of administrative component employees remained constant for all sizes of organization but did vary with the other variables.

Child found the administrative component was a heterogeneous component where the subcomponents differed considerably in their relationship with size. The subcomponents were also related to the other study variables, but no variable predicted every subcomponent. In some cases, other contextual variables were related to the subcomponent when size was not. When size was controlled, certain variables emerged as important predictors of certain subcomponents. For example, only one measure of technology, workflow rigidity, was related to 3 of the 16 subcomponents. Workflow rigidity indicates the degree to which an organization's workflow and equipment are adaptable to a variety of operations, has limited uses, and requires a rigid sequence of operations. As the rigidity of the workflow increases the size of the maintenance subcomponent increases and the size of the production planning and control and buying and stock control functions decreases. Conversely, the more flexible a firm's production operations are, the greater the need for production planning and control and buying and stock control and the less need for maintenance. Maintenance is more important in a rigid workflow sequence since any breakdown could shut down the whole production sequence. The probability of the operation being down is a multiplicative function of the individual probabilities of failure, thus more resources are devoted to decreasing the probability of failure. In a rigid sequence much of the production planning and control is built into the workflow through mechanization and there are fewer decision points about where the materials should be routed. Because the materials tend to follow fewer routes and are moved continually, there is less need for elaborate stock control. In a complex operation more different combinations of production sequences and more variety of materials are required. The implication is that the low workflow rigidity may result from a high diversity of products or numerous adaptations of a few products to meet customers' specifications. In this study all the contextual variables, with the exception of two measures of technology, were related to some subcomponent of the administrative component when organization size was held constant.

In a study of 41 manufacturing organizations in California, Freeman found a variety of technological and environmental factors to be related to the administrative component.[53] From his study he hypothesized that the administrative component will be higher when an organization employs a more highly mechanized production technology and has a more diverse environment. It will be lower when the organization is subject to stronger environmental constraints, such as having its autonomy limited by a company headquarters.

In these studies there is agreement that factors other than organization size help to determine the size of the administrative component. Child's work indicates the influential factors may be different for the different subcomponents. It seems clear that organization size is not the only factor important in determining an organization's administrative component configuration.

The Administrative Component in Summary

The research on the administrative component has been voluminous, and the understanding of its impact on changes in an organization's context and structure has been improved. But a clear understanding of the dynamics of why it changes and exactly what change can be expected has only begun. Figure 7-3 provides a summary of the studies reviewed here, and a perusal of it will indicate that there is not uniform agreement as to its relationship with other organization structural variables, organization size and contextual variables.

The major disagreement seems to be as to its relationship with organization size. Several of the studies report a negative relationship between levels of employment and the ratio of numbers employed in the administrative component to total employment. The majority of studies using ratios report a negative relationship, but it is a slim majority, and two of these—Holdaway and Blowers and DeSpelder—reported mixed results.

With the exception of DeSpelder, all the studies reporting the negative relationship have been in service organizations, such as schools and employment security agencies, or in aggregates of organizations, such as industries and school districts. Public agencies are subject to more public

figure 7-3

SUMMARY OF RESEARCH STUDIES REPORTED IN THIS CHAPTER ON THE
RELATIONSHIP BETWEEN THE ADMINISTRATIVE COMPONENT AND SIZE,
COMPLEXITY, AND CONTEXTUAL VARIABLES

Author	Organization	Variables	Relationship
Terrien & Mills	School districts	AC/E to E	Positive
Hinings	Unions	AC/E to E	Positive
Blau & Schoenherr	Unemployment agencies	AC/E, line managers excluded	Size: negative, complexity: positive
Coates & Updegraff	Banks	Administrative time to E, only administrators	Positive
Tsouderos	Volunteer associations	Number of clerical workers to E	Growth: positive, decline: negative
Holdaway & Blowers	School systems	Seven measures of AC/E to E	Mixed: only 3 neg. in growth
Hendershot & James	School districts	AC/E to E and growth rate	Size: negative, growth rate: negative
Freeman & Hannan	Schools	Number in AC to E	Growth: positive, decline: negative
DeSpelder	Manufacturing	AC/P to P in many subcomponents	Mixed
Rushing	Manufacturing industries	AC/P to P in several subcomponents	Size: negative, division of labor: positive
Pondy	Manufacturing industries	AC/P to P, complexity, and form of ownership	Size: negative, complexity: positive, ownership: positive
Child	Manufacturing	Number in AC to E in total and several subcomponents and seven contextual variables	Size: total AC and subcomponents positive, contextual: mixed
Freeman	Manufacturing	Number in AC to P and several environment and technological variables	Size: positive, environment: positive, technology: positive

AC = administrative component
E = employees (total)
P = production employees
AC/E = ratio of administrative component employees to total employees
AC/P = ratio of administrative component employees to total production employees

scrutiny, and these organizations receive their budgets from boards that may be mindful of the limits of public taxation. Since the economies to be derived from adding administrative costs are often hard to show, there may be greater reluctance to approve increases in the administrative component. But this reasoning would not apply to aggregate figures in manufacturing industries. These studies may have been done during periods of rapid expansion, and it may be that increases in the administrative component simply lagged behind increases in the direct component. The Holdaway and Blowers finding that growth rate was negatively related to the administrative ratio may support this explanation. But these explanations are tenuous, since there is little data in these studies to support them.

When one turns to the studies that have not used ratios but instead have used the numbers of employees in the administrative component or its subcomponents, the picture becomes clearer. In all these studies the relationship between size and the administrative component is positive. As the numbers of total employment or production employees increased, the size of the administrative component also increased and usually at a constant rate. Tsouderos and Freeman and Hannan did find that in periods of decline the size of the administrative component did not decrease, thus indicating that management was reluctant to let members of the administrative component go. But the overall pattern is one of a positive relationship between size and the administrative component.

It is obvious that the size of an organization exerts a powerful influence on the size of the administrative component, but the exact relationship remains a question. Some understanding of this issue can be gained if attention is focused on the problems of definition and measurement that have characterized these studies. The administrative component has been variously defined, and there is no uniform agreement as to which parts of the total component should be included. The lack of uniform definition leads to a lack of uniform measurement. Thus, although all the studies address the administrative component, they are not all analyzing the same thing.

There remains the complicating problem of how the administrative component *should* be measured relative to size or other contextual variables. Several studies have employed a ratio of administrative component personnel divided by the number of total employees. Other studies have used simply the number of administrative employees and related it to the number of employees (total or direct) or a log transformation of it.

The problem arises out of what is called definitional dependence; that is, the administrative component has been defined as being some portion of total employment. This definition only has meaning when it is compared to the total numbers employed. Since administrative categories are a part of total employment, one would expect that there would be some relationship between the two. Several of the studies have dealt with this problem by using a ratio rather than the actual number. These studies typically report a negative relationship with total employment. But several authors have argued that when this is done, one should expect a negative relationship because it is a function of the mathematics involved.[54] Thus, the consistent negative relationship that has been reported when ratios are used may be an erroneous result of the analysis techniques and measurement. The relationship with size seems so strong that until further work is done that overcomes these problems, one is forced to conclude that the administrative component grows at a rather constant rate as a function of size.

That organization size is the major determinant of the size of the administrative component has not been debated here. That it is the only determinant and that it determines the size of each of the subcomponents has been debated. There is considerable evidence that division of labor or complexity also exerts a positive effect on the indirect component. Managerial discretion and whether the organization is growing or declining seem to also affect the size of the administrative component. Perhaps the strongest evidence that size is not the sole determinant comes from the studies that desegregated the administrative component into subcomponents. It was shown that the subcomponents are not all related to size; thus, what seems to be true for the whole may not be for the parts. Child's conclusion is appropriate here:

> Possibly the only strategy for further research which offers some hope of disentangling the confusion about supportive personnel is to focus upon (1) the decisions which are taken in organizations to make changes in the numbers employed in different categories, (2) the circumstances in which they are made, and (3) the manifest and latent rationales of the decision makers.[55]

Integrating Size, Technology, and Structure

In the chapters on technology and organization size we emphasized that both factors have important effects on the structural pattern of organizations but by themselves do not determine the pattern. The point has been given credibility by arguing that other variables are also important in affecting structure. In chapters 4 and 5 on business organizational patterns the executive's belief in goals and plans as determinants of structure was emphasized. In addition, throughout these chapters it has been mentioned that the role of manager's decisions has been neglected in

figure 7-4

A GENERAL MODEL OF ORGANIZATIONAL STRUCTURE
AND PROCESS DETERMINATION

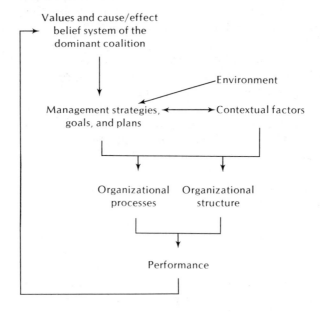

the search for an elegant theory of structural determination. Figure 7-4 presents a general model of structural and process determination in an attempt to integrate executive decision with the findings in this chapter and the previous one.

Here, it is hypothesized that two classes of variables influence managerial decisions as to organizational goals, strategies, and plans. The values and needs of members of the dominant coalition are seen as affecting the choices that executives make among the alternative strategies and goals. They are seen as having preferences and probabilities as to which alternatives will best lead to satisfying their personal needs. The process by which the individual goals of members are integrated is not specified, but it is assumed that this will occur and will approach maximizing the goals of the more powerful members.

Members also possess cause/effect belief systems as to the most appropriate means to achieve the goals and strategies. These will affect the choices about how to structure the organization and the choices about the character of the processes employed to achieve the strategies, goals, and plans. It is also hypothesized that the value and cause/effect results of belief systems will affect the executives' perceptions of the environmental conditions that are relevant to the organization's condition. These factors will lead to the executives screening out portions of the environment as well as affect the accuracy with which they perceive the environment.

Contextual factors are seen to affect the executives' choices by constraining the alternatives that are feasible for achieving goals, but the strategies, goals, and plans are also seen as affecting the contextual factors; that is, past choices as to such factors as technology, size, or ownership may constrain future choices, but the executives still have a range of choices as to the character and degree of the contextual factors such as size, diversity of operations, product sectors, and so on. Finally, both contextual and management factors are seen as codeterminants of both structure and process and as these are translated into performance. The appropriateness of past choices will be evaluated and will reinforce or conflict with cause/effect belief systems. If these systems are adjusted for incongruence, a new system will be integrated into the choice behavior.

Although this model is still crude, it does allow for a less mechanical determination of structure. Research that incorporates managerial factors along with contextual factors may increase the amount of variation in structure that can be explained beyond the present modest level.

Figure 7-5 presents a modification of Child's model by adding the above model and the other variables suggested by the present literature review. The major changes are:

1. The addition of computer usage to the contextual factors and accounting for its impact on decentralization.

2. The addition of the administrative component to structure and accounting for the effect of size, complexity, spatial dispersion, and growth phase on it, as well as the hypothesized effect of the administrative component on formalization.

3. Finally, the effect of autonomy and dependence on decentralization is added.

The major effect of these changes is to provide a more comprehensive model with the hope that it will summarize for you the relationships reported here. Although we are suggesting that these models provide a rough estimate of structural determination, we do so tentatively. The verification of some of these relationships has just begun, especially the link between management factors, contextual factors, and structure and process. Nevertheless, we believe they represent a more realistic model of structural determination than is suggested by the imperative approach.

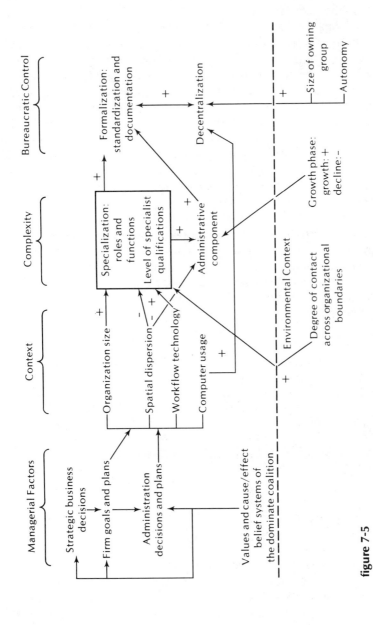

figure 7-5

A MODEL OF POSITED RELATIONSHIPS WITH ORGANIZATION STRUCTURE

NOTES

[1]John Child, "Organizational Structure, Environment and Performance: The Role of Strategic Choice," *Sociology* 6 (1972):1–22.

[2]Peter M. Blau and Richard Schoenherr, *The Structure of Organizations* (New York: Basic Books, 1971).

[3]D. S. Pugh, D. J. Hickson, C. R. Hinings, and C. Turner, "The Context of Organization Structures," *Administrative Science Quarterly* 14 (1969):91–114.

[4]Richard H. Hall, Eugene Haas, and Norman J. Johnson, "Organizational Size, Complexity, and Formalization," *American Sociological Review* 32 (1967):903–12.

[5]Richard H. Hall, *Organizations: Structure and Process* (Englewood Cliffs, N. J.: Prentice-Hall, 1972).

[6]Howard E. Aldrich, "Technology and Organizational Structure: A Reexamination of the Findings of the Aston Group," *Administrative Science Quarterly* 17 (1972):26–43.

[7]See Blau and Schoenherr, *The Structure of Organizations* for a more complete statement.

[8]Joan Woodward, *Industrial Organization: Theory and Practice* (London: Oxford University Press, 1965); and Joan Woodward, ed., *Industrial Organization: Behavior and Control* (London: Oxford University Press, 1970).

[9]David J. Hickson, Derek S. Pugh, and Diana Pheysey, "Operations Technology and Organization Structure: An Empirical Reappraisal," *Administrative Science Quarterly* 14 (September 1969):378–98.

[10]Edward Harvey, "Technology and the Structure of Organizations," *American Sociological Review* 33 (April 1968):247–59.

[11]William L. Zwerman, *New Perspectives on Organization Theory* (Westport, Conn.: Greenwood Publishing, 1970).

[12]Hall et al., "Organizational Size, Complexity and Formalization."

[13]Ibid., p. 911.

[14]Ibid., p. 912.

[15]Ibid., p. 911.

[16]Pugh et al., "Context of Organization Structures."

[17]See chapter 3 in this book for a complete description of their development, the sample, and methodology.

[18]Pugh et al., "Context of Organization Structures."

[19]Hickson et al., "Operations Technology and Organization Structure."

[20]Blau and Schoenherr, *The Structure of Organizations.*

[21]Ibid., p. 57.

[22]John Child and Roger Mansfield, "Technology, Size and Organization Structure," *Sociology* 6 (1972):369–93; John Child, "Predicting and Understanding Organization Structure," *Administrative Science Quarterly* 18 (June 1973):168–85.

[23]Ibid.

[24]Ibid., p. 171.

[25]Pradip N. Khandwalla, "Mass Output Orientation of Operations Technology and Organization Structure," *Administrative Science Quarterly* 19 (March 1974):74–97.

[26]Peter M. Blau, Cecilia McHugh Falbe, William McKinley, and Phelps K. Tracy, "Technology and Organization in Manufacturing," *Administrative Science Quarterly* 21 (March 1976):20–40.

[27]John R. Kimberly, "Organizational Size and the Structuralist Perspective: A Review, Critique, and Proposal," *Administrative Science Quarterly* 21 (December 1976):571–97.

[28]Aldrich, "Technology and Organization Structure."

[29]Pugh et al., "Context of Organization Structures."

[30]Child, "Predicting and Understanding Organization Structure."

[31]John Child, "Parkinson's Progress: Accounting for the Number of Specialists in Organizations." *Administrative Science Quarterly* 18 (September 1973):328–48.

[32]Robert Coates and David E. Updegraff, "The Relationship Between Organizational Size and the Administrative Component of Banks," *The Journal of Business* 46 (October 1973):576–88; and Neil B. Murphy, "The Relationship Between Organizational Size and the Administrative Component of Banks: A Comment," *Journal of Business* 49 (January 1976):62–65.

[33]Frederic W. Terrien and Donald L. Mills, "The Effect of Changing Size Upon the Internal Structure of Organizations," *American Sociological Review* 20 (February 1955):11–14.

[34]C. Robin Hinings, Alan Bryman, and Bruce D. Foster, "Size and the Administrative Component in Churches," University of Aston in Birmingham. working paper, 1972, cited by Child, "Parkinson's Progress."

[35]Blau and Schoenherr, *The Structure of Organizations.*

[36]Paul Goldman, "Size and Differentiation in Organizations," *Pacific Sociological Review* 16 (January 1973):89–105.

[37]Ibid., p. 103.

[38]Coates and Updegraff, "The Relationship Between Organizational Size and the Administrative Component of Banks."

[39]Murphy, "The Relationship Between Organizational Size and the Administrative Component of Banks: A Comment."

[40]John E. Tsouderos, "Organizational Change in Terms of a Series of Selected Variables," *American Sociological Review* 20 (April 1955):206–10.

[41]Edward A. Holdaway and Thomas A. Blowers, "Administrative Ratios and Organization Size," *American Sociological Review* 36 (April 1971):278–86.

[42]Gary E. Hendershot and Thomas F. James, "Size and Growth as Determinants of Administrative-Production Ratios in Organizations," *American Sociological Review* 37 (April 1972):149–53.

[43]John Freeman and Michael T. Hannan, "Growth and Decline Processes in Organizations," *American Sociological Review* 40 (April 1975):215–28.

[44]Ibid., p. 227.

[45]Bruce Erwin DeSpelder, "Ratios of Staff to Line Personnel," *Bureau of Business Research,* Monograph No. 106 (Columbus: Ohio State University Press, 1962).

[46]William A. Rushing, "The Effects of Industry Size and Division of Labor on Administration," *Administrative Science Quarterly* 12 (September 1967):273–95.

[47]William A. Rushing, "Organizational Size and Administration: The Problems of Causal Homogeneity and a Heterogeneous Category," *Pacific Sociological Review* 9 (Fall 1966):100–108.

[48]Child, "Parkinson's Progress."

[49]Ibid., pp. 343–44.

[50]Louis R. Pondy, "Effects of Size, Complexity, and Ownership on Administrative Intensity," *Administrative Science Quarterly* 14 (March 1969):47–61.

[51]Ibid., p. 60.

[52]Child, "Parkinson's Progress."

[53]John Henry Freeman, "Environment, Technology, and the Administrative Intensity of Manufacturing Organizations," *American Sociological Review* 38 (December 1973): 750–63.

[54]See Child's discussion in "Parkinson's Progress" and Kimberly's in "Organizational Size and the Structuralist Perspective."

[55]Child, "Parkinson's Progress," pp. 346–47.

SUGGESTIONS FOR FURTHER READING

BLAU, PETER M., and SCHOENHERR, RICHARD. *The Structure of Organizations.* New York: Basic Books, 1971.

CHILD, JOHN. "Predicting and Understanding Organization Structure." *Administrative Science Quarterly,* vol. 18, no. 2 (1973): 168–85.

HALL, RICHARD H. *Organizations: Structure and Process,* 2nd ed. Englewood Cliffs, N. J.: Prentice-Hall, 1977.

KIMBERLY, JOHN R. "Organizational Size and the Structural Perspective: A Review, Critique, and Proposal." *Administrative Science Quarterly,* vol. 21, no. 4 (1976): 571–97.

chapter 8

THE ENVIRONMENT AND INTERORGANIZATIONAL RELATIONS

To this point in the study of organizations, we have dealt with the reasons for organizations, methods of studying them (or the lack thereof), structural design alternatives and methods including bureaucracy, and the impact of an organization's technology and size on its structure. In this chapter we focus on the organization's interaction with its environment in general, and on a specific kind of environmental interaction; the interaction with other organizations. This interaction has come to be labeled "inter-organizational relations." Both of these focuses are major areas for improving our understanding of organizations. First, in exploring these two concepts we will deal with the environment in general, then with interorganizational issues.

AN ORGANIZATION'S ENVIRONMENT

In their search for the components of a general, yet workable theory of organizational structure and process, several researchers and theorists have been impressed with the explanatory potential of the larger social milieu in which the organization is located—that is, the environment. This awareness was a long time coming in the organization literature, and the real problems have just begun in explicitly defining the impact of the environment in organizational analysis.

Current conceptualizations of environmental variables are not well integrated, and as is the case in other areas, research results are often irreconcilable. Although we recognize that we must address ourselves to variables such as environment in order to build a general theory of organizations, we are not yet sure how to measure them, how important they are relative to other macro variables—for example, size—and finally, what the dependent variables are that result from their influence. In short, we know environment counts, but how much? For what types of organizations? With what results?

229

Any discussion of the environment of an organization must begin by distinguishing between internal environments and external ones. The former, usually called organization climate, refers to the structure and process variables *internal* to the organization. Dependent variables associated with climate are usually performance and satisfaction of organization members. However, climate is *not* the subject of this chapter. The inquiry into the effects of forces *external* to an organization is our concern here.

What Is "Environment?"

The general environment that surrounds an organization can be thought to consist of the following elements:[1]

1. Physical structure
2. Social structure
3. Ecological structure
4. Legal structure
5. Cultural (including religious) structure
6. Political structure
7. Economic structure
8. Psychological structure
9. International structure

All of these "structures" may affect, to one degree or another, the formation and survival of an organization. Organizations are social systems, and as such, they are open systems dependent upon other social systems for their survival.

An organization is a subsystem of one or more larger systems.[2] Katz and Kahn suggest that "the two major sets of determinants in the initial stages of an organization are the environmental pressures, or the common environmental problem, and the characteristics and needs of the population. The environmental pressures generate task demands which are soon met by appropriate production or technical structures."[3] This perspective says that the environment is *causal* in organizational formation. Like technology and size, environment for some analysts is an imperative for organizations.

As a primitive organization develops, the need for rules and arbitration of disputes causes an authority structure to evolve, with an organizational maintenance function following soon after. Eventually, supportive structures develop within the organization to help it deal with organization/environment boundary relationships. A bit of thought suggests that all of these emergent properties of organizations *are* affected to some extent by the environment in which the development of the organization takes place.

The list of variables in the environment that affect the organization can be expanded somewhat from that given earlier by including some more abstract properties. For example, Kunkel points out the need for the appropriate value system to be present in addition to a favorable environment if people are to organize to further economic or social development.[4] Chamberlain also discusses the impact of the value system of a culture on the organized ways in which a society within the culture goes about achieving its economic objectives. Through its legal and political mechanisms (which reflect values), society imposes restriction on the size and behavior of economic and social organizations. These restrictions are again a result of bargaining power and compromise between the organization and its environment. Both the society and the organization "attempt to modify the system of relationships in ways which are to their respective advantage"—each "uses" the other.[5]

A good example of this kind of environmental variable is the effect of different cultural roles in different countries on the use of the bureaucratic model of organization.[6] In Peru it was found that the bureaucratic form worked less well than a flat structure with a minimum of hierarchical relations and a maximum of negotiating and information exchange relations. The key point is that the appropriateness of the Weberian model of organization for developmental organizations should be questioned. Sometimes organizations built according to such a model may be detrimental to the implementation of developmental change. The "best" form is situational, depending on the environment; "different types of organizations may be conducive to different types of change in different types of environments."[7]

Such approaches to the interaction between environment and the organization are quite different than the early views of organization, notably the rational views of Taylor (1911), the classical views of Fayol (1949) and Weber (1947), and even the human relations theorists—for example, Roethlisberger and Dickson (1939). They envisioned the organization as a closed system. In other words, only forces *internal* to organizations were considered important in understanding them in these analyses. For such purposes definitions of the environment were unimportant.

Eventually sociologists began to analyze organizations as social units existing in a society and interacting with other such units, as well as containing several social groups interacting within each of them. The two theoretical orientations, which advanced those views and became the forerunners of current environmental ideas, have been called the natural system perspective and the open system perspective.[8]

Natural Systems. The natural system view holds that an organization is an "organic entity," which changes and grows as its environment is changed. This perspective was introduced in chapter 1 under the topic of growth. In the natural system view organizational changes are not so much planned changes as they are evolutionary ones. Michels' view of the evolution of liberal organizations into oligopolies over time[9] and Selznick's view of institutions as natural, responding, and adapting organisms are examples of this orientation.[10] Haire's biological growth models are illustrations of how organizations, viewed as being living organisms or natural systems, change over time and adapt to their surroundings.[11]

The natural system view is incorporated into the analysis of Talcott Parsons as he views organizations as *social systems* that must perform certain functions for their social milieu if they are to survive.[12] His famous AGIL variables—that is, adaptation, goal-achievement, integration, and latency—outline these necessary functions (see Mouzelis for an expansion of these ideas).[13] That organizations exist in environments, which present the forces to which they must adapt, is thus the cornerstone of the natural system view. Adaptation techniques, such as cooptation, the absorption of troublesome environmental elements into the organization in order to better control them have been analyzed in rich case studies.[14]

The natural systems perspective has been criticized for ignoring rational planning and the formal structure of organizations and for using vague and abstract concepts, but it has been instrumental in the formulation of organization theory since its theorists were among the first to recognize the importance of external influences on organizations.

Open Systems. The open system view of organizations described in chapter 2 is usually traced back to general systems theory. The concepts are based on the notion that the diverse disciplines of the social and behavioral sciences may be bridged if general propositions can be developed that show interdependencies and similarities of social systems across levels—for example, the group, the organization, the society. Because "an organization theory" would necessarily be an interdisciplinary endeavor and because explanatory concepts are required at several levels of analysis, this general systems view has important potential applicability for the study of organizations.

The recognition that elements both internal *and* external to an organization interact and are interdependent is a consequence of the views of systems theory advanced by Boulding[15] and Miller[16] and made most explicit for sociocultural systems by Buckley[17] and for organizations in general by Katz and Kahn.[18] The views of Katz and Kahn have greatly influenced organization analysis by outlining the illustrative open system characteristics of organizations. They are viewed as input-throughput-output systems, which take energy from their environments and eventually return it. Thus, they are "open" systems; they operate on the principle of equifinality, which allows the same end position to be reached by several means—for example, different structures—with no one best set of means seen for all organizations. Open organizations must develop feedback and monitoring systems to "map" their environments, sense its changes, and respond accordingly.[19]

These open systems views, like those of the natural system perspective, obviously place an enormous weight on the external environments of organizations as being influential for their internal functioning. But they have often used vague terms and concepts that are difficult to measure and thus deter research in these areas.

After the realization of the importance of external environmental influences was developed from the natural systems and open systems perspectives, the remaining tasks for organizational analysts were to refine these ideas in order to create specific categories of environmental impact on organizations and to provide supporting data for these views.

Specification of Environmental Effects

Through case studies, Emery and Trist developed a typology of organizational environments in which the environments were seen as being causal for the organizations within them.[20] This is the argument for an environmental imperative. Results were ordered on a continuum from "static," or "routine," to "dynamic," or "turbulent," environments. The latter type is characteristic of today's complex organizations in which environments present constraints that influence the primary goal-setting and goal-achievement processes of organizations. Certain techniques, such as cooptation, coalitions, coalescing, and bargaining are often used as the organization attempts to attain a degree of autonomy in its environment. Block 8-1 shows Emery's and Trist's environmental dimensions.

Environment/Structural Match

One way in which the environment is thought to affect organizations is through the appropriateness or inappropriateness of the match between the organization's structure and the environment. Complex environments are thought to compel flexible, open organizations for success. However, Osburn found that predicting the performance of county antipoverty agencies on this basis was somewhat different based upon what definition of complexity was used. He concluded that the *combined* impact of *general environmental conditions* (socioeconomic development of the county and the occupational mix in the county) and the *reliance* or dependence of the agency on other external units were the best measures of complexity in his study.[21] Given these findings, it may well be that the concept of environmental complexity must be defined for each organization or set of organizations to determine the optimal structure to match the environment.

Khandwalla has suggested that an organization's strategy can be viewed as a response to its environment. He suggests that a comprehensive or

EMERY'S AND TRIST'S TYPOLOGY OF ENVIRONMENTS

Type One—Placid, Randomized. This is the simplest environment. The organization cannot predict the environment but can operate independently of it as in the economists' pure competition market. Organizations can exist as single, small units.

Type Two—Placid, Clustered. The environment is still not rapidly changing but is somewhat more predictable. The organization survives by correctly predicting the environment, and therefore, planning becomes very important. Organizations are larger and more hierarchical to accommodate this need.

Type Three—Disturbed, Reactive. In this environment there are a number of similar organizations that must be considered by the focal organization. The ability to predict the environment is confused somewhat by these other organizations. This is similar to the economist's oligopolistic market. Flexibility is important if the organization is to survive, and this encourages decentralization.

Type Four—Turbulent Field. This highly complex, rapidly changing environment is a result of (1) interconnectedness of organizations, (2) more interdependence between society and economic organizations, and (3) the increased use of research and development to meet competition. The result for organizations is greatly increased uncertainty.

Source: F.E. Emery and E.L. Trist, "Causal Texture of Organizational Environments," *Human Relations* (February 1965): 21–32. Used with permission of Plenum Publishing.

multifaceted strategy indicates a dynamic, complex, uncertain environment. His test of this idea on 79 firms generally confirmed this view. [22]

Decision Points

Miles, Snow, and Pfeffer suggest that we can best understand the organization's adaptation to environmental demands by focusing on the decision points where this occurs. [23] These decision points are:

1. The decisions by which the organization selects a portion of the total environment as its particular arena of activity—that is, its domain—and chooses a basic strategy for managing the domain

2. The decisions by which the organization establishes an appropriate technology for implementing its basic operating strategy

3. The decisions by which the organization creates a structure of roles and relationships to control and coordinate technology and strategy

4. The decisions made to assure organization continuity—the capacity to survive, adjust, and grow. [24]

These decision points are under the influence of top executives but are constrained somewhat by previous decisions and environmental conditions.

Change and Environment

Katz and Kahn have made a case for the primacy of external influences over internal ones as being explanatory variables for organization change:

> It is our thesis, however, that these sources of internal strain (horizontal and vertical strain within and between intraorganization units) are not the most potent causes of organizational change. The set of conditions which we have called changed inputs from without are the critical factors in the significant modification of organizations. [25]

Another writer, Shirley Terreberry, has suggested the environment may be the *major* cause of change in organizations. She proposes, but does not test, the hypothesis that "organizational change is largely externally induced." [26]

Technology and Environment

In the effort to delineate precisely what effects environmental influences may take, we turn again to the classic work of James D. Thompson. Thompson's work is of interest here not only because he has recognized the importance of external influences, but also because he has attempted to link them theoretically to another important variable—technology (see chapter 6).

Crucial to the portion of Thompson's views dealing with environmental impact is the concept of domain (mentioned earlier and reviewed here). Domain is the point at which the organization is dependent on an element of its environment—that is, another organization, a group, and so on. To the degree the organization requires resources from the domain and there are no other elements that can provide the particular resource needed, the organization is dependent on the domain.[27] Thompson notes that by the use of such techniques as contracting, coopting, and coalescing with other units, organizations increase their power in the environment or domain by decreasing their dependency on other elements.

For Thompson the integration of technology and structure with environmental influence comes from the notion of constraints (fixed limits to action) and contingencies (opportunities) provided by the environment, as noted above. Since Thompson sees organization as only a partially open system, it must be able to protect its core technology from the environment. Technology represents the struggle for rationality, a powerful norm in organizational life and a criterion for effectiveness. Thus, as far as technology is concerned, the organization tries to be relatively closed in that it attempts to protect itself from outside threats to its basic task.

This is accomplished primarily through the manipulation of the organization's structure, by such devices as vertical integration or decentralization, which allows the environment to be coopted, exploited, and otherwise monitored while the rational technology is "buffered" from external influences. This entire process is the essence of administration according to Thompson's scheme. Although this view is only a capsule account of Thompson's well-developed ideas, it illustrates the integrative nature of his conceptualization and the importance of the environment in the study of organizations.

Organizational Reactions to the Environment

How are environmental demands felt in the organization's internal structure and processes? This important question was asked by Paul Lawrence and Jay Lorsch some years ago.[28] Lawrence and Lorsch engaged in a two-phase research study. The first phase consisted of several case studies of organizations in order to conceptualize qualitative differences in organizational environments. Environmental conditions were seen to change at differing rates over time, were seen to dictate differing time spans for feedback regarding decisions made by those members of organizations within them, and were seen to possess differing degrees of uncertainty about events occurring in them. Furthermore, Lawrence and Lorsch broke total environments into three subenvironments that an organization may face. These consisted of market, technical/economic, and scientific sectors. Any of these subenvironments may be seen as dominating an organization's total environment at any one time, depending on the industry in which it exists. Block 8-2 reviews the major concepts that resulted from the work of Lawrence and Lorsch.

It should be noted that certain of Lawrence and Lorsch's concepts and

A REVIEW OF LAWRENCE AND LORSCH: ENVIRONMENTAL INFLUENCE ON ORGANIZATION

In the first phase of their research Lawrence and Lorsch also developed their two major concepts—differentiation and integration. The former refers to the differing cognitive and emotional orientations among members of different departments as they see different aspects of their environments as dominant and try to cope with them. These orientations manifest themselves as different goal orientations (those of their own department of the entire organization), different time horizons (short or long term), and different interpersonal relations stances (task or relationship oriented). Integration was defined as the quality of the state of collaboration among departments, as well as the techniques used to achieve this collaboration and, hence, resolve interdepartmental conflict. These techniques could include, for example, formal roles, rules, the reward system, influence of an "integrator" or an "integrator's" influence based on his expertise.

As they moved into phase two of their research, Lawrence and Lorsch began to hypothesize how these concepts—environment, differentiation, and integration—would interact in organizations. Their general hypothesis was that as external environment changes, uncertainty, and time span for receiving feedback increased, internal differentiation would also increase. Furthermore, differentiation and the need for integration were directly related.

To test their theory, they selected two organizations, one deemed effective and one ineffective (based on sales, profit, and rate of product changes) from each of the following three industries: plastics, food, and containers. These were chosen as they represented, respectively, environments with different amounts of change and uncertainty to the organizations within them.

Lawrence and Lorsch used interviews and questionnaires to gather data from several managers in each organization regarding its environment and internal structure and process. They found, as expected, that there were indeed differences between the two organizations in each industry and across industries themselves. The effective organizations had high differentiation and integration. In the competitive and uncertain plastics industry, the most differentiation was required, with time frames, interpersonal orientations, and structures across departments most heterogeneous. Therefore, the most integration was also required here, as hypothesized. This integration was accomplished with formal integrating departments, with integrators possessing positional influence from their expertise and with confrontation tactics used to resolve conflict, as opposed to attempts to "smooth it over."

What can we infer from this research? First, as was advocated by several authors mentioned in this chapter, an organization is an open system. Its external environment has considerable impact on its internal structure and process. In addition, as Joan Woodward concluded from her research, effective internal process does not automatically follow from the classical organizational design principles. In short, there is more than one way to design an organization and the characteristics of its external environment are a powerful determinant, as Lawrence and Lorsch have found. Thus, a "contingency theory" of organization was beginning to develop which allowed for several different types of organization to be effective, the proper type depending upon a host of variables, some already identified and measured and others merely hypothesized, of which environment and technology are an important subset.

Based on Paul R. Lawrence and Jay W. Lorsch, *Organization and Environment* (Cambridge, Mass.: Division of Research, Graduate School of Business Administration, Harvard University, 1966). Paul R. Lawrence and Jay W. Lorsch, "Differentiation and Integration in Complex Organizations," *Administrative Science Quarterly* 12 (June 1967): 1–47.

operational definitions have been questioned and have led to failures in replicating their findings by subsequent researchers.[29]

Environmental Uncertainty

Up to this point we have mentioned uncertainty in an organization's environment only in passing. Thompson and Lawrence and Lorsch built their ideas of environment's influence on the organization on this concept. However, measurement of the concept presents some problems. A study by Downey, Hellriegel, and Slocum concluded that uncertainty concepts as presently used in organization theory are rather ambiguous.[30]

Yet the idea of environmental uncertainty is important to understanding organizations and is receiving a good bit of notice in the literature of today. We felt it sufficiently important to include a recommendation for additional reading that describes the variable further for those readers who are interested. The Downey, Hellriegel, and Slocum article in the recommendations for additional reading at the end of the chapter does just that.

A Special Case of Environmental Influence: Culture

A special case of environmental relations at the organizational level, which we will expand upon at this point, is that pointed out by "cross-cultural" studies. The Whyte study mentioned earlier is one of these. Specifically, these inquiries attempt to delineate the effects on organizational level variables that can be traced to the specific sociocultural milieu in which an organization is found.

Much confusion has surrounded the definition of cross-cultural studies. For example, a major study by Haire, Ghiselli, and Porter used data from organizations in several cultures, but it focused on individual level variables—that is, attitudes—not on organizational level variables, such as structure or technology.[31] It can be argued that there is as much to be gained at the macro level by cross-cultural organizational studies as there is at the micro level of organization studies.

Udy's study of several nonindustrial societies is an example of this type of work.[32] Udy found that the cultural context—that is, kinship ascription, community obligation, and so on—affected such organizational-level variables as reward administration, specialization, and emphasis on performance. More recently, sophisticated methodology and data analysis in cross-cultural studies have shown the sociocultural milieu to influence interaction patterns of workers on the job,[33] the relative emphasis on goal-setting in organizations across cultures,[34] and the differences in formal structures of complex organizations across cultures.[35] These obviously affect managers who might be designing organizations under different cultural conditions.

What have we learned from this work on the environmental variable, culture? There are those who feel that culture, however defined, is an *overriding* determinant of organizational behavior.[36] The research results from the studies noted above suggests more similarity on organization-level variables across cultures than differences. Perhaps we can explain the inconsistencies between these research results and some theoretical views by noting that we would, a priori, expect little difference to emerge from studies done on homogeneous samples—that is, large, complex manufacturing organizations—in industrialized societies—that is, the United States, Japan, Great Britain. Perhaps the lack of significant differences found in some research is not due to homogeneous samples but rather to confounding methodological issues. Our measures of culture may be too gross to detect possible cultural effects that exist; our translation of concepts across languages may be too imprecise, therefore not allowing subtle cultural differences to emerge. And our sampling techniques may not be random and therefore preclude a proper test of theory positing cultural differences.[37]

Abbeglen's studies of Japanese factories and a number of subsequent studies as well indicate that cultural norms provide a problem in observing much of what is considered standard procedure in organizational life in the United States.[38]

The meteoric rise of multinational corporations, coupled with the more aggressive posture of foreign governments toward any corporate incursions, leave no doubt as to the importance of considering political and ideological, as well as socioeconomic variables, in organizational practice and analysis. In short, the effects of the external environment on organization structure and functioning are becoming more and more pervasive as the entire world "fills up" with complex organizations.

To build a general theory of organizations, it seems necessary to include a cultural environment variable, at least in a moderating or intervening position between relevant independent and dependent variables. However, the *exact* nature of this variable has yet to be determined by either theory or research. Methodologically, our efforts in cross-cultural studies are deterred by difficulty in measurement and translation, as noted above. On the practical level, we must begin to answer questions regarding the universality of organization design and other such critical issues that will require an understanding of the effect of culture.

EXAMPLES OF ENVIRONMENT INFLUENCING ORGANIZATION

Up to this point we have reviewed the academic literature regarding the influence of the environment on an organization. We can conclude from our review that the organization is *indeed* affected by the environment in which it operates but that specifying the relationship beyond that point is very contingent and still developing.

We turn from the review of the literature to more specific treatment of the question: Just how does the environment affect the organization's structure and processes? We will consider two examples.

Government and Regulatory Agencies

In the United States an excellent example of how the environment causes changes in structure is provided by new government positions on certain areas relative to organizations. Three specific examples are OSHA,

EEOC, and EPA. The structural results of these three environmental changes for most organizations has been to:

1. Require new skills not directly contributing to production resulting in more specialized roles and complexity as well as increases in the supportive component.

2. Require more formalization and standardization because additional new policies and rules are required to deal with these issues and to see that the firm complies.

3. Early after the regulations appear there is an increase in centralization because top executives are held responsible to ensure compliance and avoid errors. Later, as the policies and intent are transmitted, decentralization of authority occurs.

From this example we can see how the structure of the organization as well as a number of processes have been changed. Next let's consider a related environmental variable and some possible consequences.

Density of Relationships

Another environmental organizational concept can easily be illustrated with concrete business examples. Organizations can vary in the "density" of the network of relationships they have with other organizations. Some may have many sources of supply for inputs to their conversion process and many "markets" for their outputs. Others may have few of each or some combination thereof. The relationships can result in major differences.

1. Suppliers to one or a few large customers, such as Sears or the auto manufacturers, have few customers, which makes each more important; thus, sales and marketing require fewer people and more control vested in the top. The president may even do all the selling.

2. If the firm has many suppliers with different quality standards, it must develop more specialized and formalized buying procedures to ensure that quality and contracts are met.

3. A varied product line increases the number of relevant distributors and market sectors. This multiplies the number of environments the organization must have contact with and monitor leading to a product organization.

4. Banks are regulated or affected by over 15 different banking agencies. One bank has had to create one four man unit just to survey changes in regulations, interpretations, and cases. The unit compiles a 15 page report each week for the bank managers.

Obviously density of relationships can have a rather major impact on structure and processes. These are just a few selected examples to illustrate the importance of environmental influence. Many others could be described. Even if it isn't an imperative in all cases, the environment of an organization is an extremely important variable for understanding organizations.

INTERORGANIZATIONAL RELATIONS

The views presented above reflect the effects of external environmental influences on organizations, but there is a special case of environmental influence that has received much attention lately. That is the particular influence of *other organizations* on the structure and process of a focal organization. This is usually analyzed under the rubric of *interorganizational relations*. The recent proliferation of both theoretical and empirical work in this area suggests that a separate treatment of the topic is appropriate, which we will undertake now.

Whether they are profit, nonprofit, governmental, or other, all organizations are influenced by elements of the task environment. The task environment contains diverse organizational contacts such as customers or "publics," suppliers, competitors, regulatory groups or sponsors, and many others, which are generally classified under the category of "other organizations." The topic is expanded in the second dialogue selection.

Environments and Interorganizational Relations

One of the generally accepted propositions about organizations mentioned earlier is that they seek to avoid uncertainty.[39] Yet Terreberry argues strongly that organizations face an increasingly turbulent environment as they evolve, which will result in increased uncertainty for the organization.[40] Terreberry further notes that as organizational environments evolve, the change in the environment is characterized by a change in the important constituents of the environment. Conditions arise in which *other formal organizations* become the important factors in the focal organization's field. The critical organizational responses involve complex operations requiring sequential choices based upon the calculated action of other organizations and counteractions.[41] Hence, the concern with other organizations tends to grow, and interorganizational relations take on more importance as an organization evolves.

In studies with sixteen social welfare and health agencies Michael Aiken and Gerald Hage report that organizational interdependence, as measured by the number of joint programs in which these organizations engage, tends to increase as organizations become more complex. They state:

> Our assumptions helped to explain the increasing frequency of organizational interdependency, especially that involving joint programs. As educa-

tion level increases, the division of labor proceeds (stimulated by research and technology), and organizations become more complex. As they do, they also become more innovative. The search for resources needed to support such innovations requires interdependent relations with other organizations. At first, these interdependencies may be established with different goals and in areas that are more tangential to the organization. Over time, however, it may be that cooperation among organizations will multiply, involving interdependencies in more critical areas and involving organizations having more similar goals. It is scarcity of resources that forces organizations to enter into more cooperative activities with other organizations, thus creating more integration of organizations into a community structure. The long-range consequence of this process will probably be a gradually heightened coordination in communities. [42]

Richard Hall notes that if organizations do become more complex because of pressures (internal or external), the result will be more joint programs and continued development of interorganizational relationships, perhaps at an increasing rate.

> This would, in the long run, lead to a society in which the web of interrelationships between organizations would become extremely intricate and the total society more organizationally dense. . . . The short-run implication of these findings would seem to be that the more complex the organization is, the more complex it will become since the development of new programs and interorganizational relationships both lead to additional complexity. [43]

Pfeffer and Leblebici note that an analogy may be drawn between the behavior that occurs among groups of individuals and behavior that occurs among groups of organizations. A basic concept involved in organizing is that over time individual social units find it mutually advantageous to interlock their behaviors to stabilize patterns of action and interaction. Once these patterns are stabilized, uncertainty is reduced. [44] As noted earlier, organizations as well as individuals tend to seek uncertainty reduction.

To order the opinions of these organization theorists, it appears that as organizational environments evolve, they become more turbulent and, therefore, less certain. Then as organizations begin to feel pressure both internally and externally, they develop interorganizational relationships or ties with other organizations in the environment to reduce this uncertainty. In the long run this leads to what has been called the organizational society; organizations and their ties proliferate, and we see an increasingly complex web of organizations in the total society. An example of what happens as organizations try to deal with one another within this web can be found in Block 8-3 in a case study reported by Marshall Dimock.

block 8-3

A CASE STUDY OF ONE ORGANIZATION'S
INTERORGANIZATIONAL RELATIONS

The outwardly unified appearance presented by large bureaucratic systems of organizations can be very misleading. Subsystems may interact viciously with one another, and intersystem conflict is always present. Marshall Dimock's case study illustrates the jurisdictional conflicts in which RMO (Recruitment and Manning Organization) of the War Shipping Administration was involved shortly after its creation during World War II. RMO was created to prevent shipping delays through the recruitment, training, and placement of qualified seamen for the shipping industry in the United States.

The main source of manpower besides "retired" seamen with land jobs was the Coast Guard-run training program for seamen. This caused a concern within RMO since "planning forceful action requires an integration not possible under divided authority," and this was clearly divided authority.

Within WSA, a parallel organization (The Division of Operations) existed, and its director insisted that RMO confine its activities to fulfilling the recruitment needs determined by the Division of Operations. This was considered unsatisfactory by RMO because the only way in which they "could be sure of giving satisfactory service was to deal directly with the ship operators" and not through an intermediary. It was felt this question closely affected RMO's survival.

Maritime Labor Unions believed that a government sponsored manning program was a potential threat to their welfare. Union officials, although not openly hostile, were suspicious. Because ship operators felt that RMO's attitude of attempted cooperation with the unions meant that it was controlled by the unions, they were lukewarm in their support of the programs. A final area of potential competition and conflict was with the U.S. Navy which had, since the World War I, been interested in taking over operation of the Merchant Marine. This, of course, further affected the survival of RMO.

RMO felt a need to "round out" its jurisdiction and protect its program. The first step was to stabilize RMO's position within the War Shipping Administration. Confrontation with the Operating Division in the presence of the WSA Chief resulted in RMO having jurisdiction "until the men crossed the gangplank." RMO had won round one.

Next, union officials had to be convinced that RMO would not put

244

them out of business. This was done by instituting a series of policies spelling out relations between the two organizations and implementing reciprocal relations in certain areas. This was not only acceptable to the unions but was handled in a way that the ship operators felt the relationship was acceptable to them as well—round two to RMO. By working through the Bureau of the Budget and arguing that a seaman personnel program could not be effectively operated unless it was unified, RMO was able to eventually wrest away from the Coast Guard that training function—round three.

The potential Navy takeover of the Merchant Marine was countered by emphasizing with comparison studies the greater efficiency with which RMO could do the job and the difference between Navy operations and civilian cargo handling operations—round four.

Dimock concludes this case study with the observation that power relationships are inherent in organizational life, and that clashes between competing organizations or subsystems of one organization are the "stuff from which such power conflicts are fashioned." The case provides a very interesting view of interorganizational relationships and the attempts of a focal organization to deal on its terms with other organizations in its environment.

Based on Marshall E. Dimock, "Expanding Jurisdictions: A Case Study in Bureaucratic Conflict," *Reader in Bureaucracy,* edited by Robert K. Merton et al. (Glencoe, Ill.: The Free Press, 1952), pp. 282–91.

Managing the Interorganizational/ Environment Problem

Given the need for rationality that most organizations are thought to have and the threat of uncertainty from the environment, what can an organization do to manage the problem?

Pfeffer suggests that firms face two problems in their interorganizational relationships: (1) managing uncertainty caused by the unpredictable actions of competitors and (2) managing the uncertainty caused by noncompetitive interdependence from other organizations.[45] He suggests that in either case the same set of strategies are available:

1. Merger
2. Joint ventures
3. Interlocking directorates
4. "Selective recruiting" of top executives
5. Regulation—government enforces stability
6. Other political activity to reduce competition

To this list we can add *pricing agreements; associations,* such as the Society of Automotive Engineers, to set standards, police members, and so on; *growth* to become the dominant force in the market; and development of *special units* to monitor the environment, such as a forecasting department. All of these things have the same end point—to reduce uncertainty in the environment and to make management of the environment/organization interface (including the interorganizational portion of the environment) easier.

Approaches to Ordering
Interorganizational Dimensions

Marrett has identified five principal interests reflected in the literature on interorganizational relations.[46] These are distinguished one from the other mainly on the units of analysis used. Figure 8-1 shows Marrett's classification of the principal approaches to viewing interorganizational relations and the representative variables that have been used in attempting to specify these relations.

An explanation of Marrett's classification scheme follows. The first approach classifies studies that have analyzed the characteristics of a given organization that affect or are affected by interactions with other organizations. Such things as organizational complexity, innovativeness, the degree of openness of communication, and so on, have been studied in this light. This viewpoint tends to see organizational conditions and processes in relation to interchange among formal groups.

The second category is the classification scheme Marrett calls comparative organizational. It requires that interacting organizations be compared on certain attributes. In using this approach, one does not study an organization independently of the other organization with which it is interacting.

A third approach is termed relational because it focuses on the linkage between the organizations. Neither the individual organization nor the comparative properties of the organizations are critical to this study. It is the network of relations, the traits and changes among organizations that is the unit for study.

The fourth area, labeled formal contextual properties, focuses on the context within which the focal organization operates. Some of the analysis in this area has centered on the organizational and interorganizational characteristic of the context in which a given interaction takes place. Some of the variables include the channels and types of influences on interorganizational relations exerted by the surrounding organizational world. One such study deals with the idea that a history of organizational activity affects new activity among organizations.

figure 8-1

PRINCIPAL APPROACHES TO INTERORGANIZATIONAL RELATIONS AND REPRESENTATIVE VARIABLES

Interorganizational Properties	Comparative Properties	Relational Properties	Formal Contextual Properties	Nonorganized Contextual Properties
Complexity Innovativeness	Similarity of goals Complementarity of resources (Reid, 1964)	Formality Embeddedness	Extralocal integration Local integration	Demographic structure Economic conditions (Clark, 1965)
Openness of communication (Aiken & Hage, 1968)		Intensity (Leadley, 1969)	(Turk, 1970)	
Access to outside resources (Levine & White, 1961)	Compatibility of philosophies (Miller, 1958)	Reciprocity (Johns & Demarche, 1951)	Size of organizational set (Evan, 1965)	Concentration of resources (Evan, 1965)
Autonomy from parent body (Johns & Demarche, 1951)	Similarity of structures (Levine & White, 1963)	Cooperativeness (Black & Kase, 1963)	History of interlocking relations (Aiken & Alford, 1970)	Community support (Levine & White, 1963)
Nature of laws, rules, norms (Guetzkow, 1966)		Symmetry (Guetzkow, 1966)		

Source: C. B. Marrett, "On the Specification of Interorganizational Dimensions," *Sociology and Social Research* (October, 1971): p. 85, used with permission.

The fifth approach (nonorganized contextual properties) suggests that there are other elements in the environmental setting that can affect interorganizational relations. These elements, however, are not formal organization but social processes and conditions. Such things as broad societal changes, growth of the population, or, more generally, the "field" within which organizations are embedded are viewed as being significant in the explanation of interorganizational relations.

Marrett notes that although the literature is organized by these five different approaches, the approaches are not in conflict. In fact, they should be viewed as complementary approaches to the study of interorganizational relations. A total analysis of interorganizational relations requires a thorough understanding of the interplay between variables operating at all levels.

Another attempt to provide some order to the field of interorganizational relations is made by Negandhi.[47] He suggests three levels in the development of interorganizational studies:

1. Examination of the impact of external environmental factors on the organization's internal properties

2. Examination of group interaction among social units or relationships between and among organizations

3. Examination of interorganizational relations at the social systems level or a focus on organizations as subsystems of a larger social system

This approach to providing order to the field in Negandhi's book is built around a number of examples of studies at each level.

Litwak and Hylton differentiate between interorganizational analysis and intraorganizational analysis.[48] This differentiation is based on two points. First, in interorganizational analysis it is assumed that a situation of partial conflict is not unusual or unsuitable—for example, competition between firms. From this point of view the elimination of conflict is not necessarily important since it is unlikely to lead to such things as murders, etc. By contrast, intraorganizational analysis assumes that conflicting values lead to a breakdown in the organizational structure, and, therefore, impairs the ability to function. The second point holds that interorganizational analysis stresses the study of social behavior under conditions of unstructured authority. For example, relations between nations provides a kind of model; a certain amount of coordination is necessary, yet no formal authority exists by which cooperation can be imposed. By contrast, in most intraorganizational analysis, it is assumed that a well-defined authority structure exists, and as a result, formal authority plays a larger role in explaining behavior within organizations.

Coordination Among Organizations

Of course, coordination *within* an organization is reached through the efforts of the authority structure or managers. But what procedures ensure that *organizations* will cooperate with one another when no formal authority exists to force them to do so? Litwak and Hylton mention one such mechanism—the coordinating agency. The coordinating agency's major purpose is to order behavior between two or more formal organizations by communicating pertinent information, by adjudicating areas of dispute, by providing standards of behavior, by promoting areas of common interest, and so on.

The Litwak and Hylton study found evidence for the hypothesis that coordinating agencies will develop and continue to exist if formal organizations are partly interdependent, if they are aware of this interdependence and if the coordinating agency can develop standardized units of behavior for the organizations whose activities it is coordinating. This allows the agency to develop specialists who can be of service to the coordinated organizations. There are numerous examples in both the public and private sector of these coordinating agencies having developed.

Conflict Among Organizations

A certain amount of conflict among organizations is probably inevitable, and limited interorganizational conflict is not always bad. Assael provides us with an interesting study of what he calls the "constructive role of interorganizational conflict."[49] By observing the highly visible automobile industry and drawing conclusions from what he finds, Assael provides five differences between constructive and destructive interorganizational conflict.

Assael's study indicates that conflict between organizations may have constructive consequences. His study deals with conflict between automobile manufacturers and their dealers in the New York City area in the mid-1960s. His methodology included extensive open-ended interviewing with 81 franchise dealers representing the four domestic car manufacturers and with nine field representatives of the manufacturers.

Conflict between organizations seems to be an inevitable outgrowth of functional interdependence, and the potential for conflict is especially high in systems of selective and exclusive distribution such as the automobile industry. Automobile distribution is characterized by an exclusive franchise system that requires close interaction between manufacturers and dealers. The auto industry is a particularly good subject for analysis because the conditions existing in this industry are typical of other industries using exclusive forms of distribution.

This case study indicates that interorganizational conflict can, under certain circumstances, be very functional for the continued effective operation of the concerned organizations. Assael's characterization of the conditions necessary for constructive interorganizational conflict provides a useful conceptual framework in which to view one form of interorganizational relations conflict. Block 8-4 summarizes these conditions.

---

block 8-4

RESULTS OF ASSAEL'S STUDY

Based on a review of the pertinent works of large-system sociologists and the data from his study, Assael concludes that the differences between constructive and destructive conflict can be conceptualized in five dimensions:

1. *Critical Review of Past Actions.* Constructive conflict promotes a critical inquiry into organizational policies. It leads management to review the policies that are in dispute and may lead to a general review of related areas, forcing recognition of the interdependence of the parties in conflict. In the automobile industry complaints from dealers about their relationship with manufacturers led to congressional hearings. General Motors, under the pressure of impending legislation, reacted by liberalizing franchise provisions and granting many of the demands that the dealers had made. Ford and Chrysler duplicated many of these provisions within two years. After these initial policy adjustments were made, further changes continued even after the governmental pressure had abated. General Motor's continuing changes may have reduced the potential for future conflicts. In this instance, dealers developed a much more favorable view of GM. However, a critical review of organizational policies does not necessarily ensure a resolution of existing conflicts. Both Ford and Chrysler managed to foster new conflict areas through their policy review. Such a policy review is a necessary, but by no means sufficient, indicator of constructive interorganizational conflict.

2. *System Communication and Outlets for Grievances.* Interorganizational communication is particularly difficult because organizations are often ignorant of each other's attitudes and economic policies. GM's management, for example, was genuinely surprised by the intensity and pervasiveness of their dealers' complaints. One outcome of the governmental pressure and the subsequent policy review was generally improved communications between the General Motors' manufacturing and the General Motors' distributing organizations. Ford dealers also described improved communications. In contrast, Chrysler dealers reported no formalized means of communication or adjudication. Assael feels that a number of the Chrysler dealers may have reflected accumulated hostility resulting from the lack of any outlet to express grievances.

3. *Resource Allocation.* Constructive conflict results in a more "equitable" allocation of system power and resources. Conflict between interdependent organizations may be viewed as an attempt to achieve a reallocation of system resources. General Motors did reallocate some responsibilities to the dealer such as administration of local advertising, service and warranty policies, and greater latitude on new cars, parts, and accessories. However, Chrysler, and to lesser extent Ford, ignored this extremely sensitive area. Assael notes that it is possible that factory policies in the Chrysler organization were being rejected outright by six or seven Chrysler dealers based on their previous disenchantment with the manufacturer.

4. *Standardization of Conflict Resolution.* Constructive conflict results in a standardization of procedures for resolving conflict. Such routine interaction will facilitate resolution of future conflict. In the attempt to resolve the initial conflicts, the Automobile Dealers Association resorted to political pressure through the legislative system. This application of political power was more effective in causing manufacturers to reexamine policies than in producing legislation; but it did return the resolution of the conflict to the industry. The weakness of the original conflict resolution mechanism made it necessary for dealers to appeal to external power for support. Later, it became possible to develop internal mechanisms for conflict resolution by improving channels of communication between the organizations.

5. *Balance of Power.* Constructive conflict creates countervailing power. The conflict described in the study reflected the mobilization of political and economic power by the dealers, yet countervailing power did not result in the permanent capture of power from the manufacturer. The reallocation of power that did result was primarily from the willingness of the manufacturers to exercise some restraint in the applications of power. However, arbitrary use of power seems to preclude constructive conflicts in most cases.

Based on Henry Assael, "Constructive Role of Interorganizational Conflict," *Administrative Science Quarterly* 14 (December 1968): 573–81.

Interorganizational Coalition Formation

Early in the study of formal organizations, March and Simon noted that interorganizational conflict often involved questions about the bargaining processes and coalition formation between organizations. Thompson's discussion of technology and uncertainty as determinants of organizational actions also included the constructive coalition as a central variable, especially in relation to organizational goal determination. Thompson noted that coalition behavior is critical to our understanding of complex organizations.

Wahba and Lirtzman have formulated and tested a theory of organizational coalition formation.[50] They feel that organizational coalition formation should be placed in its proper organizational context. It doesn't occur in vacuums, and it does interact with environments. Therefore, some environmental variables must be taken into account.

Certainty and uncertainty have been identified as relevant environmental variables. Organizational coalitions formed under conditions of certainty or uncertainty have had these conditions taken into account relative to their success. Under conditions of certainty or uncertainty the probability of success may be calculated and applied to the success of the coalition. Therefore, it is possible to calculate the expected utility of the coalition for each member.

According to Wahba and Lirtzman, coalitions are formed to maximize the expected utilities. Coalitions with the highest expected utilities are the most likely to be formed. The expected utility for a given coalition is obtained by multiplying the utility of each possible consequence by its probability of success and summing these products across all the possible consequences. The expected utility for coalition X is:

$$CEU = (P_{s/x})(U_{s/x}) - (P_{f/x})(U_{f/x})$$

CEU = coalition expected utility where:

$P_{s/x}$ = probability of success of coalition X

$U_{s/x}$ = utility to coalition X given success

$P_{f/x} = (1 - P_{s/x})$ is the probability of failure of X

$U_{f/x}$ = utility to coalition X given failure

In a test of their coalition formation theory, Wahba and Lirtzman found that the results generally supported their CEU theory of predictions. Coalitions are formed to maximize the expected utility, and the coalitions with the highest expected utility are formed with the highest observed frequency.

The implications of their study for interorganizational relations are interesting. Social and business organizations are engaged in hierarchical relationships as well as vertical interactions with other organizations. Coalition may result in definition of the market share size, pricing policy, territorial considerations, and so on. A coalition among dealer organizations was formed in the Assael study when the expected utility of opposing the auto manufacturers was great enough. The findings in this study, although experimental, provide a beginning of understanding for coalition behavior in these and similar situations. This study also provides further verification that organizations, regardless of present degree of environmental uncertainty, tend to act to increase the level of operational certainty and to reduce the amount of uncertainty present in the environment. The Duncan selection in the Dialogue of section four is an excellent piece on coalition formation that expands this discussion.

Internal Effects of Interorganizational Relations

An interesting recent study by Pfeffer shows some of the internal consequences of interorganizational relations for the focal organization.[51] He studied Israeli organizations and concluded that the behavior of managers in organizations seems to be affected by pressures or influences from other organizations.

The effects of the influence of various external organizations on a focal organization can easily be observed in certain organization actions. For example, the focal organization may be influenced (financially) by a union demanding a wage increase or by a municipal government offering tax incentives.

Pfeffer concluded that interdependence of organizations resulting from interactions with each other results in behavioral and attitudinal effects that can be identified. The unequal interdependence observed in his sample of Israeli managers stemmed from the need of a focal organization to be socially legitimate, its need for financing, its need for political connections, and its trade with other organizations. Behavioral manifestations of the interdependencies formed were observed primarily in the way managers spent their time. The amount of time spent with representatives of external organizations was positively correlated with the amount of preceived interdependence with these external organizations. Attitudinal manifestations of external organizational influence were noted in the amount of the influence the managers of focal organizations felt the external organizations possessed and in the constraints that these organizations were thought to have placed on the decision making of the managers of the focal organization.

Conclusions

The external environment of an organization is probably causal in some circumstances and certainly problematic. This statement finds much agreement among researchers and theorists. But conflicts arise as we begin

(1) to specify the explanatory strength of the environmental variables under observation relative to other variables and (2) to specify precisely what resultant effects on organization structure and process these variables may have.

But such controversies should not obscure the progress we have made. We have begun to investigate very complex variables at high levels of abstraction with rigor. We have dispelled some important earlier notions concerning the universal applicability of many concepts and constructs in organizational analysis and have replaced them with more realistic ones in light of current research findings.

Some of the problems associated with this area have been identified by Howard Aldrich.[52]

1. While researchers agree on the need to study populations of organizations and to conceptualize interorganizational research problems in terms of population level processes, difficulties are encountered in *measuring* the properties of networks of organizations. New methodologies must be developed if researchers are ever to get beyond the stage of analyzing the simple dyadic interaction of organizations.

2. A second very real problem in studying interorganizational relationships is related to the multiple frames of reference present when organizations of dissimilar objectives and technologies are studied. Indeed, a major problem in the past has been that of focusing on a realistically limited range of organizational types.

3. Another major problem is determining which data should be considered accurate and valid indicators of interorganizational relations. Perceptual data has been used in the past, but unfortunately, perceptual and objective data do not always agree. For example, a study by Jackson indicated that people view the same organizational climate differently based upon their level of conceptual functioning.[53]

4. A final problem is the need to study the process of interorganizational interaction rather than take only a cross-sectional view. There is a general dissatisfaction with most static analysis because organizations are constantly moving in and out of relationships with other organizations. However, the problem is how to get at this process using current methodology.

The promising directions for work in this area seem to be those in which conceptually we begin to develop multilevel and multicausal models of the configurations of these systematic variables in order to show the interactions that occur between organizations and their environments.

NOTES

[1]Narendra K. Sethi, "A Research Model to Study the Environmental Factors in Management," *Management International Review* 10 (1970): 75–86.

[2]Daniel Katz and Robert L. Kahn, *The Social Psychology of Organizations* (New York: Wiley, 1966), p. 58.

[3]Ibid., p. 78.

[4]John H. Kunkel, *Society and Economic Growth* (New York: Oxford University Press, 1970).

[5]Neil W. Chamberlain, *Enterprise and Environment: The Firm in Time and Place* (New York: McGraw-Hill, 1968), p. 144.

[6]William Foote Whyte, "Models for Building and Changing Organizations," *Human Organization* 26 (1967): 22–31.

[7]S. N. Eisenstadt, "Some Reflections on the Variability of Development and Organizational Structures," *Administrative Science Quarterly* 13 (1968): 491.

[8]J. E. Haas and T. E. Drabek, *Complex Organizations: A Sociological Perspective* (New York: Macmillan, 1973).

[9]R. Michels, *Political Parties*, trans. Eden Paul and Cedar Paul (New York: The Free Press, 1949).

[10]P. Selznick, *TVA and the Grass Roots* (Berkeley: University of California Press, 1949).

[11]Mason Haire, "Biological Models and Empirical Histories of the Growth of Organizations," *Modern Organization Theory*, ed. M. Haire (New York: Wiley, 1959).

[12]Talcott Parsons, *The Social System* (New York: The Free Press, 1951).

[13]N. Mouzelis, *Bureaucracy and Organization* (Chicago: Aldine, 1967).

[14]P. Selznick, *Leadership in Administration* (Evanston, Ill.: Row, Peterson, 1957).

[15]K. Boulding, "General Systems—The Skeleton of Science," *Management Science* 2 (April 1956): 197–208.

[16]J. C. Miller, "Toward a General Theory for the Behavioral Sciences," *American Psychologist* 10 (September 1955): 514.

[17]W. A. Buckley, *Sociology and Modern Systems Theory* (Englewood Cliffs, N. J.: Prentice-Hall, 1967).

[18]Katz and Kahn, *The Social Psychology of Organizations*.

[19]Ibid., chapter 2.

[20]F. E. Emery and E. L. Trist, "Causal Texture of Organizational Envirnonments," *Human Relations* 18 (February 1965): 21–32.

[21]R. N. Osborn, "The Search for Environmental Complexity," *Human Relations* 29 (1976): 179–91.

[22]P. N. Khandwalla, "The Techno-Economic Ecology of Corporate Strategy," *Journal of Management Studies* (February 1976): 62–75.

[23]R. E. Miles, C. C. Snow, and J. Pfeffer, "Organizations and Environment: Concepts and Issues," *Industrial Relations* (October 1974): 244–64.

[24]Ibid.

[25]Katz and Kahn, *The Social Psychology of Organizations*, p. 448.

[26]Shirley Terreberry, "The Evolution of Organizational Environments," *Administrative Science Quarterly* 12 (March 1968): 609.

[27]J. D. Thompson, *Organizations in Action* (New York: McGraw-Hill, 1967).

[28]Paul R. Lawrence and Jay W. Lorsch, *Organization and Environment* (Cambridge, Mass.: (Harvard University Press, 1966).

[29]See Henry Tosi, Ramon Aldag, and Ronald Storey, "On the Measurement of the Environment: An Assessment of the Lawrence and Lorsch Environmental Uncertainty Questionnaire," *Administrative Quarterly* 18 (March 1973): 27–36.

[30]H. K. Downey, D. Hellriegel, and J. W. Slocum, Jr., "Environmental Uncertainty: The Construct and Its Application," *Administrative Science Quarterly* (December 1975), 613–29.

[31]M. Haire, E. Ghiselli, and L. Porter, "Cultural Patterns in the Role of the Manager," *Industrial Relations* 2 (1963): 95–117.

[32]S. Udy, "Administrative Rationality, Social Setting, and Organization Development," *American Journal of Sociology,* 68 (1962) 299–308.

[33]W. H. Form, "Technology and Social Behavior of Workers in Four Countries: A Sociotechnical Perspective," *American Sociological Review* 37 (December 1972), 727–38.

[34]G. W. England and R. Lee, "Organization Size as an Influence on Perceived Organization Goals: A Comparative Study Among American, Japanese, and Korean Managers," *Organizational Behavior and Human Performance* 9 (1973), 48–58.

[35]C. J. McMillan, D. Hickson, C. Hinings, and R. Schneck, "The Structure of Work Organizations Across Societies," *Academy of Management Journal* 16 (December 1973): 555–69.

36Michel Crozier, *The Bureaucratic Phenomenon* (Chicago: University of Chicago Press, 1964); and H. A. Landsberger, ed., *Comparative Perspectives on Formal Organizations* (Boston: Little, Brown, 1970).

37P. S. Goodman and B. Moore, "Critical Issues of Cross-Cultural Management Research," *Human Organization* 31 (Spring 1973): 39–46.

38J. C. Abbeglen, *The Japanese Factory* (Glencoe, Ill: The Free Press, 1958).

39Richard M. Cyert and James G. March, *A Behavioral Theory of the Firm* (Englewood Cliffs, N.J.: Prentice-Hall, 1963).

40Terreberry, "The Evolution of Organizational Environments," p. 595.

41Ibid., p. 596.

42Michael Aiken and Gerald Hage, "Organizational Interdependence and Intraorganizational Structure," *American Sociological Review* 33 (December 1968): 928–29.

43Richard Hall, *Organizations: Structure and Process* (Englewood Cliffs, N.J.: Prentice-Hall, 1972), p. 153.

44Jeffrey Pfeffer and Huseyin Leblebici, "Executive Recruitment and the Development of Interfirm Organizations," *Administrative Science Quarterly* 18 (December 1973): 449.

45Jeffrey Pfeffer, "Beyor.d Management and the Worker: The Institutional Function of Management," *Academy of Management Review* (April 1976): 36–46.

46Cora Bagley Marrett, "On the Specification of Interorganizational Dimensions," *Sociology and Social Research* (October 1971): 85.

47A. R. Negandhi, *Interorganizational Theory* (Kent, Ohio: Kent State University Press, 1973), p. 4.

48Eugene Litwak and Lydia F. Hylton, "Interorganizational Analysis: A Hypothesis on Coordinating Agencies," *Administrative Science Quarterly* (March 1962): 395–420.

49Henry Assael, "Constructive Role of Interorganizational Conflict," *Administrative Science Quarterly* 14 (December 1968): 573–81.

50Mohammed A. Wahba and Sidney I. Lirtzman, "A Theory of Organizational Coalition Formations," *Human Relations* 25 (December 1972): 515.

51Jeffrey Pfeffer, "Interorganizational Influence and Managerial Attitudes," *Academy of Management Journal* 15 (September 1972): 317–30.

52Howard E. Aldrich, "Inter-Organizational Analysis: Some Problems and Issues Facing the Field." A summary of remarks presented at the Section Day Program of the Organizational and Occupations Section of the ASA Meetings, New York City, August 27, 1973.

53John H. Jackson, "Conceptual Systems and Organizational Climate," unpublished doctoral dissertation, University of Colorado, Boulder, 1973.

SUGGESTIONS FOR FURTHER READING

ALDRICH, HOWARD, and PFEFFER, JEFFREY. "Environments of Organizations." In *Annual Review of Sociology.* edited by I. A. Inkeles. Palo Alto, Calif: Annual Reviews, 1976.

DOWNEY, H. K.; HELLRIEGEL, DON and SLOCUM, JOHN. "Environmental Uncertainty: The Construct and Its Application." *Administrative Science Quarterly,* vol. 20, no. 4 (1975): 613–29.

HALL, RICHARD H. *Organizations: Structure and Process,* 2nd ed. Englewood Cliffs, N.J.: Prentice-Hall, 1977.

PFEFFER, JEFFREY. "Beyond Management and the Worker: The Institutional Function of Management." *Academy of Management Review* (April 1976), pp. 36–45.

chapter 9

INTRAORGANIZATIONAL ISSUES:
Power, Control, and Rules

This chapter concerns itself with three important intraorganizational phenomena—*power, control,* and *rules.* The topics are related since control is difficult without power of some sort, and rules are a common kind of control.

These three topics were selected for discussion here from the multitude of potential intraorganizational issues because of their acceptance by some as imperatives for organization and because of their high visibility in organizations. Everyone at one time or another has felt the power of another person or unit in an organization and has been subject to control and rules. Furthermore, an understanding of these topics better prepares a manager or administrator to deal with them in the design or implementation of organizational policy and programs.

POWER

Why does power exist in organizations? Perhaps because given a choice between chaos and order, organization members have opted for order and stability, which relies to a great extent on power.[1] Such an answer assumes power is very important in organizations. But is it? A review of the factors involved in the formation and survival of organizations leads directly to a discussion of power as a primary ingredient. Among the authors who argue for the centrality of power in organizations are Berle,[2] Carzo and Yanouzas,[3] Hall,[4] and Etzioni.[5]

The formation of an organization has been described as the direct result of a person's desire for power or the things that power can provide; "a person desiring power provides a viable idea system and gains power from that system by forming and operating an organization."[6] They argue that in order to be viable, the idea system must be attractive to potential recruits whose loyalty is necessary to make the system operational. However, since organizations have tremendous potential for satisfying individual needs, power becomes "a sort of social energy that can do the organization's work . . . power transforms diverse individual desires into cooperative activities for mutual benefit."[7] The continuing operation of an organization depends on the ability of organizational power holders to maintain an adequate amount of combined individual power directed toward organizational goals. In sum, then, "power is required to *inaugurate* an association in the first place, to *guarantee* its continuance, and to *enforce* its norms . . . circumstance(s) require continual readjustments of the structure of every association . . . and it is power which sustains it through these transitions."[8]

Special Problems in Studying Power

A major problem encountered in the study of power within organizations stems from an historical aversion to openly discuss matters of power.[9] This bias on the part of researchers has been reinforced by an emphasis on positivism,[10] and a preference for dealing with theories that can be operationally defined and quantified. Unfortunately, power is extremely difficult to identify and measure objectively. Thus, the aversion to dealing directly with power has retarded efforts to establish a bank of theoretical and empirical studies relating specifically to intraorganizational power.[11]

Despite the fact that power is recognized as an important variable, there is much confusion as to exactly how it affects the organization. This confusion may be a result of power's multidimensional nature.

Definition and Measurement

There is the obvious need to define *power* and a related term, *influence,* and there is a less obvious, but equally important, need to define the boundaries of intraorganizational power. Finally, there is a need to define the exact unit of analysis we are looking at—that is, is power a property of groups, individuals, or both?

Rather than review all the definitions of power present in the literature (see Votaw[12] for a review of these), a basic definition of power as *the potential determination of behavior of one social unit by another*[13] will be used as a point of departure. Influence will be referred to as the *actual determination of behavior.*[14]

The controversies surrounding the definitions of power and influence generally center on certain modifications of this basic definition, as noted by Tedeschi.[15] Possible relationships that can be subsumed under the intraorganizational power label include individual/individual, individual/group, or group/group relationships. Related to this is the choice of direction of influence—that is, downward, lateral, or upward.

The choice of an acceptable unit of analysis has evoked much debate.

Some authors are vehemently opposed to considering any unit other than the individual. Berle, for example, argues that despite the fact that intraorganizational power relationships may be between groups, power is ultimately a personal phenomenon.[16] On the other hand, Perrow argues that power can be thought of as a property of groups but that particular caution must be taken in attempting to generalize from individual characteristics of power relationships to relationships of groups. He suggests that the problem with studying intraorganizational power stems in part from:

> the persistent attempt to define power in terms of individuals and as a social psychological phenomenon. . . . the term (power) takes on different meanings when the unit, or power holder, is a formal group in an open system with multiple goals, and the system is assumed to reflect a political-domination model of organization, rather than only a cooperative model. Some meanings of the term that come from an interpersonal viewpoint are irrelevant in this case; others are magnified.[17]

The apparent conflict of views is undoubtedly a result of conclusions drawn from different definitions of power and will presumably be resolved only when (and if) the controversy over the "proper" definitions of terms is resolved.

Carzo and Yanouzas provide a discussion of the various methods used to measure power relationships between individuals, which focuses on the use of probabilities of power attempts being successful—that is, resulting in the desired behavior of the target.[18] They conclude that the development of an overall measure of individual power is formidable, since it requires comparisons of individual power, which involves the assessment of differences in (1) the sources or bases of power, (2) the means or sanctions used in the power relationship, (3) the scope of their power, (4) the number of comparable respondents (targets), and (5) the amounts of power.

The point of the foregoing discussion, of course, is that power, which seems a simple enough concept, is actually quite hard to pin down and measure.

**COMPONENTS OF POWER
RELATIONSHIPS:
SOURCE, METHOD, AND RECIPIENT**

Structure in the formal organization is based on the relationships among jobs as designated in an organizational chart. Structure in the informal organization is based on friendships, and structure in the "power organization" is based on the control of valued resources by certain members of the organization.[19] A power structure in the sense used here is formed when there are two or more unequal power relationships. Emerson suggests that a power relationship consists of a relationship in which one unit (let's say sales) controls the resources needed by another unit (production) in the attainment of its (production's) goals, and production is therefore dependent upon sales for gratification of certain needs.[20] The view that the ability of one agent to exert influence or power over another arises from the control of valued resources and results in a dependency relationship appears to be generally accepted among writers on power. However, it seems that the critical point is not that influence arises out of dependence relationships but that the dependence relationship arises, at least in part, out of a natural desire for order and stability, which is presumably accommodated by the formation of these relationships.[21]

The Source

The two major considerations that must be made relative to the source of power are: (1) resources—that is, the things which determine a unit's *ability* to exert influence—and (2) motivations—that is, the things that determine a unit's *willingness* to exert influence.[22]

Resources

Power literature is full of discussions of the resources that can be used as potential sources of influence; these resources, however, have the common characteristic of mediating the goals of the target. The range of resources noted in the literature includes personal, institutional, and situational resources. Personal attributes and abilities that have been used or developed as bases of power are described in Jacobson's exhaustive review of the literature.[23]

Institutional and situational resources have been regarded as the more important bases of power in studies of organizations, especially with respect to considerations of power in the formal organizational authority structure.[24] Although it may be that a categorization of these sources of influence is limited without the specification of a particular institution, it is nevertheless useful to review some of the possible sources available in business organizations. In particular, it is useful to discuss the bases of power associated with the "power of position,"—that is, those resources that are institutionally allocated to the individual holding a certain position.

Jacobson's review of the literature on this subject reveals several such institutional resources that go with position power:

1. Formally designated position within the communication network
2. Formal title of the position one holds
3. Rewards over which the source has control by virtue of his official position—for example, praise, appreciation, respect, promotion, or opportunities for education
4. Punishments over which the position holder has control—for example,

demotion, criticism, allocation of unpleasant tasks, or enforcement of unpleasant rules

5. Formally designated physical location within the organization and the associated access to valued information or persons

Situational resources are defined as those resources controlled by a job incumbent or group member that have not been officially allocated but that come naturally with the position of the group or individual within the organization. This set of resources is particularly important in the lateral or upward influence relationships and includes such things as access to information, persons, or instrumentalities[25]; the ability to cope with uncertainty, to determine the workflow of other departments or individuals, and to be regarded as irreplaceable.[26] It is important to note that these sources of power that are allocated informally are not particularly unlike those that are formally allocated.[27]

Motivation

A power source must not only have control of valued resources, it must also be willing to use them. The strength of such motivations are thought by some authors to be offset by the costs involved in engaging in a particular influence attempt.[28,29,30] Kipnis argues that the power holder's motivations must outweigh the costs associated with the use of power resources if an influence attempt is to be made. These costs arise when the powerholder must:

1. Ignore the "propriety of the act"—for example, when the need to evoke the desired behavior of another conflicts with personal impulses toward equality

2. Develop the needed self-confidence and/or other required personality characteristics

3. Violate group, institution, or society norms that prohibit the use of certain resources—for example, punishment that is not understood in advance of its use[31]

In addition to the rather qualitative costs described above, it is obvious that the power holder may be inhibited in its use of a certain resource by the realization that its use may cause the resource to be "used up," as would be true for certain types of rewards such as money.

The Method

In addition to identifying the possible resources under the control of the source and analyzing the strength of the various motivations, it is necessary to identify the set of alternative mediating activities through which the power holder can affect the target of power.

Modes of Influence

Several systems of classification of the possible mediating activities, or means of influence, have been advanced in the literature. Cartwright summarizes three of these (those of Russell, Gilman, and Harsanyi) by suggesting that most of the means by which an agent (O) can influence the target (P) fall within one of the following four categories.[32]

> **1.** O exercises physical control over P's body as in the case of the soldier or policeman who uses a gun or brute strength to control the behaviors of others.
>
> **2.** O exercises control over the gains and costs that P will actually experience, as in the case of the employer who keeps employees in line by either firing or praising them.
>
> **3.** O exercises control over the information available to P, as when O controls the inputs that determine P's perception of his environment.
>
> **4.** O makes use of P's attitude toward being influenced by O, as in the case where P believes that O has a legitimate right to influence him and uses this knowledge to obtain the desired behavior from P.

Cartwright acknowledges the fact that these types of influence are not mutually exclusive and may therefore be found together in any particular social situation. He also notes that it is not uncommon to observe a pattern in the use of these modes of influence in organizations, in which the use of the "harder" types (control over people's bodies) is followed by the use of "softer" types (control of information) as the organization becomes more sophisticated.

Tedeschi et al. have presented a categorization of influence modes that appears to be particularly useful in evaluating types of influence that are used in organizations.[33] They distinguish between influence modes in which the source actually mediates reinforcements and those in which it merely mediates the target's impression of what the reinforcements will be without actually controlling them directly. They also distinguish between influence modes in which the source does not conceal the fact that it is attempting to influence the target (open influence) and those in which the source believes the target to be unaware of the influence attempt (manipulation). The possible modes of influence can then be thought of as falling into one of the categories shown in Figure 9-1.

In Figure 9-1 threats and promises offer punishment for noncompliance and rewards for compliance, respectively. These threats and promises may be either tacit or explicit. Reinforcement control is the open use of warnings and punishments, which are less tangible but which are nevertheless valued—for example, verbal reinforcements such as praise or lack of criticism. Information control refers to an attempt to manipulate the behavior of the target, without its knowledge, by controlling its

figure 9-1

CATEGORIES OF INFLUENCE

Control of the Environment	Open Influence	Manipulation
Yes	Threats and promises	Reinforcement control
No	Persuasion: warnings and mendations	Information control: 1. Cue control 2. Filtering of information 3. Warnings and mendations

perception of the environment. In cue control the source capitalizes on a target's tendency to evoke the desired behavior in response to a certain cue, which the source can control. Filtering occurs through the source's ability to censor information about the environment and to control the gatekeepers of the organizational information.

The Recipient or Target

Adoption of the notion that the power of an agent resides in the dependency of the recipient[34] suggests that any discussion of a power relationship is incomplete without a consideration of the target's role in the relationship. The specific factors requiring attention are the target's evaluation and perception of the source and the processes within the recipient that determine his tendency to resist the influence attempt.

Evaluation of Source

A useful way of analyzing the reasons behind a target's compliance with a specific influence attempt is to characterize the recipient's evaluation of the source's power using the well-known French and Raven power typology, in which the source's power is defined from the recipient's perspective.[35] The five bases of power considered in this typology are: reward, coercive, referent, legitimate, and expert power.

Reward power is based on the target's belief that the source can mediate rewards for him. Thus, the source must have control over the resources that are valued as rewards to the recipient, and the target must believe that he will receive these rewards for conformity. The use of this type of power is limited to situations in which the source can monitor and record the behavior of the target. Increased use of rewards is thought to increase reward power by improving the target's evaluation of probabilities associated with conforming behavior resulting in rewards.[36]

Coercive power is based on the target's conception of the source's ability to mediate punishments or negative valences. Again, the source must have control over the punishments, and the target must believe that failure to conform will result in the delivery of punishments. As in the case of reward power, the range of coercive power is limited to those situations in which the target believes the source can monitor his behavior.

Referent power is based on the target's identification with the source. Identification refers to the target's desire for oneness with the source and is a property of groups and individuals. If the source is an individual, the target may want to become closely associated with him; if it is a group, the target may wish to become a member. The target thus believes that if he acts and thinks as the source does, the source will accept him; this acceptance on the part of the source is presumably rewarding to the target and therefore satisfies a target need.

Legitimate power is the power stemming from internalized values in the target that dictate that the source has a legitimate right to exert influence on the target and that the recipient has an obligation to accept the influence. The three bases of legitimate power are cultural values, acceptance of social structure, and assessment of the source as having legitimate power through its appointment by a legitimizing agent accepted by the target.[37] Since legitimate power is based on internalized values, its success does not depend on observability.

Expert power is based on the target's perception of the source's special knowledge or expertise. The range of expert power is restricted to those areas that the recipient believes to be the source's areas of expertise, and any attempt to use this type of power outside that area reduces its potency.[38]

Tendency to Resist

The tendency to resist arises from the fact that the source's action is designed to evoke a change in the recipient's behavior, whereas the recipient undoubtedly has a bias toward the present state; that is, the target's beliefs, attitudes, and behavior may be anchored according to its own experience and reality, its needs and internalized values, its defense mechanisms, states previously induced by other agents, and its reference groups.[39]

Studies relating resistance to conformity and target characteristics have noted that resistance tends to increase when a target has support to resist, a high degree of self-confidence, a publicly announced commitment to resist, a need for independence, or a high power status.[40]

VERTICAL POWER RELATIONSHIPS

Much of the research dealing with power in organizations focuses on the power relationship between superiors and subordinates.[41] The resources most often considered in evaluating the superior's power relate to the institutionally allocated sources—for example, control of rewards and punishments, position in the communication network, and so on. In addition, personal characteristics (expertise, attractiveness, and confidence) are regarded as important secondary sources of power. The subordinates' resources are of the situational type (access to information, access to important people) and the personal type (attractiveness, eagerness to work, expertise).

The modes of influence chosen by the superior depend on the presence or absence of conflict. Open influence modes (rewards and mendations) will be used in the absence of conflict and threats and warnings in its presence. Subordinates probably choose modes of influence according to their access to information; modes requiring the use of information (persuasion and information control) will be chosen by those in central positions within the communication network.[42]

The recipient's evaluation of the source's power will depend on the recipient's perception of the source's control of resources. From the subordinate perspective, there does not appear to be any a priori reason for eliminating any of the French and Raven power types, since the superior can conceivably be attributed with any of them. From the perspective of the superior, it would seem logical to dismiss the legitimate form of power from consideration, since subordinates are not ordinarily considered as sources of authority.

There seems to be a temptation in the literature to assume that the low-power member in the superior/subordinate relationship is the subordinate, since power-balancing discussions implicitly describe reactions of subordinates vis-à-vis superiors.[43] Indeed, Cotton suggests that the two common power balancing techniques found in organizations are the emergence of status and the formation of coalitions. It would be expected that subordinates whose level within the organization is not at the bottom of the organizational chart would prefer the emergence of status style and that the low position members would choose the coalition style (as evidenced by labor unions).

HORIZONTAL POWER RELATIONS

Studies of horizontal power relationships focus on administrative/professional relationships, and interdepartmental (staff/line, and other subunit/subunit) relationships. These studies emphasize the conflict that presumably arises out of unbalanced power relationships.

An important contribution to the study of lateral power relationships was made by Dalton with a study of staff/line relationships.[44] Dalton indicates that conflicts arise when staff members attempt to implement their ideas into the line functions, as required in their job descriptions. The resources used by the line and staff members are different. Staff controls valued information and expertise and the ability to inflict criticism on line for use of outmoded methods; line controls a valued reward in promotions. According to Hall, the motivations behind the exertion of influence were assumed by Dalton to be the same. "Both sets of managers seek income, promotion, power in the organization."[45]

In situations in which conflict was recognized, line could be expected to use open modes of influence based on threats (no promotions), whereas staff could be expected to use open modes of influence based on their control of valued information (warnings regarding the consequences associated with the use of outmoded production methods). In situations in which conflict was not perceived, line might be expected to use open modes based on promises (leave us alone and you will be promoted), whereas staff could be expected to use open modes based on their access to information (rewards relative to the benefits associated with the use of the new method).

Evaluation of the types of power attributed to each group by the other would suggest that line was regarded as possessing reward power and, perhaps, legitimate power; staff was regarded as possessing expert power and, perhaps, coercive power. Since line is typically allocated the authority position in the line/staff relationship (staff is supportive), staff can be expected to engage in power-balancing activities.

Professionals and Administrators

Analysis of another lateral power relationship—the professional/administrator relationship—yields much the same results as the line/staff relationship. Again, the resources available to the two groups differ. Professionals rely on expert knowledge; administrators rely on resources, such as control over promotions, official title, access to top decision makers. Motivations for exerting influence are probably similar to those identified in the line/staff relationship. However, it would be likely to observe the operation of the other motivation, role behavior, since persons in either position are presumably seeking gratification of higher order needs that may be accommodated by acceptable job performance.

In situations in which conflict is present between the two groups, one can expect to find professionals choosing modes of influence stressing negative consequences and information control, and administrators can be expected to choose modes based on threats. In the absence of conflict, promises and rewards would be more likely.

Strategic Contingencies Theory

These two examples of horizontal power relationships fit neatly into a package designed by Hickson et al. for describing the resources involved in intraorganizational power relationships (interdepartmental relationships). Their "strategic contingencies theory" hypothesizes that the power of a subunit within an organization is a function of the number of strategic contingencies controlled by that subunit.)[46] A strategic contingency refers to a subunit's ability to cope with uncertainty given that it is not easily replaceable and that it is central in the workflow of the organization. The coping with uncertainty in their model can be regarded as control of valued information—for example, the maintenance department is the only one that knows how to fix critical machinery. It can be regarded as the ability to acquire critical resources for the organization—for example, ability to obtain grants and contracts—or it can be regarded as the ability to determine the acceptance of the organization's output in the environment—for example, ability to acquire customers.

The value of this theory could perhaps be expanded by including an examination of the effect of the other components of the power relationships—that is, the means of influence used and the reactions of the low-power members to the dominant department. For example, do departments choose the same types of influence methods as individuals? Indeed, are the modes of influence described above relevant to a discussion of groups or only to individuals? Do low-power departments attempt to balance power using the emergence of status and coalition formation strategies?

CONCLUSIONS ON POWER

Power is a central ingredient in understanding organizational processes, but its *exact* impact on the organization is difficult to identify. Despite unresolved issues, an attempt has been made here to characterize commonly observed power relationships within organizations by examining the characteristics of the components of the relationship—the source, the method, and the recipient. Power relationships are based on personal and situational factors that cannot be separated from the institutionally determined components of the relationships. Regardless of desirability of defining power structures in terms of officially designated authority structures, such a definition involves also separating the effects of formal and informal organizational processes, which cannot, in good faith, be done.

The efforts of researchers, such as Hickson et al. and Salancik and Pfeffer,[47] to evaluate power relationships based on the power holders' ability to cope with uncertainty (or chaos) are at least consistent with a belief in the existence of power as an alternative to disorder. Continued efforts directed along this line are likely to increase our knowledge of how little we can ever know about power.

At the beginning of this chapter we offered a definition of power. This definition was selected because it avoids a major problem of focus found in some definitions. The focus of many definitions is on direct interpersonal relationships, which can mislead one into thinking that all exercise of power in organizations takes place through a direct contact. The choice of strategies, goals, policies, rules, procedures, technology, spatial arrangements, and reward systems all influence the role prescriptions and constraints placed upon the members of an organization. Yet these are all impersonal means of influencing. If these decisions influence behavior, then power has been exercised without direct interpersonal contact.

The personnel department and the executive committee that set a policy of retirement at age 65 have exercised power. A university curriculum planning committee that determines the courses and standards that students must follow to obtain a degree constrains the choices of students indirectly. The executive decision to abandon a particular product may make an engineer's knowledge and skills obsolete in that company and force his decision to change specialties or leave the firm. The exercise of such power is subtle, often unrecognized, and usually indirect and anonymous. The use of definitions that focus on direct interpersonal relationships have diverted attention away from the more impersonal modes of exercising power. In large organizations an understanding of the exercise of impersonal power may be critical to understanding how the organization can and does operate.

CONTROL

The structural aspects of bureaucratic control have been discussed in several previous chapters. Those discussions will not be repeated here, but you may wish to refer to chapters 6 and 7 to review the impact of technology and size on control and the role of formalization and decentralization in achieving bureaucratic control.

The terms *power, influence,* and *authority* are often used in much the same way as *control.* The result can be confusing. Tannenbaum suggests:

> It is the function of control to bring about conformance to organizational requirements and achievement of the ultimate purposes of the organization. The coordination and order created out of the diverse interests and potentially diffuse behaviors of members is largely a function of control. It is at this point that many of the problems of organizational functioning and individual adjustment arise.[48]

Control is the link between the inputs, processes of conversion, and the outputs of the organization. Control attempts to continually *adjust* the conversion processes of the organization to achieve the desired output. In order to do this, information on the degree of goal achievement at any given time is needed. The sources of such information form the foundation for a classification of control types. If the information comes from examining output, it is a *feedback* control. If the information comes from inputs, it is classified a *feedforward* control.

Feedback Controls

The essential difference between feedback and feedforward is the time frame of the measurement. Feedback is information provided to a unit on the nature of its outputs. Outputs include everything that the unit produces—ranging from such highly tangible items as the number of automobiles assembled to such intangibles as the level of job satisfaction achieved. Since feedback is information about output, it is a measure of what has *already been processed* by the organization. Feedforward, centered on inputs, is a measure of *future* performance rather than past performance. One of the most desirable aspects of feedback is its measurability. Even though we may be dealing with a highly intangible output, it is fixed since we are dealing with a past event. Feedforward must rely on a predictive model of some sort. If the explanative power of the model is less than complete, there is uncertainty as to the measurement of output. This means that given that same unit of measurement, units of demand, dollars of sales, and so on, feedback measurements will be inherently more reliable.

Since the measurement of feedback relies on past output, there will be a time lag between the occurrence of an event and its detection. Koontz and Bradspies explain,

> Unfortunately, a feedback loop must sense some error or deviation from desired performance *before* it can initiate a correction. This is, of course, after the fact. Moreover, since correction takes some time to become effective, the deviation tends to persist. The costs incurred in many cases increase directly with the duration of the error.[49]

This implies two things for an organization using feedback for control. First, a short feedback loop is preferable to a long loop, given the same cost. Secondly, even if the feedback cycle were shortened to the point of being able to obtain instantaneous feedback, or real time operations, the adjustment time will still allow a time delay.

Feedforward Control

Unlike feedback, feedforward monitors the input into the process rather than output. Koontz and Bradspies indicate that this will eliminate the delays encountered with a feedback system.

Feedforward control aims at meeting the problem of delay in feedback systems by monitoring inputs and predicting their effects on outcome variables. In doing so, action is taken, either automatically or by manipulation, to bring the system output into consonance with the desired standard before measurement of the output discloses deviation from standard.[50]

The advantage of feedforward is clear; it prevents deviation in output by prediction of output variations through monitoring of systems inputs.

For feedforward control to be successful, two things are needed. First is a good measure of inputs. This is not easy in many cases. Consumer demand is an input for a business organization, yet it is difficult to predict both the amount and kinds of products demanded. Even when dealing with easily measured physical units, other problems can arise when a variation is detected. For example, a manufacturer knows there will be a steel strike, but he can only guess at its duration. The second element is an understanding of the effects of resource variations. This requires a good understanding of the organization's processes and how they are integrated. Thus, feedforward effectiveness will depend on the ability to measure input variations and to predict their effects.

The weakness of feedback—time lag—is the strength of feedforward. Likewise, the weakness of feedforward—unreliable information—is the strength of feedback. Thus, the two information-gathering systems complement each other, and it is often wise to use both. Both feedback and feedforward collect information for control and thus share many of the same organizational problems. Goals must be clear so that the proper information can be gained. The information that is collected must translate into meaningful standards for the operating units.

Behavioral or Output Control

If a manager wants to control something, he can control either the *output* or the *behavior* by which the output is achieved. By controlling the output, it is hoped that the proper processes will be used. Similarly, controlling behaviors or processes assumes the result will be the desired output. For this reason, these types of controls are often viewed as substitutes for each other.

However, the assumption that controlling only the output or the behavior will control the entire process is not always valid. Controls on only the behavior may not ensure that there is an adequate volume or quality of output, and merely examining the output tells nothing of the time that may have been wasted in the production process. Because controls on either output or behavior alone are not likely to provide adequate control, both types are used in any extensive control system.

The limited range of the two types is not the only reason that they tend to be found together and not substituted for each other. A recent study by Ouchi and Maguire indicated that there are several other reasons. In a study of 197 divisions of 5 department stores, they found that the greater the superior's knowledge of the subordinate's tasks, the greater the tendency to use behavioral control.[51]

They found two other interesting associations with the type of control used. First, output controls become more important and increase in use the higher one goes in the organization's hierarchy. The popular management-by-objectives ideas are output oriented rather than aimed at controlling behaviors. Ouchi and Maguire also found that subordinates tended to use the same control method as their superior. If the subordinate thought that the superior did not know the specifics of the operation, the subordinate would provide him with *output* data rather than behavioral data.

It was earlier indicated that both types of control were needed in a good control system because they measured different things. Research has revealed, however, that different managers will have different preferences for the type of control. It becomes quite possible that two separate managers will require two different controls for a given process, Ouchi and Maguire supported this when they found that behavior and output controls were not used as substitutes but rather, were used independently.

This situation can cause serious problems. The employee responsible for a given production function may find his behavior controlled such that his options to meet quality or quantity standards are very limited; yet, he is still responsible for the output. Ouchi and Magure suggest that:

> Salespersons, for example, are subject to intense amounts of both behavior and output control. This often creates a "double bind" in which the salesperson is paid on the basis of net sales volume, but is closely supervised and forced to spend time on inventory, housekeeping, and other tasks that compete for their selling time.[52]

The appropriateness of behavioral versus output controls must be considered when designing a control system for an organization.

CONTROL SPECIFICITY

How much and how detailed must controls be? Undercontrol can cause operational problems. Cost overruns, inadequate output, quantity or quality, and the inability to adjust to change may all be caused by undercontrol. Tannenbaum found that people's "ideal" control system typically calls for more than the existing amount of control.[53] Control provides organizational members with a structure; they know what is expected of them and what the organization wants. Undercontrol fails to provide this structure and places the organizational member in an uncertain situation.

Overcontrol can be responsible for operational problems, excessive paper work, high control costs, low productivity, and a lack of innovation.[54] Arguing against too much control, Newman suggests that the level of specificity of the controls should be kept low so that the number of control standards is low.

> Experience indicates that most people can give serious attention to only four to six different objectives. This rule of thumb suggests that controls above four or six in number should seek merely an adequate level of performance. Even four controls may be too many if they deal with complex and urgent matters.[55]

Control systems are usually custom designed for the process they control, thus only the most general guidelines can be applied when discussing how specific the controls should be. Behavioral controls cut down on the flexibility of the process because certain behaviors are mandatory. Thus, in programs that require great creativity, rather general *output* controls should be used.[56]

The costs of control should always be compared with the benefits likely from the control. This can be a complex matter since a manager or administrator cannot deal only with specific controls but with entire control systems. Block 9-1 illustrates with a case study of two control systems in two state-run liquor store systems.

This study points out not only the impact of control systems but the effects of specificity of controls. Both states had similar markets, distribution systems, and identical products. The major difference was the control system. By using behavioral controls to closely control errors, State A's managers did not develop the innovations or achieve the productivity of the State B group. This confirms two of the points discussed above, organization members can deal with a relatively small number of control constraints simultaneously—for example, the State A managers let volume and productivity slide so they could meet the error controls—and controls of a specific nature tend to restrict the manager's options and thus his innovation.

Control Curves

The main tool for the simultaneous study of the distribution and absolute level of control is the control curve (See Figure 9-2). The vertical axis represents the amount of control as perceived by the subject group. The

block 9-1

A COMPARISON OF TWO CONTROL SYSTEMS

State A's liquor sales were about $200 million, and State B's sales were about $80 million per year. The sales in State A, however, were only 2 percent of the state's total revenue, whereas 20 percent of State B's revenue came from their liquor operations. Since the operations in B were relatively more important than A's, one would expect State B to maintain a tighter control system to protect their revenues. Surprisingly, this was not the case.

State B established and periodically revised a target number of bottles to be sold by the entire state. These were never broken down into targets for individual stores. State A had no overall statewide target but had specific controls on the ratio of employees to the number of bottles sold. State B operated on a two-year budget, whereas A budgeted every year. State B had an automated inventory system that automatically sent inventory to the store based on sales. In State B the manual for operations was 50 pages, consisting mostly of *general* principles of management. State A, on the other hand, had a 250 page manual of *explicit* instructions covering most of the operation.

In State A the liquor commission audited the books yearly, the district supervisor twice a month, and the store manager audited daily. The liquor commission maintained records on both the store's and the manager's errors. State A required 15 times as many reports and spent 20 times as much for error detection as State B.

State A operated under better market conditions, with a greater population density and a clause that allowed unprofitable operations to be taken over by supermarkets in the area. Yet, in spite of these differences, State B's performance was much better. State B sold twice as many bottles per employee, was more innovative, and had growth when the sales for A had remained constant. State B had less than half the overhead of State A; an administrative burden of 2.2¢ vs. 5¢ per bottle.

A sample of 44 managers in State B were matched by store volume with a sample of 68 managers in A and given an attitude survey. The managers in State B were more committed to error control than in A even though State A had more explicit error controls. The B managers worked longer hours and were twice as productive, yet expressed more willingness to work even more hours than their State A counterparts.

Based on William E. Turcotte, "Control Systems, Performance and Satisfaction in Two State Agencies," *Administrative Science Quarterly* 19 (March 1974):60–73.

figure 9-2

CONTROL CURVES

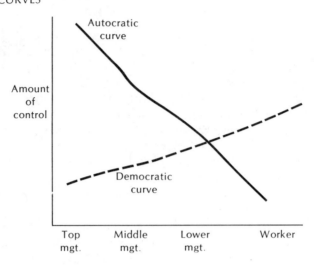

Autocratic curve

Amount of control

Democratic curve

Top mgt.　Middle mgt.　Lower mgt.　Worker

horizontal axis represents the levels of hierarchy in the organization. The slope of line indicates the general distribution of control. A positive slope indicates that control is mostly in the lower levels, and the organization is said to have a "democratic" control structure. A negative slope represents an autocratic control structure.

Much of the empirical work with control curves has been done by Arnold Tannenbaum and his associates.[57] They have hypothesized two basic relations. First, that the more absolute control present in an organization, the more effective it would be. Second, that the more democratic the control structure, the more efficient the organization and the more satisfied the members.

Most organizations' control curves are negatively sloped. The "ideal" curves desired by the members are more positively sloped than the actual curve. Yet the rank and file seldom want reductions in the levels of control exercised by the upper levels, meaning that, in general, a higher total amount of control is desired. The curves of voluntary organizations and unions tend to vary much more than business organizations.[58]

The empirical research on these notions, although not entirely consistent, seem to indicate that the effectiveness of organization is positively related to the total amount of control and not related to the democratic distribution of control. McMahon and Perritt took a different approach to control curves. They included the agreement between upper and lower levels on the distribution of control as a variable. Their 1971 study of two

274

firms found that they both had the same mean amount of perceived control, yet the one with greater concordance (more agreement between upper and lower levels as to the distribution of control) scored significantly higher on their measures of effectiveness.[59] The study also supported the earlier conclusion that the slope has no relation to effectiveness.

A second, larger study covering 12 plants, was conducted by McMahon and Perritt in 1973 that weakened their concordance theory. In this study the only significant predictor of organizational performance was the *amount* of control. There was interaction that supported both the slope and concordance as secondary predictors but only when used with the total amount of control.[60]

Criticism of Control-Curve Research

One of the criticisms of control-curve research is that the data represent not real control but only perceived control. It may be quite inaccurate to ask the third-floor janitor how much influence the company president has over the vice-president of marketing. The problem becomes worse if one considers that all the observations are equally weighted, and members at the lower levels vastly outnumber upper level personnel.

Another question is, "What is being measured?" Control and effectiveness are not the same concepts, but in the perceptions of organizational members, they may be. If an organization is operating effectively, it may be that most members would say that there is a high degree of control. On the other hand, when things are going badly, perhaps members might say, "something isn't being controlled."

CONCLUSIONS ON CONTROL

The hypotheses regarding the superiority of democratic distributions of control has not been supported by empirical studies. The hypothesis that the level of concordance between organizational levels lead to effectiveness isn't strongly supported. The only relationship that has stood under empirical examination is that organizational effectiveness is related to the absolute level of perceived control.

Specific controls can be classified according to their information source—either feedback or feedforward controls. Controls are directed at either behavior or output, and they differ in their specificity.

These dimensions appear (without having been tested) to be independent of each other. If so, we have a system of classification for controls. They are either feedback or feedforward, behavior or output, and they will vary along a continuum of specificity. This suggests some unresolved questions about control. How do different organizations compare in their relative use of feedback and feedforward, behavior and output controls, and use of relative specificity? Is any one mix of control dimensions more effective in certain organizations? The dimensions suggested by the typology developed here may have no more explanatory power than did the democratic theory of control, but they do provide an interesting basis for future research. We now turn to another "imperative" intraorganizational issue—rules.

RULES

Rules play a variety of roles in organizations. One major role is that of controlling behavior and processes. Rules are often identified with bureaucracies. For our purposes, the terms *rules, procedures,* and *policies* will be essentially synonomous in the use given to them here.

A survey of the literature on rules reveals three major areas of study: rule making, rule adherence, and rule deviation. We will take the position that these topics are roughly associated with a hypothesized life cycle of a rule—namely, creation, acceptance, and rejection. This proposed correlation between topics in the literature and the hypothesized life-cycle stages will be used as the basic framework within which rules are analyzed. Answers to three questions concerning these stages provide a basis for identifying three general roles that rules perform in an organization: Why are rules made? Why are rules observed? Why are rules ignored? Rules are made to initiate change; they are observed to ensure stability and reduce tension; and they are ignored because adherence creates tension. A general understanding of the consequences of having no rules provides an important perspective from which to consider the remaining topics.

Perrow provides an analysis of the condition of organizations that do not have rules.[61] He claims that rules reduce the dependency of an organization on machines or professionals (whose rules are built in), provide near uniformity of personnel, and can provide total isolation from the environment.

An organization that is entirely automated has no need for rules that specify various performance characteristics, since the rules are built into the machines. When machines replace people, the need for rules relating to human interaction are eliminated. Perrow suggests that hiring professionals serves a similar purpose, since professionals have rules inculcated into them during their training. In either case, he points out that both machines and professionals are expensive substitutes for rules, and their use is logically limited to cases in which they are either less expensive or there is no real choice.

An organization that relies entirely on personnel whose physical, intellectual, and personality characteristics were identical would have little need for rules. However desirable such a state of affairs may be, the possibility of it occurring seems so slight as to make it only a theoretical alternative to rules and not a real one.

An organization that is totally unaffected by its environment would not need rules concerning its relationship to the environment or changes occurring within it. Whether such an organization would ever form is doubtful, and its survival is even more doubtful. Hence, this alternative to rules must be eliminated on both theoretical and practical grounds.

Since organizations having the above characteristics are either un-desirable or nonexistent, Perrow feels that an organization *must* have rules. Failure to explicitly define rules, he argues, results in the unfortunate situation in which employees are forced to learn the unstated policies à la Pavlov.[62] Thus, he views rule making as an essential organizational activity that reduces a socially unacceptable dependence on completely automated factories run by uniform personnel in an unchanging environment. Per-row's approach to the question of why there are rules can be reversed; that is, rules exist as substitutes to machines and professionals and as a means of dealing with variations in people and environments.

As a practical matter, there is some question as to whether or not rules are actually substitutes or adjuncts to machines and professionals. Pugh et al. found a positive relationship between the number of specialists in the 52 organizations studied and the degree to which procedures were standard-ized.[63] In another study formalized procedures for hiring and promotion in government finance departments were found to be positively associated with the degree of automation and the proportion of the staff required to have bachelor's degrees.[64] This discrepancy between theory and practice is probably due to the inescapable fact that people responsible for making machines and acting as professionals are not perfect; hence, they cannot be perfect substitutes for anything.

WHY ARE RULES MADE?

New rules fulfill individual as well as organizational needs. It has been noted, for example, that successors often become preoccupied with rules and rule making because of the needs that rule making satisfy.[65] A study of the succession of school superintendents specifies that new rules serve new incumbents well.[66]

Gouldner suggests the informal group and its norms may constitute an equivalent to bureaucratic rules and may therefore be used to initiate required changes in the special cases where they are available to the successor.[67] However, in the absence of informal mechanisms, rules can serve as a practical means of formalizing proposed changes, obtaining reactions to them, and incorporating them into the bureaucratic process.

Rules are observed by the organization as a whole because of their stabilizing effect; that is, rules reduce the variability of human behavior, making it easier to predict the results of organizational activities. They are observed by individuals within the organization because compliance reduces tensions that may result from not following the rules.

Weber's characteristics of bureaucracy suggests that "there is the principle of fixed and official jurisdictional areas, which are generally ordered by rules, that is, by laws or administrative regulations.[68] He further specifies that the authority to give commands necessary for the discharge of official duties is strictly defined by rules concerning the coercive means that may be used by proper officials. Weber also specifies that the management of the office follows general rules, which are more or less stable, more or less exhaustive, and which can be learned. He suggests that rules are necessary to enable people to make decisions more objectively by eliminating the "personal, irrational, and emotional elements which escape calculation."[69]

Other Things Rules Do

Weber's stress is on rules as a means of maximizing bureaucratic efficiency by reducing the inevitability of human variability that exists in their absence. This aspect of rules, although somewhat less elaborately defined, is also recognized by other authors as the common sense reason for the existence of rules.

Rules define the employee's task as well as shape and specify authority relationships. This function of rules is appropriate in situations where informal group norms are ineffective in allocating work responsibilities; rules are thus necessary to ensure the calculability of results. It has also been said that rules serve to "cut the Gordian knots."[70] A rule requiring that A be done instead of B in the situation where both have negative aspects but neither is better or worse than the other not only eliminates the time-consuming need for difficult decisions but also assures predictability of results.

Rules also serve to depersonalize decision making. A study by Haas and Collen found that the degree of formalization of administrative practices in the teaching departments of a large Midwestern university were more closely related to the repetitiveness of decision making than to the size of the department.[71] In another study, the relationship between size, organizational complexity, and formalization lead researchers to conclude that one way in which organizations limit individual discretion is through formalization of procedures and penalties for rule violation.[72]

Melcher describes a role of rules in bureaucracies, attributed to Merton.[73] He notes that the stability of a bureaucracy depends upon the participants developing a strong commitment to their jobs and a clear recognition of the limits to their authority and competence. However, these sentiments to conform to rules originally designed to achieve organizational goals may shift to an emphasis on conformity for reasons that are independent of the organizational goals. Merton's theory is that the emphasis on reliability of behavior that rules require may have an unintended effect that March and Simon summarize in the following way:

> The choice of a desired alternative reveals additional desirable consequences not originally anticipated. The instrumental activity has, therefore, positively valued consequences even when it does not have the originally anticipated outcomes. It is this latter phenomenon (secondary reinforcement) that is operating. . . . The organizational setting brings about new personal or subunit consequences through participation in organizationally motivated actions.[74]

So, a possible side effect of rules may be that they can take on a terminal value of their own in addition to the instrumental value for which they were instituted—that is, reducing tensions. Gouldner concludes that rules are functional insofar as they reduce status-located tensions stemming from close supervision and organizational tensions stemming from interaction of different values, ambiguous legitimacy of authority, unreciprocated expectations, decline in informal interaction, discontinuity in the hierarchy of authority, limited communications, challenge to managerial expertise, and incongruence of organizational and group goals.[75]

If the instrumental value of rules to the organization is to maximize efficiency by assuring predictability of results, then the terminal value of rules may well be to reduce the tensions that the emphasis on predictability creates. If predictability means that subordinates must comply with orders that threaten their status as equals, rules mitigate the tensions arising from this. If it means that subordinates must comply with orders imposed on them by outsiders whose goals do not coincide with theirs, rules ease the tension associated with such an imposition. If subordinates must be coerced in order to comply with organizational goals, rules eliminate the tensions created by "illegitimate" punishments. If subordinates must be bribed for cooperation, rules provide the mechanism for the operation of such bargaining. And finally, if subordinates are required to engage in activities that serve only to ensure security to the individual and nothing more, rules stipulate the minimum performance necessary to meet the individual's goal. The reduction of tensions created by the use of rules that enhance predictability is presumably stabilizing to the organization as a whole, at least in the short run. Hence, the direct and indirect use of rules as stabilizing agents is a primary role of rules in organization.

The focus on the effect of rules at the formal organizational level so far has been on the initiation of changes and the regulation of activities and relationships to ensure predictability. However, if goal congruence exists between the organization and its participants and if rules are designed to apply to circumstances that no longer exist, the instrumental value of the rule is presumably lost, and the inevitable result is rule deviation. Hence, the saying that "rules are made to be broken" does indeed apply to most organizations. Rule deviation can be viewed as a symptom of the presence of tension and the attendant need for change in the rule and/or the conditions that create the tension.

Inaccurate Assumptions

There is empirical evidence to support the notion that rule deviance will occur as a result of rules based on inaccurate assumptions. Blau's study of a government agency concluded that "adjustments" to official procedures had to be made in the interest of operating efficiency because the characteristics of the industry served were not incorporated into the procedures.[76] A study purporting to duplicate Blau's research made a similar conclusion with respect to adjustments, except that it was further observed that not all the necessary adjustments were made to counteract the inaccurate assumptions built into the procedures.[77] A study of the Navy dispursing officer illustrated a situation in which the dispursing officer's status was related to how well he responded to requests from superiors, subordinates and other groups.[78] This ability, however, depended upon the functioning of well-established informal procedures that were not consistent with the official procedures.

To summarize, if current conditions do not correspond to the conditions assumed to be present when the rule was initiated and if the rule serves to impede the sincere efforts of groups or individuals to attain the organizational goals, the rule can be regarded as a source of tension; the inevitable deviation from the rules may be recognized as a symptom of the need for change.

Vulnerability of the Group

Vulnerability of an organizational group to the rules is a factor brought out in Carlson's study of school superintendents cited previously. In situations in which obedience to rules will neither affect the formal status of the individual or group, their method of work, or their responsibility and chain-of-command relationships, vulnerability to the rules is limited.

In such cases violation of the rules is likely to occur especially when it is not convenient to be obedient. As an example, Carlson cites the difference in vulnerability to rules of teachers and school administrators.[79] Teachers are at the bottom of the professional hierarchy; surveillance of their work is impossible; and the principal can presumably intervene to corrupt the intent of rules. Hence, there is little to gain by adherence to rules and little to lose in ignoring them. School administrators, however, can be demoted and are readily susceptible to surveillance; thus, rules can affect the way in which they perform their work, their status, and their position in the professional hierarchy. They are, therefore, highly vulnerable to rules and their tension creating potential.

Communication Channel

Another factor, the communication channel used when designing the rule was investigated by Melcher.[80] The hypothesis was that the use of formal channels of communication in establishing rules to govern situations is acceptable and results in the creation of little tension. Rules designed to regulate controversial situations in which goal congruence of the affected groups or individuals is a problem should be decided upon at the informal level and legitimized using formal channels. He suggests that tension can arise in the process of using the formal level to achieve a consensus regarding nonroutine issues because open confrontations between groups or individuals may result in permanent damage to interpersonal relations.

The presence of the conditions cited above—that is, rules that incorporate invalid assumptions, high vulnerability to rules, and improper use of formal communication channels—increases the probability that rules will create tensions that can only be alleviated through change. Why don't needed changes automatically occur under these tension-exacting conditions? The answer to this question leads one back to the nature of rules; that is, they are highly interdependent. Perrow succinctly summarizes this notion:

> Rules are like an invisible skein which bundles together all the technological and social aspects of an organization. As such, rules stem from past adjustments and seek to stabilize the present and future. When things are different in the future, an attempt to change these tough invisible threads means that all kinds of practices, bargains, agreements, and payoffs will tumble out of the web and must be stuffed back in again.[81]

CONCLUSIONS ON RULES

The role of rules in an organization is rather straightforward. They initiate changes, provide stability, and create tension. This apparent contradiction among the functions of rules is simply a reflection of the continual battle being waged within an organization between the various forces of stability and flexibility. It has been assumed (1) that all bureaucratic rules can serve all three of these general purposes sometime during their life cycle and (2) that any one rule need not be classified into a single category at any one point in time.

This latter assumption leads to the necessity of discussing the complications created by individuals or groups within an organization and their reaction to rules. At the informal level in a bureaucracy the role of rules may be largely unrelated to the intent of the formal organization. Intense vulnerability of individuals to rules or the inappropriate use of formal channels of communication may lead to tension at an individual level even though the rules stabilize at the organizational level. Conversely, rules that create tension for the organization as a whole—that is, those based on inappropriate assumptions—may be stabilizing to the individual because of their tension-reducing capacity. That is, a rule may have taken on a terminal value of its own that may be either unrelated to or contrary to the attainment of organizational goals.

Ultimately, the stage in the rule life cycle to which a rule is assigned in the bureaucracy depends on the relative strength of the conflicting forces. A rule will be observed when the organizational or individual benefits (stability) derived from adherence exceed organizational or individual costs (tensions) associated with adherence; a rule will be ignored when the costs exceed the benefits.

It should be recognized, however, that this simplistic cost/benefit evaluation of rules does not explicitly occur. The process of evaluation is complicated by the interdependent nature of rules. If the effect of a single rule could be isolated from all the others, the tensions and stability associated with it could presumably be evaluated precisely, but rules tend to hinge on one another. The ultimate dilemma faced by an organization with respect to rules may well be how to impose change needed to alleviate tension created by a rule without simply shifting the tension to another rule that previously existed primarily as a stabilizing agent.

NOTES

[1]Adolph A. Berle, *Power* (New York: Harcourt, Brace & World, 1967), p. 7.

[2]Ibid.

[3]R. Carzo and J. N. Yanouzas, *Formal Organizations: A Systems Approach* (Homewood. Ill.: Irwin, 1967).

[4]Richard H. Hall, *Organizations: Structure and Process* (Englewood Cliffs, N.J.: Prentice-Hall, 1972).

[5]Amitai Etzioni, *A Comparative Analysis of Complex Organizations* (New York: The Free Press, 1961).

[6]H. G. Hicks and C. R. Gullet, *Organization: Theory and Behavior* (New York: McGraw-Hill, 1975), p. 261.

[7]Ibid.

[8]Robert Bierstedt, "An Analysis of Social Power," *American Sociological Review* (1950), p. 246.

[9]Hicks and Gullett, *Organization*, p. 235.

[10]D. Cartwright, "Influence, Leadership, and Control," *Handbook of Organizations*, ed. J. G. March (Chicago: Rand McNally, 1965).

[11]D. J. Hickson, R. C. Hinings, C. A. Lee, R. E. Schneck, and J. M. Pennings, "A Strategic Contingencies Theory of Intraorganizational Power," *Administrative Science Quarterly* 16 (June 1971):216–29.

[12]Dow Votaw, "What Do We Believe About Power?" *California Management Review* 8 (Summer 1966):74–75.

[13]Hickson et al., "A Strategic Contingencies Theory," p. 218.

[14]Henry L. Minton, "Power and Personality," *The Social Influence Processes*, ed. J. T. Tedeschi (Chicago: Aldine, 1972).

[15]J. T. Tedeschi, ed., *Perspectives on Social Power* (Chicago: Aldine, 1974).

[16]Berle, *Power*, p. 37.

[17]Charles Perrow, "Departmental Power and Perspective in Industrial Firms," *Power in Organizations*, ed. M. N. Zaled (Tennessee: Vanderbilt University Press, 1970), p. 84.

[18]Carzo and Yanouzas, *Formal Organizations*, pp. 209–20.

[19]Ibid., p. 193.

[20]R. M. Emerson, "Power Dependence Relations," *American Sociological Review* 27 (1962):31–41.

[21]Karl E. Weick, *The Social Psychology of Organizing* (Reading, Mass.: Addison-Wesley, 1969), p. 45.

[22]Cartwright, "Influence, Leadership, and Control," pp. 5–11.

[23]W. B. Jacobson, *Power and Interpersonal Relations* (Belmont, Calif.: Wadsworth, 1972).

[24]David Kipnis, "The Powerholder," *Perspectives in Social Power*, ed. J. T. Tedeschi (Chicago: Aldine, 1974), pp. 82–124.

[25]David Mechanic, "Sources of Power of Lower Participants in Complex Organizations," *Administrative Science Quarterly* 7 (1962):349–64.

[26]Hickson et al., "A Strategic Contingencies Theory."

[27]Hall, *Organizations*, p. 231.

[28]G. C. Homans, *Social Behavior: Its Elementary Forms*, rev. ed. (New York: Harcourt Brace Jovanovich 1974).

[29]J. C. Harsaryi, "Measurement of Social Power, Opportunity Costs, and the Theory of Two Person Bargaining Games," *Behavioral Science* 7 (1962):67–81.

[30]J. Thibaut and H. H. Kelley, *The Social Psychology of Groups* (New York: Wiley, 1959).

[31]Kipnis, "The Powerholder," pp. 91–92.

[32]Cartwright, "Influence, Leadership, and Control," pp. 12–13.

[33]Tedeschi, *The Social Influence Processes* (Chicago: Aldine, 1972), pp. 291–98.

[34]Emerson, "Power Dependence Relations," p. 32.

[35]J. R. P. French and B. H. Raven, "The Bases of Social Power," *Studies in Social Power*, ed. D. Cartwright (Ann Arbor, Mich.: Institute for Social Psychology, 1959), pp. 150–67.

[36]Cartwright, "Influence, Leadership, and Control," p. 28.

[37]Jacobson, *Power and Interpersonal Relations*, p. 59.

[38]Ibid., p. 60.

[39]Cartwright, "Influence, Leadership, and Control," p. 33.

[40]Jacobson, *Power and Interpersonal Relations*, pp. 62–65.

[41]Etzioni, *A Comparative Analysis of Complex Organizations;* Mechanic, "Sources of Power."

[42]Mechanic, "Sources of Power."

[43]Chester Cotton, "Measurement of Power Balancing Styles and Some of Their Correlates," *Administrative Science Quarterly* 2 (1976):307–9.

[44]Melville Dalton, *Men Who Manage* (New York: Wiley, 1959).

[45]Hall, *Organizations*, p. 221.

[46]Hickson et al., "A Strategic Contingencies Theory," p. 22.

[47]G. R. Salancik and J. Pfeffer, "The Bases and Use of Power in Organizational Decision Making and the Case of a University," *Administrative Science Quarterly* 19 (1974):453–73.

[48]Arnold S. Tannenbaum, *Control in Organizations* (New York: McGraw-Hill, 1968), p. 3.

[49]Harold Koontz and Robert Bradspies, "Managing Through Feedforward Control," *Business Horizons* (June 1972).

[50]Ibid., p. 29.

[51]William G. Ouchi and Mary Ann Maguire, "Operational Control: Two Functions," *Administrative Science Quarterly* (December 1975).

[52]Ibid., p. 563.

53Tannenbaum, *Control in Organizations*, pp. 80–81.

54William E. Turcotte, "Control Systems, Performance and Satisfaction in Two State Agencies," *Administrative Science Quarterly* 19 (March 1974):60–73.

55William H. Newman, *Constructive Control: Design and Use of Control Systems* (Englewood Cliffs, N.J.: Prentice-Hall, 1975), p. 35.

56Ibid., chapter 7.

57Tannenbaum, *Control in Organizations.*

58Ibid., chapter 5.

59J. Timothy McMahon and G. W. Perritt, "The Control Structures of Organizations: An Empirical Examination," *Academy of Management Journal* (September 1971), 327–39.

60J. Timothy McMahon and G. W. Perritt, "Toward a Contingency Theory of Organizational Control," *Academy of Management Journal* (December 1973), pp. 624–35.

61Charles Perrow, "There Ought to Be a Rule," *Complex Organizations: A Critical Essay,* (Glenview, Ill.: Scott, Foresman, 1972), pp. 23–32.

62Perrow, "There Ought to Be a Rule."

63D. S. Pugh, D. J. Hickson, and C. R. Hinings, *Writers on Organizations* (Baltimore: Penguin Books, 1971), pp. 19–29.

64Peter M. Blau and Marshall W. Meyer, *Bureaucracy in Modern Society,* 2nd ed. (New York: Random House, 1971).

65Alvin W. Gouldner, *Patterns of Industrial Bureaucracy* (New York: The Free Press, 1954), p. 94.

66Richard O. Carlson, *Executive Succession and Organizational Change* (Chicago: Midwestern Administration Center, University of Chicago, 1962), pp. 24–25.

67Gouldner, *Patterns of Industrial Bureaucracy,* p. 164.

68Max Weber, "Bureaucracy," *Organizations: Structure and Behavior,* vol. 1, 2nd ed., ed Joseph A. Litterer (New York: Wiley, 1969), pp. 29–39.

69Ibid., p. 35.

70Perrow, "There Ought to Be a Rule," p. 31.

71J. Eugene Haas and Linda Collen, "Administrative Practices in University Departments," *Administrative Science Quarterly* 8 (June 1963):44–60.

72R. H. Hall, Norman J. Johnson, and J. Eugene Haas, "Organizational Size, Complexity and Formalization," *American Sociological Review* 32 (December 1967):903–12.

73Arlyn J. Melcher, "Rule Orientation: The Reliance on the Formal System," *Structure and Process of Organization: A Systems Approach* (Englewood Cliffs, N.J.: Prentice-Hall, 1976), p. 340.

74March and Simon, "The Dysfunctions of Bureaucracy," p. 32.

75Gouldner, *Patterns of Industrial Bureaucracy,* p. 240.

76Peter M. Blau, *The Dynamics of Bureaucracy* (Chicago: University of Chicago Press, 1955).

77Harry Cohen, *Demonics of Bureaucracy: Problems of Change in a Government Agency* (Ames: Iowa State University Press, 1965).

78Ralph H. Turner, "The Navy Disbursing Officer as a Bureaucrat," *American Soicological Review* 12 (June 1974):342–48.

79Carlson, *Executive Succession and Organizational Change,* pp. 30–31.

80Melcher, "Rule Orientation," p. 349.

81Perrow, "There Ought to Be a Rule," p. 29.

SUGGESTIONS FOR FURTHER READING

McMahon, Timothy J., and Perritt, G. W. "The Control Structures of Organizations: An Empirical Examination." *Academy of Management Journal* 14 (September 1971):327–39.

Tannenbaum, Arnold S. *Control in Organizations.* New York: McGraw-Hill, 1968.

Zald, M. N., ed. *Power in Organizations.* Nashville, Tenn.: Vanderbilt University Press, 1970.

section three   DIALOGUE

In section three we have discussed the major factors that have been thought to constrain the decision maker in building a viable organization. Throughout this stream of literature the missing link has been the role that the executive plays in determining structure. Typically the executive's discretion has been seen as limited in choosing the structural characteristics. The first dialogue selection has been chosen to provide an additional counterpoint to such arguments. Building on the conceptual work of John Child, Montanari has conducted studies that indicate that the "imperatives" may play a lesser role in the determination of organization structure than the "strategic choices" of executives. In this piece he provides us with the theoretical model upon which his research has been grounded. It represents one of the few attempts to link together executive decision making, organization structure, and contextual variables.

The second reading that appears in dialogue three is devoted to expanding our coverage of interorganizational relationships. Relationships between organizations have been assuming greater significance with the proliferation of governmental organizations. Just as increased complexity and differentiation increases the need for coordination within an organization the increased complexity within modern societies has placed a premium on interorganization planning and coordination. There has also been an increase in joint efforts by business and government to solve many problems. One place where interorganizational relations differ from relationships within the organization is the autonomy of the respective organizations. Van De Ven's article is an attempt to define ways in which the character of inter organizational relationships may be understood.

OPERATIONALIZING STRATEGIC CHOICE

JOHN R. MONTANARI

What factor(s) actually determine the most effective structural design for an organization? This question has continued to fascinate students of management theory over the decades. The standard bureaucratic model is inappropriate in many contemporary situations and therefore cannot serve as the universally optimal structural configuration as originally proposed. Subsequent open systems perspectives of the organization encouraged researchers to examine a wide range of variables in an effort to explain the difference in organization structures. The resulting studies demonstrated that factors associated with the organization's context were highly related to several dimensions of organization structure. These results fostered an imperative view of structural determination. According to proponents of this view, the firm's size, technology, or environment dictates the appropriate structural arrangement. To date, imperative models have been able to explain only 50 percent to 60 percent of the variability in structures of firms surveyed (Child, 1972; Pugh, 1973).

A recent study by John Child (1972) proposes that conditions in the firm's environment may actually define a range of structural alternatives within which the senior executive has discretionary freedom. Child labeled this conceptualization 'strategic choice" and suggests that it may be the missing variable in present imperative models. The objective of this paper is to critically evaluate the strategic choice construct and analyze its role in the structural determination process.

THE IMPERATIVES

Three factors that are typically used to describe the context of the organization are its size, technology, and environment. The imperative perspective refers to the proposition that one of these contextual factors operates as the exclusive predictor of organization structure. Several organization theorists have promoted one or the other contextual factor based on results of their empirical studies.

Organization Size

Studies conducted by the Aston Group (Pugh et al., 1969; Inkson et al., 1970; Child & Mansfield, 1972) provide the foundation for the size impera-

---

This reading was *written for this text* at the request of the book's authors because of Montanari's ground breaking attempts to demonstrate the significance of the executive's strategic choice in the determination of the organization's structural characteristics.

tive. These researchers report results showing a high correlation (.69) between size and their composite structure dimension (structuring of activities). The addition of technology to the analysis did not significantly increase the coefficient value. Subsequent research also supports the importance of size in structural determination . (Holdaway et al., 1975; Mindlin & Aldrich, 1975; Blau et al., 1976; Evers et al., 1976). However, many of the size studies have been questioned on the basis of unreliable measures of technology (Aldrich, 1972; Child & Mansfield, 1972), environment (Mindlin & Aldrich, 1975), and structure (Holdaway et al., 1975). For example, Holdaway et al. (1975) could not reproduce the Aston results using a sample of 23 colleges and technical institutions. These results suggest that technology indirectly influences the size/structure relationship.

Organization Technology

Woodward (1958, 1965) serendipitously discovered linear and curvilinear relationships between her scale of technical complexity and several measures of organization structure. Although J. D. Thompson (1967) added theoretical support for the importance of technology, her study continues to provide the bulk of the empirical justification for the technology imperative. Attempts to further validate Woodward's research have been, for the most part, unsuccessful (Pugh et al., 1969; Hickson et al., 1969; Child & Mansfield, 1972; Negandhi & Reimann, 1973; Khandwalla, 1974; Blau et al., 1976; Evers et al., 1976). Either size emerges as a superior predictor to technology, or results fail to support the importance of technology. However, theoretical treatises on the technology imperative continue to proliferate.

Organization Environment

The most influential study with respect to the environment imperative was conducted by Lawrence and Lorsch (1967). Founded on an open systems view of the organization, this imperative proposes that characteristics of the firm's environment, specifically the level of uncertainty present, determine the appropriate structure. A majority of the research reported focused on attempts to verify the two dimensional conceptualization of environment postulated by Lawrence and Lorsch and others (J. D. Thompson, 1967; Duncan, 1972; Jurkovich, 1974).

Studies investigating the environment imperative have been criticized for using inconsistent measures of environment and structure. Attempts to determine the validity of the two dimensional conceptualization by comparing the manager's perceptions of uncertainty with objective measures of the environment do not strictly support this interpretation. Also, when size and technology were introduced into the analysis, confusing results were obtained.

Organization Structure

Organization structure is a multidimensional concept that describes both the anatomical shape of the organization and the patterns of authority and communication relationships present. Although organization form has been investigated in over 20 studies, there exists a general lack of agreement among management theorists as to what should be included in an operational definition of organization structure. Sixteen separate dimensions and over 25 different definitions for structure appear in the literature. Figure 1 provides a summary of the most frequently used definitions of structural dimensions.

Imperative Models

Figure 2 is an illustration of present imperative models. These models postulate that one of the three previously discussed contextual factors is the single most important predictor of organization structure. Implicit in the imperative theories is the proposition that a strong positive relationship exists between structural adaptation and organization effectiveness. In other words, the firm that achieves the best match between the demands imposed by its size, technology, or environment will be most effective. Several empirical studies (Woodward, 1958; Lawrence & Lorsch, 1967; Keller et al., 1974; Reimann, 1975) support this proposition.

STRATEGIC CHOICE

Several recent theoretical studies have renewed interest in the role of the manager in determining the structure of his or her organization unit. Classical management theorists acknowledged the importance of the executive in the principles of scientific management. Subsequent schools of management thought have emphasized the individual/structure and context/structure relationships while neglecting the impact of the decision maker on structure. In 1962 Chandler reported a study that analyzed the components of strategy and structure in several major United States firms. He concluded that an organization's structural configuration is influenced by prior strategic decisions of the top executive team.

John Child (1972) builds on Chandler's "structure follows strategy" observations to develop the concept of strategic choice. This author postulates that members of the top executive team have some "freedom of maneuver" or range of discretion with respect to organizational factors of scale of operations, technology, structure, and human resources. This range is defined primarily by conditions present in the firm's environment. Figure 3 is an illustration of Child's construct. He summarizes:

figure 1

DIMENSIONS OF ORGANIZATION STRUCTURE

---

1. Vertical span—number of levels in the authority hierarchy from the bottom to the top levels, inclusive (Reimann, 1974).

2. Span of control—measure of the limits of hierarchical authority exercised by a single manager or how many subordinates an individual manager can or should supervise (Ouchi & Dowling, 1974).

3. Formalization—extent to which the employee's role is defined by formal documentation (Reimann, 1974). Proportion of codified jobs in the organizational unit (Hage, 1965).

4. Standardization—measured by the range of variation that is tolerated within the rules defining the jobs (Hage, 1965).

5. Differentiation (vertical)—degree of cumulative authority and responsibility resting in the various levels of the hierarchy (Reimann, 1974).

6. Differentiation (horizontal)—the number of specialty functions represented in a firm (Weber, 1947).

   —differences in departmental manager's orientation toward particular goals, time requirements and interpersonal relationships (Lawrence & Lorsch, 1967).

7. Integration—the quality of the state of collaboration that exists among departments that are required to achieve unity of effort (Lawrence & Lorsch, 1967).

   —the basis for coordination between organizational units, either plans or feedback (Perrow, 1970).

8. Centralization—the proportion of occupants or jobs whose occupants participate in decision making and the number of areas in which they participate (Hage, 1965).

   —concentration of power arrangements (Thompson, 1967).
   —(a) locus of decision making with respect to policies, (b) degree of information sharing between levels, and (c) degree of participation in long-range planning (Reimann, 1974).

9. Administrative ratio—ratio of number of line supervisors, managers, and staff personnel to the total of employees (Reimann, 1974).

10. Professionalization—involves both structural and attitudinal dimensions. The structural dimension incorporates:
    (a) creation of full-time occupation, (b) establishment of a training school, (c) formation of professional associates, (d) formation of a code of ethics. The attitudinal dimension involves: (a) use of the professional organization as a major reference, (b) belief in service to the public, (c) belief in self-regulation, (d) sense of calling to the field, (e) autonomy (Hall, 1968).

11. Structuring of activities—degree to which the intended behavior of employees is overtly defined by task specialization, standard routines, and formal paper work (Pugh et al., 1969).

12. Line control of workflow—degree to which control is exercised by line personnel instead of through impersonal procedures (Pugh et al., 1969).

289

13. Specialization—(complexity) number of occupational specialties (Aiken & Hage, 1971; Hage, 1965; Reimann, 1974).

   —degree to which highly specialized requirements are spelled out in formal job descriptions for various functions (Reimann, 1974).

14. Stratification—difference in rewards between jobs and the relative rates of mobility between them (Hage, 1965).

15. Autonomy—extent to which management had to refer certain typical decisions to a higher level of authority.

16. Delegation of authority—ratio of number of specific management decisions the executive delegated to the number he had to make (Reimann 1974).

---

figure 2

PRESENT STRUCTURE MODEL

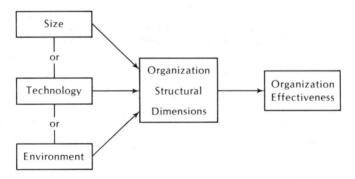

We have argued that the analysis of organization and environment must recognize the exercise of choice by organizational decision makers. . . . The critical link lies in the decision maker's evaluation of the organization's position in the environmental areas they regard as important, and in the action they may consequently take about its internal structure. (Child, 1972; p. 10)

Thus, Child implies that the introduction of strategic choice into the structural determination paradigm will substantially improve its predictive power.

Several issues, fundamental to further investigation of Child's construct, were not discussed in his treatise. First, what are the assumptions underlying his conceptualization? Child appears to assume a limited time perspective in this formulation. His model is only descriptive of the organization's initial formation or when *major* modifications in the firm's posture are being considered. In other time periods, once personnel are hired and capital

figure 3

ILLUSTRATION OF CHILD'S CONCEPTUALIZATION

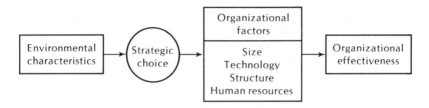

resources committed, the manager may be severely constrained with respect to his discretionary range for size and technology. Thus, in most situations the manager's structural choices are constrained by the firm's present size and technology in addition to the environment.

Child also assumes that the organization is sufficiently large in terms of assets and employees to allow size and technology changes. Barriers to entry into a new technology or market may appear insurmountable for a small firm. These same barriers present less of an obstacle for a larger organization. Lastly, a labor intensive technology is assumed in Child's model. The inertia characteristic of capital intensive technologies may not permit a major change in technology or size in the short term. This discussion of the assumptions implicit in Child's conceptualization of the strategic choice construct suggests that, in most time periods, size and technology act to constrain the manager's range of discretion rather than being determined by strategic choice as Child proposes.

Secondly, Child develops the strategic choice concept but does not provide an operational definition that permits empirical investigation; that is, if managerial discretion is the primary structural determinant, then how does it operate? How is it manifested in decisions and measured for research purposes?

Anderson and Paine (1975) provide partial answers to these questions in their perceptually based strategy model. These authors postulate that response patterns of policy makers affect several "strategic properties" including organization form (structure). Response patterns of policy makers are influenced by their perceptions of uncertainty in the environment and their perceived need for internal change. In actuality, however, only when environmental conditions are perceived as problematic do they encourage structural responses by the executive. If the existing structure is judged to be adequate for the present business situation, then the manager will not engage in structural modification. Therefore, strategic choice is operationally defined here as the manager's predisposition to use structural modification to solve organizational problems.

A question regarding the imperative status of strategic choice naturally precipitates from this discussion. Is Child's construct a fourth imperative as he appears to imply? Current research does not support the imperative perspective in general. A recent study (Montanari, 1976) indicates a codeterminant role for contextual and managerial discretion factors. The primary predictor of structure was found to vary as a function of the structure dimension being analyzed. For three dimensions (specialization, formalization, and autonomy) managerial discretion emerged as the dominant predictor. Size exclusively determined the vertical span dimension. Technology moderated the determinant/structure relationship for centralization, delegation of authority, and hierarchical control; that is, for one technology type a contextual factor predicted structure, whereas discretionary factors determined structure for the remaining technology types. Based on results of this study, the imperative perspective of structural determination should be superseded by a contingency oriented view.

A CONTINGENCY THEORY

The development of a novel structural determination theory will contribute to our present knowledge base only if it is theoretically sound and empirically testable. This requires that it build on existing theory and research and be formulated in a manner that can be investigated using current research methodology. It is believed that the theory herein developed fulfills these criteria.

The contingency theory of structural determination proposed here states that whether contextual or managerial factors predict structure depends on the technology used and the structural dimension in question. Consistent with past theory, appropriate structure design is hypothesized to result in superior organization performance. An illustration of the model evolving from this theory statement is shown in Figure 4. It meets the requirements of a contingency model in that relationships proposed are conditional with respect to technology type and structural dimension. This model is not proposed as a comprehensive representation of the decision process used to design an organization's structure. Factors such as the organization's stated objectives and traditional management styles also influence a firm's structural makeup. Rather, the theory discussed here is intended to extend current structural determination theories to include managerial influences and encourage future empirical investigation.

Contextual Factors

Contextual factors shown as causal are consistent with past theory and research. Aston research previously reviewed provides strong support for the importance of size in explaining the variability in organization structures. Montanari (1976) reports results of an empirical study in which size was the dominant predictor of the vertical span structure dimension. Size alone explained between 50 percent and 59 percent of the vertical span variance in firms surveyed. Size also emerged as a primary predictor for three other dimensions, but technology moderated these relationships.

Environmental uncertainty has been the focus of much current research. The work of Reimann, Negandhi, and Montanari (Negandhi & Reimann, 1973; Reimann, 1975; Montanari, 1976) provide substantial evidence of the central role of the environment in determining the level of centralization present in the firm. However, this contextual factor failed to display dominance for any other structural dimension. The strength of the environment/centralization relationship demands its inclusion here.

Managerial Factors

Child's strategic choice construct was discussed in detail in a preceding section of this study. Strategic choice was defined as the manager's predisposition to use structural modification to solve organizational problems. However, two other managerial factors also influence the ultimate structural design of the organization. First, managers must perceive that their power positions within the firm are strong enough to attach a high subjective probability to the implementation of their structural preferences. If this is not the case, then these managers would not actively promote their recommendations. Secondly, Lawrence and Lorsch (1967) report that the executive's functional orientation (department) exerts a strong influence on structural characteristics. Task requirements and traditional work methods dictate that research and development units display less rigid, formalized structures. Conversely, production units can benefit from more standardized job descriptions and less autonomy.

Contextual and managerial factors are presented as codeterminants of structure. Limited research (Gomolka & Alutto, 1974; Montanari, 1976) supports this formulation. The relationship between these factors has received very little attention in organization theory literature. Child (1972) proposes that environmental demands determine the manager's strategic choice. It is also conceivable that other intrapersonal factors—for example, manager's cultural background, education, previous experience, and so on—influence the manager's perceptions of environmental conditions. This possible dual interaction of causal factors is represented by a dashed-double-headed arrow in Figure 4.

Moderating Factors

As previously discussed, the direct determinant role of technology has generally not been supported subsequent to Woodward's (1958, 1965) research. Hickson et al. (1969) imply a moderating effect for technology. Their data suggests that the proportion of the organization unit's functions that are workflow centered effects the strength of the size/structure rela-

figure 4

A CONTINGENCY MODEL

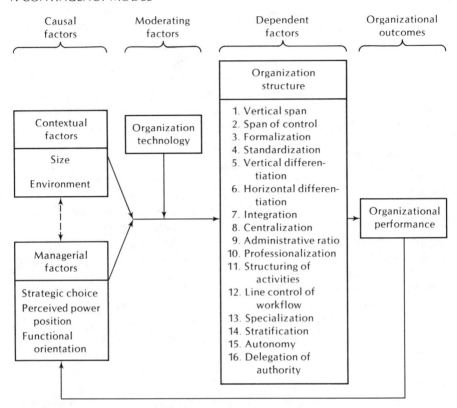

Causal factors   Moderating factors   Dependent factors   Organizational outcomes

Contextual factors

Size

Environment

Managerial factors

Strategic choice
Perceived power position
Functional orientation

Organization technology

Organization structure

1. Vertical span
2. Span of control
3. Formalization
4. Standardization
5. Vertical differentiation
6. Horizontal differentiation
7. Integration
8. Centralization
9. Administrative ratio
10. Professionalization
11. Structuring of activities
12. Line control of workflow
13. Specialization
14. Stratification
15. Autonomy
16. Delegation of authority

Organizational performance

tionship.[1] Also, Holdaway et al. (1975) could not replicate Aston results obtained on primarily manufacturing firms in an educational setting. Lastly, Montanari (1976) directly tested the moderating influences of technology. Results were supportive of a moderating role for technology for three of the seven structure dimensions investigated.

Dependent Factors

Sixteen structure dimensions appearing most frequently in the literature are defined in Figure 1 and delineated in Figure 4. The contingency theory hypothesizes that the causal factor mix and the strength of relationships depend on which dimension is being considered. In addition, the moderating effect of technology is present for some dimensions and not others.

Decisions on the structural configuration of the organization unit are not

[1]This is a different interpretation of the Hickson et al. results than proposed by the authors. Their use of correlational analysis and recent research evidence suggests that this interpretation is more feasible.

the only issues of strategic importance to the firm that are subject to contextual and managerial influences. Market and product expansion opportunities are constrained or enhanced by the size of the firm and conditions in its environment. Another example is the level of organizational resources expended for nonprofit socially responsible projects. This decision is greatly influenced by consumer attitudes (environment) and the executive's personal value set (manager's predispositions). One could point to many other strategic decision areas that are influenced by both contextual and managerial factors, but the focus of this paper is on structural determination. The point to be made here is that the contingency model is flexible enough to accommodate the interactive effects of management and context on several decision areas.

Organization Performance

Structural determination theory and research is legitimated, in a practical sense, by its impact on organizational performance. The executive continually strives to adapt his organization to current business conditions. The relevancy of these conditions to organizational success can best be analyzed by expressing them in terms of the firm's constituency. This constituency is composed of several diverse special interest groups—for example, customers, employees, stockholders, and society in general.

An organization's effectiveness is measured in terms of the favorableness of constituency behavior. The marketing effort is successful if sales meet or exceed expectations (customers). The production function contributes to overall organizational effectiveness if efficiency objectives are achieved (employees and suppliers). The availability of equity capital is dependent, to a great extent, on stock market behavior (stockholders). Lastly, the organization is compelled to operate under the laws of the host country. If society, as represented by government, imposes excessive regulations on the firm, then its effectiveness and survival may be jeopardized.

Strategic choices of the executive are formed in part by past experiences. A structural modification that resulted in improved performance is remembered and repeated. If a change is unsuccessful another structural design will be forthcoming. Also, the manager's perceptions of his or her power among colleagues is enhanced by past structural successes. The prudent manager learns from experience, and experience is measured in terms of the efficacy of past decisions. This supports the presence of a feedback loop from performance to managerial factors in Figure 4.

PAST, PRESENT, AND FUTURE

In sum, organization theory literature postulates the three contextual factors of size, technology, or environment as exclusive determinants of organization structure. These imperative models have been able to explain approximately half of the variability in organization structures. John Child (1972) proposed that managerial discretion (strategic choice) would account for a substantial amount of the unexplained variance. Child, however, failed to provide an operationalization of his concept. This report refines and expands the strategic choice construct. Furthermore, a contingency theory of structural determination is developed and discussed.

The contingency theory presented here was generated on the basis of two criteria. Strengths of prior studies were incorporated where feasible. This provides a sound methodological base for research on the contingency model. In addition, relationships were stated in unambiguous terms and operational definitions provided to facilitate future research. Thus, a firm theoretical foundation has been laid for empirical research on the contingency theory of structural determination. There remains only for organization theory researchers to accept the challenge and design empirical studies to validate the paradigm presented here.

BIBLIOGRAPHY

1. AIKEN, MICHAEL, and HAGE, JERALD. "The Organic Organization and Innovation." *Sociology* 5 (1971): 63–82.
2. ALDRICH, HOWARD E. "Technology and Organization Structure: A Re-examination of the Findings of the Aston Group." *Administrative Science Quarterly*, vol. 17, no. 1 (March 1972): 26–43.
3. ANDERSON, CARL R., and PAINE, F. T. "Managerial Perceptions and Strategic Behavior." *Academy of Management Journal*, vol. 18, no. 4 (1975): 811–23.
4. BLAU, PETER M.; FALBE, C. M.; MCKINLEY, W.; and TRACY, P. K. "Technology and Organization in Manufacturing." *Administrative Science Quarterly* 21 (1976): 20–40.
5. CHANDLER, ALFRED D. *Strategy and Structure.* Cambridge, Mass.: The M.I.T. Press, 1962.
6. CHILD, JOHN. "Organization Structure, Environment and Performance: The Role of Strategic Choice." *Sociology* 6 (1972): 1–22.
7. CHILD, JOHN, and MANSFIELD, R. "Technology, Size and Organization Structure." *Sociology* 6 (1972): 369–93.
8. DUNCAN, R. B. "Characteristics of Organizational Environments and Perceived Environmental Uncertainty." *Administrative Science Quarterly*, vol. 17, no. 3 (1972): 313-27.
9. GOMOLKA, EUGENE G., and ALUTTO, J. A. "Personality and Organizational Structure: An Empirical Investigation." Unpublished Working Paper, #183, presented at the Eastern Academy of Management Meeting, College Park, Maryland, May 1974.
10. EVERS, FREDERICK T.; BOHLEN, J. M.; and WARREN, R. D. "The Relationships of Selected Size and Structure Indicators in Economic Organizations." *Administrative Science Quarterly*, vol. 21, no. 2 (1976): 326.

11. HAGE, JERALD. "An Axiomatic Theory of Organizations." *Administrative Science Quarterly* 10 (1965): 289–320.

12. HALL, RICHARD. "Professionalization and Bureaucratization." *American Sociological Review* 33 (1968): 92–104.

13. HICKSON, DAVID; PUGH, D. S.; and PHEYSEY, D. C. "Operations Technology and Organization Structure: An Empirical Reappraisal." *Administrative Science Quarterly,* vol. 14, no. 3 (1969): 378–98.

14. HOLDAWAY, EDWARD A.; NEWBERRY, J. F.; HICKSON, D. J.; and HERON, R. P. "Dimensions of Organizations in Complex Societies: The Educational Sector." *Administrative Science Quarterly* 20 (1975): 37–58.

15. INKSON, J. H.; PUGH, D. S.; and HICKSON, D. J. "Organization Context and Structure: An Abbreviated Replication." *Administrative Science Quarterly* 15 (1970): 318–29.

16. JURKOVICH, RAY. "A Core Typology of Organization Environments." *Administrative Science Quarterly,* vol. 19, no. 4 (1974): 380–94.

17. KELLER, ROBERT T.; SLOCUM, J.W. JR.; and SUSMAN, G.T. "Uncertainty and Type of Management System in Continuous Process Organizations." *Academy of Management Journal,* vol. 17, no. 1 (1974) 56–68.

18. KHANDWALLA, PRADIP N. "Mass Output Orientation of Operations Technology and Organization Structure." *Administrative Science Quarterly,* vol. 19, no. 3 (September 1974): 74–97.

19. LAWRENCE, PAUL R., and LORSCH, J. W. *Organization and Environment.* Homewood, Ill.: Irwin, 1967.

20. MINDLIN, SERGIO E., and ALDRICH, H. "Interorganizational Dependence: A Review of the Concept and Reexamination of the Findings of the Aston Group." *Administrative Science Quarterly* 20 (1975): 382–92.

21. MONTANARI, JOHN R. "An Expanded Theory of Structural Determination: An Empirical Investigation of the Impact of Managerial Discretion on Organization Structure." Unpublished D.B.A. Dissertation, University of Colorado, Boulder, Colorado, 1976.

22. NEGANDHI, ANANT R. and REIMANN, B. C. "Correlates of Decentralization: Closed and Open Systems Perspectives." *Academy of Management Journal,* vol. 16, no. 4, (1973): 570–82.

23. OUCHI, WILLIAM G., and DOWLING, J. B. "Defining the Span of Control." *Administrative Science Quarterly,* 19 (1974): 357–65.

24. PERROW, CHARLES. *Organizational Analysis: A Sociological View.* Belmont, Calif.: Wadsworth, 1970.

25. PUGH, D. S.; HICKSON, D. J.; HININGS, C. R.; and TURNER, C. "The Context of Organizations." *Administrative Science Quarterly,* vol 14, no. 1 (March 1969): 91–114.

26. PUGH, D. S. "The Management of Organization Structures: Does Context Determine Form." *Organizational Dynamics* (Spring 1973): 19–34.

27. REIMANN, BERNARD C. "Dimensions of Structure in Effective Organizations: Some Empirical Evidence." *Academy of Management Journal,* 17 (1974): 693–708.

28. REIMANN, BERNARD C. "Task Environment and Decentralization: A Cross National Replication." *Human Relations,* vol. 27, no. 7 (1975): 677–95.

29. THOMPSON, JAMES D. *Organizations in Action.* New York: McGraw-Hill, 1967.

30. WOODWARD, JOAN. *Management and Technology.* London: Her Majesty's Stationery Office, 1958.

31. WOODWARD, JOAN. *Industrial Organization: Theory and Practice.* London: Oxford University Press, 1965.

ON THE NATURE, FORMATION, AND MAINTENANCE OF RELATIONS AMONG ORGANIZATIONS

ANDREW H. VAN DE VEN

How does one understand, quantify, and examine relationships among two or more organizations linked together as an action system to solve complex problems or attain joint goals? What factors are important for explaining how and why these action systems voluntarily develop and are maintained over time? This article attempts to answer these questions for practical and theoretical reasons. The questions are of particular interest to public-sector organizations and officials attempting to mobilize coordinated action among local human service organizations for coping with health, welfare, manpower, and other social problems too complex for any one agency to solve by itself. The premise is that many complex problems of a community can be dealt with effectively (however defined) through joint inter-agency planning and programming, because the resources and expertise needed to cope with the problems are contained within autonomous organizations and vested interest groups.

While this article does not question this important premise, it does *propose a theory for explaining how and why relationships among two or more human service organizations voluntarily emerge, and how they function over time.* Little is objectively known about this more limited set of issues. Knowledge of the inter-organizational field is still at a primitive stage (42).[1] No generally accepted framework, theory, or methods have emerged from research or practice. Therefore, the main attempt of this article is to build a partial foundation for studying inter-organizational relationships (IR). The article (a) suggests a framework for viewing an IR as a social action system, (b) operationally defines its dimensions in terms of structure, process, and ends, and (c) presents a theory to describe how and why IRs develop and are maintained over time.

THEORETICAL FRAMEWORK

An inter-organizational relationship (IR) occurs when two or more organizations transact resources (money, physical facilities and materials, customer or client referrals, technical staff services) among each other. An IR can be temporary or long-lasting. Although the nature of this relationship and the behavior of organizations within it can be examined from a number of

[1]Numbers refer to the bibliography at the end of the article. [*Editors.*]

Source: Academy of Management Review 1 (October 1976):24-36. Reprinted by permission.

perspectives (3, 31, 39), a useful relationship can be conceptualized between two or more organizations as a *social action system*. An IR is defined as a social action system on the premise that it exhibits the basic elements of any organized form of collective behavior.

1. Behavior among members is aimed at attaining collective and self-interest goals.
2. Interdependent processes emerge through division of tasks and functions among members.
3. An IR can act as a unit and has a unique identity separate from its members.

When two or more organizations become involved in a relationship, they create a social system. The actions of the organizational parties are interdependent, and over time, member organizations or their representatives take on specialized roles and develop behavioral expectations of each other regarding the rights and obligations of membership in the IR (19). Clark suggests that two or more agencies bind themselves together by performing specialized activities to attain an objective for a limited period of time, often by the terms of a contract (6, p. 234).

The end objective of organizations involved in an IR is the attainment of goals that are unachievable by organizations independently. For example, Litwak and Hylton (24) and Levine and White (23) suggest reasons for human service organizations to join together: (a) to establish a clearinghouse for client referrals, (b) to promote areas of common interest, (c) to jointly obtain and allocate a greater amount of resources than would be possible by each agency independently and (d) to adjudicate areas of dispute or competition. Warren, et al. (43) describe the more frequent occurrence of a single organization that sets out to pursue some objective which it cannot achieve by itself. It initiates contacts with other organizations to secure help; if successful, these contacts result in formation of a pair-wise relationship, usually short-term and ad hoc.

The social structure among organizations in a social action system is such that the system can act as a *unit*. This implies that many activities in an IR cannot be explained simply by analyzing the behavior of member organizations. Collective events arise out of the actions of the social system and are formally a property of the IR itself (9). Warren, et al. observe that:

> one can describe and analyze as a single system of inter-action any group of organizations whose properties may differ from those of the interacting organizations themselves and cannot be reduced to properties of these individual organizations (42, pp. 54–55).

To attain its goals as a unit, a social action system adopts a structure and process for organizing member activities. *Structure* refers to administrative arrangements established to define the role relationships among members.

Process, conceptualized as a flow of activities, refers to the direction and frequency of resources and information flowing between members. Thus, the structure and process of an IR is the "organizational form" for inter-organizational collaboration. Since an IR exhibits the basic elements common to any organized form of collective behavior, the analytic dimensions commonly used to measure social structure and process should also apply to an IR.

Structural Dimensions of an IR

There is a growing consensus among organization theorists that formalization, complexity, and centralization capture the major dimensions of social structure (38). While these dimensions have been used extensively to define and measure intra-organizational structure, the contribution is to generalize and operationalize them so they can be used to study IRs.

Formalization is the degree to which rules, policies and procedures govern the inter-agency *agreement* and *contacts* (25). An inter-agency agreement exists if any form of expression has been made between the parties regarding the terms of their relationship. Its formalization increases as the agreement is verbalized, written down, contractual, and mandatory. Two indicators of the formalization of inter-agency contacts are the extent to which rules, policies, and procedures are established to transact activities between parties, and the extent of procedures (e.g., agendas, minutes, etc.) followed by a committee or group that governs the IR.

Centralization refers to the locus of decision making in a collectivity. The degree of hierarchy of authority is the conventional measure of centralization within organizations (4, 15, 16). However, Litwak and Hylton point out that intra-organization analysis departs from inter-organization analysis in that the latter stresses the study of social behavior among autonomous agencies under conditions of non-hierarchical authority (24, p. 396). Clark (8) suggests that studies of interorganizational decision making should first determine: "Who governs, when, where, and with what effects?" and Rossi (32) asks: "Who influences what?"

Warren's concept of "concerted decision making" over time appears useful for examining the locus of decision making in an IR (41, pp. 148–167). He begins with the observation that individual organizations in an inter-agency relationship will continue to maximize their self-interests, but certain aspects of decision making are pooled.

> What earlier were individual agency decisions now become inclusive decisions; which itself constitutes an enterprise (the IR) with its own system of differentiated roles and task and maintenance functions. Initially the structure of inclusive decision making is customarily very weak, with a minimum of authority, a high salience for self-orientation among parties, and a consequent difficulty in making concerted decisions that are not in accord with the self-

interests of all the parties. As the inclusive organization (the IR) grows in strength in relation to its members, it begins to take on the characteristics of a formal organization. To the extent that it does so, the organizational model for concerted decision making, as developed in administrative theory, becomes increasingly relevant (41, p. 166).

The centralization of an IR is defined as the degree of inclusive or concerted decision making by member agency representatives. Concerted decisions are normally made by a committee or board of individuals representing member agencies. In this context centralization can be measured as the perceived degree of influence by these individuals in making decisions that are binding upon the member agencies.

The *structural complexity* of a collectivity refers to the number of differentiated elements that must be contended with and integrated in order for an IR to act as a unit. Two indicators measure the structural complexity of an IR: the number of organizations involved in the IR, and the number of different issues or tasks on which the IR is based.

Although size is often used as a predictor rather than an indicator of structural differentiation within organizations (4, 17), Litwak and Hylton (24) and Evan (11) have suggested that the number of organizations in an IR is an important indicator of the complexity of inter-agency relationships. The simplest form of IR is the dyad, where two organizations need only to consider each other in defining their roles and expectations. Following the deductive reasoning of Graicunas (13), arithmetic increases in the number of agencies involved in an IR are accompanied by exponential increases in the total number of possible contacts among agencies. Applying his formula, $C = n(2^n/2 + n - 1)$, an IR consisting of only $n = 5$ agencies may have to contend with a potential complexity of 100 different forms of contacts (C) among its members! The number of different issues or tasks on which relationships among organizations are based indicates IR functional differentiation. As the number of different projects, activities, and problems undertaken by an IR increases, the complexity of the relationship increases.

Process Dimensions of an IR

Most researchers studying IR have been more concerned with whether an actual flow of resources or activities occurred between agencies than whether a structural arrangement for coordination was established. This concern for the *process* of coordination is justified, because structural arrangements for coordination are often dismal failures in attaining tangible results. Warren and his associates (43) found that out of a total of 406 reports of structured coordination, only 125 instances of positive tangible results were obtained, and 29 of these were tautological references to improved communications. Thus, a study of an IR should also examine the dynamic activities that actually occur within it.

Flows of resources and information between organizations appear to be the major processes within an IR. *Resource flows* are the units of value transacted between agencies (such as money, physical facilities and materials, customer or client referrals, technical staff services). The major dimensions for measuring resource flows between agencies are their direction (20, 30, 35), intensity (2, 11, 25) and variability (18, 22). *Information flows* are messages or communications about the units of exchange or the nature of the relationship, transmitted between organizational parties through a variety of media (e.g., written reports and letters, phone calls, face-to-face discussions, group or committee meetings). The major dimensions for measuring information flows between agencies are their *direction* (2, 25) and *intensity* (22, 23, 42).

There are three reasons why resource and information flows are believed to be the major processes in an IR. First, resource and information flows are the basic elements of activity in organized forms of behavior. Without them a social action system would cease to exist; whatsoever remained would be relics of past behavior (38).

Second, systems theorists have emphasized the parallel functions of task instrumental and pattern-maintenance activities of collectivities (21, 27, 40). Task-instrumental functions are manifest in resource flows. Without some on-going transaction of resources, it is highly probable that one or more agencies will terminate their membership in an IR. The comment, "We coordinated but nothing happened" exemplifies this lack of task-instrumental concern. Maintenance functions are manifest in information flows between organizational parties in a relationship. In the absence of information flows necessary for maintaining and integrating resource flows, it is highly probable that one or more agencies will lose sight of their purpose for being and acting in an IR. As a result means and ends become inverted, and member agencies soon perceive the IR to be an aimless series of threatening and chaotic resource transactions.

Third, with resource and information flows one can examine process dynamics within an IR from two different perspectives: a single agency or the social action system as a whole. The more *intensively* or *frequently* a single organization transacts resources and communicates with other member agencies, the greater the strategic position or power of that agency in the IR. Conversely, the lower its frequency of resources and information flows with other agencies, behaviorally speaking, the more isolated is that agency. The *direction* of resources and information flows to and from an agency indicates the role it performs in the social action system. If more resources and messages flow from an agency than into it, the agency is a sender or director. Alternatively, if it receives more resources and communications than it sends, the agency is a receiver or follower.

For the IR as a whole, the *direction* of resources and information flows identifies the patterns of transactions among agencies. The intensity of resources and information flows indicates the degree of activity of the social action system; i.e., the strength of task-instrumental and maintenance activity in the IR. The *variability* of resource flows and the ratio of written communications to personal and group contacts are indicators of the degree of routinization of IR relationships. Moreover, by measuring the *intensity* and *direction* of inter-agency information and resource flows in complex IRs, one can identify and quantify coalitions that may differ in degrees of linkages, from tightly to loosely joined coalitions within the overall network (3).

SUMMARY

This framework for conceptualizing a relationship among two or more organizations as a social action system is based on the premise that an inter-organizational relationship exhibits the basic common properties of any form of organized collective behavior: behavior is aimed at a goal, interdependence exists between members, and it can act as a unit with an identity separate from its members. Operating from this premise, an IR can be studied by defining and quantifying its dimensions in terms of structure (formalization, centralization and complexity) process (direction and intensity of resource and information flows) and ends (perceived effectiveness of the inter-agency relationships).

A THEORY ON THE FORMATION AND
MAINTENANCE OF IRs

Returning to the questions which motivated this investigation—How and why do relationships among human service organizations voluntarily develop? How does an IR function, grow, adapt, and dissolve?—a theory or testable model on IR will now be developed.

Figure 1 summarizes the variables in the model. Five situational factors explain why and how inter-agency relationships develop. The model hypothesizes that variations in the structure and process of a network can be largely explained by five situational factors. Over time, feedback on perceived effectiveness is expected to influence the other variables in the model. Definitions and justifications for the variables in Figure 1 are discussed and overall hypotheses about their inter-relations developed. Figure 2 presents the basic assumptions or premises used to explain how and why an IR emerges and functions. These assumptions provide the arguments for hypotheses to be tested.

Why and How Do IRs Emerge?

Organizations do not coordinate for coordination's sake. Instead, organizations strain to maintain their autonomy (12) (assumption A). Autonomy means that organizations are capable of choosing the course of action they desire to pursue (7, 23). From an agency's point of view, to become involved in an inter-agency relationship implies (a) that it loses some of its freedom to act independently, when it would prefer to maintain control over its domain and affairs, and (b) that it must invest scarce resources and energy to develop and maintain relationships with other organizations, when the potential returns on this investment are often unclear or intangible. For these reasons an agency prefers not to become involved in an IR unless it is compelled to do so.

figure 1

DIMENSIONS IN MODEL ON FORMATION AND MAINTENANCE OF IRs

Situational Factors
1. *Resource Dependence*
   Agency's need for external resources
   Agency's need for other agencies in the environment
2. *Commitment To Problem Issue or Opportunity*
   Perceived commitment to resolve environmental needs or realize opportunities
3. *Awareness*
   Knowledge of environmental needs, problems, or opportunities
   Knowledge of services and goals of other agencies
   Personal acquaintance of agency representatives
4. *Consensus*
   Agreement among agencies on solutions to environmental needs or problems
   Agreement on services and goals among agencies
   Conflict on means and ends
5. *Domain Similarity*
   Sameness of goals, services, staff skills, and clients of agencies

Process Dimensions
1. *Intensity of Resource Flows*
   Amount of resource flows among agencies
2. *Intensity of Information Flows*
   Frequency of communications among agencies

Structural Dimensions
1. *Formalization of IR*
   Of inter-agency agreements
   Of inter-agency contacts
2. *Centralization of IR*
   Extent inter-agency committee decisions are binding upon members
3. *Complexity of IR*
   Number of agencies in IR
   Number of projects and tasks undertaken by IR

Outcome Dimensions
1. *Perceived Effectiveness*
   Extent agencies carry out commitments and believe relationships are worthwhile, equitable, productive, and satisfying.

Two reasons appear sufficiently compelling for inter-agency activity to emerge: (a) *an internal need for resources* or (b) *a commitment to an external problem or opportunity* (assumption B). Generally, the first reason is generated internally within organizations to achieve their self interests, while the latter is externally stimulated with information about problems, needs or opportunities in the overlapping domains of organizations. The former is often a product of internal organizational planning and change;

figure 2

ASSUMPTIONS AND HYPOTHESES ABOUT THE EMERGENCE AND FUNCTIONING OF INTER-AGENCY RELATIONSHIPS

Assumptions

  A. Organizations strain to maintain their autonomy.
  B. Organizational needs for resources and/or commitment to an external problem or opportunity are the compelling reasons for IR emergence.
  C. Resource dependence or problem commitment, awareness, and consensus among parties are necessary conditions for IR emergence.
  D. Organizations maximize gains and minimize losses in becoming involved in IRs.
  E. Increases in the size of an IR and in the amount of resource flows between agencies increases problems of integration and pattern maintenance.
  F. IRs emerge incrementally and grow with successful previous encounters at coordination.

Hypotheses in Resource Dependence Model

  1. The greater the resource dependence, the greater the frequency of inter-agency communications.
  2. The greater the frequency of inter-agency communications, the greater the awareness of other agencies and the greater the consensus among parties.

Hypotheses in System Change Model

  3. The greater the frequency of inter-agency communications, the greater the awareness and commitment to environmental problems or opportunities.
  4. The greater the commitment to environmental problems or opportunities, the greater the consensus among agencies.

Hypotheses on Emergence and Structure of Inter-Agency Relationships

  5. The intensity of an IR is a function of resource dependence, awareness, issue commitment, and consensus.
  6. There is a concave ($\cap$ shaped) relationship between domain similarity and the intensity of an IR.
  7. The greater the number of agencies in an IR, the greater the formalization and centralization of the IR.
  8. The greater the resource intensity of an IR, the greater the formalization and centralization of the IR.
  9. The greater the perceived effectiveness of an IR at time 0, the greater the interdependence, and issue commitment among the agencies at time 1, over time periods 0, 1, 2, ... n.

---

and the latter arises from inter-organizational planning and change. While the former is more tangible and project oriented (43, p. 67), the latter is more diffuse and emerges out of an awareness of changing need priorities, resource distribution channels, or power relationships in the environment (10).

Thus, while resource dependence identifies the intra-organizational reason for IR, commitment to environmental problems emphasizes the larger inter-organizational field as a reason for IR (33). The relative importance of these reasons for IR differs by agency. Inter-organizational relationships are often a common product of diverse individual motivations. But to argue why either resource dependence or problem commitment is the compelling reason for IR to emerge, it is useful to treat each reason separately and to examine the different processes each entails. The processes set in motion by an agency's need for resources will be called the *resource dependence model,* while activities associated with an organization's commitment to external problems or opportunities will be called the *system change model.* Although the two models entail different assumptions and hypotheses, they become fused as one when predicting the overall emergence of IRs.

Resource Dependence Model

In varying degrees all organizations depend upon their environments (or other organizations) for personnel, information, monetary or physical resources, and clients, customers, or markets to attain their self-interest objectives (23). Guetzkow (14) notes that the roots of inter-agency activity are internal to each organization, while Aiken and Hage state that organizations are:

> pushed into such interdependencies because of their need for resources—not only money, but also resources such as specialized skills, access to particular kinds of markets, and the like (1, pp. 914–15).

If organizations were self-sustaining entities, there would be little need for inter-organization analysis (28, p. 161). Therefore it is hypothesized that the greater the resource dependence, the more organizations will engage in communications with other agencies which may lead to establishing a relationship. However, resource dependence alone is unlikely to result in the creation of an IR; also required are *awareness* and *consensus.*

Awareness—Organizations must be aware of possible sources in other agencies where their needed resources can be obtained; otherwise organizational directors are likely to conclude that the goal or need which motivates the search for resources cannot be attained. Alternatively, agencies may commit themselves to achieving goals within the limitations of their own resources. Awareness is therefore a second predictor of the formation of inter-agency relations (24, 44). Two levels of awareness appear particularly important in predicting inter-organizational activity.

At a general level is the extent to which agency boundary spanners are informed about the specific goals, services, and resources existing in other agencies. This level of awareness identifies the number of potential alternatives for obtaining needed resources (36). Because organizations attempt to minimize losses and maximize gains (assumption D), they will attempt to obtain needed resources from a number of agencies. This strategy reduces an organization's dependence on any given source (1, 23, 36); provides the opportunity to select the type of environment in which it will operate (5); and permits it to segment its sources and use unique tactics for coping with each source (34).

A more specific level of awareness is the degree of personal acquaintance between agency boundary spanners. Personal and business acquaintances between organizational coordinators become fused in the context of mobilizing inter-agency coordination (43). Boundary-spanning activity is often acted out during social, political, and recreational engagements (such as coffee breaks and luncheons). The greater the length of time and degree of intimacy in the personal relationships between organizational boundary spanners, the more similar their attitudes, values, and goals; the greater their mutual trust of one another; and as a result, the greater their predisposition to help one another out by committing their organizations to an IR.

Consensus refers to the degree to which an organization's specific goals and services are agreed upon by the parties (11). Domain consensus by organizations in a system is prerequisite to exchange (23, p. 599). Through informal communications and personal acquaintances with people in the community, organizations become aware of the services, goals, and resources of other agencies; with each setting out to sell the importance of its needs. Out of these interactions arise areas of common interest and quid pro quo compromises. The more successful each agency is in establishing awareness and consensus on the part of other agencies on joint and self-interest objectives, the greater the potential for IR to emerge. If agreement is not established or if severe conflict is encountered between the parties involved, negotiations probably will terminate and agency boundary spanners will look elsewhere to obtain needed resources.

The System Change Model

The system change model is well known to community organizers and planners (22). It is the normative externally induced model for community change often brought on with the infusion of money by a resource granting agency, or the redistribution of resource allocation channels (e.g., revenue sharing) in a target population or problem area. Information about this type of disruption, opportunity, or turbulence in the environment brought on by an external intervention sets the system change model in action. External intervention stimulates inter-agency communications, which in turn increase an organization's awareness of needs, problems, or opportunities in the environment of which it is a part. This awareness motivates organizational involvement and commitment because the environmental problems or opportunities exist in the legitimate but overlapping domains of member agencies, and because each agency will attempt to protect or enhance its domain (43, p. 44).

Although the causation is reversed, the logic in arguments for the resource dependence and system change models is basically the same. Inter-agency communications set in motion by resource dependence are *externally* directed from the organization to the environment, and the causation among variables moves from dependence to communications to awareness and to consensus. In the system change model, the inter-agency communications are *internally* directed from the environment into the organization, and causation among variables moves from communication to awareness to commitment to consensus. But in the system change model, the focus of inter-agency communications and awareness is on environmental issues, rather than intra-organizational issues, as in the resource dependence model.

At the point where consensus among the agencies is formed, the resource dependence and system change models become fused as one, to explain how and why an IR develops. The divergent motivations and objectives of agencies become fused through negotiations, bargaining and compromise, and consensus emerges on specific means and ends for joint collaboration. From the above discussion it follows that the formation of an IR is a function of resource dependence and/or commitment, awareness, and consensus.

What Kind of Agencies Will Be Joined in an IR?

Domain similarity is a qualitative indicator of the kinds of organizations likely to become jointly involved in a web of inter-relationships. Domain similarity refers to the extent to which organizations obtain their money from the same sources, have the same goals, have staff with the same professional skills, provide the same kind of services to the same clients or customers.

The evidence is conflicting on whether domain similarity helps or hinders the establishment of an IR. When agencies have similar domains in a community, they are likely to be aware of one another, and to have resources needed to help each other achieve individual goals. The greater the domain similarity, the greater the interdependence and the greater the extent and variability of exchanges (30). In this sense domain similarity facilitates IR. But similar domains also increase potential for territorial disputes and competition between agencies, thereby hindering the potential for IR to emerge (11). Over the range from low to high domain similarity, both facilitative and inhibitive processes are probably at play in different degrees. Specifically, a concave (∩ shaped) relationship between domain similarity and the amount of resource flows between agencies in an IR is hypothesized.

At the low extreme of domain similarity, organizations have nothing in common, and are likely not to be aware of one another, nor to have mutually desired resources; thus it is unlikely that an IR will emerge. At the high extreme of domain similarity, organizations are almost identical, and may either continue to co-exist in cut-throat competition which permits no transaction of resources between the agencies, or they may merge as a single organization (in which case the intra-organization level of analysis applies.) Thus, the polar ends of domain similarity are unlikely and unstable conditions for IR. Intermediate ranges of domain similarity appear to provide the most interesting and stable conditions, because in that range organizations have complementary resources, are likely to be aware of one another's interdependence, and are also likely to be involved in some competition and territorial disputes.

The Functioning of Inter-Agency Relationships

Given the existence of an IR, how does it function, grow, adapt, or dissolve over time? The last two assumptions in Figure 2 are the bases for dealing with this problem.

The defining criterion of an inter-agency relationship is the intensity of resource flows among agencies. Growth, adaptation, or dissolution of an IR can be directly monitored by observing variations in resource flows over time.

Increases in the amount of resource flows among agencies increase problems of integration and pattern maintenance of the IR (assumption E). An immediate response to the problem is to increase the frequency of communications between agencies through personal contacts and committee meetings. But personal contacts and committee meetings absorb much time and effort and are inefficient mechanisms for coordinating activities that can be standardized. Under norms of rationality, the IR coordinating committee will increase formalization by developing a set of policies and standardized reporting procedures for integrating and maintaining the higher level of resource flows. Through consent of organizational representatives on the committee, this decision binds the behavior of the members, thereby increasing centralization. Thus, the greater the intensity of an IR, the greater its formalization and centralization (hypothesis 8).

As the hypotheses in Figure 2 imply, the *timing* of activities and events is a key factor in understanding the emergence, adaptation, and growth of an IR. These processes do not occur quickly; inter-agency networks are more likely to emerge incrementally and grow with small, successful previous encounters at coordination (assumption F). The case study by O'Toole and his associates of the Cleveland Rehabilitation Complex is particularly insightful in its description of how IR occurs as a slow, flexible, developmental process with many small thrusts or activities around specific problems followed by periods to congeal new developments. O'Toole, et al. (26) emphasize that inter-agency relationships grow and build upon previous small, but successful, exchanges between agencies. Each agency is able to see coordination's positive aspects and to deal with its negative implications. Commitments and formalized arrangements are not developed prematurely, when the nature of commitment or involvement of agency participants is still unclear and provides no tangible indication of available direct benefits.

The emergence and functioning of an IR, therefore, is a cyclical process of: need for resources—issue commitments—inter-agency communications to spread awareness and consensus—resource transactions—and structural adaptation and pattern maintenance over time. What starts as an interim solution to a problem may eventually become a long-term inter-organizational commitment of resource transactions *if* previous cycles in the process are perceived by the parties to have been effective encounters. The perceived effectiveness of an IR refers to the extent to which the agencies subjectively believe that each party carries out its commitments and that the relationship is worthwhile, equitable, productive, and satisfying.

The greater the perceived effectiveness of network relationships at time 0, the greater the dependence, awareness, and consensus among the agencies at $t + 1$, over time periods $0, 1, 2, \ldots n$. An IR may also dissolve or terminate when the organizations have achieved their self-interest objectives and no longer depend upon other agency members for resources or the attainment of a joint goal, even though previous encounters were perceived as highly effective. Therefore, not all the variation in commitment or dependence in subsequent time periods is explained by the perceived effectiveness of an IR. But there is a tendency within organizations to adopt new goals, solve new problems, and market new products when previous goals have been attained, old problems solved, and old product lines terminated (e.g., the March of Dimes and other long-lasting enterprises and specially commissioned governmental agencies). As indicated by Terreberry (33), the analogous tendency is expected in IR. In the long run, historically successful IRs become meshed together in a web of interdependencies.

Conclusion and Research Directions

From the six assumptions in Figure 2, nine testable hypotheses were derived for explaining why and how inter-agency networks emerge, and how they adapt, grow, and dissolve. Additional hypotheses on the relations between variables can be deduced, but these hypotheses seem to capture the major dynamics in the emergence and maintenance of voluntary IRs.

If one adopts the perspective taken in this article, three steps appear necessary for collecting data on IRs. First, relevant organizations constituting the core system under investigation should be identified. In many large IRs, the total number of member agencies is so great that it seems wise not to study them all. Limited evaluation resources and manpower forbid it. Therefore, researchers will need to adopt decision rules for determining what agencies to include and exclude in a study of large IRs. A useful appendix in Warren, et al. (43) provides a starting point to identify criteria for a purposive sampling scheme. The objective is to select a broad variety of agencies which are representatives of the total population of agencies in an IR. To the extent that appropriate selection criteria have been developed, one can draw inferences from the sample of agencies to the population of agencies in the action system.

Second, the respondents in each agency who are most knowledgeable about their agency's relations with other organizations in the system should be identified. Aldrich (3) suggests that boundary spanners are the most appropriate informants about an agency's IRs. In complex organizations boundary spanning roles are differentiated, and seldom is one boundary spanner knowledgeable about all the different functions or activities inherent in one pair-wise inter-agency relationship, let alone the total cluster of relations maintained by the organization with all other agencies in the social action system.

For example, a relationship maintained by the Department of Public Welfare (DPW) with another agency often includes many functions (e.g., licensing, funding transactions, and technical assistance), and different boundary spanners within DPW are responsible for each function. Boundary spanning responsibilities in DPW with different agencies in an IR are often assigned to different people. The more complex the organization, the greater the number of informants required to measure accurately all of the roles of the organization with other agencies in the IR.

One approach to the problem is to ask the directors of each agency to nominate the individual most directly responsible for coordinating activities with each agency in the IR. Although the resulting list of informants creates a complex set of possibilities and combinations, it represents an attempt to identify the relevant actors in a realistically complex web of inter-agency relations.

Third, data should be collected by having each agency's informant(s) answer a set of questions about its pair-wise relations with each of the other agencies in the core system and about the overall functioning of the IR. With this kind of data collection strategy, one can systematically examine an IR at different levels of analysis. The smallest unit of analysis is the pair-wise relationship which can be obtained by matching and merging each agency's perceptions of the other. Because the dyad is the simplest form of a social action system, all the IR dimensions suggested here apply to the pair-wise relationship. Of course, some dimensions manifest in large IRs will be salient or emergent in dyadic relationships.

At higher levels of aggregation, dyadic relations can be grouped to permit a sociometric evaluation of the total cluster of pair-wise relations between agencies in the social action system. This article has suggested how a sociometric analysis of the flow of resources and information between agencies can provide insight into the functioning of IRs. Aldrich (2) and Van de Ven (37) have shown how network theory and matrix algebra are useful for quantifying sociometric patterns in an IR.

Finally, many activities in an IR cannot be explained simply by analyzing relationships between pairs or clusters of member agencies. Instead, many events are collective social facts which emerge out of the actions of the IR as a unit (9, 42). Therefore, a study of IRs should also examine dimensions of the overall structure and functioning of the social action system.

REFERENCES

1. AIKEN, MICHAEL, and JERALD HAGE. "Organizational Interdependence and Intra-Organizational Structure." *American Sociological Review* 33 (December 1968): 912–30.

2. ALDRICH, HOWARD. "An Organization-Environment Perspective on Cooperation and Conflict Between Organizations in the Manpower Training System." Paper presented at Comparative Administration Research Institute Conference, Kent State University, Kent, Ohio, 1972.

3. ALDRICH, HOWARD. "Organization Sets, Action Sets, and Networks: Making the Most of Simplicity," in W. Starbuck (ed.), *Handbook of Organization Design*, Vol. 1, in draft stage.

4. BLAU, PETER. *On the Nature of Organizations* (New York: Wiley and Sons, 1974).

5. CHILD, JOHN. "Organizational Structure, Environment and Performance: The Role of Strategic Choice." *Sociology* 6 (1972): 1–22.

6. CLARK, BURTON. "Interorganizational Patterns in Education." *Administrative Science Quarterly* 10 (September 1965): 224–37.

7. CLARK, PETER, and JAMES WILSON. "Incentive Systems: A Theory of Organizations." *Administrative Science Quarterly* 6 (September 1961): 129–66.

8. CLARK, TERRY. "Community Structure, Decision-Making, Budget Expenditures and Urban Renewal in 51 American Communities." *American Sociological Review* 33 (1968): 546–93.

9. DURKHEIM, EMILE. *The Division of Labor in Society* (Glencoe: The Free Press, 1947).

10. EMERY, F. E., and E. L. TRIST. "The Causal Texture of Organizational Environments," *17th International Congress of Psychology*, Washington, D.C. August, 1965.

11. EVAN, WILLIAM. "The Organization Set: Toward A Theory of Inter-organizational Relations," In James Thompson (Ed.), *Approaches to Organizational Design* (1966).

12. GOULDNER, ALVIN. "Reciprocity and Autonomy in Functional Theory," in Llewellyn Gross (Ed.), *Symposium on Sociological Theory* (1959), pp. 241-70.
13. GRAICUNAS, V. A. "Relationship in Organization," in L. Gulick and L. Urwick (Eds.), *Papers on the Science of Administration* (New York Institute of Public Administration, 1937).
14. GUETZKOW, HAROLD. "Relations Among Organizations," in R. V. Bowers (Ed.), *Studies in Behavior in Organizations* (1966), pp. 13-44.
15. HAGE, JERALD. "Axiomatic Theory of Organizations." *Administrative Science Quarterly* 10 (1965): 289-320.
16. HALL, RICHARD H. "Intra-organizational Structural Variation: Application of a Bureaucrative Model." *Administrative Science Quarterly* 7 (December 1962).
17. HALL, RICHARD H. *Organizations, Structure and Process* (Englewood Cliffs, N.J.: Prentice-Hall, 1972).
18. HALL, RICHARD H., and JOHN P. CLARK. "Problems in the Study of Inter-organizational Relationship," in A. Negandhi (Ed.), Comparative Administration Research Institute, Center for Business and Economic Research, Kent State University, Kent, Ohio, 1973, pp. 45-60.
19. HOMANS, GEORGE. *The Human Group* (New York: Harcourt, Brace, and World, 1950).
20. JOHNS, RAY, and DAVID DEMARCHE. *Community Organization and Agency Responsibility* (New York: Associated Press, 1957).
21. KATZ, DANIEL, and ROBERT L. KAHN. *The Social Psychology of Organizations* (New York: John Wiley & Sons, 1966).
22. KLONGLAN, GERALD E., RICHARD D. WARREN, and JUDY M. WINKELPLECK. "Inter-Organizational Measurement Differences Between Hierarchial Levels of Organizations." Paper presented at Rural Sociological Society Meeting, College Park, Maryland, March 30, 1973.
23. LEVINE, SOL, and PAUL E. WHITE. "Exchange as a Conceptual Framework for the Study of Interorganizational Relationships." *Administrative Science Quarterly* 5 (1961): 583-601.
24. LITWAK, EUGENE, and LYDIA F. HYLTON. "Interorganizational Analysis: A Hypothesis on Coordinating Agencies." *Administrative Science Quarterly* 6 (1962): 395-420.
25. MARRETT, CORA BAGLEY. "On the Specifications of Interorganizations Dimensions." *Sociology and Social Research,* 56 (October 1971): 83-99.
26. O'TOOLE, R., et al. *The Cleveland Rehabilitation Complex: A Study of Interagency Coordination* (Cleveland, Ohio: Vocational Guidance and Rehabilitation Services, 1972).
27. PARSONS, TALCOTT. *Structure and Process in Modern Societies* (New York: The Free Press, 1960).
28. PERLMAN, ROBERT, and ARNOLD GURIN. *Community Organization and Social Planning* (New York: John Wiley & Sons, 1972).
29. PUGH, D. S., et al. "A Concept Scheme for Organizational Analysis." *Administrative Science Quarterly* 8 (1963): 389-416.
30. REID, WILLIAM. "Inter-agency Coordination in Delinquency Prevention and Control." *Social Service Review* 38 (1964):418-28.

31. REIKER, PATRICIA, JOSEPH MORRISSEY, and PATRICK HORAN. "Interorganizational Relations: A Critique of Theory and Method." Prepared for an Organizations Day Round-Table Presentation at the American Sociological Association, Montreal, Canada, August 1974.

32. ROSSI, PETER. "Community Decision Making." *Administrative Science Quarterly* 1 (March 1957): 415-43.

33. TERREBERRY, SHIRLEY. "The Evolution of Organizational Environments." *Administrative Science Quarterly* 12 (March 1968): 509-613.

34. THOMPSON, JAMES D. *Organizations in Action* (New York: McGraw-Hill, 1967).

35. THOMPSON, JAMES D., and W. J. McEWEN. "Organizational Goals and Environment: Goal-Setting As An Interaction Process." *American Sociological Review* XXIII: 23-31.

36. TURK, HERMAN. "Comparative Urban Structure From an Interorganizational Perspective." *Administrative Science Quarterly* 19 (March 1973): 37-55.

37. VAN DE VEN, ANDREW H. "A Design for Studying Inter-Organizational Networks." Paper presented at American Sociological Association 79th Annual Conference, San Francisco, August, 1975.

38. VAN DE VEN, ANDREW H. "A Framework for Organization Assessment." *Academy of Management Review,* vol. 1, no. 1 (January 1976): 64-78.

39. VAN DE VEN, ANDREW M., DENNIS EMMETT, and RICHARD KOENIG, JR. "Frameworks For Inter-organizational Analysis." *Organization and Administrative Sciences Journal,* vol. 5, no. 1 (Spring 1974): 113-29.

40. VON BERTALANFFY, LUDWIG. "The History and Status of General Systems Theory." *Academy of Management Journal,* vol. 15, no. 4 (December 1972): 407-26.

41. WARREN, ROLAND. *Truth, Love and Social Change* (Chicago: Rand McNally, 1973).

42. WARREN, ROLAND, ANN BERGUNDER, J. W. NEWTON, and STEPHEN ROSE. "The Interactions of Community Decision Organizations: Some Conceptual Considerations and Empirical Findings," in A. Negandhi (Ed.), *Organization Theory in an Inter-organizational Perspective* (Kent, Ohio: Comparative Administration Research Institute, Kent State University, 1971), pp. 35-52.

43. WARREN, ROLAND, STEPHEN M. ROSE, and ANN F. BERGUNDER. *The Structure of Urban Reform* (Toronto: D.C. Heath, 1974).

44. WHITE, PAUL, SOL LEVINE, and GEORGE VLASEK. "Exchange As a Conceptual Framework for Understanding Inter-Organizational Relationships: Applications to Non-Profit Organizations." Paper presented at the Comparative Administrative Research Institute Conference, Kent State University, 1971.

section four

At this point in our exploration of organizations, we might consider how they have managed to stay around as long as they have. Certain specific examples of organizational longevity go back hundreds of years. It seems reasonable to assume that those having survived not only met their own goals (which generally include *survival* either explicitly or implicitly) but met some of society's goals as well. But there is more to surviving than simply meeting goals. Organizational operations must have been within the bounds of effectiveness and efficiency to survive.

Chapter 10 considers the twin topics of goals and effectiveness. It's difficult to consider the two apart, but to avoid circular reasoning (effectiveness is the attainment of goals, goals can only be attained if the organization is effective), we will propose some additional bases for viewing effectiveness in organizations.

Chapter 11 deals with survival and change in organizations. The ability or lack of it to change often determines whether or not an organization will survive in a dynamic environment.

The objective for this section is to answer the general question: What is required for an organization to survive?

ORGANIZATIONAL
CONTINUITY

chapter 10

ORGANIZATIONAL
GOALS
AND EFFECTIVENESS

The twin topics of *goals* and *effectiveness* are treated together here because organizations usually rely on how well goals have been met to determine how effective they have been. Furthermore, managers tend to think and talk in terms of goals and goal achievement for their organizations.

Effectiveness is a topic that managers and administrators in all organizations are concerned with to some extent. Yet despite its importance the characteristics of an effective organization are neither universally recognized nor always readily apparent. Fortunately, a growing body of knowledge about effectiveness in organizations is being developed to provide guidance for managers and administrators. In this chapter we will attempt to help you understand effectiveness in organizations or in specific units or programs housed in organizations. Some of the concepts have come from nonprofit-oriented organizations where a special set of problems exist in measuring effectiveness.

Effective organizational performance has a direct bearing on the well-being of society since organizations both take from and return to the society certain products or services. Furthermore, for a good quality of life, society requires effective organizations to provide goods and services. In fact, society may try to achieve many of its goals through its organizational subsystems—for example, equal employment opportunity. Organizations can exercise a good deal of leverage in such areas, and the behavior of organizations can be more easily policed by society than the behavior of individuals.

It is important to make a distinction between the concepts of effectiveness and efficiency. Although the words are related, there are some important differences. Organizations can be effective but highly inefficient or highly efficient but ineffective. Effectiveness is commonly referred to as the degree to which predetermined goals are achieved, whereas efficiency refers to the "economical manner" in which goal-oriented operations are carried out, something of an input/output ratio.

An organization must be able to achieve its objectives or goals within the constraints of limited resources, since none of the resources provided by an organization's environment are truly unlimited. The level of output an organization achieves with its limited resources determines its *efficiency*, and the extent to which it is successful in doing what it set out to do determines its *effectiveness*.

Disagreements over the definition of effectiveness arise from the fact that organizations and the people that run them often have *multiple* and *conflicting* goals. Even the definition of the organization's goals may be subject to differing viewpoints: those of society, client groups, employees, or managers, to name but a few. If agreement cannot be reached on goals, agreement on effectiveness (at least as measured by goal attainment) is impossible.

THE GOAL, COMPARATIVE, AND SYSTEMS APPROACHES TO EFFECTIVENESS

We will place views of organizational effectiveness into one of three categories: goals, comparative, or systems approaches. First, in the goals approach one can compare stated goals and objectives with the actual *attainment* of those goals and objectives. This is the traditional and typical view of effectiveness. It suffers from the problems suggested above (whose goal and who's going to do the measuring?).

An organization's goal accomplishment is a necessary condition for effective performance with the goal approach. The basic *activities* in which all organizations must engage help determine what organizational goals might be, therefore what performance must be, and therefore, effectiveness. These activities can be roughly classified as follows:

1. Acquiring resources
2. Making efficient use of inputs relative to outputs
3. Producing outputs of services or goods
4. Performing technical and administrative tasks rationally
5. Investing in the organization
6. Conforming to codes of behavior
7. Satisfying the varying interests of different people in groups[1]

Inputs of major resources—knowledge, money, people, machines, and time—are an important part of an organization's performance cycle as well, since they will determine the scope of activities.

Another approach to effectiveness matches organizations in similar situations—the *comparative* approach. For example, Organization A makes more money than Organization B; therefore, it's more effective. Paul Mott defines effective organizations as "those that produce more and higher quality output and adapt more effectively to environmental and internal problems than do similar organizations."[2] This approach has the advantage of avoiding the pitfalls of the goals approach but is limited by the ease of matching "similar" organizations. The very "effective" organization may meet this criterion but not due to its own effort. For example, luck, monopoly, or unique product might be the reason.

Although some feel that effectiveness essentially is established by the extent to which organizations or an organizational unit attains its goals, Amitai Etzioni argues that the central question in the study of effectiveness is not "how devoted is the organization to its goal" but rather "under the given conditions how close does the organizational allocation of resources approach an optimal distribution."[3]

Optimum is the key word to Etzioni. What is needed for effectiveness is a *balance of distribution* of resources among the various organizational needs, not necessarily a maximum satisfaction of any one activity.[4] Etzioni's viewpoint is expressed by others as well and can be viewed as an argument for seeing organizations as *systems* and evaluating organizational performance on this basis rather than on the basis of goal attainment or comparison with other organizations.

This *systems view* of organizations, as suggested in a previous chapter, assumes that the organization is one of a number of elements that interact *interdependently*. The organization takes inputs from the environment and returns them as output. An organization remains effective as long as it uses its resources in an efficient manner and continues to contribute to the larger system.

Of course, feedback is an important concept in viewing an organization as a system. Feedback comes to the organization as commentary on its services, projects, or products. Feedback is crucial in helping the organization learn from experiences with the environment so it can develop the means for adjusting to the environmental demands. Therefore, rather than viewing an organization's effectiveness as merely the extent to which it attains its goals, the systems approach suggests that effectiveness can be viewed in terms of optimizing and maintaining elements of the input-process-output-performance cycle—as well as the extent to which an organization adjusts to feedback from the environment.

EFFECTIVENESS OVER TIME

A great deal remains to be done through research to pinpoint all the components of effectiveness. Effectiveness dimensions and the interrelationships among them are not yet completely clear. However, one dimension that is generally agreed upon is *time,* since a final test of organizational effectiveness is whether or not it is able to sustain itself over time in the environment.

Survival is the long-run (and ultimate) measure of organizational effectiveness. Yet for most management decisions, this is an insufficient indicator to use for decisions in the short run, since long-run indicators may come too late. Possible short-run indicators of effectiveness include organizational production, efficiency, and satisfaction.[5] (See Figure 10-1.) Other indicators can be thought of as intermediate. These include adaptation to environmental changes and the internal development of the organization.

As shown in Figure 10-1, the short-run criteria for effectiveness are as follows:

1. *Production*—reflects the ability of an organization to produce the quantity and quality of output (whatever it is) that the environment demands.

2. *Efficiency*—can be defined as the ratio of outputs to inputs.

3. *Satisfaction*—the conceptualization of the organization as a social system requires that some consideration be given to the benefits received by an organizational participant as well as by the customers. Satisfaction is the label for this criterion, and its measures include attitude data, turnover, absenteeism, tardiness, and grievances.

Intermediate indicators of effectiveness are:

1. *Adaptiveness*—refers to the extent to which the organization can and does respond to changes that are either internally or externally induced.

2. *Development*—an organization must invest in itself; the purpose of de-

figure 10-1

ORGANIZATIONAL EFFECTIVENESS AND THE TIME DIMENSION

Time	Short-Run	Intermediate	Long-Run
Criteria	Production Efficiency Satisfaction	Adaptiveness Development	Survival

Source: G. L. Gibson, J. M. Ivancevich, and J. H. Donnelly. *Organizations: Structure, Processes, and Behavior* (Dallas: Business Publications Inc., 1976), p. 65.

1. *Management Team*
To create a management team that continually stimulates individual growth and team effort aimed at a high level of performance.

2. *Finances*
To keep the charges to patients as low as possible consistent with quality care. Make enough income to pay operating costs and provide capital expenditures as needed.

3. *Innovation*
To find new developments that improve our service.

4. *Service*
To maintain a friendly and efficient atmosphere for patients and visitors. To cultivate in the public at large an attitude of respect and confidence in our operations.

5. *Physical Facilities*
To maintain the best possible physical facilities, equipment, and supplies for patient care.

velopment is to enhance the capability of the organization to survive in the long run. Development may include training programs for managerial and/or nonmanagerial personnel, or organizational development efforts.[6]

These criteria for effectiveness can be translated into goals or objectives for an organization or a specific organizational subunit. For example, a nursing home might formulate certain goals/objectives that also serve as criteria for the evaluation of effectiveness. Block 10-1 shows an example of such goals. They provide a basis for measuring effectiveness through the goal approach.

A CLOSER LOOK AT GOALS

Etzioni defines a goal as "an image of a future state."[7] This definition might include goal statements about a single variable such as profit or the complex satisfying of multiple criteria of the systems theory model.

However, formal statements of goals do not necessarily resemble the goal that the organization is actually working toward. Perrow's distinction between "official" and "operational" goals has been accepted by many.[8] Official goals are those that can be formed in annual reports and other such material for public consumption. Operational goals can be discovered by watching what an organization actually does. How resources are allocated can be an indication of operational goals as they are often not explicitly stated.

It is useful to try to understand the way in which the goals of organizational members and groups become organizational goals. Hall suggests "the goal of an organization is an *abstraction* distilled from the desires of members and pressures from the environment and the internal system."[9] This process of abstraction however has not been studied empirically to date.

Using Goals for Measuring Effectiveness

We suggested earlier that the use of goals for measuring effectiveness is limited. Official goals can be easily identified but may at times bear little resemblance to the operational goals of the organization. Yet, operational goals are difficult to determine. One reason is that goal formation is motivated, and measurement of behavior alone cannot differentiate among motives behind goals.

With multiple goals, determining effectiveness by the goal approach becomes all but unmanageable. Assume that the operational goals could be isolated and that the level of achievement for each could be measured; it may be that meeting one goal to its fullest will cause another not to be fully met. For example, maximizing quantity goals may compromise quality goals for a manufacturing organization.

As long as all other achievement levels stay the same when one goal is more completely met, additional achievement in any amount is *better*. But if one goal achievement indicator drops while another rises, is the organization better or worse off? Is quantity "better" than quality? Only by knowing exactly what the utility of each goal for the organization is at that particular level of achievement can the problem be solved.

Yet despite these and other problems associated with using goals and goal attainment as the basis for measuring effectiveness, it is the most common approach to viewing effectiveness. As noted earlier other approaches have been proposed. Some of these approaches have been empirically tested and some have not, but to really understand the issues involved, let us now briefly review some of the more important literature on organizational effectiveness.

A REVIEW OF SELECTED EFFECTIVENESS LITERATURE

Direct studies of organizational effectiveness are somewhat limited in their numbers. Many schemes for viewing effectiveness in organizations are "conceptual" in nature; that is to say, they have been theoretically and logically derived but have not yet been tested empirically. Other views *are* based upon empirical evidence. This distinction will be emphasized in reviewing selected efforts from the effectiveness literature (see Figure 10-2). Comparative and systems approaches have been combined since both have elements of the systems approach.

Conceptual Goal-Oriented Approaches: James L. Price

One of the most extensive literature surveys of organizational effectiveness has been done by James L. Price in his book, *Organizational Effectiveness*. Price adheres to a goal-oriented approach and does no empirical hypothesis testing, so his contribution is classified in the conceptual goal-oriented category. He provides an inventory of propositions specifying the determinants of organizational effectiveness as defined by their level of goal attainment.

Price's inventory is compiled from a review and analysis of 50 studies. The model he develops is comprised of a dependent variable (effectiveness), and five intervening independent variables: productivity, morale, conformity, adaptiveness, and institutionalization. Price structures his model to include the following organizational systems: the economic system, the political system, internal and external, the control system, and the population and ecology or environmental system (see Figure 10-3).

figure 10-2

A SCHEME FOR ORDERING SELECTED EFFECTIVENESS LITERATURE

	Type of Study	
	Conceptual	Empirical
Goal	Price	Mahoney and Weitzel
System	Seashore and Yuchtman Schein Caplow Prasad	Georgopoulous and Tannenbaum Friedlander and Pickle Mott

Price provides a rather lengthy list of propositions derived from reviewing very carefully the literature on organizational effectiveness. For our purposes, we will include only a few to demonstrate his approach and call attention to some of the more important effectiveness issues.

> *Proposition 2.1.* "Organizations which have a high degree of division of labor are more likely to have a high degree of effectiveness than are organizations which have a low degree of division of labor."[10]
>
> *Proposition 3.2.* "Organizations which have a high degree of autonomy are more likely to have a high degree of effectiveness than are organizations which primarily have a charismatic type of decision making."[11]
>
> *Proposition 4.1.* "Organizations which have a high degree of autonomy are more likely to have a high degree of effectiveness than are organizations which have a low degree of autonomy."[12]
>
> *Proposition 6.2.* "Organizations which have a high degree of vertical communication are more likely to have a high degree of effectiveness than are organizations which have a low degree of vertical communication."[13]
>
> *Proposition 7.1.* "Except where there is a high degree of professionalization, large organizations are more likely to have a high degree of effectiveness than small organizations."[14]

Conceptual Systems Approaches

As noted earlier, systems theory approaches to the study of organizations assumes that an organization is a series of interrelated systems that receive inputs from the environment, process them, and return them to the environment as outputs.

Seashore and Yuchtman

Seashore and Yuchtman have taken what they label a "systems resource approach" to organizational effectiveness. Their ideas of organizational effectiveness focus upon concepts that:

1. Take the organization itself as the logical frame of reference rather than some external entity or some particular set of people
2. Explicitly treat the relations between the organization and its environment as a central ingredient in the definition of effectiveness
3. Provide the theoretically general framework capable of encompassing different kinds of complex organizations
4. Provide some guide for the identification of performance and action variables relative to organizational effectiveness and to the choice for empirical use.[15]

Seashore and Yuchtman postulate that the interdependence between an organization and its environment takes the form of an input/output transaction, which involves scarce and valued resources. The attempted

figure 10-3

JAMES L. PRICE'S EFFECTIVENESS MODEL

The Economic System

    1. Division of labor
    2. Specialized
       departmentalization
    3. Mechanization
    4. Continuous assembly

The Political System (internal)

    1. Legitimacy
    2. Rational-legal
    3. Centralization (tactical)
    4. Centralization (strategic)

The Political System (external)

    1. Autonomy
 2–5. Ideology (congruence,
      priority, and conformity)
    6. Cooptation
    7. Major elite cooptation
    8. Representation
9–10. Major elite representation and
      constituency

The Control System

    1. Sanctions
    2. Secondary norm enforcer-
      norm conformer
      relationship
    3. Graded sanctions
    4. Collectivistic sanctions
    5. Communication
 6–7. Vertical and horizontal
      communication
8–10. Instrumental, personal, and
      formal communication

Population and Ecology

    1. Size
    2. Spatial mobility
    3. Spatial mobility oriented to
      effectiveness

Intervening Variables
    1. Productivity
    2. Conformity
    3. Morale → Effectiveness
    4. Adaptiveness
    5. Institutionalization

Source: James L. Price, *Organizational Effectiveness* (Homewood, Ill.: Irwin, 1968), by permission.

acquisition of these resources leads to competition among organizations, and Yuchtman and Seashore define an organization's effectiveness in terms of the bargaining position that is attained between competing organizations.

The idea of a bargaining position implies the exclusion of any specific goal or function as the ultimate criterion for organizational effectiveness. With this approach, the key problem in assessment of effectiveness is identification of the competitive dimensions in interorganizational transactions.

A key concept for Seashore and Yuchtman is that of resources. Resources are generalized means or facilities that are potentially controllable by social organizations and that are potentially usable, however indirectly, in relationships between the organization and its environment.[16] This definition does not limit the concept of resources to physical or economic objects. One important kind of resource that organizations may compete for is human activity.

Seashore and Yuchtman suggest how one might assess organizational effectiveness by following certain steps:

1. Provide an inclusive taxonomy of resources.

2. Identify the different types of resources that are *mutually* relevant for the organizations under study.

3. Determine the relative positions of the compared organizations on the basis of information concerning the amounts and kinds of resources that are available for the organization and its efficiency in using these resources to get further resources.[17]

These authors conclude that:

The highest level of organizational effectiveness is reached when the organization maximizes its bargaining position and optimizes its resource procurement. . . . Optimum is the point beyond which an organization endangers itself because of a depletion of its resource producing environment or the devaluation of the resource, or because of this stimulation of countervailing forces within that environment.[18]

Schein

Another follower of systems theory, Edgar Schein, views a system's effectiveness as its capacity to survive, adapt, maintain itself, and grow regardless of the particular function it fulfills.[19] Schein proposes the following effectiveness criteria:

1. Adaptability—the ability to solve problems and to react with flexibility to changing environmental demands

2. A sense of identity—knowledge and insight on the part of the organization as to what it really is, what its goals are, and what it is to do

3. The capacity to test reality—the ability to search out, accurately perceive, and correctly interpret the real properties of the environment, particularly those that have relevance for the functioning of the organization.

A fourth that could be added is the degree of integration of the subparts into a total organization.

Schein argues that organizational effectiveness criteria must include *multiple* criteria like those above. Concentration on a single criterion leads to distortions in the organization's activities. He suggests that the maintenance of effectiveness is through an adaptive coping cycle. "The sequence of activities [is]. . . processes which begin with some change in some part of the internal or external environment and end with more adaptive dynamic equilibrium for dealing with change."[20] The stages in the suggested adaptive coping cycles are:

1. Sensing a change in some part of the internal or external environment

2. Importing the relevant information about the changes into those parts of the organization that can act upon it

3. Changing production or conversion processes inside the organization according to information obtained

4. Stabilizing internal changes while reducing or managing undesired by-products

5. Exporting new services, products, etc., that are more in line with the originally perceived changes in the environment

6. Obtaining feedback on the success of the change through further sensing of the state of the external environment and the degree of integration of the internal environment.[21]

Through this adaptive coping cycle, the effectiveness of the organization is either maintained or lost depending upon the sensing and use of the organization's environmental feedback.

Caplow

Theodore Caplow proposes the use of four variables to measure the effectiveness of organization:

1. Stability—a measure of the organization's ability to maintain its structure through the activities of acquiring resources, making efficient use of input, acting rationally and observing codes

2. Integration—the ability of the organization to avoid conflict among its members, primarily through communication

3. Volunteerism—an organization's ability to provide satisfaction for individuals and the desires of the members to continue their participation

4. Achievement—the net result of the organization's activity.[22]

Caplow's criteria almost suggest a goal approach, but the inclusion of stability and integration, which are systems characteristics, helps classify this as a systems approach.

Prasad

S. B. Prasad views all organizations as complex and dynamic and the successful ones as adaptive and problem solving. He recognizes that organizations are sociotechnical systems that are rationally structured and organized typically on the basis of hierarchical authority principles such as autocratic functional divisions, impersonal control mechanisms, and formal work rules.[23]

Prasad addresses organizational effectiveness by viewing three subsystems of the organization:

1. The economic subsystem, which includes all activities measurable in economic terms

2. The technical subsystem, which includes, in addition to technical outputs, design and manufacturing capabilities, market knowledge and information

3. The social subsystem, which encompasses variables of adaptability, a sense of identity, capacity to test reality, involvement and participation satisfaction, problem-solving capacity, degree of harmonious interunit relationships, goal perception, response capabilities, and a host of others.[24]

He concludes that an organization can be ineffective in either one or two subsystems without necessarily jeopardizing its total effectiveness to a significant degree. But if an organization is to maintain a high level of total effectiveness, an equilibrium of the levels of effectiveness of all three subsystems must be achieved.

What can we conclude from these "conceptual" approaches to understanding effectiveness? There are a number of both internal and external factors that are likely to be important in determining whether or not an organization is effective. Bargaining position has been suggested as a surrogate for effectiveness. Schein feels that multiple criteria are a more realistic approach, however, and places heavy emphasis on an organization's ability to accurately assess and react to its environment. Finally, we were exposed to the idea that an organization might be ineffective in one respect but still be considered effective overall.

The conceptual approaches to the study of organizational effectiveness are useful for framing the problem and defining its dimensions, but an empirical examination of the important variables holds the key to future knowledge in the area. A review of these follows.

Goal-Oriented Empirical Studies: Mahoney and Weitzel

Thomas Mahoney and William Weitzel examined organizational characteristics that managers use in judging the overall effectiveness of their organizational units. They recognized three sets of criteria in the determination of organizational effectiveness: ultimate, intermediate, and immediate. The ultimate criterion is the achievement of the "final goal," which is generally stated in broad terms and not susceptible to practical assessment. Midrange criteria (intermediate and immediate), tend to apply to the short-run assessment of effectiveness. Their concern was specifically with *measurable* midrange organizational criteria, which are used as short-run substitutes for the more subjective long-run criteria of organizational effectiveness.[25]

Mahoney and Weitzel began with 114 characteristic criteria of organizational effectiveness and investigated the relationships among them. This revealed 24 relatively independent criteria. Two different classifications of organizations—general business organizations and research and development organizational units—were used. Figure 10-4 lists the 24 items that were used to attempt to predict effectiveness. Further analysis involved investigating the relationships of these 24 midrange criteria of organizational effectiveness to management judgments about ultimate overall effectiveness of organizational units. The relative importance or weight assigned to each of the 24 variables was determined.

For the business organizations, the important variables and their weights were: productivity, support, and utilization (.42), planning (.22), reliability (.16), initiation (.12). This model shows that the primary criterion of organizational effectiveness used by business organizations is *efficient productive performance*. Associated with such performance is a high degree of manpower use, which is derived from a challenging and effective use of skills, and a manpower development program. The remaining dimensions are more indicative of organizational behavior than output and can be viewed as criteria concerned with organizational *adaptiveness* and future *survival*.

The important variables for the research and development unit were: reliability (.43), cooperation (.27), development (.19). An effective research and development unit has as its primary criterion of organizational effectiveness the factor of *reliability*. Productivity and planning are so closely related to reliable performance in organizations of this nature that they account for no independent explanation of effectiveness.[26] The second criterion—coordination—is the result of the coordination of scheduling and flexibility in changing and adjusting assignments. The third criterion significant in research and development units was the continuing development of members' skills. It should be noted that the research and development model is probably a reasonably good surrogate for many professional, nonprofit organizations.

figure 10-4

MAHONEY AND WEITZEL DIMENSIONS
OF ORGANIZATIONAL EFFECTIVENESS

Dimensions

Flexibility. Willingly tries out new ideas and suggestions; ready to tackle unusual problems.

Development. Personnel participate in training and development activities; high level of personnel competence and skill.

Cohesion. Lack of complaints and grievances; conflict among cliques within the organization.

Democratic supervision. Subordinate participation in work decisions.

Reliability. Meets objectives without necessity of followup and checking.

Selectivity. Does not accept marginal employees rejected by other organizations.

Diversity. Wide range of job responsibilities and personnel abilities within the organization.

Delegation. High degree of delegation by supervisors.

Bargaining. Rarely bargains with other organizations for favors and cooperation.

Emphasis on results. Results, output, and performance emphasized, not procedures.

Staffing. Personnel flexibility among assignments; development for promotion from within the organization.

Coordination. Coordinates and schedules activities with other organizations, utilizes staff assistance.

Decentralization. Work and procedural decisions delegated to lowest levels.

Understanding. Organization philosophy, policy, directives understood and accepted by all.

Conflict. Little conflict with other organization units about authority or failure to meet responsibilities.

Personnel planning. Performance not disrupted by personnel absences, turnover, lost time.

Supervisory support. Supervisors support their subordinates.

Planning. Operations planned and scheduled to avoid lost time; little time spent on minor crisis.

Cooperation. Operations scheduled and coordinated with other organizations; rarely fails to meet responsibilities.

Productivity-support-utilization. Efficient performance; mutual support and respect of supervisors and subordinates; utilization of personnel skills and abilities.

Communication. Free flow of work information and communications within the organization.

Turnover. Little turnover from inability to do the job.

Initiation. Initiates improvements in work methods and operations.

Supervisory control. Supervisors in control of progress of work.

Source: J. A. Mahoney and William Weitzel, "Mangerial Models of Organizational Effectiveness," *Administrative Science Quarterly*, vol. 14, no. 3 (September 1969), by permission.

Figure 10-5 summarizes the Mahoney and Weitzel findings. One explanation of differences between the two models is related to the concept of an ultimate criterion. The ultimate criterion of the general business model being economic, it closely agrees with profit, productivity, and efficiency criteria. Certain behavioral characteristics are related to the economic criteria and somewhat predictive of them. The research and development units show a more "professionally" oriented view of the ultimate criterion. Profit, productivity, and performance are secondary relative to the behavioral characteristics of reliable performance, cooperative relationships, and level of professional competence and development.

figure 10-5

ORGANIZATIONAL EFFECTIVENESS IN GENERAL BUSINESS AND RESEARCH AND DEVELOPMENT MODELS

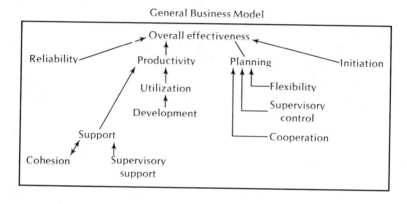

General Business Model

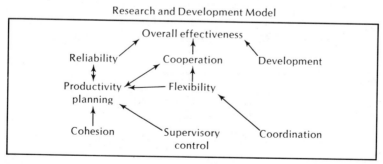

Research and Development Model

Source: J. A. Mahoney and William Weitzel, "Managerial Models of Organizational Effectiveness," *Administrative Science Quarterly,* vol. 14, no. 3 (September 1969), by permission.

Systems-Oriented Empirical Studies:
Georgopoulous and Tannenbaum

In their study of organizational effectiveness, Georgopoulous and Tannenbaum pursued three major objectives: (1) to examine the concept of effectiveness and to provide a definition derived from the nature of organizations, (2) to develop operational criteria and to measure the concepts in a specific industrial setting, and (3) to evaluate these criteria and operations in terms of the operational character.[27]

Organizational effectiveness was designed as "the extent to which an organization as a social system, given certain resources and means, fulfills its objectives without placing undue strain upon its members."[28] This concept of effectiveness subsumes the following criteria: (1) organizational productivity, (2) organizational flexibility in the form of successful adjustment to internal organizational changes and successful adaptation to externally induced change, and (3) absence of intraorganizational strain or tension and of conflict between organizational subgroups.

The organization studied was a firm that specialized in the delivery of retail merchandise. The structure included subsystems called "stations," and these stations were structurally homogeneous and organizationally parallel. The tasks in all stations were similar, and were uniform.

Overall station effectiveness was obtained through independent judgment of a group of experts. Judges rated the stations from best to worst. Average ranking of each station's effectiveness was obtained from the arithmetic average of the ratings. The three criterion variables used were station productivity, intraorganizational strain, and flexibility. Figure 10-6 presents the rank order correlations among criterion variables and the measures of organizational effectiveness. Effective stations were more productive, lower in intergroup strain, and somewhat more flexible than noneffective stations. The authors concluded that the operations they measured proved reliable indicators and that the criteria used related significantly to an independent evaluation of effectiveness by experts.

figure 10-6

CORRELATIONS AMONG CRITERION VARIABLES AND ORGANIZATIONAL
EFFECTIVENESS COMPONENTS

Effective Components	Criterion Variables		
	Station Productivity	Intergroup Strain	Station Flexibility
Station effectiveness	.73	−.49	.39
Station productivity	—	−.48	.35
Station intergroup strain	—	—	−.70

Friedlander and Pickle

In addition to viewing the total organizational system and its interde-pendency with its environment, Friedlander and Pickle attempted to define the criteria of organizational effectiveness to reflect those interdependen-cies. Their criteria contain elements of the organization's contributions to society as well as those that describe maximization of returns to the organization from society. The purpose of the study was to explore the concept of total organizational effectiveness by studying the relationship between internal and external system effectiveness.[29]

Effectiveness was determined by the degree to which the needs of "components" were fulfilled in their transactions with the organization. Internal components were those within the formal boundaries of the organization transacted by exporting and importing energy. The study included 97 firms, each of which had one level of management and employed from four to fifty employees.

Analysis of the data indicated that organizations were able to satisfy both societal and employee needs in only a moderate number of instances. Only community and consumer satisfaction relate consistently to em-ployee satisfaction. This is a possible indicator that organizations that recognize and fulfill community needs are likely to be effective in fulfilling employee desires as well. Significant relationships were found between employee satisfaction and owner fulfillment.

Conclusions drawn from the study show only a moderate number of relationships between the degree to which the organization concurrently fulfills a need of its internal subsystem components (employees and its owner) and the components of its larger society. Evidently, organizations find it difficult to fulfill simultaneously the variety of demands made upon them,[30] or to quote John Child, "on the whole though, the message of these findings seems clear. If you want to manage a successful business, concentrate on a few key objectives and avoid distractions."[31]

Mott

Paul Mott's study points to the importance of measuring effectiveness internally and externally since they may not be at all the same thing. The object of Mott's study was to develop questionnaires, which when com-pleted by members of an organization, would provide a measure of organizational effectiveness. Similar to the ideas of Georgopoulous and Tannenbaum, Mott's criteria of organizational effectiveness consist of production, adaptability, and flexibility. Productivity is perhaps the most studied single variable in effectiveness literature. Productivity for Mott is a component variable of both efficiency and effectiveness.

Mott tested a series of hypotheses on productive organization, including the effect of the task on productivity.[32] The nature of the task being performed in an organization has implications for the proper design of the organization. He defined a highly *structured* task as one that specifies in precise detail the activities associated with the roles and relationships among roles. For example, a football play or an assembly line operation is a situation in which the various role holders have been told precisely what to do and how their tasks relate to those of others around them, and indeed, such structure is necessary to getting the job done. Other tasks, however, are inappropriate for the design of rigid roles and role relations because of an unpredictable environment, and greater reliance must be placed on individuals who can improvise to adjust to new problems and opportunities, such as an architect designing a new building. The extent to which a task is structured will determine the conditions that relate to high productivity and high effectiveness in an organization.

The following hypotheses, which include a consideration of the level of structuring in the task, were generally supported by the data from Mott's study.

1. When task structuring is high, productivity is positively related to:
   a. formal coordination
   b. level of workers' skills
   c. conditions for achieving negotiated orders
   d. clarity of an adherence to rules governing work
2. When task structuring is high, productivity is not necessarily related to:
   a. managerial awareness of problems
   b. managerial success of solving problems
   c. perceptions about the reasonableness and empathy of top managers (rational trust)
   d. clarity of objectives
3. When task structuring is high, productivity is negatively related to:
   a. intra-unit conflict
   b. conflicting priorities
4. When task structuring is low, productivity is related to:
   a. formal coordination
   b. conditions for achieving negotiated orders
      (1) coordination by avoidance
      (2) problem solving at low echelons
      (3) ease in exchanging ideas and information
   c. levels of workers' skills
   d. clarity of objectives
5. When task structuring is low, productivity is not necessarily related to:
   a. managerial awareness of problems
   b. managerial success at solving problems
6. When task structuring is low, productivity is negatively related to:
   a. interunit conflict
   b. conflicting priorities.[33]

Mott's evidence suggested that with appropriate safeguards workers' subjective judgments provide a "fairly valid measure of effectiveness." The major safeguard required is an outside evaluation of the effectiveness of the unit under study. This evaluation will reveal any disagreements between inside and outside evaluators over the criteria of effectiveness.[34] It should be noted that Mott provides primarily an *internally oriented* view of effectiveness.

Conclusions from Empirical Effectiveness Studies

The empirical studies on effectiveness that have been reviewed here suggest several concluding notes. First, different kinds of organizations are likely to have different criteria for effectiveness. For example, business organizations are likely to find production efficiency based measures most important, whereas "professional" organizations are more likely to emphasize reliability, cooperation, and professional competence in determining effectiveness.

A number of different criteria for effectiveness have been suggested. *External* criteria include adaptiveness, bargaining position for resources, the ability of the organization to accurately perceive reality, and the "achievement" of the organization. *Internal* criteria include morale, voluntarism (almost a turnover measure), stability, low stress, and matching type of task to individual work role structuring.

It has been suggested that an organization need not be 100 percent effective in *all* potential areas of effectiveness but rather attempt to optimize effectiveness among economic, technical, and social concerns.

We make the distinction here between internal and external effectiveness because it seems that they can be quite different. Mott suggests that a measure of internal effectiveness (employee opinions) is a reasonably good external measure as well. We feel that more evidence is necessary before that statement can be carved in stone.

Regardless of which specific criterion an organization has chosen to define effectiveness, it must be measured. For certain organizations, this presents very special problems. This is especially true of nonprofit organizations as we will discuss next.

NONPROFIT ORGANIZATIONS:
SPECIAL PROBLEMS IN EFFECTIVENESS

The evaluation of effectiveness is of concern to organizations in the public as well as private realm. Private "for-profit" organizations have a particular advantage in measuring overall performance since their performance is subject to easier measurement. The "bottom line" on an income statement gives organizations in this category a good (at least partial) measurement of their effectiveness. Most public or nonprofit organizations do not have the benefit of a bottom line; however, this does not negate the *need* for evaluation of the organization's success or lack of it.

Three general classes of nonprofit organizations can be identified. One is *voluntary* organizations. A high percentage of adults belong to voluntary associations of one sort or another. Consider, for example, the number of fraternal orders, trade unions, trade associations, professional associations, chambers of commerce, women's organizations, and so on, to which a large percentage of persons may belong.

The single largest nonprofit organization (or group of organizations) is the federal government. The number of agencies and employees connected with this operation, along with its yearly budget, is quite large. Not only are purely "governmental" positions, such as elected and appointed officials and civil service employees included here, but also the aggregation of personnel connected in some way with the armed services. State, county, and city governments also employ large numbers of people. These *governmental entities* form the second nonprofit category of organizations.

Finally, a "hidden" classification of nonprofit organizations remains. Many groups and operations with profit-oriented business firms do not lend themselves to profit measurement of performance. These *staff organizations* (or suborganizations), such as research and development, legal department, administrative services, and so on, share many of the maladies of more orthodox nonprofit organizations.

Need for Good Effectiveness Measures

Two factors point to the need for greatly increased study of the effectiveness of nonprofit organizations:

1. Nonprofit organizations are so numerous, large, and important that they touch the lives of each of us every day with major impacts, whether it be through our own association with them or our need to operate within their constraints.

2. For the most part, they have been frustrated in their efforts to measure effectiveness. Evaluation of their operations has had many serious problems.

In 1969 the Urban Institute made an extensive study of federal program evaluation and concluded that "the most impressive finding about the evaluation of social programs in the federal government is that substantial work in this field is almost nonexistent."[35] However, in 1972 a resurvey of the field revealed quite a different picture—funds committed to evaluation had mushroomed, and many evaluation studies had been completed.[36] This seems to indicate that evaluation has firmly established itself since 1969 in both the budget and administrative realms of the federal government—one very major segment of nonprofit organizations. However,

> there is little evidence to show that evaluation generally leads to more effective social policies or programs. On the contrary, experience to date strongly suggests that social programs have not been as effective as expected and had *not* improved in performance following evaluation.[37]

This indicates that evaluation of effectiveness by itself is not enough. The concern must be with *effective* evaluation. For evaluation to be effective, several things must be present—most of these will be discussed later—but one of the most important will be mentioned in this context. Effective evaluation requires a *desire* on the part of the individuals who are in a position to put evaluation information to use and to make indicated changes in existing programs or procedures *for the evaluation to take place*. Evaluation of a particular program or organization activity may take place for any number of reasons. These reasons may be *organizationally* or *personally* oriented.[38] Organizational reasons might include:

1. Demonstrating to others that the program is worthwhile
2. Determining whether or not a program is moving in the right direction
3. Determining whether the needs for which the program is designed are being satisfied
4. Justifying past or projected expenditures
5. Determining the cost of a program in terms of money or human efforts
6. Obtaining evidence that may be helpful in demonstrating to others what is already believed to be true regarding the effectiveness of the program
7. Gaining support for program expansion
8. Comparing different types of programs in terms of their relative effect
9. Comparing different program messages or approaches in terms of effect
10. Satisfying someone who has demanded evidence of effect

Individually oriented reasons for evaluation include:

1. Seeing an evaluation as "the thing to do" if one wants to belong
2. Wishing to make an evaluation study as a means of bringing favorable attention, better budgets, and better staff to the unit
3. A means of gaining status and acceptance from superiors
4. Making a job easier and more interesting
5. Moving toward promotion
6. A vague but urgent need for the administrator to know if he is progressing.

It is important to identify as many reasons as possible for having an evaluation since the reasons for evaluation may govern the kind of evaluation programs selected. Furthermore, the reasons for evaluation will tend to govern the kinds of assumptions the evaluator is willing to accept or reject, the standards of judgment or values against which effectiveness will be measured, and the intensity of the investigation to be undertaken.[39]

The evaluation of an organization's effectiveness can be viewed as a complex set of processes for feeding back information to guide future action. It is the mirror image of organizational planning, since the criteria against which performance is measured are developed during the planning process.

The development of *evaluation criteria* during the planning phase is critical but often poorly done, especially in nonprofit organizations. "To plan without making *explicit* the many kinds of criteria by which a program might be evaluated leaves the planner the problem of evaluating *post hoc* without adequate information."[40]

When to Evaluate Effectiveness

The planning stage is where subsequent evaluations should first be considered. Determination should be made at that time whether or not rigorous evaluation of effectiveness is needed. There are a number of situations in which it might not be wise to commit a large amount of resources to evaluation:

1. When the cost of carrying out a rigorous evaluation is higher than the cost of the program

2. When a current program is the only strategy available and there is evidence that it may be having some effect

3. When the program is obviously desired by the community regardless of its effectiveness

4. When change of program activity would be too disruptive to other programs[41]

The important point here is that evaluation is *not* always appropriate but that when it is, the time to begin planning for measuring effectiveness is early in the program's development.

Alternative Forms of Organizational Effectiveness Measurement

In a search for accurate organizational effectiveness measures, various nonprofit organizations have arrived at several general classifications or yardsticks that they use to get an idea of their performance. Depending upon the organization at hand, one, several, or all of these types of measures may be in use.

Monetary Measures

Scales such as these center around both costs and prices. Some nonprofit organizations may price their output at such a level so as to recoup production and distribution costs but no return beyond that. This provides a measure of performance much akin to profit, where a breakeven level would be the organizational goal. Troubles may arise, however, when the organization simply cannot, by either law or conscience—for example, churches and welfare agencies—charge for their services or where their entrance into a given market would bring about competition with for-profit organizations.

In order to avoid the potentially negative impact of using real dollars, monetary "proxies"[42] or "shadow prices"[43] are sometimes used. Operations may then appear to become nothing more than a game, however, and motivational problems can arise.

Cost measurement of the expense of resources is often used as an effectiveness measurement for management. This is a particularly weak criterion. Although some organizations set a goal of holding costs down, others may view the amount of inputs as an indication of the work being accomplished. Regardless, such a measure ignores both the level and quality of output. Costs alone, therefore, cannot give a completely accurate picture of effectiveness for nonprofit organizations.

Nonmonetary Counts

The translation of amounts into dollar figures is not always possible or even wise, as much can be lost in such translation. However, quantification in other terms may be equally acceptable. Unit counts, percentage points, time expenditures, and comparative ratings of data are used by almost every organization in one form or another. For example, educational administrators can use test scores of the student body. Many organizations examine turnover and absentee rates, and so on.

Several words of caution are due, however. Simply because some measure can be quantified, it is no simple guarantee that it will provide an accurate effectiveness measure. The public relations department that counts the number of responses to a news release without ascertaining the positive/negative split is not accurately measuring the effectiveness of its operation. In addition, it should be noted that such measures are rarely focused on the "big picture." Such counts generally reveal more about efficiency than they do about effectiveness, and a large group of them may need to be examined to determine how the organization as a whole is progressing.

Subjective Analysis

Some criteria simply should not be distilled to a quantitative level. Justice would not be done if such action were taken. Two mistakes commonly occur in subjective analysis: (1) The claims of the parties involved are not verifiable. This may be due either to an honest lack of reasoning, such as a "gut feeling," or because the critical party cannot bring himself to admit the feelings that he has. In short, any subjective analysis should be backed up with some degree of logical explanation. (2) The subjective analysis may be treated as an objective measure, which, in and of itself, is a logical contradiction in that nonquantitative subjective information cannot be measured.

Models for Dealing with Effectiveness in Nonprofit Organizations

World War II brought to the forefront a need to evaluate the effectiveness of organization in the absence of profit. The PERT (performance evaluation review technique) method was designed to perform such a task. To a large degree PERT was used in federal agencies for some years. During the early 1960s PPBS (planning, programming, and budgeting system) later modified by some to PPBES (where the "e" added an evaluation stage) found favor with public sector organizations. However, as the name implies, PPBS was strictly program oriented. As such, the method was of little use in evaluating either long-range or continuous everyday or organizationwide effectiveness. In spite of these obvious shortcomings, PPBS was applied widely throughout the public sector, which subsequently uncovered its serious deficiencies as a universal model. The backlash resulted in its lessened use in the government.

Within the last ten years, cost/benefit analysis has been incorporated into government as an effectiveness model. Cost/benefit analysis is much like PPBS and PERT, although it is quite limited to use with projects rather than continuous operation. It may be of assistance in choosing the correct path to follow but does little to guide correct implementation. Furthermore, cost/benefit analysis demands quantification to an extreme degree. Such quantification may often produce contrived or misleading results.

The current trend appears to be the application of MBO (management by objectives) in nonprofit organizations. Studies of MBO in churches, government agencies, libraries, fund-raising organizations, and even fraternities abound. For the most part, these studies reveal that MBO can survive the transition from profit to nonprofit operations with few modifications.

It has been estimated that MBO is currently in use either formally or informally by about 80 percent of the industrial firms in this country.[44] This success in private industry coupled with the seeming ease of transition into nonprofit applications has led many again to hail the arrival of the "universal organizational effectiveness model."

The use of caution is important at this stage of MBO development. PPBS felt the sad effects of "bandwagon support" and has now fallen into disfavor. MBO is extremely new on the nonprofit scene, and it must gradually be adapted to a useful form for this sector. Although it has been used for a good many years in the private sector, some "bugs" still remain. Problems can be programmed into an MBO system. Although some say that MBO represents the "ideal goal-oriented model,"[45] it is tricky to install and use and warrants patience and discretion concerning its recommendation for universal application.

Most authorities agree that MBO is one of the most significant steps toward the development of a universal effectiveness model, but a great deal of further innovation and refinement needs to be done.

CONCLUSIONS ABOUT GOALS
AND EFFECTIVENESS

Much has been accomplished in the field of effectiveness study since the early days of effectiveness measurement. A search for the "sole criterion" of effectiveness has resulted in recognition of differences among kinds of organizations. The emphasis on trying to determine an effectiveness model with multiple variables, such as Mahoney and Weitzel's work, shows some promise. When such a model is developed, its components combined with management by objectives in certain organizational forms may produce what many believe to be the rudimentary form of a usable effectiveness model. Justification for such a position seems to rest on MBO's apparently high level of application and usefulness in profit and nonprofit organizations alike.

In this chapter we suggested that effectiveness can probably best be viewed *both* internally and externally and that the two are quite different. In addition to developing appropriate internal and external criteria for effectiveness, management must deal with the dilemma of finding good measures for the criteria. A number of possibilities were suggested. Finally, regardless of the criteria or measure selected, management must realize the importance of evaluating effectiveness and using the feedback if the organization is to be effective and survive in the long run.

We will make this link between effectiveness and survival stronger in the next chapter as we consider survival and change in organizations.

NOTES

[1]R. M. Gross, "What Are Your Organization's Objectives: A General Systems Approach to Planning," *Human Relations* 18 (August 1965):195–216.

[2]P. E. Mott, *The Characteristics of Effective Organization* (New York: Harper & Row, 1972).

[3]Amitai Etzioni, "Two Approaches to Organizational Analysis," in *Program Evaluation in the Health Fields*, ed. H. C. Schulberg, Alan Sheldon, and Frank Baker (New York: Behavioral Publications, 1969), p. 104.

[4]Ibid.

[5]J. L. Gibson, J. M. Ivancevich, and J. H. Donnelly, *Organizations: Structure Processes and Behavior* (Dallas: Business Publications, 1973), p. 37.

[6]Ibid., pp. 38–39.

[7]Amitai Etzioni, *A Comparative Analysis of Complex Organizations* (New York: The Free Press, 1975), p. 103.

[8]Charles Perrow, "The Analysis of Goals in Complex Organizations," *American Sociological Review* (1961):854–65.

[9]Richard H. Hall, *Organizations: Structure and Process* (Englewood Cliffs, N.J.: Prentice-Hall, 1972), p. 82.

[10]J. Price, *Organizational Effectiveness* (Homewood, Ill.: Irwin, 1968), p. 16.

[11]Ibid., p. 55.

[12]Ibid., p. 96.

[13]Ibid., p. 163.

[14]Ibid., p. 185.

[15]F. E. Seashore, and E. Yuchtman, "A Systematic Resource Approach to Organizational Effectiveness," *Administrative Science Quarterly* 32 (December 1967):377–95.

[16]Ibid., p. 156.

[17]Ibid., p. 161.

[18]Ibid., p. 160.

[19]E. Schein, *Organizational Psychology* (Englewood Cliffs, N.J.: Prentice-Hall, 1965), pp. 117–29.

[20]Ibid., p. 119.

[21]Ibid., p. 120.

[22]T. Caplow, *Principles of Organization* (New York: Harcourt, Brace & World, 1964), pp. 119–24.

[23]S. B. Prasad, "A Construct of Organizational Social Effectiveness," *Management International Review* 13 (1973):103–10.

[24]Ibid., p. 106.

[25]J. A. Mahoney and William Weitzel, "Managerial Models of Organizational Effectiveness," *Administrative Science Quarterly* 14 (September 1969):357–65.

[26]Ibid., p. 566.

[27]B. S. Georgopoulous and A. S. Tannenbaum, "A Study of Organizational Effectiveness," *American Sociological Review* 22 (October 1957):534–40.

[28]Ibid., p. 180.

[29]F. Friedlander and H. Pickle, "Components of Effectiveness in Small Organization," *Administrative Science Quarterly* 13 (September 1968):289–304.

[30]Ibid., p. 302.

[31]John Child, "What Determines Organizational Performance? The Universals Vs. It all Depends," *Organizational Dynamics* (Summer 1974):102.

[32]Mott, *The Characteristics of Effective Organizations*, p. 38.

[33]Ibid., pp. 38–39.

[34]Ibid., pp. 178–79.

[35]J. S. Wholey et al., *Federal Evaluation Policy* (Washington, D.C.: The Urban Institute, 1970).

[36]Pamela Horst et al., "Program Management and the Federal Evaluation," (Washington, D.C.: Urban Institute Reprint 162-0010-6, August, 1974), p. 1.

[37]Ibid., p. 1.

[38]A. L. Knutson, "Evaluation for What," *Program Evaluation in the Health Fields,* ed. H. C. Schulberg, Alan Shelson, Frank Baker (New York: Behavioral Publications, 1969), p. 43.

[39]Ibid.

[40]M. F. Arnold, "Evaluation of Parallel Process to Planning," *Administering Health Systems,* ed. M. F. Arnold, L. V. Blakenship, J. M. Hess (Chicago: Aldine, 1971), p. 275.

[41]Ibid., p. 281.

[42]Robert N. Dearden and John Dearden, *Management Control Systems,* 3rd ed. (Homewood, Ill.: Irwin, 1976), p. 685.

[43]Russell L. Ackoff, *A Concept of Corporate Planning* (New York: Wiley-Interscience, 1970), p. 106.

[44]John C. Alpin, Jr. and Peter P. Schoderbek, "How to Measure M.B.O. in the Public Sector," *Public Personnel Management* 5 (March/April 1976):88–95.
[45]John P. Campbell, "Contributions Research Can Make in Understanding Organizational Effectiveness," *Organization and Administrative Sciences* 7 (Spring/Summer 1976):29–45.

SUGGESTIONS FOR FURTHER READING

ETZIONI, A. *A Comparative Analysis of Complex Organizations.* Rev. ed. New York: The Free Press, 1975.

KATZ, DANIEL, and KAHN, ROBERT L. *The Social Psychology of Organizations.* New York: Wiley, 1966.

MOTT, P. E. *The Characteristics of Effective Organizations.* New York: Harper & Row, 1972.

PRICE, JAMES. *Organizational Effectiveness.* Homewood, Ill.: Irwin, 1968.

chapter 11

ORGANIZATIONAL SURVIVAL AND CHANGE

In this final chapter we approach an important topic—the ability of organizations to survive, or their failure to do so. Several books about organizations include some limited discussion of organizational survival. In this chapter we will expand this discussion and include organizational change and a very brief look at organizational development. The material on these topics is much more conceptual in nature than technology, size, and so on. There have been few empirical studies of the phenomena.

Why concern ourselves with organizational survival? The Office of Business Economics and the United States Department of Commerce gather and record the vital statistics regarding the death rate of business organizations. If we examine these statistics, one thing is very apparent. Business organizations, especially small ones, have a high mortality rate. Half of these go out of existence in the first year of operation, and only a third survive past the fourth year. And size is no guarantee of immortality since the 100 largest business firms in existence in the United States at the turn of the century could claim only two survivors as of 1968.[1]

Although most organizations are formed with the intention of long term survival (as can be seen in many corporate charters), examples of extreme organizational longevity are rare. The Catholic church, the government of England, and a business example—the Hudson's Bay Company—might be used as examples of extreme longevity. The effects of organizational demise, then, are well documented, but all the causes are somewhat less well understood.

SURVIVAL AS AN ORGANIZATIONAL GOAL

Most approaches to organizational survival treat it as an integral component of the organization's goal structure. Starbuck says that the organization may choose whether to do or not to do many things, but it must survive.[2] Kemball-Cook believes that survival need not take the form of a stated goal since it is an inherent aim of organization.[3] Other authors feel that continued survival may be used as the long-run measure of an organization's effectiveness.[4] Skibbins suggests that survival is the "most broadly acknowledged goal" of modern organization but that it is so complex and subject to such differing value-oriented interpretations that attempts at the statement of such a goal are quite superficial, or in his terms, "polite hogwash."[5]

Rothschild surmised that the primary motive of an entrepreneur may well be survival of the enterprise and that such a stance might yield incongruency with more specific organizational goals in light of a dynamic environment.[6] This argument has an interesting corollary since a paid professional manager is only an employee of the organization and may not pursue its perpetuation with the same zeal as would its creator. Rather, he might be more attuned to satisfaction of the specific objectives assigned to him. Perhaps an argument could be made that the professional manager pursues organizational survival with less zeal than the entrepreneur.

The decision as to whether survival is an organizational means or end will be left to you since in our opinion it is of interest but not critical to understanding organizations. The point of view will be taken here, however, that organizational survival is an ongoing process and that, for the most part, organizational demise is the result of either internal or external causes or a combination of the two. At this point we shall examine some of the reasons why organizations fail to survive.

SOME REASONS WHY ORGANIZATIONS FAIL TO SURVIVE

Organizations cease their existence every day. Critical financial position is probably the most frequently cited "terminal illness" for commercial organizations as well as a good many nonprofit institutions. This might be either a cause or an effect. Some organizations that suffer this condition may experience a "reincarnation" of sorts through acquisition or merger; yet, in a strict sense the original organization no longer exists. In many cases a planned, rational demise may result in effective disbandment and orderly placement of the remaining organizational components. Often, however, the end of organizational activities is *not* planned and occurs swiftly and quite blindly.

In a general sense organizations may cease to exist when they are no longer able to fill the niche they have carved in the environment or when they cannot adapt to a changing set of conditions in the environment. These are, of course, external factors, but they may be predicated on internal situations as well. For example, the inability of the organization to respond to changes may be a result of internal decay. Furthermore, if such things as organizational life cycles (chapter 1) really exist, these could play a part in explaining the survival or demise of an organization.

The reasons for organizational demise will be discussed here as external, internal, or life-cycle oriented. You are cautioned, however, that there is likely a great interdependence among these different reasons, and the distinction is made only for the sake of ordering the material.

External Factors: Environmental Change and Adaptation

The most frequently expressed reason for organizational demise centers around organizational inability to adapt to an increasingly dynamic external environment. In one sense, external forces place "claims" upon an organization.[7] In these terms the organization's survival is dependent upon:

1. The occurrence of fortunate events, such as technological advances, whereby the scarce resources attainable by the organization can be spread across more of the claims that are placed upon it

2. The ability of the organization to forecast the strength that the various environmental forces will have in enforcing their claims upon the organization

3. The ability of the organization to find new patterns of activity that will adequately meet emergent claims on them

The importance of a future-oriented "reality testing" of the environment is clear in this regard.

Adaptability

To meet environmental change, many authors stress the importance of *adaptability* for maintaining organizational effectiveness. It has been suggested that adaptability is far and away the most critical issue in determining the survival of the organization. Short-run environmental fluctuations may be tolerable without it, but flexibility to changing long-run conditions is necessary for continuation of organizational existence.[8] It is a widely held view that the environment of the future will change at an increasingly rapid rate. In speaking about organizations in this dynamic future, Leavitt, Pinfield, and Webb agree that an organization's quick and accurate response to environmental alterations will account for the lion's share of its success and continuation.[9]

From a practical management perspective, placing overly tight restrictions on an organization's environment sensing or boundary-spanning mechanisms may be as dangerous as ignoring external forces altogether. Business, legal, technical, ethical and moral, managerial, social, and international trends must all be monitored continuously and accurately. Since, as Weick has argued, the environment in which the organization operates is an "enacted" environment, the organizational units that operate at the organization's boundary with the environment will be accurate in perceiving that environment only to the extent their perceptions are not imposed upon them from within the organization. Adaptability can be severely limited by the blinders of inaccurate environmental assessment.

A number of other authors have also emphasized that the *perceived* environment is that which is acted upon by top managers and executives. What these people perceive to be true in the environment, *whether it is or not,* will determine the structures and processes that organizations develop. Needless to say, executive perception of the environment is not always completely objective or accurate. Since accurate perception of environmental changes is necessary for adaptability and survival, *reality testing* of executive perceptions by objective measures may be critical for long-run survival and short-run effectiveness.

Resistance to Change

Another popular view is that adaptability is threatened by organizational "resistance to change."[10] Although much has been written about resistance to change, there seem to be two major ideas about its existence. The first deals with *personal* resistance to change on an individual basis. (This will be dealt with briefly later in the chapter.) Another idea proposes that certain *organizational forms* are inherently resistant to change.

One can observe that all organizations today do have at least some natural tendency to resist change and that to combat such "instinctive" behavior is extremely difficult. Chris Argyris feels strongly that the most prominent culprit of such unfortunate behavior is the traditional pyramid form of the bureaucratic organization. The onslaught of an increasingly competitive environment, he believes, will soon spell the end to this form of organization.[11]

A classic article by Warren Bennis mentioned in another context earlier is often regarded as the cornerstone of the "bureaucratic doom" philosophy.[12] He proposed that within 25 to 50 years no bureaucracies will have survived because of their inbred resistance to change, as well as their inefficient operation, which poses a threat to their short-run survival. Spencer and Sofer,[13] as well as Gardner,[14] concur. Bureaucracy will fail because of resistance to change. Although the validity of such a prediction remains to be seen, Bennis himself has evidently somewhat changed this view due to his personal experiences in the State University of New York system where the bureaucratic structure has shown amazing resilience.[15]

Adaptation and Change

Indeed, within bounds resistance to change by an organization may be beneficial. One can take the position that the function of an organization is, in part, to weed out discrepant, invalid, and implausible ideas from the environment and that the wisdom of a new way of doing things should be clearly established or it isn't worth the risk of changing an acceptable situation. Theoreticians using adaptation as a focal point for studying survival have studied both its precedents and antecedents. Robbins looks for the necessary prerequisites for adaptiveness under the basic premise that survival *requires* change.[16] He does not accept the proposal that modern organizations choose to ignore their changing environment, but he assumes that they do not perceive environmental alterations because they are shielded by their own complacency. Given these assumptions, he suggests that a certain amount of conflict is beneficial to the organization because it will force the organization to keep abreast of current changes in the environment that affect it. His proposal is described schematically in Figure 11-1.

Adaptation can be thought of as a passive, evolutionary trend. But the dynamic nature of today's organizational environment may require more than passive evolutionary change. Griener contends that even the best future planning by an organization is insufficient to keep pace with the environment.[17] The organization, then, must periodically meet with the environment in stormy, critical periods of growth and change, which he refers to as "revolutions." These revolutions are beyond the control of the organization; anarchical rather than governed, they tend to put the organization "back on the track" to active adaptation and survival.

Skibbins describes three possible organizational states that relate to this environment/organizational interaction.[18] The first is "homeostasis," wherein the internal and external forces exerting pressure on the organization are in equilibrium. In the second state, "adaptation," passive change or evolution is occurring. In modern organizations, however, a third state, "radical change," must come into being when evolutionary movement is not adequate to allow the organization to remain a "going concern."

figure 11-1

CONFLICT/SURVIVAL MODEL. *Source:* Stephen P. Robbins,
Managing Organizational Conflict: A Nontraditional Approach, © 1974, p. 20.
Reprinted by permission of Prentice-Hall, Inc., Englewood Cliffs, New Jersey.

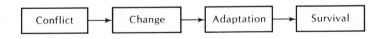

A novel view of passive and active change related to survival is taken in an article entitled, "On Spitting Against the Wind."[19] "Precarious organizations" are those classified as being on the brink of survival. One of the forces that brings about this precarious situation is an organizational incongruency with environmental pressures. Two possible methods are proposed to alleviate the situation. The first, and by far most common, is to adapt and come into line. But an alternative avenue of approach is offered, and that is for the organization to become more radical and dissident. This is done in hopes of building a strong, though small, central, loyal core around a defensive motive. Although there may be some value to this approach in some social organizations, its implications for commercial and business enterprises seems to be somewhat limited.

Certain authors treat adaptation as a by-product of good forecasting and future planning, which allows the organization to "get in on the ground floor" of any important changes. There are yet others who would extend the adaptation implementation beyond this point. Preliminary notions in this regard have been expressed by Mott et al.[20] They suggested that to assume that the environment has "fate control" over an organization missed the full potential of an organization to more fully exploit its environment by gaining some degree of control over it, thus helping to shape its future role in a somewhat "designed" environment.

This view was also popularized by Ackoff.[21] His classification of organizational planning philosophies identifies "satisficing" as the common or traditional planning method that adopted a "doing-well-enough" posture. The "optimizing" philosophy makes use of mathematical models and quantitative methods in an attempt to do the best possible job within the constraints of the present environment as they are now known. However, his "adaptivizing" philosophy pushes beyond compliance, readiness, or responsiveness to a dynamic environment. It proposes that the most attractive policy for the organization to follow is one that will allow it to shape and influence the turn of future events in their direction. There is, of course, ample evidence that this is increasingly being done, and although it may make organizational life more pleasant, some of the tactics may have socially undesirable consequences. Price fixing, market division arrangements, some kinds of lobbying, and so on are all attempts to adapt the environment to the organization. But the importance of adaptation to environmental change for organizational survival is quite clear.

The Demise of Multiorganization Systems

Regardless of how internally efficient, externally adaptable, and free of other problems a given organization may be, it is still not guaranteed survival. The future of the industry or interest within which an organization exists, as well as complementary industries or interests, such as suppliers and customers, are important. The most efficient buggy whip manufacturer in 1890 could claim that credential with little consolation in 1920. The most popular radical college newspaper of 1969 had few laurels to rest upon in 1978.

Industrywide demise is relatively rare and is probably overused as an excuse for singular organizational failures. Murdick et al. list 14 industries, each of which is characterized by both growing and dying firms.[22] An efficient organization in a dying industry may have built up an "energetic surplus" to a level that diversification into another field is a viable avenue of escape.

Even the soundness of an entire industry is of little help if the economic or social system of which it is a part cannot remain viable. For example, private business ownership disappears under communism, and the free press is lost to dictatorships of any political persuasion.

Drucker on Business Survival

Peter Drucker looks at the survival of business organizational forms common today as a function of the continuity of free enterprise.[23] He identifies threats to the survival of relatively unregulated commercial enterprise and sees a lack of understanding by both laymen and employees concerning the how and why of business operations (a social variable) as a major problem. Without such understanding, criticism and calls for increased regulation are placed upon business.[24]

Drucker proposes five functions of a "survival objective" for an organization. A stated objective level must constantly be met in all five areas. Failure in one will lead to failures in the other four, the organization, and its subsystem. Those five functions include:

1. The design of a human organization capable of joint performance, self-perpetuation, and the ability of members to work as individuals but also in common
2. "Approval" of both society and the economy as either can put the business out of existence
3. The efficient production and supply of an economic good or service
4. An ability to deal with a changing economy and changing technology through innovation
5. Profitability[25]

Although Drucker's thrust is *business* organizations, the same general criteria for survival apply to nonprofit organizations as was suggested in

Chapter 10 in the discussion of effectiveness in organizations. Ineffective organizations cannot expect to survive in the long run.

Internal Decay

Another common reason for organizational demise is a breakdown of the structures, processes, policies, and personnel within the firm to the point where the efficient/effective operation mentioned earlier is no longer attainable. This internal decay may result from lack of talent, or from apathy, stagnation, repeated mistakes, or a combination of these and other factors.

Many internal problems are closely akin to the adaptation problems discussed earlier. The organization has a need to adapt its internal structure, etc., as well as its external posture. Greiner points out some problems of internal rigidity, such as clinging to an outmoded structural form, an unbending chief executive officer who refuses to adopt new policies, and the disenchantment of young management talent who feel their suggestions are falling upon deaf ears.[26] He feels that too much emphasis can be placed on *external* adaptation, while the true potential for saving an organization lies in the development of its internal resources. He hypothesizes that internal forces are *more important* than the external ones in shaping the future of the organization.

There are many ways in which internal decay may attack the organization and a number of problems that gnaw at organizations from the inside.[27] For example, in trying to adapt to a rapidly changing environment, the organization may become unable to adjust internally due to constant shifts in policy and structure. Managers may be aware of external alterations and desire to keep abreast but have not the organizational finesse to bring the structure into congruence repeatedly within a short time frame. Changes in administrations with the resulting change in management styles, lack of goal clarity resulting in a lack of unified direction, the underdevelopment of one or more critical functional areas, and a lack of control over operations are all common problems associated with internal decay.[28]

Bennis identifies other core internal problems that are likely to face any organization. Among them he lists a difference between organizational goals and individual needs, an inequitable distribution of power or social influence throughout the organization, the lack of collaboration in resolving and managing conflicts, and the inability to devise and implement a program of revitalization to combat decay.[29]

Kemball-Cook suggests another common causal factor of internal decay: a neglect to program a succession of quality management personnel.

Such a neglect inevitably produces both knowledge and operational "gaps." If these gaps become either too important or too numerous, failure seems imminent.[30]

It is a common contention that organizational change of a planned or programmed nature is the avenue by which to escape internal decay. Suggestions of appropriate change include structural reorganizations, such as varying the amount of centralization in the organization, or altering the horizontal distribution of power among departments. But before undertaking planned internal change, it is wise to pinpoint the causal factor or factors of the decay and orient the change effort toward that problem area. "Shotgun" approaches are notable for their lack of success.

Identification of Problem Areas

How are internal problem areas to be identified? One source suggests that the things that are most important—the life and death issues of the organization—are generally those issues that are "bantered about" to the highest degree within the organization.[31] However, another view holds that those subjects, questions, and problems that may have the very survival of the organization hanging in the balance are those that are most closely guarded and "hushed up." This implies that organization members become anxious when the subject is brought up and tend to withhold comment either to avoid involvement or to screen it out of their consciousness in hopes that it will go away. That issue is clearly not yet resolved.

Problem identification and solution through *team* effort has been advocated in many quarters. The varied input of team members in an open environment is thought to help discover the roots of a problem and provide a multidimensional solution. This approach is just one of the numerous techniques that have been loosely accumulated under the banner of *organizational development*. Organization development is a collection of approaches aimed at improving the processes within a given organization. This is usually accomplished by preparing the personnel of the organization to work well together so as to be more effective.

Disciples tell us that organizational development (OD) is to be used as a preventive, as well as a restorative, measure against internal decay. A problem, of course, is that the OD methods are often not applied until the need is forced upon the organization—at which point the decay is well underway. Under such circumstances the OD "change agent" may be trying to close the gate after the horse has fled.

This section has examined hypothesized causal factors of organizational demise that may be attributed to various forms of internal decay. It seems obvious that the best way to avoid such decay is to *maintain a high level of operational efficiency, flexibility, and awareness*. Organizational development and internal reorganization of the proper scope (both large and small are possible) are two common methods for meeting these goals.

ORGANIZATIONAL LIFE CYCLES

It was suggested in chapter 1 that an organization may undergo a life cycle that is analogous to biological development. The variety of work in this area can be helpful in the search for understanding of organizational survival or demise. The life cycle line of reasoning holds that all biological organisms travel through a continuum marked by birth, life, and death.

Mason Haire did some of the pioneering work in this field with his article, "Biological Models and Empirical Histories of the Growth of Organizations."[32] His research supported the idea that organizations follow biological growth curves. In his work he introduced an important implication related to organizational demise. He explains that the administrative component in large organizations can grow to unwieldy proportions. Just as there is an absolute limit to the size of a physical structure, such as a bridge, there is an absolute limit beyond which an organization cannot support its own operations. Haire does not directly test this idea, but its introduction is of interest here.

In supporting the biological analogy, Gardner introduced an important disclaimer:

> Like people and plants, organizations have a life cycle. They have a green and supple youth, a time of flourishing strength, and a gnarled old age. . . . But organizations differ from people and plants in that their cycle isn't even approximately predictable. An organization may go from youth to old age in two or three decades, or it may last for centuries. Most important, it may go through a period of stagnation and then revive. In short, decline is not inevitable.[33]

Gardner breaks with the formality of the biological analogy by giving the organization the potential for immortality. Second, he hints that "stagnation" rather than a life cycle may be the proximate cause of death.

Chris Argyris also describes the organization as a "living system." This "living system" for Argyris is the entity composed of interpersonal relations that exist beyond the plans, written rules, and official public statements made.[34] It injects a variety of pathologies into the pure, perfect, and logically derived organization, including the retardation of information processing, attempts to stifle necessary conflict, domination by the system of its members, the breeding of low motivational attitudes a campaign for slow, cautious growth, and its own self-perpetuation.[35]

Lippitt supports the biological analogy and equates an organizational life cycle to personality development.[36] His approach to "organizational renewal" is aimed at achieving successively higher levels in the organizational life cycle while simultaneously managing each level in a different manner which is most appropriate, so as to preclude the decline of the organization. Block 11-1 contains a summary of Lippitt's stages in the

block 11-1

LIPPITT'S STAGES OF THE ORGANIZATIONAL
LIFE CYCLE

In Lippitt's view the organization passes through six critical stages that dictate different response patterns. The *first stage* deals with launching the venture. Only about one-half of the organizations formed today proceed much beyond this level. Lippitt calls the *second stage* of organization infancy "survival and sacrifice." Here the organization is constantly "teetering on a survival plateau," which calls for trade-offs of regular sacrifice in order to continue operation. The physical factors related to death at this stage include the promotion of poor products and services, a lack of planning and of foresight, an unrealistic assessment of the market, inadequate capitalization, and leadership inexperience.

The *third stage* is a drive to achieve stability. The organization cannot continually operate on the survival plateau because the deck is stacked against it. The *fourth stage* encompasses pride and perpetuation whereby the organization has a duty to perform critical self-examination to avoid its being caught blindly "out in the cold." The *fifth stage* requires the development of a uniqueness for the organization.

The *final stage* places a responsibility for the organization to return something of value to the society from which it draws its resources. This necessarily goes beyond the production of its "normal" goods and services.

Lippitt points out that although survival is a more pressing concern in the early stages, threats to continuity are real and existent in every stage presented. When a survival issue confronts the organization, realities are accepted, experience and learning are gained, and the organization remains viable as long as the proper response is initiated. When such issues are ignored or handled incorrectly, the organization fails to adjust to new realities and subsequently must either die or remain marginal, which requires continuing sacrifice.

Based on Gordon Lippitt, "Growth Stages in Organizations," *Organizational Renewal* (New York: Appleton-Century-Crofts, 1969), pp. 32–39.

organizational life cycle. Despite the number of opinions supporting life cycles, little empirical testing of the concept has been done to date.

CONCLUSIONS ON ORGANIZATIONAL SURVIVAL

Can we now assume that an organization that is *externally adaptable, internally efficient and flexible,* and on the *upswing* of its life cycle is insulated from harmful occurrences that may precipitate its demise? No. The preceding sections have covered in-depth areas of real concern to an organization's management in its striving for survival. Demise, however, can come in many forms (some of which are controllable by management, and some of which are not). *Natural disasters* can simply wipe out the holdings, market, or interest of an organization to a degree that continuity of operation is quite unfeasible. *Financial insolvency,* which is the most commonly cited reason for organizational demise, can result from many sources and can affect profit and nonprofit organizations alike. Other reasons could be listed, but the point is that there are a number of reasons for organizations going out of existence. Again, some of these are within the control of management, and some are not. The next section will concern itself with better understanding the process of organizational change.

THE PROCESS OF ORGANIZATIONAL CHANGE

The multitude of models purporting to represent the organizational change process[37] argues for one of two conclusions on the part of the student of organizational change. Either the process is not clearly understood and each additional model is a further groping attempt to create the correct model, or "correctness" in a model of organizational change is a function of the particular emphasis of its inventor or user.

The authors admit a bias toward the second of these views. Rather than attempt to view all the change models available, we will adapt one we are comfortable with and use it to explain the change process. The organizational change model proposed by Kurt Lewin will be used as a basic framework from which our discussion of the change process will be conducted.

Lewin's Change Model

Lewin's model is based on the idea that changes in organizations are precipitated by changes in the magnitude, direction, or absolute number of factors that encourage and facilitate change (driving force), by changes in the magnitude, direction, or number of factors that oppose change (restraining forces), or both.[38] See Figure 11-2 for a graphic representation. Organizational stability, or quasi-stationary equilibrium, occurs when these driving and restraining forces balance each other in such a way as to maintain a constant level of functioning for a while.

The process of change is seen as consisting of three phases: (1) unfreezing, in which the balance between restraining and driving forces is upset; (2) moving, in which driving forces are increased and/or restraining forces reduced; and (3) refreezing, in which a new equilibrium is established between the driving forces and the restraining forces.

Although the success of a change attempt depends on completion of the latter two steps (moving and refreezing), an organization's ability to adapt must first be determined by whether or not its current level of functioning can be "unfrozen." That is, if the organization neither perceives a need to change (whether or not one actually exists) nor possesses the desire or ability to alter the status quo, voluntary changes will presumably not be initiated, thus ending possible organizational adaptation before it begins. Identification of the sources of organizational resistance to change, the sources of impetus for organizational change, and the organizational characteristics that accommodate imbalance between these forces should be dealt with since obviously the balance between these forces cannot be systematically upset (unfrozen) until the sources are identified.

Before investigating these forces, however, it is essential to recognize the fact that the *order* in which these forces are brought to bear on an organization is undeterminable.[39] It is useless to attempt to establish

figure 11-2

LEWIN'S CHANGE MODEL

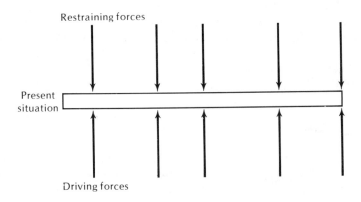

whether or not an organization first feels pressure to change and then experiences resistance in response to the method or agent engaged to eliminate the pressure, or whether the advantages of the status quo prevent the organization from perceiving the sources of impetus for change. Clearly, both considerations are important. Therefore, this chicken/egg question will be ignored, and the discussion of the relevant forces will proceed with forces for change, followed by forces for stability.

Driving Forces (Forces for Change)

As was implied by the earlier discussion, organizations managing to survive for more than a short time inevitably adapt to new external and internal environmental conditions, sometimes whether the participants and powerholders want to or not.[40] This suggests that change can come in two ways: involuntarily or voluntarily.

Involuntary changes arise for many reasons but quite commonly as a result of personnel turnover.[41] As Kaufman explains "replacement personnel in organizations are all a little bit different than their predecessors (and from each other), particularly if they are of different generations . . . they produce changes. . . . The process may be very gradual and consequently almost imperceptible. . .nevertheless, it goes on relentlessly."[42] Thus, "the regeneration of organizations" comes about quite naturally.

Another need for change is experienced by organizational participants in the form of pressures or anxieties, which are created by discrepancies between the desired (or potential) level of organization (formal or informal) functioning and the actual (or predicted) level. That is, "a motive force for change occurs in 'discrepant situations,' in cases of a difference between stimulus and a person's 'internal anchors' of attitudes, perceptions, or whatever."[43]

These discrepancies can be viewed from two perspectives: (1) perception of the potential state—where the key factor is an organization's positive (or negative) predisposition toward change in general, or (2) perception of the actual state—where the organization's internal and external environment are critical. Again, these ideas are related in an operational way to Weick's "enacted Environment" discussed in chapter 1 and referred to in several places throughout this book.

Perception of the Potential State: Attitude Set

Albanese notes that there is now a tendency on the part of some organizations to respond to the recognition of the need to function in a rapidly changing environment by assuming a positive attitude set toward change. He argues that "the main thrust . . . is toward the idea of accepting and coping with changes, and becoming more open (less restraint) to those proposed and desired."[44]

He attributes this emphasis on change found in the literature to five phenomena associated with modern organizations:

1. The urgent need for change
2. The presence of organizational slack* that gives the organization room for experimentation
3. The appeal of novelty, which presumably satisfies the organizational needs for stimulation
4. The presence of "operational theories," which allow the organization to evaluate and measure the impact of proposed changes
5. The focus of social scientists (who are in the change business) who depend on successful implementation of stability[45]

But, beyond this supposed shift in organizational attitudes toward change in general, most students of organizational change would agree that in order for specific change proposals to be successful, a more dramatic set of forces than simply a favorable attitude set toward change must be active; that is, there must be a set of forces specifically relating to existing organizational circumstances. That this is the case is evidenced by the relative emphasis in the literature on specific sources of impetus for change relative to the emphasis on these attitudinal factors.

Perception of the Actual State: Internal and External Environment

Of the factors that have been identified as contributors to the creation of a need for change, most can be categorized as being either internal or external to the organization.

Internal factors refer to those things within the organization that have a potential for creating organizational unrest and include such things as favorable experiences with organizational changes,[46] changes in organizational goals (or reordering of multiple goals),[47] incongruity of personal and organizational goals,[48] presence of innovators or eccentrics,[49] strikes, low productivity, and rising costs,[50] unfavorable organizational climate,[51] resistance to authority and other power conflicts between organizational units,[52] and other conflicting situations.

External factors, although not necessarily unrelated to the internal factors, refer to those forces in the organization's external environment

---

Organizational slack is the term used to refer to the difference between the payments required to maintain an organization and the resources obtained from the environment, which tends to increase with organizational effectiveness and success (Albanese, p. 527).

that increase the amount of uncertainty with which the organization must cope and include such things as changes in knowledge or technology, economic opportunities, distribution of political power, demographic makeup of the population, ecological considerations, and ideological and cultural factors.[53]

The important point regarding these factors, as suggested earlier in the discussion on survival, is that no one factor should be singled out as a source of pressure for change but that any number within either category can be active at any one time. Evidence suggests that successful changes are associated with cases involving both types of pressure together; unsuccessful change attempts more commonly emerge out of situations in which only one type is present.[54]

Restraining Forces (Forces for Stability)

The literature that addresses the organizational tendency to resist change focuses on resistance that arises from a pair of sources: personal and systemic. Resistance from either sector can be fully intentional, in which case the practitioner may find a rational model of the change process useful, or the resistance can be somewhat unintentional and require additional measures to bring it to the surface.

Personal Sources of Resistance

Individuals may resist specific change proposals or change in general for various reasons of which they may or may not be aware. Conscious resistance presumably arises when an individual perceives a change as a threat to the security of personal advantages associated with the status quo. Conversely, resistance may arise as a result of anticipated disadvantages that accompany change. It is not our purpose to deal with all possible sources of individual resistance to change; that is best left for a book on psychology or organizational behavior. Suffice it to say that there are a number of sources of personal resistance to change and that personal resistance *can* result in unsuccessful change attempts and often does if not dealt with properly.

Systemic Sources of Resistance

In addition to the conscious and unconscious efforts of individuals to oppose change, there are obstacles to change inherent in the organization rather than in the individuals who make it up. Such barriers to change include resource limitations, sunk costs, accumulation of official constraints, unofficial and unplanned constraints on behavior, and inter-organizational agreements.[55]

Resource Limitations

An organization's inability to acquire the means to implement restorative measures, despite a recognition of the desirability of such action, obviously impedes change. Limited natural resources, an inability to penetrate new product markets, or an inability to increase production capacity (through lack of funds or space), may all inhibit change.

Sunk Costs and Vested Interests

Change that threatens the safe return of heavy investments in the status quo is likely to be resisted by the affected parties. Commitments of time, energy, and money that have been made to ensure that the existing system will work undoubtedly explain the tendency of older people, line managers (as opposed to staff specialists), and capital-intensive organizations to resist change.

Accumulation of Official Constraints on Behavior

Organizations become enmeshed in a network of rules, regulations, and procedures that seldom become less over time. In addition to the obvious difficulty associated with attempting to change a single policy without affecting other interrelated policies, official hiring practices may endanger the chances of change attempts. This would be especially true of personnel departments that fail to hire individuals having diverse backgrounds, since it has been shown that heterogeneity increases the likelihood that new ideas emerge.

Unofficial and Unplanned Constraints on Behavior

Informal groups within an organization develop a host of customary practices that often become as rigid as law. Watson has suggested several aspects of these unofficial laws that impede change.[56] For instance, he notes that since organizational norms (which make it possible for organization members to work together) are shared, they cannot be easily changed by an individual without serious repercussions. In particular, norms regarding moral and ethical issues are especially resistant to change. Finally, he notes that changes that come to the organization from the "outside" will inevitably be met with the suspicion and hostility due all strangers.

Interorganizational Agreements

Commitments to other organizations—for example, labor unions—competitors, suppliers, customers, and public authorities (in return for licenses/permits) usually impose limitations or obligations on organizational members that also limit the range of possible changes.

According to Lewin, a change is initiated when restraining forces are reduced, driving forces are increased, or both. The simplicity of Lewin's model is somewhat complicated by the fact that voluntary change cannot be initiated until the sources of impetus for change have filtered through the mental blinders of those with the power to initiate change. In order to effectively penetrate a filter, the environmental circumstances must create a discrepancy, or lack of confirmation or disconfirmation, which then creates a desire to reduce the discrepancy.[57] In this way, driving forces become activated and upset the balance between opposing forces.

With this modification in mind, it is possible to define the determinants of organizational change as those characteristics of an organization that improve the likelihood that: (1) internal/external factors will penetrate mental blinders and become driving forces, and (2) calculated resistance and systemic barriers (restraining forces) will be reduced.

Hage and Aiken on Determinants of Change

The major systematic study of organization characteristics as they relate to the initiation of change is the work of Hage and Aiken.[58] Their study focused on the rate of program change (addition of new services or products) and its relationship to seven organizational characteristics:

1. Complexity
2. Centralization
3. Formalization
4. Stratification
5. Morale or job satisfaction
6. Rate of production
7. Efficiency

In addition to these characteristics, there is evidence to support the notion that a flexible boundary structure between the organization and its external environment is likely to be associated with organizations having high rates of change.[59]

Complexity

Complexity, defined as the level of knowledge and expertise in an organization, was found to be directly related to the rate of program change. The measures of complexity used in the Hage and Aiken study were the number of occupational specialists in the organization, the length of training required, and the degree of involvement in professional societies. The cause of the established relationship between change and complexity was thought to be associated with coordination problems and conflict between the large numbers of different specialists and with the increases in ancillary occupations needed to support them.

Further support is given to the notion that high degrees of organizational complexity are associated with higher rates of change by Hummon et al.[60] Their structural control model of organizational change posited the number of divisions that functionally differentiate the work force (along with three other independent variables) against change and found significance is in the expected direction.

Centralization

Centralization, defined as the concentration of decision making into the hands of a few persons, was found to be inversely related to the rate of program change by Hage and Aiken. Although two aspects of centralization were investigated—centralization of agencywide decisions (hiring; promotion; policy, program, and service adoption) and centralization of decisions concerning the performance of a specific job—only the agencywide decisions were found to be important in explaining the rate of program change. This centralization variable presumably reflects the notion that the power of persons to veto new ideas or fail to give them the requisite support is exercised as a means of guarding against changes that would redistribute that power; hence, few changes are considered, and even fewer are initiated.

Formalization

Formalization, defined as the degree of job codification, was found to be inversely related to the rate of program change by Hage and Aiken. Formalization presumably discourages new suggestions, new patterns of behavior, and incentive to search for better ways of performing tasks. It is important to note, however, that research relating formalization to successful implementation of changes (rather than initiation) yields opposite conclusions; that is, formalization is regarded as a necessary component of implementations of change.

Stratification

Stratification, defined as unequal distribution of rewards, status, fringe benefits, and barriers to mobility between hierarchical levels, was found to be inversely related to the rate of program change by Hage and Aiken. The explanation of this finding follows the argument given regarding the effect of centralization on program change; that is, persons with high status and salary will veto changes that threaten their advantages. In addition, it was suggested that high degrees of stratification reduce both the quantity and quality of upward communications.

Again, the Hummon et al. structural control model of organizational change lends support to the validity of this variable as an explanation of program change. In that study it was found that the mean number of hierarchical levels over all divisions had a significant negative correlation with change.

Rate of Production

The rate of production, defined as the emphasis on high volumes of production (as opposed to emphasis on quality of production), was found to be inversely related to the rate of program change by Hage and Aiken. It was presumed that changes designed to improve volume were less critical than those related to quality improvement and would therefore be made less often. Changes aimed at improving volume would also initially be met with declines in volume as individuals involved in the change process learn new skills. It would appear that the questionable rationale behind the use of this variable in explaining program change is matched only by the tentativeness of their evidence for it; that is, high volume industries have relatively smaller proportions of their budgets devoted to research and development than do low volume industries.

We suspect that the critical variable here may not be the volume of production, but rather the unit profit margin. Organizations that stress quality (low volume) presumably face more inelastic demands and have higher markups over cost—that is, more organizational slack. High-volume organizations may not enjoy the benefits of inelastic demands and may therefore have less slack. This is not to say that markups are the only determinants of organizational affluence, but it does suggest that organizational slack may be highly correlated with the Hage and Aiken volume variable. Although there is conflicting evidence as to the effect of organizational slack on program change, Wieland and Ullrich do cite two studies in which a low, positive relationship to innovation was found.[61]

Efficiency

Efficiency, defined as emphasis on cost reduction or resource conservation, was found to be inversely related to the rate of program change by Hage and Aiken. The logic behind the use of this variable is, of course, that change is not free and that even changes that are designed to reduce costs are not without their inefficiencies in the beginning. It can be argued that modern management techniques designed to improve efficiency in decision making may also increase rigidity into the decision-making process because of large investments in time and money.

Job Satisfaction and Morale

Job satisfaction, defined as satisfaction with pay, working conditions, supervisors, and peers, was found to be directly related to the rate of program change by Hage and Aiken. It was assumed that high degrees of job satisfaction were associated with high degrees of job commitment and that this commitment allowed greater perception of discrepancies between actual levels of functioning and desired levels that inevitably led to recognitions of a need for change.

Since the variable that Hage and Aiken were evidently measuring was really not job satisfaction as the term is commonly used but, rather, job commitment, it is not clear that this variable is very different from the Hage and Aiken complexity variable that measured the degree of professionalism. Indeed, there is no reason to suspect that only professionals and specialists are committed to their jobs.

Boundary Structures

Although the internal structural variables identified by Hage and Aiken provide insight into our understanding of conditions that increase an organization's propensity to change, an investigation of boundary structures as they relate to change is also enlightening. It has been suggested that rigid boundary structures between an organization and its external environment are frequently found to be associated with organizations that face heavy external pressures for change.[62] However, it has further been suggested that such a structure cannot survive under these circumstances and that heuristic or flexible structures are more functional for such organizations.

That a flexible boundary structure is an important characteristic of innovative organizations is further supported by Czepiel's study of innovation–diffusion in which a functioning interorganizational communication network was found to be active.[63]

Perhaps the most important point made in the Hage and Aiken study is that the seven variables and rate of program change are interrelated and move together in compatible ways; that is, organizations having high rates of program change are characterized as having high degrees of complexity and job satisfaction and low degrees of centralization, formalization, stratification, production (volume), and efficiency emphasis. The flexible boundary structures identified by Butkovich et al. as being associated with organizations that face high rates of change in the external environment are also compatible with the characteristics identified by Hage and Aiken.

CONCLUSIONS ON THE CHANGE
PROCESS

The current emphasis in the literature is on developing methods for organizations to deal with changes in their environments, as well as the uncertainty and ignorance related to those changes. In the preceding, an attempt has been made to identify (1) those broad categories of environmental changes that argue strongly for organizational responses, (2) those broad categories of resistance to change that argue strongly for not responding, and (3) those organizational characteristics that reflect the organization's actual tendency to respond.

It was seen that driving forces for change are expressed as tension or pressure on organizational participants who seek to be relieved via organizational changes. The specific environmental changes most pertinent to organizations include changing attitudes toward change in general and conditions in the organization's internal and external environment that deviate from desired or assumed conditions.

Restraining forces were those conditions within the organizational actors or the system that impede efforts to change. These include both built-in obstacles as well as barriers erected for specific occasions to reflect acknowledged advantages of the status quo and recognized costs of change.

Successful attempts to change organizational functioning are initiated when the balance between these driving and restraining forces is upset so that the sum of the driving forces exceeds the sum of the restraining forces. It was shown that organizations having high rates of change or relatively unstable balances between driving and restraining forces have a set of characteristics that are interrelated and compatible.

As Hage and Aiken suggest, the set of organizational characteristics associated with low rates of change tend to arise in relatively stable environments, or in the terms used in this analysis, when there is a relatively stable equilibrium between driving and restraining forces. Conversely, the set of organizational characteristics associated with high rates of program change tend to arise in dynamic environments where the balance between driving and restraining forces is easily upset.

This analysis of the change process can be used as a reminder that organizational responses to relative increases in driving forces cannot safely ignore changes in restraining forces that may also evolve. Indeed, it has been suggested that the absence of restraining forces may be an important signal calling for further investigation.[64] In addition, one author has specifically noted that resistance to change is an important ingredient in successful changes, since resistance can serve to weed out those changes that would be harmful to the organization.[65] The point is, of course, that an organization must maintain stability (balanced forces) as well as grow (unbalanced forces), and in order for organizations to perform both of these tasks, practitioners cannot concentrate on changing organization characteristics in response to environmental changes without also worrying about refreezing the new equilibrium. The discussion now turns to a very brief look at a concept that purports to deal with organizational change at the practitioner's level: organizational development (OD).

ORGANIZATIONAL DEVELOPMENT

Figure 11-3 illustrates the relationship between formal and informal organizational components.[66] The top part of the figure represents such formalized parts of an organization as structure, policies, physical facilities, job descriptions, and other tangible attributes. Organizational management can concentrate on organizational problem solving in the formalized structure, personnel changes, and so on. OD practitioners argue that response to environmental change was often made without regard for possible dysfunctional impact on other organizational systems, especially the "informal organizational" systems.

figure 11-3

FORMAL AND INFORMAL
ORGANIZATIONAL SYSTEMS

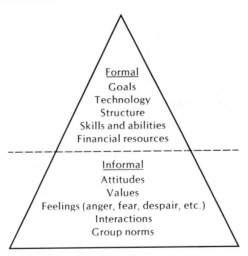

The bottom half of Figure 11-3 is concerned with the "human reactions" of organizational personnel. Interpersonal reactions and peer and work group competitions and alliances. It is argued that change in the formal structure of an organization may substantially influence the informal structure by fostering free expression and improved interpersonal relationships or dysfunctionally by developing feelings of isolation, depersonalization, and passivity. What is needed according to some OD practitioners is a balanced system that recognizes the interrelationship of formal and informal parts of an organization when planning and implementing change. Organizational development is represented as such a system.[67]

Leavitt's much reproduced diagram of the relationship that exists among the parts of the organization provides us another illustration of the potential targets for OD intervention in an organization.[68] Figure 11-4 shows those potential targets. The double ended arrows in the diagram indicate that the variables are interrelated and dependent on each other.

To attempt change in any or all of the target areas, a number of OD techniques are available. It isn't our purpose to go into great detail but for those interested in learning more about each we recommend Edgar Huse's book *Organization Development and Change*.[69] A listing of possible OD change tactics would include:

1. Sensitivity training
2. Survey feedback
3. Team development
4. Change in reward structures
5. Change in decision-making structure
6. Change in authority structure
7. Technological innovations
8. Role clarification[70]

figure 11-4

POTENTIAL OD TARGETS

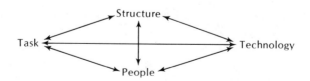

block 11-2

AN EXAMPLE OF OD: CORNING GLASS

The Corning approach to organizational development provides an example of the scope and application of organizational development techniques. Long regarded as a pace setter for organizational development, Corning is a centrally managed, highly productive diversified organization. Corning's organizational development program is a unified strategy based on Argyris' organizational culture determinants of (1) structure and technology, (2) leadership and interpersonal relationships, (3) administrative controls and regulations, and (4) human controls. Corning considers change in all four characteristics as being necessary for program success.

The Corning organizational development program views the organization as a system of interlocking subsystems that tend toward equilibrium. The intervention process at Corning initially occurred at lower levels and spread to other parts of the organization. At Corning, the attitude of top management toward organizational development is regarded as "benevolent neutrality."

Team building is the most frequently applied method of intervention; however, structural intervention usually precedes the social and interpersonal changes brought about through team building. As a general rule, Corning has found structural intervention effective with lower level employees and process intervention more effective at higher levels. Process intervention equated to decision-making activities and structural intervention with implementation of decisions. Intervention included:

1. Monthly group meetings at any level
2. Weekly meeting of plant managers and a sample of production and clerical employees
3. Technical and productivity sessions
4. Establishment of autonomous groups with total responsibility for scheduling, assembly and training
5. Allowing hourly workers to determine productivity goals
6. Redesign of personnel and pay systems to reflect performance

The Corning intervention process attempts to develop the idea that employees have a personal stake in the organizational development process.

The Corning program has resulted in quantitative improvements. For example, at Corning's Medfield plant, production rejects dropped from 23 percent to 1 percent and absenteeism from 11 percent to 1 percent in a six-month period. New product innovation increased significantly, and there was substantial improvement in the levels of cooperation between functional areas.

Based on W. F. Dowling, "Organizational Development: The Corning Approach," *Management Review* 64 (October 1975):43–52.

How Good is OD?

Because there are numerous difficulties in measuring effectiveness and evaluating the results of an organizational development program, there is little evidence on either the number of OD program failures or successes. Studies on less than 10 percent of implemented organizational development programs suggest three main reasons for program failure. These reasons are:

1. Failure of the management/consultant group to correctly tailor the program to actual needs of the organization.

2. Failure to correctly model appropriate personnel behavior in the program. Emphasis should be toward enhancement of individual motivation through increased employee participation and by developing personal growth and self-esteem.

3. Failure of the organization to structure its personnel system and its reward system for productivity.[71]

But OD efforts are successful as well. Block 11-2 gives an example of a successful OD intervention.

CONCLUSIONS ABOUT ORGANIZATIONAL DEVELOPMENT

Organizational development programs are behavioral science–oriented systems intended to facilitate the management of internal organizational change. They are methods of response to environmental changes in technology markets, social/cultural climate, and so on.

Organizational development theory began with T-group or sensitivity training; moved into team building, encounter, and confrontation groups; and is now attempting to focus on the entire organizational structure. The specific orientation toward behavioral sciences and McGregor's "Theory Y" system of participative management implies that program success is most likely in a democratic organizational climate or under persuasive leadership styles of management. A number of techniques are available. Our purpose here was merely to suggest OD as a potential approach for managing the problems of organization change, not to review it extensively.

NOTES

[1]Robert G. Murdick, Richard H. Eckhouse, and Thomas W. Zimmerer, "The Struggle for Survival and Prosperity," *Business Policy: A Framework for Analysis* (Columbus, Ohio: Grid, 1972), p. 61.

[2]W. H. Starbuck, "Organizational Growth and Development," *Organizational Growth and Development* (Middlesex, England: Penguin Books, Ltd., 1971), p. 30.

[3]R. B. Kemball-Cook, *The Organization Gap* (Beverly Hills, Calif.: Davlin Publications, 1972), p. 54.

[4]James L. Gibson, John M. Ivancevich, and James H. Donnelly, *Organizations: Structure, Processes, Behavior* (Dallas: Business Publications, 1973), p. 37.

[5]Gerald J. Skibbins, *Organizational Evolution: A Program for Managing Radical Change* (New York: AMACOM, 1974), p. 106.

[6]K. W. Rothschild, "Price Theory and Oligopoly," *Economic Journal* 42 (1947): 297.

[7]William J. Gore, *Administrative Decision-Making: A Heuristic Model* (New York: Wiley, 1964), p. 23.

[8]Louis C. Schroeter, *Organizational Elan* (New York: American Management Association, 1970), p. 87.

[9]Harold Leavitt, Lawrence Pinfield, and Eugene Webb, eds., *Organizations of the Future: Interaction with the External Environment* (New York: Praeger Publishers, 1974), p. 22.

[10]Alton C. Bartlett and Thomas A. Sayer, "Part IV," *Changing Organizational Behavior* (Englewood Cliffs, N.J.: Prentice-Hall, 1973), pp. 375–434.

[11]Chris Argyris, "Today's Problems with Tomorrow's Organizations," *Journal of Management Studies* 4 (1967):31–55.

[12]Warren G. Bennis, "The Coming Death of Bureaucracy," *Organization Structuring*, ed. H. Eric Frank (London: McGraw-Hill, 1971), pp. 9–18.

[13]Paul Spencer and Cyril Sofer, "Organizational Change and Its Management," *Organization Structuring*, ed. H. Eric Frank (London: McGraw-Hill, 1971), p. 276.

[14]J. W. Gardner, "How to Prevent Organizational Dry Rot," *Harper's* 231 (October 1965): 20–26.

[15]Warren Bennis, "The Sociology of Institutions or Who Sank the Yellow Submarine?" *Psychology Today* 6 (November 1972):112–20.

[16]S. P. Robbins, *Managing Organizational Conflict: A Nontraditional Approach* (Englewood Cliffs, N.J.: Prentice-Hall, 1974).

[17]Larry E. Greiner, "Patterns of Organization Change," *Organization Structuring*, ed. H. Eric Frank (London: McGraw-Hill, 1971), pp. 256–72.

[18]Skibbins, *Organizational Evolution*, pp. 8–9.

[19]"On Spitting Against the Wind: Organizational Precariousness and American Irreligion," *American Journal of Sociology* 71 (1966):674–87.

[20]Mary P. Mott, Harold B. Repinsky, John Riner, and Karl E. Weick, "The Research Team and Its Organizational Environment," *Studies on Behavior in Organizations: A Research Symposium*, ed. Raymond V. Bowers (Athens: University of Georgia Press, 1966), p. 149.

[21]Russell Ackoff, "Philosophies of Planning," *A Concept of Corporate Planning* (New York: Wiley-Interscience, 1970), pp. 6–20.

[22]Murdick et al., "The Struggle for Survival and Prosperity," p. 85.

[23]Peter F. Drucker, chapter 9: "Business Objectives and Survival Needs," *Technology, Management, and Society* (New York: Harper & Row, 1970), pp. 149–65.

[24]Ibid., p. 151.

[25]Ibid., p. 160.

[26]Larry E. Greiner,"Evolution and Revolution as Organizations Grow," *Harvard Business Review* 50 (July/August 1972):37–46.

27Murdick et al., "The Struggle for Survival and Prosperity."

28Ibid.

29Bennis, "The Coming Death of Bureaucracy," pp. 13–15.

30Kemball-Cook, *The Organization Gap*, p. 191.

31Mott et al., "The Research Team," p. 146.

32Mason Haire, "Biological Models and Empirical Histories of the Growth of Organizations," *Modern Organization Theory*, ed. Mason Haire (New York: Wiley, 1959), pp. 272–306.

33Gardner, "How to Prevent Organizational Dry Rot," p. 20.

34Argyris, "Today's Problems," p. 239.

35Ibid., pp. 240–42.

36Gordon Lippitt, "Growth Stages of Organization," *Organizational Renewal* (New York: Appleton-Century-Crofts, 1969), p. 27.

37See John W. Hunt, *The Restless Organization* (Sydney: Wiley, Australasia Pty. Ltd., 1972), pp. 301–447, for a good review of these models.

38Kenneth D. Benne and M. Birnbaum, "Principles of Changing," *The Planning of Change*, ed. K. Benne, W. Bennis, and R. Chin (New York: Holt, Rinehart & Winston, 1969), pp. 328–35.

39Robert C. Shirley, "Model for Analysis of Organizational Change," *MSU Business Topics* 22 (Spring 1974):60–68.

40Herbert Kaufman, *The Limits of Organizational Change* (University, Alabama: University of Alabama Press, 1971).

41George F. Wieland and Robert A. Ullrich, *Organizations: Behavior, Design, and Change* (Homewood, Ill.: Irwin, 1976), p. 459.

42Kaufman, *The Limits of Organizational Change*, p. 42.

43Robert T. Golembiewski, *Renewing Organizations: The Laboratory Approach to Planned Change* (Itasca, Ill.: F. E. Peacock, 1972), p. 101.

44Robert Albanese, "Overcoming Resistance to Stability," *Business Horizons* 13 (April 1970):35–42, reprinted in N. Margulies and A. Raia, eds., *Organizational Development: Values, Process, and Technology* (New York: McGraw-Hill, 1972), pp. 527–30.

45Ibid.

46A. S. King, "Expectation Effects in Organizational Change," *Administrative Science Quarterly* 19 (June 1974):221–30.

47Jerald Hage and Michael Aiken, *Social Change in Complex Organizations* (New York: Random House, 1970).

48James V. Clark, "A Healthy Organization," *California Management Review* 4 (Summer 1962), reprinted in K. Benne, W. Bennis, and R. Chin, eds., *The Planning of Change* (New York: Holt, Rinehart & Winston, 1969), pp. 282–97.

49Kaufman, *The Limits of Organizational Change*, p. 44.

50Greiner, "Patterns of Organization Change."

51Donald Helriegal and John W. Slocum, *Management: A Contingency Approach* (Reading, Mass.: Addison-Wesley, 1974), pp. 427–51.

52Donald A. Schon, *Technology and Change: The New Heraclitus* (New York: Dell, 1967), p. 64.

53Joseph R. Martino, *Technological Forecasting for Decision Making* (New York: American Elsevier, 1972).

54Greiner, "Patterns of Organizational Change."

55These items and the following discussion are suggested by Kaufman, *The Limits of Organizational Change*; and Kast and Rosenzwerg in their book *Organization and Management: A System Approach*. (New York: McGraw-Hill, 1974), pp. 572–98.

56Goodwin Watson, "Resistance to Change," *Concepts for Social Change*, ed. Goodwin Watson (Washington, D.C.: National Training Laboratories, 1966), reprinted in K. Bennis, W. Benne, and R. Chin, eds., *The Planning of Change* (New York: Holt, Rinehart & Winston, 1969), pp. 493–96.

57Edgar H. Schein, "The Mechanisms of Change," *Interpersonal Dynamics*, ed. W. Bennis, Schein, Steele and Berlew (Homewood, Ill.: The Dorsey Press, 1964), reprinted in K. Bennis, W. Benne, and R. Chin, eds., *The Planning of Change* (New York: Holt, Rinehart & Winston, 1969), p. 98.

58Much of the following discussion owes its substance to Hage and Aiken, *Social Change in Complex Organizations* and to the review of their work in Wieland and Ullrich, *Organizations*, pp. 447–55.

[59]Paul Butkovich, Marion Sullivan, and Boris Astrachan, "Boundary Structures and Responses of Community Mental Health Centers to Pressures for Change," *Academy of Management Proceedings* (New York: Holt, Rinehart & Winston, 1969), pp. 62–78.

[60]Norman P. Hummon, Patrick Doreian, and Klaus Teuter, "A Structural Control Model of Organizational Change," *American Sociological Review* 40 (December 1975): 813–24.

[61]Wieland and Ullrich, *Organizations*, p. 458.

[62]Butkovich et al., "Boundary Structures and Responses."

[63]John A. Czepiel, "Patterns of Interorganizational Communications and the Diffusion of a Major Technological Innovation in a Competitive Industrial Community," *Academy of Management Journal* 18 (March 1975):6–24.

[64]Albanese, "Overcoming Resistance to Stability."

[65]Donald Klein, "Some Notes on the Dynamics of Resistance to Change: The Defender Role," *Concepts for Social Change*, ed. Goodwin Watson (Washington, D.C.: National Training Laboratories, 1966), reprinted in K. Bennis, W. Benne, and R. Chin, eds., *The Planning of Change* (New York: Holt, Rinehart & Winston, 1969), pp. 498–507.

[66]Wendell L. French and Cecil H. Bell, Jr., *Organizational Development* (Englewood Cliffs, N.J.: Prentice-Hall, 1973), p. 18.

[67]A. F. Hollingsworth and J. W. Haas, "Structural Planning in Organizational Development," *Personnel Journal* 54 (December 1975):614.

[68]H. Leavitt, *Managerial Psychology*, 3rd ed. (Chicago: University of Chicago Press, 1972), p. 263.

[69]Edgar F. Huse, *Organizational Development and Change* (New York: West, 1975).

[70]Ibid., p. 306.

[71]M. G. Evans, "Failure in Organizational Development Programs: What Went Wrong?" *Business Horizons* 17 (April 1974):19.

SUGGESTIONS FOR FURTHER READING

FRENCH, W., and BELL, C. *Organizational Development*. Englewood Cliffs, N.J.: Prentice-Hall, 1973.

HAGE, HAROLD, and AIKEN, MICHAEL. *Social Change in Complex Organizations*. New York: Random House, 1970.

HUSE, EDGAR F. *Organizational Development and Change*. St. Paul: West Publishing, 1975.

section four   DIALOGUE

Section four has focused on the expected outcomes of good organization design: the continuing existence of the organization. What organizations seek to achieve is becoming clearer, but how the various possible outcomes become the goals of the organization and which ones come to predominate is not as yet clear. The goal formation and selection process has been a relatively neglected area of study in organization theory. In the dialogue selection by Duncan you are exposed to one view of how goals are formed. You may wish to argue that the goals of many organizations—business, for example—are well known and understood. But a quick review of the literature will show that not all writers are willing to accept the premise that profit is the sole goal of all businesses. Even if one were to accept profit as a common goal, there are still many alternative routes to its achievement, and each such alternative could become the operational goal for an organization. Duncan's reading provides us with a way of understanding how an organization arrives at its goals.

A common thread throughout all organization theory literature has been a concern for organizational effectiveness. The goal of organizational research is first to understand organizations, but ultimately it is to be able to manipulate them so as to improve their performance. Most of the current research has focused on understanding rather than manipulating organizations. The article by Child represents one of the most extensive attempts to link organizational characteristics with performance. Although the field is not at the point where its knowledge can be used to manipulate with precision, the work reported by Child offers promise that it may eventually occur. His article is an appropriate summary for this book on organization theory since he summarizes and interrelates the major points we have made in the preceding chapters.

ORGANIZATIONS AS POLITICAL COALITIONS:
A Behavioral View of the Goal Formation Process

W. JACK DUNCAN

Within the contemporary theory of formal organization, much is said of the importance of organizational goals. It has been noted, for example, that goals are instrumental in defining the organization in its environment so as to establish legitimacy, to provide for the coordination of diverse subunits, and to establish the standards for performance evaluation (17).

When reading the literature on goal formation, one is impressed with two factors. First, everyone agrees that to accurately understand organizational processes, one must recognize the importance of goals. Second, although goals are universally accepted as basic to organization and management, little attention has been directed toward a systematic theory of goal formation. Thus, on one hand, we concede the importance of goals, while on the other hand we do little to explain how they come into being.

In this paper an attempt will be made to examine and expand one view of organizational goal formation. This view is labeled the political theory because of the way in which goals are said to emerge. The thesis is not new. It is hoped, however, that the process will provide some perspectives that are seldom scrutinized with any degree of seriousness.

SOME PRELIMINARY CONSIDERATIONS

Before we can examine the political theory of goal formation we must set the stage for the discussion by answering two critical questions. The first is the pragmatic issue of why such a topic is worthy of discussion. The second question is a historical one because it provides some insight into how the problem of goal formation has been traditionally resolved.

The Question of Relevancy

Organizational goals are theoretically important at two interrelated levels of analysis. At the intraorganizational level it is difficult to imagine a more important question than the one that asks how organizational goals are formulated. Why, for example, does one organization favor owners in the conduct of its affairs and another favor employees? Or, why is one organization dedicated to healing while another is created for the purpose of destruction?

At the interorganizational level, the problems are equally compelling.

Source: Journal of Behavioral Economics (Summer 1976):25–44, by permission.

Why do union-management relations exhibit changing trends over time? Why do government agencies interact closely with some organizations and very little with others? Obviously, to answer questions of this nature, and related ones at the intraorganizational level, a number of political, environmental, philosophical, and sociological factors must be considered. A few of the more important will occupy our attention in forthcoming sections of the paper.

Conventional Wisdom

Historically, several assumptions have been advanced about organizational goal formation so that seemingly more important administrative issues could be examined. Perhaps the most familiar picture of goal formation is that proposed by microeconomic theory. For purposes of analytical simplicity and theoretical necessity, economic theory proposes the profit-maximization assumption. In the case of noneconomic organizations, utility is substituted in the maximization calculus.

Modern developments in decision theory have challenged the maximization hypothesis (9). Even more important is the growing emphasis on the incongruency between various normative performance criteria that view conflict, rather than coordination, as the natural state of affairs (11, 32).

If we leave economics and move to more applied organizational behavior and theory, we find only slightly more attention is directed toward a systematic theory of goal formation. Here, the attention is directed toward the behavioral processes that describe how organizational goals emerge.

One of the frequently proposed theories is that organizational goals can be effectively viewed as a summation or composite of the individuals' objectives within the group (18). Various studies in noneconomic organizations have been frequently referenced to support this proposition (1, 7, 8).

The alternative argument, sometimes referred to as the natural systems view, visualizes organizational goals as distinct from the objectives of individual members. As with the previous case, empirical studies and holistic theories have been advanced in support of the independence view (21, 38, 42).

GOAL FORMATION AS A POLITICAL PROCESS

The modern behavioral theory of the firm was the first important conceptual model of decision making to question the conventional maximization assumption of normative management theory (9). Although the logic is sound, theoretical extensions and empirical testing of the alternative view have been lacking. Because of this, we must briefly look at the implications at a rather simplistic plane.

Triads, Coalitions, and Coalitions of Coalitions

A triad is a three-person group (25, 31). Coalitions are goal-oriented alliances among individuals with different interests that are formed to mobilize joint resources so as to influence the outcome of a contest and divide the spoils of victory (15, 29). The goal of a coalition is to increase its power vis-à-vis other groups.

One of the most useful schema for analyzing coalition formation in simple three person groups was advanced by Caplow (1968). Although he proposed a variety of alternative patterns, we can illustrate the point by looking at only three cases.

Let us assume initially that we have three individuals. We will refer to them as A, B, and C. We will further assume that individual power is distributed as follows:

$$A > B > C \text{ and}$$
$$A < (B + C)$$

Schematically, this means that A has more power than B who has more power than C. However, the combined power of B and C is greater than that of A. In this case, the likely coalition is B and C against A. It is also possible that A would align with B or C to negate the possibility of a BC coalition.

It might also be possible to confront a situation where $A > B > C$ but the combined power of B and C is equal to that of A. Or, more formally, $[A = (B + C)]$. In this case, there is less likelihood of a coalition since an alignment of B and C can only neutralize the power of A. A, in turn, has little reason to form an alliance except to block a neutralizing BC coalition.

A final relevant possibility is where $A = (B + C)$ and $B = C$. In this case, a basically indeterminant situation exists. A may align with B or C to overpower the isolate or B and C might form a coalition to neutralize the power of A.

We could continue to look at the other theoretical combinations. However, the point is simply that the types of coalitions likely to emerge in triads depend on the relative power distributions of all parties. Since the goal is to win a contest, pragmatic power issues become the important factors for consideration.

In order to extend the analysis to the interorganizational level, it is possible to look at coalition patterns in triads from a group perspective. This can be done with the aid of Figure 1.

This figure shows a hierarchical pattern of power structures that are extremely important to a dynamic theory of goal formation. At the bottom of the diagram are three coalition patterns in triads. When two members of a triad align against the third they form an interest group as shown at the second level of the hierarchy. Realistically, we might visualize three work groups that could be affected by a proposed fringe benefit alteration. The coalition in work-group one forms in such a way to favor the change. The alignment in work-group two chooses to oppose the alteration. The third coalition decides to assume an apathetic posture and not become involved.

At the second level the three coalitions form a larger interest group with other combinations of workers in the organization possessing similar values. When, at this level, it becomes obvious that the pro and con forces are offsetting one another, political bargaining begins again with the hostile parties. In this case, the supporters of the change align with the apathetic group to form a viable political force to push for the alteration. In this case the apathetic group possesses considerable power because the polar groups must fight for its support.

More systematically, the process of goal formation has been viewed as following a similar pattern. March (1962) proposes a theory of the business firm as a political coalition taking essentially the same approach. The organization is viewed as consisting of a number of groups such as owners, managers, suppliers, employees, governmental agents, etc. The result of a complex bargaining process determines, to a great extent, the objectives pursued by the firm.

To this point, most of what has been said makes sense at the intuitive level. What is missing is a description of the dynamics of the process. Such questions as why does individual A align with B against C, or why do owners align with consumers against employees under certain conditions at a higher hierarchical plane, have yet to be answered. To provide insight relating to these questions, the logic of coalition formation must be carefully examined.

LOGIC OF COALITION FORMATION

Schachter (1972) itemizes several factors that must be considered in analyzing the political logic behind coalition formation. These factors include the minimum size or resource principle, cohesion, ideology, and stability and change. Each of these variables will be examined in some detail.

Minimum Size or Resource Principle

Coalition formation is best viewed as a pragmatic-rational process where the goal is to maximize the group's power relative to resource input (14). Although there are a variety of available theories such as Caplow's (1956) maximum control argument, Shapley and Shubik's (1954) pivotal power concept, and Komorita and Chertkoff's (1973) bargaining theory, Gamson (1961) has proposed a useful framework for describing the rational calculus. According to Gamson (1961b) the resources, and thus the power, each individual or group possesses are constant in the short run. Thus, the coalition that will form is the one with the smallest possible resource pool necessary to ensure a winning outcome. This assumes, of course, that the spoils of victory are divided according to the resource inputs of the members of the winning coalition. By keeping the total resource input minimum, members of the winning group ensure themselves a greater proportion of the resulting payoff.

Abstractly, let us assume that owners (A) control six units of power, employees (B) control five units of power, and consumers (C) control three units of power and that eight units are needed to control the $3 million of profit available to the firm. There are three possible coalitions, *AB, BC,* and *AC.* Under a *BC* coalition *A* receives none of the profits while *B* would receive $3 million × 5/(5 + 3) or $1.875 million and *C* would receive $3 million × 3/(5 + 3) or $1.125 million.

In the *AC* coalition *B* would receive none of the profits, while *A* would obtain $3 million × 6/(6 + 3) or $1.998 million, and *C* would receive $3 million × 3/(6 + 3) or a little over one million dollars. Under the *AB* coalition, *C* would receive none of the profits, *A* would obtain $3 million × 6/(6 + 5) or $1.635 million, and *B* would control $3 million × 5/(6 + 5) or $1.362 million.

If we analyze the possibilities, *A* would prefer the *AC* coalition, *B* would prefer the *BC* alignment and *C* would also maximize its gains under the *BC* coalition. As Gamson predicts, it is the *BC* coalition, with the fewest total resources (eight), that occurs, since it is preferred by both *B* and *C.*

Cohesion

The size principle is closely related to the cohesiveness of the coalition. Although the quest is toward the smallest possible winning combination, when the coalition is too small to ensure a victory, it must extend its boundaries. As a coalition becomes larger, heterogeneity increases with a resulting decrease in intragroup cohesiveness. The trade-off is clear. Cohesion is more difficult to obtain in heterogeneous alliances but small homogeneous groups have difficulty exercising far ranging power, because they include few members from different, but necessary, interest groups (36). A group of plumbers, for example, can develop a cohesive, unified attack but may have difficulty obtaining the support of other groups within the organization necessary to offset the power of owners or customers. This, no doubt, is part of the motivation for industrywide unions that may be less cohesive but more powerful. The smaller the group, the greater the unity necessary to win (30).

Heterogeneous coalitions show less concern for ideology, because intragroup competition develops among the diverse groups (34). Perhaps the greatest political danger is that of a landslide victory by opposing groups. When a coalition becomes fragmented, competition develops between radical factions for the support of members toward the middle of the

figure 1

EMERGENT POWER STRUCTURES IN ORGANIZATIONS

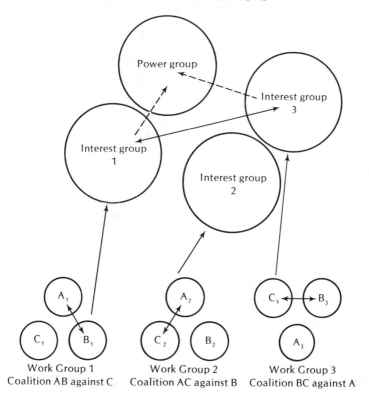

Work Group 1   Work Group 2   Work Group 3
Coalition AB against C Coalition AC against B Coalition BC against A

ideological continuum. The vacuum is easily filled by the opposition as is illustrated with Lyndon Johnson's landslide victory in 1964 and Richard Nixon's in 1972 (43).

Ideology

Ideologies can take a variety of forms. Lipset and Rokkan (1967) propose several ideological bases for political cleavages. Some of the more important include socioeconomic alliances, sectional or regional groupings, and ethnic associations. Their "other" category can be altered by referring to it generally as philosophical cleavages. The importance of each is illustrated by briefly reviewing the factors sequentially.

Socioeconomic Alliances. In the interorganizational as well as the intra-organizational context alliances may develop for socioeconomic reasons. One of the most important factors relates to the occupation of the individuals. Some would even argue that occupation is the single most influential factor on a person's life (33). Education, because of its effect on occupation and income, is also important. Various studies have been conducted that display a number of relationships between socioeconomic status, political affiliation, and voting behavior (39).

Sectional Groupings. Regional alliances can be easily observed in studies of voting behavior. One region of a country may display distinct political orientations while other areas exhibit different preferences (3, 25). Within organizations, geographically proximate workers may form alliances against other areas according to plant locations, subsidiary operations, and regional offices.

Ethnic Associations. Ethnic groupings may be national, racial, linguistic, and so on in character. Immigrant workers have traditionally formed certain alignments against domestic counterparts. Although workers, as a group, possess a unity and commonality of interest, their power is frequently reduced through Irish, Jewish, Polish, or similar groupings (23, 35). Racial coalitions have also, at times, strengthened or weakened larger political groups depending on the type and direction of their behavior.

Philosophical Cleavages. Philosophically, it may be easier for students to align with professors than university administrators. In the larger political arena, Democrats are stereotyped as favoring the working class while the Republicans are considered the "rich man's" party (19).

Stability and Change

Political coalitions are dynamic phenomena. Some are temporary and constantly changing. They may be formed to respond to the demands of the moment as when consumers and employees align to block owners' attempts to invest profits in a way that works to the disadvantage of the two groups (22). At other times, coalitions may be standing and make decisions on issues with only infrequent review of their actions (2). This would be true of faculty groupings within institutions of higher learning.

Once political coalitions form, they face situations similar to firms operating in oligopolistic markets. They must remain sensitive to the actions of other coalitions even though the membership's alternatives are limited (36). Pragmatically, the cleavages resist polarization so as not to risk a defeat by bringing about intracoalition conflict.

COALITIONS AND GOAL FORMATION:
APPLICATIONS FOR A THEORY OF
ORGANIZATION

To this point an attempt has been made to discuss key elements in the theory of coalition formation. Now, we shall examine two areas of application within the broader theory of organization. The first application relates specifically to the goal formation process while the second reveals the importance of the interface between organizational goals and environmental factors. This latter issue represents an extension of the goal formation process.

Coalitions and Goals: The Political Perspective

Writers on the theory of organization have long been interested in the politics of collective behavior. When viewing organizational behavior from this perspective, the emphasis is on power and bargaining processes. The result has been a recognition that politics is not unique to political bodies but an integral part of all organizational processes. Jay (1967) makes the point effectively by stating that "a corporation is not something different from a state with some interesting similarities; it is a state with a few unimportant differences" (20, p. 3).

In recognition of political realities, Cyert and March (1963) and March (1962) have chosen to include the coalition view of goal formation as part of their behavioral theory of the firm. In this formulation the decision maker is visualized as the administrative rather than the economic man who "satisfices" instead of maximizing goal accomplishment. Although there are several reasons why this "satisficing" occurs, one of the most basic is the political process by which organizational goals emerge.

The behavioral theory of the firm pictures the organization as a series of coalitions or interest groups such as owners, fellow decision makers, employees, etc. These groups politically interact through a bargaining process with the result being a compromised goal, or set of goals, rather than a single maximizing objective that responds completely to the interests of a single group.

Empirical investigations have confirmed that decision makers are, in fact, influenced by a variety of interest groups (13). The extent to which the various values are considered in the decision process depends on the power possessed by each group (12). The process, however, is distinctly political and clearly contained within the framework of political coalitions.

Some of the advantages of viewing the behavioral theory of the firm from this perspective are obvious. Since coalitions are to be analyzed as factors in the goal formation process, it would be helpful to identify how and why alliances develop. By applying the theory likely coalitions can be predicted on the basis of the minimum size principle; their cohesiveness and strength can be speculated by looking at the degree of homogeneity; and the socioeconomic, sectional, ethnic, and philosophical bases for the existent groupings can be examined.

Goals and Environmental Externalities

Dow and Duncan (1974) have provided a behavioral interpretation of the expected patterns of response decision makers exhibit toward important external forces such as changing social philosophies. Behavioral science research suggests, for example, that managers confronted with conflicting group expectations will behave consistently with groups that maintain the greatest influence on the individual (6).

The example of the decision maker in the profit-oriented firm can be used to illustrate this point. Assume that the firm is under pressure to control the pollutants emitted from its production process. As an individual *qua* citizen, the decision maker is a member of the larger society and is concerned with the survival of the socio-political and economic systems. As a member of the management team, he or she is concerned with the efficiency and profitability of the organization. The result is a political dynamic that ultimately influences the decision maker's behavior.

In a speculative sense, it could be argued that observations of reality suggest that many decision makers feel at least a nominal association with the larger system known as society. It is doubtful, however, that they are influenced as much by this macro "abstraction" as by the management team or the owner coalition. Thus, society is seen as a membership group. Owners and fellow managers, on the other hand, are accurately labeled reference groups because they are more emotionally and cognitively significant to the decision maker (41).

If we visualize a situation where community pressure emerges demanding a reduction in the pollution level, the significance of the various groups can be easily predicted. Social psychology would argue quite accurately that the decision maker will behave in a manner consistent with the desires of the reference group. From a political perspective Converse and Campbell (1968), in a study of voting behavior, illustrate how individuals displaying a strong association with a particular group vote consistently with collective goals more often than persons with nominal group affiliations.

An additional illustration of the reality of organizational coalitions and their effect on the behavior of complex structures can be inferred from the frequently cited study of George England (13). In this study, over 1000 decision makers were surveyed and asked to specify the primary values influencing their behavior. The results clearly illustrated that managers viewed owners as the primary coalition or reference group. Employees and society were less influential.

Specifically, England noted that high importance was assigned to owner-oriented performance criteria such as efficiency, productivity, profit maximization, growth, industrial leadership, and stability. Employee and social welfare were found near the end of the list of influential factors. Duncan (12) has reported consistent findings in diversified industrial samples.

Thus, the perspective provided by the theory of political coalitions can be useful in describing some important processes in the organization's interaction with environmental externalities. This provides additional potential for the pragmatic value of an understanding of the nature of coalitions in describing the larger theory of formal organization.

CONCLUSIONS

The theory of formal organization has devoted much attention to the importance of organizational goals. More than one writer has accurately made the point that without well defined objectives the entire management process has little or no meaning. In spite of the universal importance placed upon goals, little work has been done on the development of a systematic theory of organizational goal formation. This paper has proposed one approach to this complex subject.

There are, of course, other ways in which one might view the goal formation process. However, when examining the alternatives the political view appears to possess certain parsimonious and pragmatic advantages. Goal formation is, in fact, a political process and bargaining among diverse interest groups can be easily observed in reality. For this reason, it becomes useful to draw upon the political theory of coalition formation to provide insights into this important area of organization theory. Also, with a review of the state of the art, it is hoped that empirical research will be stimulated to test if, in reality, the tenets of political theory apply at the level of organizational analysis.

REFERENCES

1. BECK, BERNARD. "Organizational Goals and Inmate Organization." *American Journal of Sociology* 72 (1966): 522–34.
2. BURHAM, W. D. "American Voting Behavior and the 1964 Election." *Midwest Journal of Political Science* 12 (1968): 1–41.
3. CAMERON, D. R., J. S. HENDRICKS, and R. I. HOFFENBERT. "Urbanization, Social Structure, and Mass Politics." *Comparative Political Studies* 5 (1972): 259–91.
4. CAPLOW, THEODORE. *Two Against One: Coalitions in Triads* (Englewood Cliffs, N.J.: Prentice-Hall, 1968).
5. CAPLOW, THEODORE. "A Theory of Coalitions in the Triad." *American Sociological Review* 21 (1956): 489–93.
6. CONVERSE, P., and A. CAMPBELL. "Political Standards in Secondary Groups," *Group Dynamics*, 3rd ed., eds. D. Cartwright and A. Zander (New York: Harper & Row, 1968), pp. 199–224.
7. COTTON, W. R. "Unstated Goals as a Source of Stress in an Organization." *Pacific Sociological Review* 8 (1962):29–35.
8. CRESSEY, D. R. "Achievement of an Unstated Organizational Goal: An Observation on Prisons." *Pacific Sociological Review* 4 (1958): 29–35.

9. CYERT, RICHARD, and JAMES MARCH. *A Behavioral Theory of the Firm* (Englewood Cliffs, N.J.: Prentice-Hall, 1963).

10. Dow, L. A., and W. J. DUNCAN. "Economic Neoliberalism: A Behavioral View of the Sportsmanship Assumption." *American Journal of Economics and Sociology* 33 (1974): 351-65.

11. DUNCAN, W. JACK. *Decision Making and Social Issues* (Hinsdale, Ill.: Dryden Press, 1973).

12. DUNCAN, W. JACK. "Organizational Goals and the Process of Value Determination in Management Decision Making." *Managing the Changing Organization,* eds. D. F. Ray and T. B. Green (Atlanta: Southern Management Association, 1974), pp. 228-34.

13. ENGLAND, G. W. "Organizational Goals and the Expected Behavior of American Managers." *Academy of Management Journal* 10 (1967): 107-17.

14. FLANAGAN, S. C. "Theory and Method in the Study of Coalition Formation." *Journal of Comparative Administration* 5 (November 1973): 267-75.

15. GAMSON, W. A. "A Theory of Coalition Formation." *American Sociological Review* 26 (1961a): 373-83.

16. GAMSON, W. A. "An Experimental Test of A Theory of Coalition Formation." *American Sociological Review* 26 (1961b): 565-73.

17. GLUECK, WILLIAM F. *Business Policy: Strategy Formation and Executive Action* (New York: McGraw-Hill, 1972).

18. GRAHAM, GERALD H. "Approaches to Organizational Goal Formation." *Southern Journal of Business* 4 (1969): 1-11.

19. INGLEHART, RONALD, and AVRAN HOCHSTEIN. "Alignment and Dealignment of the Electorate in France and the United States." *Comparative Political Studies* 5 (1972): 343-70.

20. JAY, ANTHONY. *Management and Machiavelli* (New York: Holt, Rinehart & Winston, 1967).

21. KAST, F. E., and J. E. ROSENZWEIG. "General Systems Theory: Applications for Organization and Management." *Academy of Management Journal* 15 (1972): 447-65.

22. KEY, V. O., JR. *The Responsible Electorate* (New York: Vintage Books, 1966).

23. KOLODNY, RALPH. "Ethnic Cleavages in the United States." *Social Work* 14 (1969): 13-24.

24. KOMORITA, S. S., and J. M. CHERTKOFF. "A Bargaining Theory of Coalition Formation." *Psychological Review* 80 (1973): 149-62.

25. LINDEEN, J. W. "Longitudinal Analysis of Republican Presidential Electorial Trends, 1896-1968." *Midwest Journal of Political Science* 16 (1972): 110-20.

26. LINDSAY, J. S. B. "On the Number in A Group." *Human Relations,* 25 (1972): 50-61.

27. LIPSET, S. M., and STEIN ROKKAN. *Party Systems and Voter Alignments* (Englewood Cliffs, N.J.: Prentice-Hall, 1967).

28. MARCH, J. G. "The Business Firm as a Political Coalition." *Journal of Politics* 24 (1962): 662-78.

29. MCGREGOR, E. B., JR. "Rationality and Uncertainty at National Nominating Conventions." *Journal of Politics* 35 (1973): 459-78.

30. MELTZ, D. B. "Legislative Party Cohesion: A Model of the Bargaining Process in State Legislatures." *Journal of Politics* 35 (1973): 647–48.

31. MILLS, T. M. "Coalition Patterns in Three Person Groups." *American Sociological Review* 19 (1954): 657–67.

32. MOONEY, JAMES D. *The Principles of Organization,* Rev. ed. (New York: Harper & Row, 1947).

33. MURPHY, R. J., and R. T. MORRIS. "Occupational Status, Subjective Class Identification and Political Affiliation." *American Sociological Review* 26 (1961): 383–92.

34. ORBELL, J. M., and GEOFFREY FOUGERE. "Intra-Party Conflict and the Decay of Ideology." *Journal of Politics* 25 (1973): 435–45.

35. PALLEY, H. A. "The White Working Class and A Strategy of Coalition for Social Development." *Social Science Review* 47 (1973): 241–55.

36. ROSE, RICHARD, and DEREK URWIN. "Social Cohesion, Political Parties and Strains in Regimes." *Comparative Political Studies* 2 (1969): 19–30.

37. SCHACHTER, H. L. "Educational Institutions and Political Coalition." *Comparative Educational Review* 16 (1972): 462–73.

38. SELZNIK, PHILIP. "Foundations of the Theory of Organization." *American Sociological Review* 13 (1948): 30–38.

39. SHAFFER, W. R. "Political Continuity in Indiana Presidential Elections." *Midwest Journal of Political Science* 16 (1972): 705–15.

40. SHAPLEY, L. S., and M. SHUBIK. "A Method for Evaluating the Distribution of Power in A Committee System." *American Political Science Review* 48 (1954): 787–92.

41. SIEGEL, A. E., and S. SIEGEL. "Reference Groups, Membership Groups, and Attitude Change." *Journal of Abnormal and Social Psychology* 60 (1957): 360–64.

42. SIMON, HERBERT A. "On the Concept of Organizational Goal." *Administrative Science Quarterly* 9 (1964): 1–12.

43. WHITE, T. H. *The Making of the President, 1972* (New York: Bantam Books, 1973).

WHAT DETERMINES ORGANIZATION PERFORMANCE?
The Universals vs. the It All Depends

JOHN CHILD

One school of management thought maintains that, irrespective of the circumstances, certain factors, attributes—call them what you will—universally determine the performance of any organization. The opposing school (newer, and perhaps for that reason just as doctrinaire) argues that universals are not reflections of reality, that the effect of any factor on organizational performance varies with the objectives, size, markets, and other characteristics of the particular organization. This is the contingency school.

Which school is correct? Research, including our own investigations, discourages dogmatism, permits tentative generalizations, and indicates strongly the need for further research. Based on the research to date, however, ten propositions are advanced here about the factors that determine organizational performance; half of these propositions refer to universal attributes, while the other half lend themselves to a contingency approach to organizational performance.

But first, a few caveats that qualify what follows.

The question of what determines the levels of performance achieved by organizations still defies a sure answer. The problem is extremely complex because, as Jonathan Boswell said in his *The Rise and Fall of Small Firms,* "A vast number of influences on performance are at work. Some of these are quantifiable, others aren't; some are external to the firm, others are internal and managerial, and of the latter many are subtly interwoven."

Both universalistic and contingency perspectives assume that it is possible to identify factors that will to some degree determine levels of performance. A major difficulty, however, lies in the fact that performance is not simply a dependent variable. The performance levels achieved by an organization constitute a vital input to stimulate them to make adjustments in policies and modes of operation. These adjustments may be an attempt to correct a poor level of performance or to accommodate the consequences of good performance, such as a growth in scale, and so to sustain the favorable trend. In other words, it is unrealistic to regard performance *only* as a variable dependent on other factors.

This conclusion has important implications for the interpretation of the kind of data it has been practicable to obtain in most research studies. These data are cross-sectional in nature, deriving from measurements taken in a single time period, rather than from a close examination of how performance and other variables change in association with one another over time. Within certain limits, such studies can provide useful clues as to what factors are associated with different levels of performance, but they cannot address the question of how performance acts as part of a continuing cycle of organizational change. This means that they cannot demonstrate what causes good or bad performance. Problems of interpretation will therefore arise.

For instance, in my own research into 82 British companies, I found that less profitable and slower-growing firms used manpower budgets and other cost controls more than did high performers. The implications of this correlation are ambiguous. To what extent do manpower budgets contribute to lower performance because of their intrinsic inflexibility and because they focus managers' attention on departmental considerations, rather than on broader needs? On the other hand, to what extent is manpower budgeting instituted or intensified as a response to poor performance, in an attempt to keep manpower costs to a minimum and to control a staffing situation that may be getting out of hand? My impression is that in practice a period of poor performance often stimulated an intensification of financial controls.

These introductory remarks contain the elements of a simple framework that will be used to bring together the more salient research findings on the performance of organizations. This framework is sketched out in Figure 1 in terminology that applies particularly to business organizations. Briefly, the strategy and plans that are formulated are regarded as major determinants of an organization's activities, and hence a critical influence on its eventual performance. Strategic decisions are responses to pressures imposed on managers by the various participants within the organization and its environment, with managers' own stakes in ownership being a strongly influencing factor. The design or organization structure in the light of situational contingencies is included as a potential determinant of how effectively the tasks of the organization are carried out. The quality of management is regarded as a pervasive element that can affect all aspects of organizational behavior.

The managerial, strategic, and organizational factors that have emerged as correlates of performance will now be discussed separately. . . .

MANAGERIAL CORRELATES OF PERFORMANCE

"The good manager" is the keynote of one of the most popular universalistic theories about performance. This theory holds that the successful leadership of any organization will depend on the presence of certain qualities of character, drive, competence, and dedication among its managers. Thus, a British survey carried out in the early 1960s concluded that "thrusting" managerial attitudes "are considerably more likely to lead to high and

figure 1

PERFORMANCE IN THE CONTEXT OF ORGANIZATIONAL BEHAVIOR

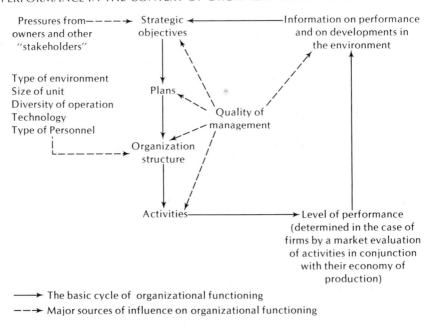

⟶ The basic cycle of organizational functioning

⟶ Major sources of influence on organizational functioning

profitable growth than are the sleepy attitudes and practices with which they are contrasted."

Youth, technical qualification, and a stake in the ownership of the organization are among the factors often thought of as promoting more effective management. For example, in recruiting, the relative merits of youth, with its supposed adaptability and energy, as against the experience of more mature applicants, have often occasioned debate. What are the facts?

Proposition 1: Organizations run by younger teams of top managers will tend to achieve higher levels of performance.

The journal *Management Today* found in its 1973 survey of the boards of the 200 largest British companies that those having the oldest boards showed lower profitability and growth than companies with the youngest directors. As the journal put it, there was no refutation here of "the common-sense view that companies dominated by conservatively reared older men are less likely to produce dynamic performance."

Our research at the Aston Management Centre did not find that the age of senior managers correlated systematically with company profits, but it did relate to growth in sales, income, and assets measured over a five-year period. In each one of six industries sampled, younger managements typically achieved higher rates of company growth. At their best, the "young Turks" achieved quite outstanding growth performances. Although there was a lot of variation in the levels attained, the least successful young teams did no worse than the least successful older managements. Two economists, Peter Hart and John Mellors, have also independently looked at the age of company chairmen and the growth of net assets in four British industries and reached the same conclusion: The growth of companies controlled by older men tends to be slower, although less volatile.

So a fairly general link seems to exist between youthful management and more rapid growth. But how should we interpret this observation? After all, it may signify little more than that faster-growing companies recruit and promote younger people more rapidly into senior vacancies. Is youth among managers just a consequence of growth already achieved?

Favoring this argument is the fact that managers in faster-growing companies tended to have had shorter periods of service with the company and to have reached their present posts via fewer intermediate positions. On the other hand, they had not on the whole been in their present jobs for any less time than had managers in slow-growing companies.

The personal qualities that we found to characterize younger managers support the view that age is, indeed, an operative influence. Younger managers were more likely to press actively for change and innovation within their companies. They questioned prevailing systems of formal rules and authority more keenly. They also had greater confidence in their own abilities to succeed in the high positions they held than did older managers. The confident attitudes and behavior found among younger managers are just the kind likely to promote a striving for innovation and rapid growth.

Comparisons of individual companies illustrate these general findings. An example is the best and the worst performers among the 15 insurance companies in the Aston study. Let us call them Company A and Company B. These two organizations had such distinctive climates that they were immediately apparent to the visitor. In Company A, the high performer, there was an atmosphere of business, yet the staff appeared relaxed, friendly, and well turned out. Despite the hustle and bustle, appointments were always kept punctually and staff members seemed to know of and take an interest in each other's movements. The initial appearance of Company B to the visitor was in marked contrast. Staff members were casual to the point of indifference; there was little animation in their behavior; the whereabouts of senior managers were often unknown (particularly around the middle of the day); and appointments were not kept on several occasions.

Company A's senior management team had an average of 34 years, compared with 50 years in Company B. When we applied statistical measurements of attitudes and behavior, the managers in the two companies contrasted sharply. In Company A, formal rules and routines were adhered to with less than half the degree of rigidity found in Company B. Some 50 percent more pressure for change and innovation was reported among managers in Company A. The young management team in that company expressed itself as being almost twice as ready to take risks when necessary, and also preferred to have more variety and challenge in its work. It is worth noting that a study by Victor Vroom and Bernd Pahl of 1,500 managers from 200 U.S. companies found a consistent and significant relationship between younger age and a greater willingness to take risks.

I have devoted some space to the question of youthful management because it may be an influence on performance that applies in most types of organization and upon which managers can act. Research findings to date point to the need for career systems that allow young people of proven ability and appropriate experience to advance rapidly to senior positions. The other side of this coin is the justification of the practice found in some American corporations where, after the age of 50 or so, senior executives may be transferred into less demanding positions.

In British industry, the rapid promotion of able men and women who are still in their prime is slowly becoming more usual, but a planned transfer of older people to less responsible positions, as opposed to more brutal methods like dismissal or compulsory early retirement, is not. This always tends to be resisted by the older executives who hold power in company managements, and it is important for transfers of this kind not to entail a loss of remuneration and privilege. The question remains, nevertheless, whether holding down top management positions is to be primarily a reward of age and long service or a recognition of who is best able to meet the requirements of the job—quite possibly a relatively young man.

Proposition 2: Organizations run by formally better-qualified teams of top managers will tend to achieve higher levels of performance.

The reasoning behind this proposition is the straightforward notion that the possession of formal qualifications is likely to indicate that managers have a certain level of attested expertise and ability. This potential influence on levels of performance cannot, of course, be entirely separated from the age factor, since younger managers tend more often to possess these formal qualifications than do older managers.

Some evidence emerges from British studies that the financial success of companies is generally greater when a relatively high proportion of their directors have formal professional qualifications. D. P. Barritt found this to be the case after studying the profits of larger British companies in the 1950s. More recently, in the mid-1960s, a study by Roger Betts of 23 companies, chiefly in construction and plastics, found that those achieving a higher rate of growth in profits had a greater average number of formal qualifications held per director. In both industries, the successful companies had a significantly higher proportion of directors concerned with research and development and (it appeared) possessing scientific qualifications.

There is some support, then, for the proposition that formally qualified management teams will achieve superior performance. And the balance within top executive or directorial teams of types of qualifications may also relate to success. For example, in the study by Betts just cited, there was evidence that poor-performing companies had a heavy weighting of men with production and engineering backgrounds. Another study of 93 major British companies achieving the highest and lowest rates of return on capital during the period 1966–72 found that the high performers had more directors with accounting qualifications, while the low performers had more directors with engineering qualifications. This proportionate relationship of directors' qualifications appeared to be more closely associated with organizational performance than the total number of qualifications within the board.

Proposition 3: Organizations run by managers with a substantial personal stake in their ownership will tend to achieve higher levels of performance.

A major theme in writings on the "managerial revolution" is that managers who do not have a significant personal stake in the ownership of corporations will devote more attention to objectives other than the maximization of profit. One such objective is growth, which many commentators have concluded will furnish considerable advantages to managers in terms of higher remuneration, prestige, sense of achievement, and so on.

A number of studies have been made in the United States and Britain of the relation between the control of companies and their levels of performance. Overall, the results suggest that companies with a concentration of ownership control (rather than dispersed ownership) tend to have higher rates of profit *and* higher rates of growth, but differences in levels of performance have often not been significant, and the measures of ownership influence have been formalistic and indirect.

In our studies, we have found that where there was a greater concentration of ownership control, chief executives attached particularly great importance to maximizing profits and growth: There were, however, no significant links between the ownership control factor and rates of profit actually achieved, and the only significant link with growth was found in the tendency for owner-controlled companies to have a more rapid growth in net assets over a five-year period.

Rather fewer studies have looked at managers' stockholdings in relation to company performance, but the results that emerge are more clear-cut, indicating that when managers have greater personal stake in ownership, the performance of companies tends to be superior. For example, a study by Steve Nyman of the 100 largest British commercial and industrial companies found that higher levels of stockholding by directors were significantly associated with higher rates of growth. A larger stake in ownership was also associated with the achievement of higher rates of profit, although this result was only just statistically significant. Given higher growth and higher profitability, it is not surprising that a greater stake in ownership was also associated with a higher stock market rating and a higher price-earnings ratio.

In short, there is a clear tendency for the company in which control is linked with a stake in ownership to be a superior performer. The motivational implications of this relationship for all types of organizations are significant, since they suggest that whenever managers have a direct personal stake in the success of an undertaking, its performance will be enhanced. There is also a suggestion here that the objectives held by managers may influence the performance of their organizations, which leads us to a consideration of strategic factors.

Proposition 4: The performance standards set by an organization's management will be influenced by the norms of performance among other organizations of a similar type.

Strategy deals with the objectives established for an organization and the effort to attain them. For example, if we establish the objective of sustaining a given annual rate of growth, this may mean diversification into a faster-growing industry in order to achieve the objective. There is ample evidence that normal rates of profit and growth vary among industries and that these variations can have an important influence on the performance of firms, especially smaller ones whose activities are usually confined to a single industry. In addition to reflecting certain shared economic circumstances having to do with size of markets, growth of overall demand, structure of the industry, and so forth, the differentiation of company performance levels by industry also reflects the presence of shared standards by which many firms are content to judge themselves. This phenomenon—of managements' assessing performance against localized, rather than general, standards—is likely to be even more widespread outside the business sphere, where mechanisms to enforce universal economic standards such as stock market ratings are absent. It is this consideration that underlies the proposition made above.

We also expect that the mix of objectives held by an organization's senior managers will have an impact on its performance. The exact formulation of objectives may well result from an appraisal of what can realistically be attained in the light of the organization's previous performance. The type of objectives held by top management is, nevertheless, likely to be an active influence upon performance because of the ways in which objectives shape plans and activities. Moreover, the singlemindedness of managements is important, first because effort may be dissipated in trying to achieve too many different aims at once, and second, because the more conflict among senior managers over objectives, the less integrated will be their efforts toward reaching a common goal. Hence, we arrive at the fifth proposition.

Proposition 5: The less dispersed top-management objectives are and the more agreement there is among senior managers as to which objectives have priority, the more successful the organization will be in attaining them.

Chief executives in our study of British firms were asked to rate the importance to their companies of ten possible objectives, scoring each of them separately along five-point scales. Nearly all of the respondents gave very high priority to maximizing net profit over the long term (five years) and to achieving a high rate of growth. Because of this strong measure of agreement, the rating of these objectives did not discriminate between successful companies and others.

The evaluation of certain other objectives did differentiate. In the more profitable companies, with above-average rates of return for their industries on sales and on net assets, chief executives attached lower importance to a high level of distributed dividends, but greater importance to a high level of rewards and benefits for employees. In more profitable firms they also showed less concern for the company's prestige. In the faster-growing companies, chief executives attached low importance to maximizing short-term profits over a 12-month period, to paying out a high level of dividends, and to "service to the wider community."

A comparison of three sugar confectionary companies with contrasting performance profiles illustrates these points in greater detail. Company X was a poor performer by any criterion. Company Y had an outstanding growth record and had maintained an average level of profitability. Company Z was highly profitable and had achieved an average level of growth. As Figure 2 shows, the chief executive of all three companies attached considerable importance to major objectives such as maximizing long-term profitability, growth, and market share. In Company X, however, the chief executive hardly discriminated in his assessment among these objectives and others in the list we gave him. In the two better-performing companies, less importance was attached to objectives like prestige, a high dividend payout, and service to the community. In growth-Company Y, innovation was given a high rating. In Company Z, which was securing high margins on high-quality traditional lines, less emphasis was given to growth and market share than in Company Y, and somewhat more stress was placed on maximizing profits in the short term.

Findings like these, even though they concern chief executives' views alone, suggest that the mix of strategic objectives selected for a business may influence its performance. In the sample as a whole, the companies achieving greater commercial success were those whose top managements were more singleminded in pursuing longer-term profit and growth objectives. Chief executives in these companies also paid considerable attention

figure 2

RATING OF OBJECTIVES IN THREE CONFECTIONERY COMPANIES

Objective	Ratings of Importance*		
To Maximize:	Company X	Company Y	Company Z
1. Net profit over five years	5	5	5
2. Rate of growth	5	5	4
3. Market share	4	5	4
4. Employee rewards	4	5	5
5. Net profit over one year	5	3	4
6. Prestige	5	3	2
7. Innovation	4	5	2
8. Assets and reserves	4	2	1
9. Dividends distributed	4	2	1
10. Service to the wider community	4	1	1

*5—extremely important; 4—very important; 3—moderately important; 2—not very important; 1—not at all important

Company X was a small, family firm with low profitability and low growth, old product and old technology. Company Y was an American-owned firm of small to medium size, with average profitability and rapid growth, some new products and advanced technology. Company Z was a medium-size subsidiary, with high profitability and average growth, and traditional high-quality products, enjoying high margins on low-cost technology.

to the building up of internal strengths, such as providing favorable conditions for employees and retaining surpluses within the business to finance further profitable expansion.

In companies where chief executives attach more importance to external points of reference, such as prestige, serving the community, and paying higher dividends, financial performance tends to be poorer. Whether this association between a lower concern for external interests and superior performance can continue through the 1970s, with the present growing insistence on company social responsibility, remains to be seen. On the whole, though, the message of these findings seems clear: If you want to manage a successful business, concentrate on a few key objectives and avoid distractions. This also implies, of course, that careful thought should be given to the selection of key objectives in the first place.

Further support for Proposition 5 comes from a study by David Norburn, who compared 21 British companies with varying levels of financial performance. He found that the more successful companies were characterized by a greater degree of consensus among top executives about who was responsible for setting long-term objectives and about the priority of objectives their organizations should follow. In poor-performing organizations he found both more disagreement and a wider spread of objectives. Norburn also found that successful company managements possessed better information on their environments. It is likely that superior, well-integrated information will assist managers to agree on which objectives deserve priority.

There are more strategic factors associated with performance than can be considered here, but there is enough evidence to indicate that as a general rule, attention to the formulation of strategy will have beneficial effects on performance. For instance, the systematic planning of expansion policies among American firms is related to superior economic performance. A comparative study of acquisition behavior among American companies carried out by Igor Ansoff and his colleagues lends further support to Proposition 5, because the firms more successful in terms of profit and growth were found to have restricted their attention to a more limited range of possible acquisitions and to have evaluated these more thoroughly.

ORGANIZATION STRUCTURE AND PERFORMANCE

Managerial attributes and the quality of strategy appear to have some relation to levels of performance in most organizations, even though the organizations differ in their environment, diversity, size, technology, and personnel. When we turn to a third possible influence on performance, the design of organization structure, we find most authorities taking the view that the type of situation is vital. This is the contingency approach mentioned earlier, which states that the design of organization most appropriate for high performance can be formulated only with contingent circumstances in mind. According to this theory, there are no general principles of organization.

The argument goes as follows: Contingent factors such as the type of environment or the size of the organization have some direct influence on levels of success. There may, for example, be economies of scale open to the larger organization. Certain environments, such as particular industries, may be more beneficent and provide greater opportunity. Second, it is assumed that a set of structured administrative arrangements consciously adapted to the tasks that are to be done, to the expectations and needs of people performing the tasks, to the scale of the total operation, to its overall complexity, and to the pressures of change being encountered will themselves act to promote a higher level of effectiveness than will a structure illsuited to these contingencies. Organization structure is seen in this way to modify the effects of contingencies upon performance. Last, the all-pervasive quality of management affects both strategic decisions as to the type of conditions under which the organization will seek to operate and the design of its internal structure.

Environment

According to contingency theory, different approaches to organizational design are conducive to high performance, depending on whether or not the environment in which the organization is operating is variable and complex in nature, or stable and simple. Variability in the environment refers to the presence of changes that are relatively difficult to predict, involve important departures from previous conditions, and are likely, therefore, to generate considerable uncertainty.

Complexity of the environment is said to be greater the more extensive and diversified the range of an organization's activities, which correspondingly take it into more diverse sectors of the environment. These diverse sectors are all relevant areas of external information that it should monitor. There is evidence that the degree of environmental variability is a more important contributor to uncertainty among managerial decision makers than is complexity. I shall discuss variability now and return to complexity in a later section on diversity of operations.

Proposition 6: In conditions of environmental variability, successful organizations will tend to have structures with the following characteristics: (1) arrangements to reduce and to structure uncertainty; (2) a relatively high level of internal differentiation; and (3) a relatively high level of integration achieved through flexible, rather than formalized, processes.

This mouthful of a proposition attempts to distill the essence of what we know so far about a highly complex issue. Among possible arrangements to reduce and structure the uncertainty generated by a changing environment are a closer liaison with the separate independent organizations upon which one's own organization is highly dependent as supplier or customer (even to the extent of vertical or horizontal integration), and attempts to secure a better quality of intelligence from outside the organization.

The critical nature of a variable environment and the need for liaison with outside organizations and for a significant intelligence activity all mean that an organization is under pressure to employ specialist staff in boundary or interface roles—that is, in positions where they form a link with the outside world, scooping in and evaluating relevant information. This may well take the form of setting up more specialist departments and thereby increasing the internal differentiation of the organization.

If there are many new significant external changes to which an organization has to adapt, and if it has become fairly differentiated to cope with these, then there will be all the more need to achieve a degree of integration among its personnel that not only offsets their specializations from one another but, over and above this, permits them to react swiftly to new developments in a coordinated manner. Flexible, rather than highly formalized, methods of coordination and information-sharing will be required. This generally means a greater amount of face-to-face participation in discussions and decision making, with an emphasis on close lateral relations among members of different departments instead of formal links up and down hierarchies or via periodic formal meetings. This mode of working also implies a higher degree of delegation, particularly when it comes to operational decisions.

Various studies that have examined organizational performance in relation to structure and variable environments have produced sufficiently consistent findings to support the conclusions we have just made. Each study, of course, examines the structural elements I have mentioned in more detail. In the United States there is the well-known work of Paul Lawrence and Jay Lorsch, as well as studies by Robert Duncan, Pradip Khandwalla, Anant Negandhi, and Bernard Reiman, among others. Of British studies, Tom Burns' and G. M. Stalker's is the best known.

Our own research at Aston indicated that companies in the variable science-based environment characterizing electronics and pharmaceuticals that were achieving above-average levels of growth tended to rely less on formal procedures and documentation than did slow-growing companies. Among firms in more stable environments, high-growth companies relied more (but only marginally so) on formalized methods of integration than did less successful firms.

These organizational differences between high- and low-growth companies located in contrasting environments were most marked in certain areas of management. Within the stable sector, faster-growing companies had significantly more formalization in the production area, especially in matters like defining operator tasks, training operators, and recording their performance. The faster-growing companies in variable environments particularly made little use of formal training procedures, standardized routine personnel practices, and formal hierarchical channels for communication or seeking and conveying decisions.

Size of Unit

Here the major proposition is this:

Proposition 7: Organizations that increase their degree of formalization to parallel their growth in size will tend to achieve higher levels of performance.

Critics contend that the problem of the large organization is the dead weight of bureaucratic administration that it takes on. In an attempt to hold together its many divisions and departments, the large organization emphasizes conformity to the rules, a trait that has prompted the observation that "a new idea has never come out of a large corporation." Many studies of organization have confirmed that large scale does indeed breed bureaucracy in the form of highly compartmentalized jobs and areas of work, elaborate procedural and paperwork systems, long hierarchies, and delegation of routine decisions to lower-level managers within precise discretionary limits.

Much as critics may decry bureaucracy, we found that in each industry the more profitable and faster-growing companies were those that had developed this type of organization in fuller measure with their growth in size above the 2,000-or-so employee mark. At the other end of the scale, among small firms of about 100 employees, the better performers generally managed with very little formal organization. The larger the company, the higher the correlation between more bureaucracy and superior performance.

Poorly performing large companies tend to specialize their staff less, to have less developed systems and procedures, and to delegate decision making less extensively. It is also worth noting that among the poorly performing companies the strength of the relation between changes in size and changes in structure is noticeably reduced, compared with that among high performers.

Comparisons of larger companies within the same industry clearly illustrate this trend. For example, we studied three of the largest national daily newspaper groups. One was the superior performer by a substantial margin, in terms of growth, return on net assets, and return on combined circulation plus advertising sales. Although this particular group was the smallest of the three big companies in numbers employed, it operated a highly formalized type of organization—it had developed a more elaborate set of procedures and systems covering a wider range of activities than had the other two companies, and it relied heavily on written communication and records. Indeed, its most distinguishing feature lay in this heavier use of documentation, especially job descriptions, manuals, work records, and the like.

The newspaper industry represents a relatively stable environment. When the nature of each organization's environment is taken into account, as well as its size, the association between organization and performance becomes more complicated. The need for companies operating in a more variable environment to keep a check on the formality in their organization, especially its routine-enforcing elements, probably explains why it is the successful companies in a more stable environment that most rapidly take on a formal bureaucratic type of structure as they grow larger. The rate at which companies tend to develop bureaucratic structures as their size increases varies according to the environment and performance in the following sequence from low to high: below-average performers in stable environments; below-average performers in variable environments; above-average performers in stable environments.

Managers, it appears from our research, have to take note of multiple contingencies, such as environment plus size, when planning the design of their organization. When there is not much variability in the environment, the need to develop organization to suit size becomes relatively more dominant. In this environment, the better-performing companies tend to develop formalized structures at a faster rate as they grow than do poor performers. When the environment is a variable one, however, these differences in structural development are reduced, because the contingency of coping with uncertainty tends to offset the contingency of coping with large scale. We found that in a variable environment, the rate of increase in formalization accompanying growth in scale is higher for good performers, but the absolute level of their formalization only reaches that of poor-performing companies at a size approaching 10,000 employees. The picture is complex indeed, as most practical managers are well aware!

Diversity of Operations

Now comes the eighth proposition:

Proposition 8: Organizations that group their basic activities into divisions once these activities become diversified will tend to achieve higher levels of performance.

This proposition expresses the fundamental argument for the divisionalized organizational structure that has become the dominant form among large business firms today and that can also be seen in some large public undertakings. Organizations having a spread of different products or services, and having outlets in a number of regions, operate in a complex total environment. Such organizations are also likely to be large. Because of both their size and their diversity, they will almost certainly experience communications difficulties.

To overcome these problems, it is logical to create decentralized, semi-autonomous operating units or divisions, for these can group formal relationships in a way that reflects the necessities of exchanging information and coordination around common problems. These commonalities may center around product groups, favoring a product division type of organization, or they may center on geographical regions, favoring an area division structure. If both product and regional coordination are equally vital, then a mixed, or "grid," structure may be logical.

The detailed research of John Stopford and Louis Wells supports the argument that these divisionalized arrangements work. American multinational corporations that have divisionalized their structures in response to a diversity of activities tend to be superior performers. The more successful firms have in most cases adopted the kind of divisionalization—international divisions, global area divisions, global product divisions, mixed or grid structures—that considerations such as product diversity and level of involvement in foreign business would logically dictate.

Technology

This brings us to the ninth proposition:

Proposition 9: Organizations that design their work flow control and support structures to suit their technologies will tend to achieve higher levels of performance.

The term technology is employed in almost as many different senses as there are writers on the subject. The analyses offered by Charles Perrow and Joan Woodward are the best known and best developed. Perrow's definition of technology in terms of variability of inputs and availability of known techniques to handle these comes close to what most have in mind when they speak of variability in the environment and its generation of uncertainty. To this extent, Perrow's recommendations for structural design tend to be borne out by the findings of studies on organizational performance under different environmental conditions.

Woodward's view of technology is based on the physical organization of work flows. Does the organization have heavy plant and a rigid sequence of production, as in car assembly? Or does it have fairly light plant and flexible production, as in the manufacture of some electronic instruments and in service industries? Woodward's pioneering studies suggested that when organizations design structural attributes to fit their technologies, they secure a superior level of performance. Unfortunately, neither Woodward nor subsequent investigators adopting her approach have employed precise measures of performance.

The research we conducted indicated that the pattern of specialization in production and ancillary areas such as production control and maintenance was predictable in terms of the technology employed. In addition, the proportion of total employment allocated to some of the ancillary functions varied along with differences in technology. For example, more rigid technologies, such as those of a process type, tend to have relatively few production control specialists and internally specialized production control departments. Most control is actually built into the technology itself.

These associations between technology and the structure of employment lead one to ask whether, along with environment, size, and diversity, there is some logic of adjustment to contingencies here. If there is, does the extent predict differences in their performance?

The closeness of fit between technology and the pattern in which roles were specialized did not vary significantly between good- and poor-performance companies. What did distinguish the more successful firms was that they tended to vary their investment in manpower devoted to production support activities according to differences in their technology. For instance, among companies using heavy plant and more rigid production systems, the more profitable and faster-growing ones had significantly larger percentages of their total employment given over to maintenance activities.

In other words, allocation of manpower in relation to technological requirements appears to improve performance.

Type of Personnel

Now let's consider the last proposition:

Proposition 10: Organizations that adopt forms of administrative structure consistent with the expectations and perceived needs of their personnel will tend to achieve higher levels of performance.

This proposition is a cornerstone of the behavioral study of organizations. Readers of *Organizational Dynamics* will already be familiar with the work of Chris Argyris, Frederick Herzberg, Rensis Likert, Douglas McGregor, and others who have argued for structures and styles of management that secure a higher degree of commitment to the organization from employees by more adequately meeting their expectations and their needs as mature adults. In a broader context, moves to enrich jobs and the developments in industrial codetermination now under way in Europe also reflect an implicit faith in Proposition 10, since they start from the premise that employees' expectations and perceived needs are not being fulfilled adequately by existing organization forms.

The results of many research studies indicate that the proposition is valid. Indeed, some would call it a truism. While it is unnecessary to review familiar ground, some qualifications are in order. The proposition refers to the expectations and perceived needs of personnel. This reference to the perceptual level is important, for whatever the order of man's universal psychological needs, it is clear that different types of people do not have the same requirements of their work at the conscious perceptual level. One has only to compare the professional employee with the manual worker to realize that sociocultural factors are crucial in shaping different expectations as to what constitute legitimate conditions of work. Similarly, research of a cross-cultural nature has indicated that different supervisory styles are effective with employees located in different cultural milieux where different attitudes toward work and authority are evident. In short, Proposition 10 indicates that managements need to spend time ascertaining the expectations of different groups among their employees if they want to have a reliable idea of which arrangements will secure the willing commitment of those employees.

CONCLUSION

I have discussed ten propositions, of which half support the universalistic argument on organizational performance and half support the contingency argument. These two arguments have sometimes been regarded as completely opposed, but the findings of research indicate several ways in which they are compatible.

In essence, the contingency approach stresses that managers should secure and evaluate information on their operating situation and that they should adapt the design of their organizational structure when necessary. It will quite possibly prove to be a general rule that managerial qualities such as the personal flexibility and drive associated with youth or the thrust for performance spurred on by a personal stake in stock appreciation enhance a company's ability to adjust to new contingencies. This is a universalistic type of statement, which includes two of the propositions I have advanced; it is nevertheless quite compatible with a contingency view of organizational design.

A further example of compatibility between the two arguments can be provided. The priority top managements give to different objectives is probably a factor that always influences the performance profiles that they attain. At the same time, the performance of only two companies having identical sets of objectives is unlikely to be the same, because this will also be determined by how they decide to adjust to prevailing contingencies.

The practical implications of the first five universalistic propositions have already been discussed. The first two draw attention to the desirability of selecting and developing managers who possess a combination of relative youth and relevant qualifications. Proposition 3 supports the general thrust of research on motivation and reward by indicating that the performance of organizations is enhanced when they grant their managers a sizable personal stake in their development. The fourth and fifth propositions indicate how the objectives management selects can shape performance, and how a greater degree of boardroom consensus over objectives will increase the chances of achieving good performance. These last two propositions speak for the practical importance of good communication, information sharing, and other hallmarks of effective integration among top executives.

The thrust of the last five propositions and supporting research, is that the design of organization is likely to influence a company's performance. The problem has to be worked out in the context of each company's own circumstances. Several evaluations have to be made before deciding on the form of organization that is most appropriate. First, we must assess the nature of present and future contingencies. In other words, just what kind of institution are we, and what do we want to be in terms of markets, size, type of production, and so on? Second, what are the organizational requirements imposed by relevant contingencies? For example, a large unit will have particular problems of coordination and communication. What alternative organizational designs might satisfy these requirements?

Third, if different contingencies pose the dilemma of conflicting requirements, what policies could we formulate to modify the contingencies themselves? Some companies, for example, that seek to enter a faster-growing but more variable market or that seek to combine successful new product development with economies of large-scale, standardized "bread and butter" operations are finding that they can circumvent the size contingency by setting up small, internally flexible, venture-management units or similar companies-within-companies.

The important point is that there are usually several ways of securing an effective match between a company's internal organization and the contingencies it faces. This fact tends to be overlooked by those who share the present-day public concern about large bureaucratic firms and other institutions. A bureaucracy can be operated in different ways, and not necessarily with the proverbial "dead hand." And even if large scale brings too much bureaucracy to permit desirable levels of participation and sensitivity to change, there are in most areas of activity various possibilities for devolving units into smaller ones without incurring any loss in their efficiency.

In conclusion, it is already possible to identify certain managerial and organizational factors that are related to company performance, but in the future it will be necessary to go further and initiate experiments and changes in these variables that, it is hoped, will demonstrate how far they actively determine performance. It is, however, abundantly clear that company performance is not the prey of random and uncontrollable forces.

BACKGROUND

This article is largely based on a research program involving 82 British companies selected among six industries to provide contrasting environments. Two of the industries were in the service sector: advertising and insurance (predominantly ordinary life insurance). Four were manufacturing, with two of these being science based—electronics (predominantly instruments and components) and pharmaceuticals. The other two manufacturing industries were chocolates-and-sweets and family newspapers. The companies chosen provided a clustering within each industry around six different size levels, of 150, 300, 500, 1,000, 2,500, and 6,000 employees.

Information on the organization, technology, location, scale, ownership, policy, and background of each company was obtained chiefly through interviews with its senior managers and specialists. In 78 of the companies, the researchers followed up this investigation within one to two weeks with a questionnaire to senior and departmental managers asking them about the nature of their jobs, their personal attitudes towards matters such as change and innovation, and how they would characterize typical behaviors at their level in the company. Completed replies returned by 787 of the 888 managers contacted were the source of data on managerial characteristics. Statistics on the profit and growth performance of the companies were collected from their internal records and accounts.

Most writings on the performance of organizations have been by economists, who have only infrequently examined managerial or organizational
factors. Robin Morris and Adrian Wood, in editing *The Corporate Economy*
(Macmillan, 1971) have, however, drawn together recent theoretical and
empirical studies that take such factors into account. Jonathan Boswell's *The
Rise and Decline of Small Firms* (Allen and Unwin, 1973) examines the
performance of small firms in Britain, giving particular attention to problems
of management succession. *Attitudes in British Management* (Penguin,
1966) contrasts "thrusting" and "sleeping" managerial attitudes, which it
claims are associated with marked differences in company performance.
Paul R. Lawrence and Jay W. Lorsch, in *Organization and Environment*
(Harvard Business School, 1967), provides a classic statement of the contingency approach. Within the contingency school, Tom Burns and G. M.
Stalker, in *The Management of Innovation* (Tavistock, 1961), consider the
implications of environmental differences. John M. Stopford and Louis T.
Wells, in *Managing the Multinational Enterprise* (Basic Books, 1972), con-
centrate on diversity of operations, while Joan Woodward's *Industrial
Organization: Theory and Practice* (Oxford University Press, 1965) reports
studies on technology, organization, and performance. More detailed accounts of the author's own research into performance will appear in the
Journal of Management Studies in October 1974 and February 1975.

NAME INDEX

SUBJECT INDEX

Uncertainty, 193. *See also* Environment; Interorganizational relations

Vertical integration. *See* Technology
Vertical span. *See* Organization size; Technology

Woodward studies. *See* Organization size; Technology
Workflow integration. *See* Technology
line control of, 92–95, 204